GET RESULTS!

English
Thesaurus

GET RESULTS!

English Thesaurus

GEDDES & GROSSET

Published 2001 by Geddes & Grosset

© 1998 Geddes & Grosset,
David Dale House, New Lanark ML11 9DJ, Scotland

First published 1998
Reprinted 1999, 2001 (twice), 2002, 2003 (twice)

ISBN 1 85534 379 7

Printed and bound in Poland

A

abandon vb **1** (*abandon his wife and children*) desert, leave, forsake, depart from. **2** (*abandon the attempt*) give up, drop, discard, (*inf*) scrap.

abate vb (*The storm abated*) die down, lessen, ease, decrease, diminish, moderate, wane.

abbreviate vb (*abbreviate a word or phrase*) shorten, reduce, cut, cut short, cut down, contract.

abdicate vb **1** (*The king abdicated in 1936*) give up, resign, stand down, retire, quit. **2** (*abdicate responsibilities*) give up, renounce, relinquish.

abdomen n (*a pain in the abdomen*) stomach, belly, (*inf*) tummy, (*inf*) insides, intestines.

abduct vb (*abduct someone else's child*) kidnap, carry off, seize, hold as hostage, (*inf*) snatch.

ability n (*a performer of great ability*) talent, skill, expertise, cleverness, competence.

able adj (*an able pupil*) clever, talented, capable, competent.

abnormal adj (*an abnormal thing to do*) unusual, strange, odd, peculiar, queer, extraordinary.

abolish vb (*abolish smoking in public*) do away with, put an end to, end, stop, eliminate.

abridge vb (*abridge the book for children*) shorten, cut down, condense, compress.

abroad adv (*go abroad on holiday*) overseas, to a foreign country, to a foreign land, out of the country.

abrupt adj **1** (*come to an abrupt end*) sudden, quick, hurried, hasty, swift, rapid, unexpected, unforeseen. **2** (*an abrupt reply*) curt, blunt, brusque, short, rude. **3** (*an abrupt slope*) steep, sheer, sudden, precipitous.

absent adj (*absent from school*) not present, away, off, missing, truant.

absent-minded adj (*so absent-minded that she didn't hear what people were saying to her*) distracted, preoccupied, absorbed, vague, inattentive.

absolute adj (*absolute trust*) complete, total, utter, out and out, outright, perfect, unqualified, sheer.

abstain vb (*abstain from voting/abstain from drinking*) refrain, desist, hold back, keep from.

absurd adj (*absurd plan*) ridiculous, foolish, silly, idiotic, stupid, nonsensical, senseless, crazy, ludicrous, harebrained.

abundance n (*there was food in abundance*) plenty, plentifulness, profusion, (*inf*) heaps, (*inf*) bags, (*inf*) oodles.

abundant adj (*an abundant supply of fresh food*) plentiful, ample, large, great, copious, lavish, profuse.

abuse vb **1** (*abuse children*) mistreat, maltreat, ill-treat, ill-use, injure, hurt, harm. **2** (*abuse power*) misuse, misapply, misemploy, mishandle. **3** (*abuse the person who ran into his* *car*) swear at, curse, insult, rebuke.

abuse n **1** (*child abuse*) mistreatment, maltreatment, ill-treatment, ill-use, injury, hurting, harming. **2** (*the abuse of power/the abuse of alcohol*) misuse, misapplication, misapplying, mishandling.

abysmal adj **1** (*abysmal ignorance*) utter, extreme, complete, thorough, profound. **2** (*an abysmal performance*) dreadful, appalling, very bad, worthless.

accelerate vb **1** (*The car accelerated*) speed up, go faster, go quicker, pick up speed. **2** (*accelerate the process of change*) speed up, hasten, hurry along, expedite, spur on.

accent n **1** (*a Birmingham accent*) way of speaking, pronunciation, inflection, enunciation. **2** (*The accent is on the first syllable*) stress, emphasis, force, accentuation. **3** (*the accent must be on efficiency*) emphasis, stress, importance.

accept vb **1** (*accept the gift*) receive, take, take receipt of. **2** (*accept their decision*) agree to, consent to, comply with, acquiesce in, concur with, endorse.

acceptable adj **1** (*a very acceptable gift*) welcome, agreeable, delightful, pleasing, pleasant, desirable. **2** (*work that is not acceptable*) satisfactory, good enough, adequate, passable, tolerable.

access n **1** (*no direct access to the building from the main road*) entry, entrance, way in, admittance, approach.

accessible adj (*accessible sources of information*) attainable, available, reachable, obtainable.

accessory n **1** (*accessories for an electric drill*) attachment, fitment, extra, addition, adjunct. **2** (*accessories to the crime*) accomplice, associate, confederate, abettor.

accident n **1** (*people injured in the mining accident*) casualty, disaster, catastrophe, calamity, mishap. **2** (*old friends who met by accident*) chance, fate, good fortune, luck, (*inf*) fluke.

accidental adj (*accidental death/an accidental meeting*) chance, unintentional, unintended, unexpected, unforeseen, unplanned, unpremeditated.

accommodation n (*find accommodation for the homeless*) housing, lodging, shelter, board, quarters, (*inf*) digs.

accompany vb (*accompany her to the dance*) partner, escort, go with, go along with.

accomplice n (*an accomplice in crime*) confederate, accessory, collaborator, abettor, ally, helper, henchman, (*inf*) sidekick.

accomplish vb (*accomplish a task*) finish, complete, do, perform, execute.

accomplished adj (*an accomplished pianist*) skilled, skilful, expert, gifted, talented, masterly.

accomplishment n (*person of many accomplishments*) talent, gift, ability, skill, attainment, achievement.

account n **1** (*give a full account of the accident*) statement, report, description, record, story, tale. **2** (*send in the account for the work done*) bill, invoice, charges.

accumulate vb **1** (*rubbish accumulating in the streets*) gather, collect, pile up, build up. **2** (*accumulate many books over the years*) gather, collect, amass, stockpile, hoard.

accredited adj (*an accredited representative of the firm*) official, authorized, legal, approved, certified.

accurate adj **1** (*accurate measurements*) correct, precise, exact, right, errorless. **2** (*an accurate description*) correct, exact, close, true, faithful, strict.

accusation n (*deny the accusations*) charge, allegation, imputation, incrimination.

accuse vb **1** (*accuse her of murder*) charge, indict, arraign. **2** (*accuse the boys of breaking windows*) blame, put the blame on, lay the blame on, hold responsible for, hold accountable for, lay at the door of.

accustom vb (*accustom herself to her new surroundings*) adapt, adjust, acclimatize, get used to.

accustomed adj **1** (*our accustomed route home*) usual, normal, customary, regular, habitual, routine. **2** (*accustomed to public speaking*) used to, in the habit of, familiar with, acquainted with.

ache vb (*My head aches*) hurt, be sore, be painful, throb.

ache n (*an ache in his back*) pain, soreness, throbbing, twinge, pang.

achieve vb (*achieve one's aim*) accomplish, reach, attain, gain, obtain, acquire.

achievement n (*proud of his achievements on the sports field*) accomplishment, attainment, deed, act, effort, feat.

acid adj **1** (*an acid taste*) sour, tart, sharp, bitter, vinegary. **2** (*acid remarks*) sharp, sarcastic, caustic, trenchant, acerbic.

acknowledge vb **1** (*acknowledge a letter*) answer, reply to, respond to. **2** (*acknowledge defeat*) admit, accept, recognize, grant, concede.

acquire vb (*acquire enough money*) obtain, get, come by, gain, procure.

acquit vb (*the judge will acquit the accused*) clear, set free, release, discharge, pardon, absolve, exonerate.

act vb **1** (*act like a fool*) behave, do, operate. **2** (*act quickly to put out the fire*) take action, move, be active, perform. **3** (*act the part of Peter Pan*) play, perform, enact. **4** (*act in a new play*) be an actor, play a part, perform.

act n **1** (*a brave act*) action, deed, undertaking, feat, exploit. **2** (*enjoy the magician's act*) performance, show, turn, routine. **3** (*an act to forbid smoking*) law, ruling, rule, regulation, order, bill, decree, statute.

acting adj (*the acting head teacher*) temporary, interim, substitute.

action n **1** (*His action saved their lives*) act, deed, move, behaviour, undertaking, feat, exploit. **2** (*a film full of action*) activity, movement, liveliness, energy, vitality.

active adj **1** (*active children tiring their mothers/lead active lives*) energetic, full of energy, lively, busy, nimble, (*inf*) on the go. **2** (*sports clubs which are still active*) in action, working, operating, in operation, functioning.

activity n **1** (*city streets full of activity*) movement, bustle, hustle and bustle, liveliness. **2** (*activities enjoyed after school*) pastime, interest, hobby, pursuit, project.

actual adj **1** (*The actual cost was far less than the newspapers reported*) real, true, genuine, authentic. **2** (*no actual evidence of burglary*) existing, definite, certain, positive, concrete.

actually adv (*The boy seems unhealthy but he is actually quite well*) really, in fact, in reality, in truth, truly.

adapt vb **1** (*adapt the scheme to suit younger children*) adjust, alter, change, convert, modify, vary, reshape, remodel. **2** (*find it difficult to adapt to a new way of life*) adjust, fit in, accustom oneself, become accustomed to, acclimatize.

add vb **1** (*add some more details to the report*) put in, include, append. **2** (*add the rows of figures*) add up, count, count up, (*inf*) tot up, total. **3** (*Money problems added to his worry*) increase, augment, amplify, intensify, aggravate.

addicted adj (*be addicted to alcohol*) dependent on, (*inf*) hooked on.

addiction n (*try to cure his drug addiction*) dependence, dependency, craving, habit.

additional adj (*require additional supplies*) more, extra, further, supplementary.

additive n (*additives listed on food labels*) supplement, preservative.

address n **1** (*find out his address*) where one lives, home, house, residence. **2** (*the address of the company's head office*) location, place, whereabouts. **3** (*unable to read the address on the parcel*) label, directions, inscription. **4** (*the head teacher's end-of-term address*) speech, talk, lecture.

address vb **1** (*address a parcel*) write the address on, label, write the directions on, direct, inscribe. **2** (*How do you address a bishop?*) name, call, speak to, write to, describe. **3** (*address one's remarks to the manager*) direct, communicate, convey, send.

adequate adj **1** (*adequate supplies for the week*) enough, sufficient, ample. **2** (*workers who are not adequate*) fit, able, competent, qualified, (*inf*) up to scratch.

adhesive n (*an adhesive to stick the tiles to the wall*) glue, cement, gum, fixative.

adjacent adj (*living in the adjacent house*) adjoining, next, next door, neighbouring, bordering.

adjourn vb (*adjourn the meeting till the next day*) break off, discontinue, defer, postpone, put off, shelve.

adjudicate vb (*adjudicate at the singing contest*) judge, arbitrate, referee, umpire.

adjust vb **1** (*unable to adjust to the new situation*) adapt, become accustomed to, accustom oneself to, get used to, acclimatize. **2** (*adjust the saddle of the bike*) alter, change, modify, rearrange.

administration n (*in hospital administration*) management, direction, government.

administrator n (business administrators) manager, director, executive, controller.

admire vb 1 (admire her hat/admire the view) express admiration of, approve of, like, compliment, praise. 2 (admire their courage) approve of, respect, think highly of, appreciate, applaud, praise, esteem.

admit vb 1 (admit his guilt/admit that she could be wrong) acknowledge, confess, own up, reveal, make known, declare, disclose, divulge. 2 (a ticket that admits only one person) let in, allow in, allow entry, permit entry.

admittance n (no admittance to the private building) entry, right of entry, entrance, access.

adolescence n (a young person just reaching adolescence) teenage years, (inf) teens, growing up.

adopt vb 1 (adopt a child) take as one's own, take in, take care of, be adoptive parents to. 2 (adopt a parliamentary candidate) select, choose, pick, vote for. 3 (adopt modern customs/adopt a foreign style of dress) assume, take on, take over, affect, embrace, espouse.

adorable adj (an adorable little baby) lovable, sweet, dear, darling, delightful, appealing, charming, enchanting, winsome.

adore vb 1 (They adore their children) love dearly, be devoted to, dote on, cherish, idolize. 2 (adore ice cream) like very much, love, be fond of, enjoy, relish. 3 (adore God) worship, praise, glorify, revere, venerate.

adorn vb (flowers adorning the room/ adorn the Christmas tree with lights) decorate, embellish, ornament, beautify.

adroit adj (her adroit handling of the situation) skilful, skilled, deft, expert, clever, able, adept.

adult adj 1 (adult people) grown-up, (fml) of age. 2 (adult trees) mature, fully grown, developed.

advance vb (The armies advance) move forward, go forward, proceed, press on, forge ahead, make progress.

advance adj 1 (the advance party) leading, first, in front. 2 (advance warning) early, previous, prior, beforehand.

advanced adj 1 (advanced technology) progressive, modern, up-to date, ultra-modern, sophisticated, avant-garde. 2 (advanced studies/schoolwork that is more advanced) higher-level, complicated, difficult.

advantage n 1 (one of the advantages of being tall) benefit, asset, good point, blessing, boon. 2 (have an advantage over his rivals) superiority, ascendancy, supremacy, upper hand. 3 (There is little advantage in going into business with her) benefit, profit, gain, good.

advantageous adj 1 (an advantageous position) favourable, helpful, beneficial, useful. 2 (advantageous to his hopes of promotion) of benefit, beneficial, of assistance, useful, valuable.

adventure n 1 (tell her grandchildren of her adventures at sea) exploit, escapade, deed, feat, experience. 2 (a journey full of adventure) risk, precariousness, danger, hazard, peril, uncertainty.

adventurous adj (an adventurous life) risky, precarious, dangerous, hazardous, perilous.

adversary n (their adversaries in the battle/her adversary in the tournament) opponent, enemy, foe, antagonist, rival.

adversity n 1 (a homeless person leading a life of adversity) misfortune, illluck, bad luck, trouble, hardship, distress, misery. 2 (many adversities in his life) misfortune, mishap, setback, trial, disaster, catastrophe, calamity.

advertise vb (advertise a new product) promote, give publicity to, publicize, (inf) push, (inf) plug.

advice n (give careers advice/get advice on a personal problem) guidance, counselling, counsel, help, suggestions, hints, tips.

advisable adj (Such action is not advisable) desirable, wise, sensible, prudent, suitable, appropriate, recommended.

advise vb 1 (advise them on future careers) give advice to. give guidance on, guide, counsel, give recommendations, offer suggestions, give hints. 2 (advise carefulness) recommend, suggest, urge, commend, advocate.

advocate vb (advocate spending less money) advise, recommend, suggest, urge, press for, favour, support.

affable adj (an affable neighbour/in an affable mood) friendly, amiable, genial, cordial, pleasant, agreeable, good-natured, sociable, courteous.

affair n 1 (It's my affair) concern, business, matter, responsibility. 2 (The sacking of the boss was an unfortunate affair) event, happening, occurrence, incident, episode, state of affairs.

affect vb 1 (a tragedy which affected all of us) have an effect on, influence, have an influence on, act on, work on, change, alter. 2 (a disease affecting his stomach) attack, infect. 3 (We were deeply affected by the orphan's sad story) move, touch, upset, disturb, trouble, stir.

affected adj (an affected way of speaking) pretentious, artificial, false, pretended, unnatural, assumed.

affection n (feel affection for his children) love, fondness, caring, devotion, liking, warmth.

affectionate adj (an affectionate farewell) loving, fond, devoted, tender, warm.

afflict vb (people afflicted by a terrible disease) trouble, distress, trouble, torment, plague.

affliction n (the afflictions associated with old age) trouble, disorder, disease, ailment, pain, suffering, hardship.

affluent adj (affluent people living in expensive houses) wealthy, rich, well-off, prosperous, well-to-do, (inf) well-heeled.

afford vb (unable to afford a new car) buy, purchase, pay for, pay the price of, meet the expense of.

affront n (sexist remarks that are an affront to women) insult, offence, slight, snub, indignity.

afraid adj 1 (afraid of the wild animal/afraid to enter the haunted house) frightened, scared, nervous, terrified, apprehensive, fearful. **2** (*I'm afraid that I cannot help you*) sorry, regretful, apologetic, unhappy.

age n **1** (*the wisdom that comes with age*) old age, maturity, seniority, advancing years. **2** (*in the Elizabethan age*) era, period, epoch, time.

agency n (*an advertising agency*) organization, business, firm, company, office, bureau.

agenda n (*on the agenda for tonight's meeting*) programme, schedule, timetable, list.

agent n **1** (*an insurance agent/a travel agent*) representative, negotiator, operator, (*inf*) rep. **2** (*an enemy agent*) spy, (*inf*) mole, (*inf*) spook.

aggravate vb **1** (*aggravate the situation/ aggravate the illness*) make worse, worsen, exacerbate, intensify, increase. **2** (*inf*) (*children aggravating their mother with their noise*) annoy, irritate, anger, exasperate, provoke, get on someone's nerves.

aggravate should be used in the meaning of 'annoy' only in informal situations, such as in speech or personal letters between friends. Many people regard this as a wrong use of the word and it should be avoided in formal writing, such as essays.

aggressive adj **1** (*people getting aggressive when they get drunk*) quarrelsome, argumentative, belligerent, pugnacious. **2** (*aggressive salesmen/aggressive young workers seeking rapid promotion*) assertive, forceful, dynamic, thrusting, (*inf*) pushy.

aghast adj (*aghast at the decision to close the local steelworks*) horrified, appalled, astounded, amazed, shocked, flabbergasted.

agile adj (*old people still agile/agile young gymnasts*) active, nimble, lithe, supple, sprightly.

agitate vb **1** (*The news agitated her*) upset, work up, fluster, perturb, ruffle, disconcert, flurry, excite. **2** (*demonstrators agitating for more nursery schools*) campaign, argue.

agonizing adj (*an agonizing pain*) excruciating, painful, unbearable, insufferable, piercing.

agony n (*accident victims in agony*) suffering, pain, torture, torment, distress, anguish.

agree vb **1** (*agree with your suggestions*) concur, comply, accord. **2** (*agree to your demands*) consent to, accept, assent to, acquiesce in. **3** (*accounts of the accident that do not agree with each other*) match, accord, correspond, coincide, tally, (*inf*) square.

agreeable adj **1** (*We are agreeable to your coming with us*) willing, amenable, compliant, consenting, assenting, accommodating. **2** (*an agreeable occasion*) pleasant, delightful, enjoyable, pleasurable. **3** (*an agreeable young man*) pleasant, likable, amiable, friendly, nice, affable.

agreement n **1** (*all in complete agreement*) accord, assent, concurrence, harmony, unity. **2** (*sign an agreement to purchase*) contract, compact, covenant, pact, pledge, deal.

aid vb **1** (*aid the rescue workers*) assist,

help, support, lend a hand. **2** (*medicine to aid his recovery*) assist, help, speed up, hasten, expedite, facilitate.

aid n **1** (*stop to give aid to a motorist who had broken down*) assistance, help, support, a helping hand. **2** (*give aid to poor countries*) assistance, help, contributions, subsidy, gift, donation. **3** (*a hospital aid*) helper, assistant, girl/man Friday.

ailment n illness, complaint, disease, disorder.

aim vb **1** (*aim a gun at*) point, direct, train, level. **2** (*aim to get there before dark*) plan, intend, propose, try.

aim n (*their aims in life/Their aim is to make a lot of money*) goal, ambition, objective, object, target, purpose, intention, plan, aspiration, design, desire.

aimless adj **1** (*lead an aimless life*) pointless, purposeless, futile, undirected. **2** (*aimless young people wandering the streets*) unambitious, drifting, wandering.

air n **1** (*fly through the air*) atmosphere, sky. **2** (*an air of loneliness about her*) impression, appearance, atmosphere, mood, quality, look, feeling. **3** (*playing a sad air on the piano*) tune, melody, song, theme.

air vb **1** (*air clothes/air a room*) ventilate, freshen. **2** (*air one's views*) make known, make public, publicize, voice, express, vent, communicate, reveal.

aisle n (*the aisles in planes/trains*) gangway, passageway, passage, corridor.

alarm vb (*alarmed by a loud bang in the night*) frighten, scare, startle, terrify,

unnerve, disturb, upset.

alarm n **1** (*a burglar alarm/a fire alarm*) alarm signal, alarm bell, danger signal, siren, warning. **2** (*a burglar causing alarm in the neighbourhood*) fear, fright, apprehension, terror, panic, disturbance, anxiety, upset, disquiet.

alert adj (*stay alert when on sentry duty*) awake, wide awake, aware, attentive, watchful, wary, observant, vigilant.

alien adj **1** (*alien lands*) foreign, overseas. **2** (*find themselves in an alien environment*) strange, unfamiliar, unknown.

alien n **1** (*aliens deported from the country at the start of the war*) foreigner, non-native. **2** (*aliens from another planet*) extraterrestrial, (*inf*) little green man.

alight vb **1** (*alight from the bus*) get off, dismount, descend. **2** (*butterflies alighting on leaves*) land, come down, come to rest, settle, touch down.

alike adj (*sisters who are very much alike*) like, similar, the same, identical, indistinguishable.

alive adj **1** (*soldiers wounded but still alive*) living, live, breathing, (*inf*) in the land of the living. **2** (*streets alive with shoppers*) crowded, packed, teeming, swarming, overflowing, thronged, (*inf*) crawling.

allegation n (*deny their allegations that he was a thief*) claim, charge, accusation, declaration, assertion, statement.

allergic adj (*allergic to cows' milk*) hypersensitive, sensitive.

alley n (*attacked in a dark alley leading*

off the high street) alleyway, lane, passage, passageway, backstreet.

alliance n *(foreign countries forming an alliance against the enemy)* union, association, league, coalition, federation, partnership, affiliation.

allot vb *(allot work to each of the students/allot grants of money to those in need)* allocate, distribute, give out, share out, dispense, apportion.

allow vb 1 *(allow them to use her swimming pool)* let, permit, give permission to, authorize, *(inf)* give the go-ahead to. 2 *(allow half a roll of wastepaper for wastage)* plan for, make provision for, provide for, take into account, take into consideration.

allowance n *(a dress allowance)* money, payment, remittance, contribution, grant, subsidy.

allude vb *(He alluded to the history of the town in his speech)* refer to, mention, mention in passing, touch upon, make an allusion to.

alluring adj *(a woman of alluring beauty)* attractive, fascinating, charming, enchanting, captivating, bewitching, beguiling, tempting.

ally n *(their allies in the war)* confederate, associate, collaborator, partner, friend.

almost adv *(almost four o'clock/almost two miles long)* nearly, close to, just about, around, not quite, practically, approximately.

alone adj 1 *(go to the party alone)* by oneself, unaccompanied, unescorted, companionless. 2 *(left all alone by her father's death)* solitary, lonely, isolated,

desolate, deserted, forlorn. 3 *(He alone can answer the questions)* only, solely, just.

aloof adj *(People who are aloof do not have many friends)* distant, remote, unresponsive, unapproachable, standoffish, unsociable, unfriendly, cold.

aloud adv *(cry aloud)* out loud, audibly, clearly, distinctly.

also adv 1 *(buy a bed and a wardrobe also)* too, as well, besides, in addition, into the bargain. 2 *(He's poor; also he's ill)* furthermore, besides, moreover, in addition.

alter vb 1 *(alter the dress)* change, adjust, modify, convert, reshape, remodel, vary, transform. 2 *(The village has scarcely altered)* change, become different, vary.

alteration n 1 *(make alterations to the dress/make alterations to the letter)* change, adjustment, modification, amendment, revision, variation. 2 *(the alteration of his appearance after his illness)* change, difference, variation, transformation, metamorphosis.

alternative n *(offer an alternative on the menu for vegetarians)* choice, option, possibility, preference.

altitude n *(the altitude of the ski-resort)* height, elevation.

altogether adv 1 *(six of us altogether)* in all, all told, in total. 2 *(not altogether sure)* completely, quite, entirely, totally, thoroughly, absolutely, fully, perfectly.

always adv 1 *(We always shop there)* regularly, invariably, consistently, unfailingly, repeatedly, without exception. **2** (*She's always cheerful*) continually, continuously, constantly, incessantly, perpetually. **3** (*promise to love her always*) forever, forever and ever, evermore, eternally, endlessly, everlastingly.

amaze vb (*His sheer stupidity amazed us*) astonish, astound, surprise, dumbfound, flabbergast, daze, shock, stun, (*inf*) stagger, nonplus.

amazing adj (*have an amazing memory*) exceptional, extraordinary, remarkable, phenomenal.

ambiguous adj (*Her message was ambiguous*) unclear, uncertain, doubtful, dubious, vague, obscure, puzzling, perplexing, enigmatic, abstruse.

ambition n **1** (*young members of the firm full of ambition*) aspiration, drive, striving, force, enterprise, enthusiasm. **2** (*Her ambition is to go on the stage*) aim, goal, objective, purpose, intent, dream, hope.

ambitious adj (*ambitious people seeking promotion*) aspiring, forceful, purposeful, enterprising, go-ahead, assertive.

ambush n **1** (*terrorists waiting in ambush for the soldiers*) hiding, concealment, cover. **2** (*lay an ambush for the enemy soldiers*) trap, snare, pitfall.

amiable adj (*in the company of amiable people*) friendly, pleasant, agreeable, charming, good-natured, sociable, genial.

amnesty n (*declare an amnesty for all political prisoners*) general pardon, pardon, reprieve, forgiveness, absolution.

among/amongst prep **1** (*a house among the trees/live among enemies*) in the midst of, amid, amidst, surrounded by, in the thick of. **2** (*divide it among you*) between, to each of.

amount n (*a small amount of wood/a large amount of attention*) quantity, mass, measure, volume, extent.

amount vb (*The bill amounted to hundreds of pounds*) add up to, total, come to, run to.

ample adj **1** (*ample food for everyone*) enough, sufficient, plenty, adequate, more than enough. **2** (*an ample supply of money*) plentiful, abundant, copious, liberal, generous, lavish. **3** (*her ample bosom*) large, big, substantial.

amplify vb **1** (*amplify the sound level*) make louder, increase, boost, augment. **2** (*amplify your suggestion*) expand, enlarge on, elaborate on, develop.

amputate vb (*The surgeon had to amputate his leg after the accident*) cut off, remove, sever, excise.

amuse vb **1** (*try to amuse the children on a cold, rainy day*) entertain, occupy, interest, divert. **2** (*The comedian's jokes amused everyone*) make laugh, entertain, cheer up, delight.

amusement n **1** (*various forms of amusement in the holiday resort*) entertainment, diversion, fun, interest, pastime, hobby, recreation. **2** (*smile with amusement at the comedian's jokes*) laughter, mirth, hilarity, pleasure, enjoyment.

amusing adj (*an amusing story*) funny, humorous, comical, entertaining, hilarious.

analyse vb (*analyse the election results*) examine, study, investigate, enquire into, dissect.

anarchy n **1** (*The fall of the government was followed by a period of anarchy*) absence of government, lawlessness, revolution. **2** (*anarchy on the streets when the police went on strike*) lawlessness, disorder, chaos, confusion, mayhem.

ancestor n (*trace his ancestors back to the time of Queen Anne*) forbear, forefather, progenitor, forerunner, predecessor.

ancestry n (*She is of royal ancestry*) descent, extraction, origin, derivation, parentage, blood, family tree.

ancient adj **1** (*ancient customs*) very old, age-old, time-worn. **2** (*in ancient times*) earliest, early, primeval, prehistoric. **3** (*His ideas on fashion are ancient*) antiquated, old-fashioned, out-of-date, outdated, outmoded, obsolete.

and conj (*my family and I*) along with, with, together with, as well in, in addition to, plus.

angel n **1** (*angels in heaven*) seraph, cherub, archangel, guardian angel. **2** (*My kind neighbour is an absolute angel*) saint, gem, dear, darling.

anger n (*feelings of anger at cruelty to animals*) annoyance, rage, fury, indignation, wrath, irritation, ire.

anger vb (*They were angered by his rudeness*) annoy, infuriate, enrage, irritate, incense, madden, provoke, rile.

angry adj (*angry mothers scolding their children*) annoyed, cross, furious, in-furiated, indignant, irate, livid, enraged, wrathful, incensed, (*inf*) mad.

anguish n (*The children were in anguish when their pet died*) agony, suffering, pain, torment, torture, distress, misery.

animated adj (*an animated discussion*) lively, spirited, excited, enthusiastic, passionate, fiery, dynamic, energetic.

annexe n (*add an annexe to the house*) extension, wing.

annihilate vb (*annihilate the enemy army*) destroy, wipe out, exterminate, eliminate, obliterate, eradicate.

announce vb (*announce that the president was dead*) make known, make public, proclaim, publish, broadcast, report, state, declare, reveal, disclose.

announcement n (*an announcement of the president's death*) report, statement, notice, proclamation, declaration, bulletin, communiqué, intimation.

announcer n (*a BBC announcer*) commentator, presenter, newsreader, newscaster, broadcaster, reporter.

annoy vb **1** (*Her attitude annoyed her parents*) anger, infuriate, enrage, irritate, incense, madden, provoke, rile. **2** (*Don't annoy your mother while she is working/children annoying the dog*) bother, disturb, pester, worry, torment, tease.

annul vb (*annul the marriage/annul the agreement*) declare null and void, nullify, invalidate, cancel, rescind, revoke.

anomaly n (*anomalies in the tax system*) abnormality, irregularity, deviation, aberration, oddity, peculiarity, inconsistency.

anonymous adj (*The money for the charity was from an anonymous donor*) unnamed, nameless, unknown, unidentified, incognito.

another adj 1 (*another cup of tea*) additional, second, further. 2 (*go another time/get another car*) different, some other.

answer vb 1 (*answer the question*) reply to, give a response to, respond to, retort. 2 (*answer our requirements*) meet, satisfy, fulfil, fill, serve. 3 (*a man answering the description issued by the police*) fit, match, correspond to, be like.

answer n 1 (*receive no answer to his question/waiting for an answer to his letter*) reply, response, acknowledge, retort, rejoinder. 2 (*the answer to the puzzle*) solution, explanation.

antagonism n (*a great deal of antagonism between the two sides*) hostility, opposition, animosity, antipathy, enmity, dissension, conflict, friction.

anthology n (*an anthology of poetry*) collection, selection, miscellany, compendium.

anticipate vb 1 (*The organizers are anticipating a large audience for the concert*) expect, foresee, predict, forecast, look for, await. 2 (*anticipate his opponent's move*) forestall, intercept, prevent, (*inf*) beat someone to it.

anticipation n 1 (*buy champagne in anticipation of victory*) expectation, prediction. 2 (*girls full of anticipation*

before the dance) expectancy, hopefulness, hope.

anticlimax n (*After all the fun of planning the actual holiday was rather an anticlimax*) disappointment, let-down, disillusionment.

antiquated adj (*children thinking that their parents have antiquated ideas/an antiquated television set*) out-of-date, old-fashioned, outmoded, outworn, obsolete, archaic, passé.

antique adj (*antique furniture*) old, antiquarian, vintage, early.

antisocial adj 1 (*antisocial people who dislike parties*) unsociable, reserved, aloof, withdrawn, retiring, uncommunicative, unfriendly. 2 (*Playing loud music late at night is an example of unsocial behaviour*) disruptive, disorderly, lawless, unruly, obstreperous.

antithesis n (*The antithesis of good is bad*) opposite, reverse, converse, inverse, other extreme.

anxiety n (*full of anxiety about the lateness of her husband*) worry, concern, uneasiness, disquiet, nervousness, apprehension, tenseness.

anxious adj 1 (*anxious parents out looking for their children*) worried, concerned, uneasy, nervous, apprehensive, fearful, tense. 2 (*anxious to learn*) eager, keen, longing, avid.

apart adv 1 (*blow the place apart*) to pieces, in pieces, to bits, asunder. 2 (*a couple living apart*) separated, separately, divorced. 3 (*a man standing apart at the party*) to one side, aside, separately, by oneself.

apathy n (*Because of apathy many*

people did not vote) lack of interest, indifference, unresponsiveness, unconcern, lethargy.

apex n **1** (the apex of the triangle) top, tip, pinnacle, vertex, peak. **2** (the apex of his career) peak, summit, top, zenith, acme, apogee.

apologetic adj (feel apologetic for the trouble which they caused) sorry, regretful, contrite, remorseful, repentant, penitent, rueful.

apologize vb (apologize for his error) say one is sorry, express regret, ask forgiveness, (inf) eat humble pie.

apology n (accept his apology for his wrongdoing) regret, regrets.

appalling adj **1** (an appalling accident) shocking, frightful, horrifying, terrible, dreadful, awful, ghastly. **2** (a piece of work that is quite appalling/appalling behaviour) very bad, unacceptable, unsatisfactory, intolerable.

apparent adj **1** (It was apparent that she was unwell/problems that were apparent from the start) obvious, clear, plain, evident, discernible, perceptible, manifest. **2** (He eventually saw through her apparent sincerity) seeming, ostensible, outward, superficial.

apparition n (They thought they saw an apparition in the graveyard) ghost, spectre, phantom, spirit, wraith, (inf) spook.

appeal n **1** (make an appeal for help) request, call, plea, entreaty, supplication. **2** (a possibility that holds little appeal for her) attraction, attractiveness, charm, allure, interest. **3** (He has been convicted of the crime but the case is going to appeal) review, reconsideration, re-examination.

appear vb **1** (A figure appeared out of the mist) come into view, come into sight, emerge, materialize, surface. **2** (The visitors were very late but they finally appeared) come, arrive, make an appearance, turn up, (inf) show up. **3** (She appeared rather thoughtful) seem, look, have the appearance of, have the air of, give the impression of. **4** (He once appeared in a production of 'Hamlet') act, perform, play, take part in.

appearance n **1** (the sudden appearance of the police) arrival, advent, materialization, surfacing. **2** (having an appearance of sadness) look, air, expression, impression, manner. **3** (His statement had the appearance of truth but it was a lie) semblance, outward appearance, guise, show, pretence.

appease vb (try to appease his angry wife by giving her flowers) calm down, placate, make peace with, pacify, soothe, conciliate, mollify, propitiate.

appetizer n (serve smoked salmon as an appetizer) starter, hors d'oeuvre, antipasto.

appetizing adj **1** (an appetizing dish) tasty, mouth-watering, flavoursome, delicious. **2** (appetizing smells coming from the kitchen) tempting, inviting, enticing, alluring.

applaud vb **1** (The audience applauded) clap, give a standing ovation to, (inf) to give a big hand to. **2** (Everyone applauded his courage) praise, admire, compliment on, commend, acclaim, extol, laud.

appliance n (electrical appliances in the kitchen) gadget, tool, implement, apparatus, device, machine.

applicant n (applicants for the job) candidate, entrant, competitor, interviewee.

apply vb **1** (apply for a job) put in an application for, ask, put in for, try for. **2** (apply ointment to the sore) put on, rub in, cover with, spread, smear. **3** (have to apply force to open the box) use, employ, administer, utilize, exercise, bring to bear. **4** (These regulations do not apply) be applicable, be relevant, be pertinent, be apposite, be appropriate.

appoint vb (appoint a new manager) name, select, choose, pick, elect, designate, nominate.

appointment n **1** (have a business appointment this afternoon/a dinner appointment) meeting, engagement, date, rendezvous, assignation. **2** (take up his new appointment as manager) job, post, position, situation, place.

appreciate vb **1** (appreciate offers of help) be grateful for, be thankful for, be appreciative of, give thanks for. **2** (appreciate the urgency of the situation) recognize, acknowledge, realize, know, be aware of, be conscious of, understand. **3** (appreciate good wine) value, prize, treasure, respect, hold in high regard, think highly of, enjoy, take pleasure in. **4** (a house that has appreciated in value over the years) increase, gain, grow, rise.

apprehensive adj (apprehensive at the thought of going into hospital) frightened, fearful, scared, nervous, anxious, worried, uneasy, concerned.

apprentice n (find work as an apprentice in the garage) trainee, learner, beginner, probationer, novice.

approach **1** vb (visitors approaching the house) come/go near, draw near, move towards, advance towards. **2** (beggars approaching strangers to ask for money) go up to, speak to, talk to, engage in conversation, address, hail. **3** (approach the task with energy) set about, tackle, begin, start, commence, embark on, make a start on. **4** (temperatures approaching freezing point) come close to, come near to, approximate.

approach n **1** (the approach to the house) driveway, drive, access, entrance, entry, way in. **2** (a new approach to education) method, system, technique, procedure, style, mode, way. **3** (make approaches to the government for money) application, appeal, advances, overtures.

appropriate adj (an appropriate time/an appropriate reply) suitable, fitting, proper, right, apt, apposite, opportune.

approval n **1** (The audience showed its approval by applauding) favour, liking, admiration, appreciation, approbation, regard. **2** (The committee gave its approval to their plans) acceptance, agreement, consent, assent, sanction, authorization, (inf) the go-ahead, the green light, (inf) the OK.

approve vb **1** (unable to approve of their actions) think well of, think highly of, think favourably of, look upon with favour, like, admire, hold in high regard. **2** (*The committee approved her plans*) accept, pass, agree to, consent to, assent to, sanction, authorize, (*inf*) give the go-ahead to, give the green light to.

approximately *adv* (*a distance of approximately five miles*) about, just about, around, roughly, nearly, close to, almost, more or less, in the neighbourhood of, in the region of, circa.

apron *n* pinafore, overall, (*inf*) pinny.

apt *adj* **1** (*apt to lose his temper*) inclined, given, likely, liable, ready, disposed, prone. **2** (*an apt comment*) appropriate, suitable, fitting, applicable, relevant, apposite. **3** (*an apt pupil*) clever, bright, intelligent, quick, able.

aptitude *n* (*have an aptitude for word games*) talent, gift, flair, skill, ability, capability, bent, knack.

arbitrary *adj* **1** (*a purely arbitrary decision/The choice of players seemed arbitrary*) personal, subjective, discretionary, unreasoned, unsupported, random, chance, whimsical, capricious, erratic. **2** (*an arbitrary ruler*) despotic, tyrannical, absolute, autocratic, dictatorial, domineering.

arbitrate *vb* (*asked to arbitrate in the dispute between union and management*) adjudicate, judge, adjudge, umpire, referee.

arc *n* (*the arc of a rainbow*) curve, bow, arch, bend, crescent, semi-circle.

arch *vb* (*a cat arching its back*) curve, bend, bow, arc.

archaic *adj* (*archaic language/archaic attitudes*) old, out-of-date, old-fashioned, outmoded, antiquated, passé, obsolete, (*inf*) old-hat.

architect *n* **1** (*the architect of the new church*) designer, planner, building consultant. **2** (*the architect of the new scheme*) author, originator, planner, creator, founder, instigator, prime mover.

archives *npl* (*study the archives of the firm*) records, annals, chronicles, register, documents.

arctic *adj* (*arctic temperatures*) freezing, frozen, frigid, icy, glacial, frosty, chilly, cold.

ardent *adj* (*an ardent supporter of the local football team*) passionate, avid, fervent, zealous, eager, enthusiastic, keen.

arduous *adj* (*an arduous task*) difficult, hard, taxing, laborious, strenuous, tough, onerous, burdensome, tiring, exhausting, gruelling, Herculean.

area *n* **1** (*live in a pleasant area of the city*) district, part, region, quarter, neighbourhood, locality, sector, zone, territory. **2** (*a specialist in the area of computing*) field, sphere, department, discipline, realm, sector. **3** (*measure the area of the room*) dimensions, extent, size, expanse. **4** (*the changing area of the swimming pool*) section, part, portion, space.

arena *n* (*the sports arena*) ground, field, stadium, ring.

argue *vb* **1** (*Brother and sister are always arguing*) quarrel, disagree, bicker, squabble, wrangle, fight, dispute, (*inf*) fall out. **2** (*He argued that his method* *was the best*) assert, declare, maintain, hold, claim, contend.

argument n 1 (*children having an argument over toys*) quarrel, disagreement, squabble, wrangle, fight, dispute. 2 (*the argument against the new scheme*) reasoning, line of reasoning, reasons, grounds, case, defence, evidence, proof.

argumentative adj (*argumentative people/an argumentative mood*) quarrelsome, belligerent, disputatious, contentious, combative, litigious.

arid adj 1 (*arid areas of the world*) dry, dried up, desert, waterless, parched, barren. 2 (*an arid discussion*) uninspiring, uninteresting, dull, dreary, dry, colourless, lifeless, boring, monotonous, tedious.

arise vb 1 (*deal with any problems that arise*) appear, make an appearance, come to light, crop up, turn up, emerge, occur. 2 (*matters arising from our discussion*) result, proceed, follow, stem, originate, emanate, ensue.

aristocracy n (*a member of the British aristocracy*) nobility, peerage, gentry, upper class, high society, (*inf*) upper crust.

arm n 1 (*have an arm amputated*) upper limb. 2 (*an arm of the civil service*) branch, offshoot, section, department, division, sector.

arm vb (*arm oneself with a gun/arm oneself with a stick to protect oneself against attack*) provide, supply, equip, furnish.

armaments npl (*a military armaments store*) arms, weapons, firearms, munitions.

armistice n (*the armistice that ended the war*) truce, ceasefire, peace.

armour n (*knights wearing armour*) armour plate, chain-mail, coat of mail, mail, protective covering.

arms npl 1 (*soldiers laying down their arms*) weapons, firearms, guns, armaments. 2 (*the family arms*) coat of arms, emblem, crest, insignia, heraldic device.

army n 1 (*the invading army*) military force, troops, soldiers. 2 (*armies of tourists on the island in the summer*) horde, crowd, host, multitude, swarm, throng, mob.

aroma n (*the aroma of freshly baked bread*) smell, scent, fragrance, perfume, odour, bouquet.

aromatic adj (*aromatic spices*) fragrant, sweet-smelling, scented, perfumed, piquant, spicy, pungent.

around adv 1 (*turn around*) in the opposite direction, in reverse. 2 (*around nine o'clock/around five miles away*) approximately, roughly, close to, near to, nearly, circa. 3 (*flowers planted around the tree*) about, on all sides of, on every side of, surrounding, circling, encircling. 4 (*newspapers scattered around the room*) about, here and there in, all over, everywhere in, in all parts of.

arouse vb 1 (*The noise aroused the neighbours*) rouse, awaken, waken, wake, wake up. 2 (*behaviour arousing suspicion/actions arousing panic*) cause, induce, stir up, provoke, call forth, whip up.

arrange vb 1 (*arrange the books*) put in

order, set out, order, sort, organize, group, classify, categorize. **2** (*arrange a meeting*) fix, fix up, organize, settle on, plan, schedule.

arrangement n (*make an arrangement to meet tomorrow*) preparations, plans, provisions, agreement, deal, contract.

arrest vb **1** (*Police arrested the thieves*) take into custody, take prisoner, detain, seize, capture, catch, (*inf*) run in, nick. **2** (*try to arrest the spread of the disease*) stop, halt, bring to a halt, end, check, nip in the bud.

arresting adj (*her arresting appearance*) striking, noticeable, conspicuous, impressive, remarkable, extraordinary, unusual.

arrival n **1** (*the arrival of winter*) coming, advent, appearance, occurrence. **2** (*several new arrivals in the village*) newcomer, incomer, immigrant.

arrive vb **1** (*arrive at their destination*) reach, come to, attain. **2** (*when mother arrives*) come, get here, appear, put in an appearance, turn up, come on the scene, (*inf*) show up.

arrogant adj (*a very arrogant young woman/have a very arrogant manner*) haughty, proud, conceited, vain, self-important, egotistic, overbearing, condescending, disdainful, snobbish, supercilious, imperious, presumptions, bumptious, boastful, (*inf*) cocky, (*inf*) stuck up.

art n **1** (*studying art at college*) painting, drawing, visual arts. **2** (*the art of conversation*) skill, craft, aptitude, knack, technique, facility, talent, flair, gift.

artful adj (*get his own way by artful means*) cunning, crafty, wily, sly, deceitful, scheming, shrewd, ingenious, clever.

article n **1** (*a range of articles going on sale*) thing, object, item, commodity. **2** (*an article in the newspaper on violence*) item, piece, story, feature, report, account, write-up.

artificial adj (*artificial flowers/an artificial beard*) manmade, synthetic, imitation, simulated, ersatz, mock, sham, fake, bogus, counterfeit, (*inf*) phoney.

ashamed adj (*She was obviously ashamed of what she had done*) sorry, shame-faced, abashed, repentant, penitent, remorseful, sheepish.

ask vb **1** (*We asked where they were going*) inquire. **2** (*They asked a favour from her/You should ask for more money*) request, demand, apply for, beg for, plead for. **3** (*The police asked him about his movements on the night of the murder*) question, interrogate, cross-examine, give the third degree to, pump, (*inf*) grill.

assault vb (*They assaulted the old man to get his wallet*) attack, set upon, strike, hit, (*inf*) mug.

assemble vb **1** (*The children assembled in the school hall to hear the news*) gather, come together, congregate, convene. **2** (*He is assembling the evidence for the prosecution*) get together, gather together, collect, accumulate, amass. **3** (*You buy the furniture in a flat pack and have to assemble it yourself*) put together, fit together, construct, build, erect.

assist vb (*He assisted the doctor to care*

for the accident victims) help, aid, give assistance to, lend a hand to, support.

associate vb 1 (*She associates home with security*) connect, link, relate. 2 (*The clubs are associated in some way*) connect, link, join, attach, affiliate. 3 (*He associates with crooks*) mix, keep company with, socialize, fraternize.

astonish vb 1 (*Their boldness astonished us*) amaze, astound, dumbfound, stun, surprise.

attach vb 1 (*They should attach luggage labels to their suitcases*) fasten, tie, secure, stick, affix. 2 (*We attach no importance to that*) place, lay, put, apply, ascribe.

attend vb 1 (*He is unable to attend the meeting*) be at, be present at, put in an appearance at, be there/here. 2 (*She promised to attend to the matter immediately*) deal with, see to, cope with, handle. 3 (*You should attend to what your teacher says*) pay attention to, pay heed to, heed, listen to, take note of.

attitude n 1 (*I don't like her attitude to people from other countries*) view, point of view, opinion, outlook, thoughts, ideas. 2 (*She stood in an attitude of thought*) stance, pose, position.

attractive adj 1 (*She is a very attractive girl*) good-looking, pretty, beautiful, handsome. 2 (*That is an attractive idea*) appealing, pleasing, tempting.

authentic adj (*He is the authentic heir to the estate*) real, genuine, rightful, lawful, legal, valid.

authority n 1 (*He does not have the authority to stop us going*) power, right, control, force, influence. 2 (*We have the authority of the king to be present*) permission, sanction, authorization, (*inf*) say-so. 3 (*He is an authority on local history*) expert, specialist, pundit.

available adj 1 (*have to make do with the material that is available*) obtainable, handy, to hand, accessible, ready. 2 (*There are still tickets available*) free.

average adj 1 (*She was of average height for her age*) normal, typical, ordinary, common. 2 (*Her work was just average*) run-of-the-mill, mediocre, unexceptional.

awful adj 1 (*She has an awful cold*) dreadful, nasty, unpleasant, troublesome, bad. 2 (*in the awful presence of God*) awesome, awe-inspiring.

awkward adj 1 (*They arrived at an awkward time*) inconvenient, difficult, problematic. 2 (*She is a very awkward child and keeps bumping into things*) clumsy, ungainly, inelegant, gauche. 3 (*It is an awkward piece of furniture*) clumsy, unwieldy.

B

baby n (*babies in their prams*) infant, child, toddler.

babyish adj (*older children acting in a babyish way*) childish, immature, infantile, juvenile.

back n 1 (*the back of the building*) rear, far end. 2 (*the back of the envelope*) reverse, other side. 3 (*break his back in the accident*) spine, backbone.

back adv (*without looking back*) backwards, behind, to the rear.

back vb 1 (*back the plan*) support, give support to, help, assist, encourage, favour. 2 (*look for someone to back the theatrical production*) finance, subsidize, sponsor. 3 (*back the horse*) bet on, place a bet on, gamble on. 4 (*back the car out of the garage*) reverse, drive backwards.

backer n (*the backers of the theatrical production*) sponsor, promoter, financier, benefactor, (*inf*) angel.

background n 1 (*people from a wealthy background*) upbringing, family circumstances, environment, experience. 2 (*photographed against a white background*) setting, backdrop, scene. 3 (*in the background of the photograph*) rear, distance.

backlog n (*a backlog of work*) accumulation, stockpile, arrears, (*inf*) mountain.

backward adj 1 (*a backward look*) to the rear, rearward. 2 (*a backward area of the world*) underdeveloped, slow, retarded, unprogressive.

bacteria npl (*bacteria from rotting food*) germs, micro-organisms, (*inf*) bugs.

bad adj 1 (*bad people*) wicked, evil, immoral, wrong, sinful, dishonest, dishonourable, criminal, (*inf*) crooked, naughty, mischievous. 2 (*a bad accident*) serious, severe, terrible, shocking, appalling. 3 (*a bad performance*) poor, unsatisfactory, inadequate, inferior, substandard, defective, shoddy, (*inf*) lousy. 4 (*Smoking is a bad habit*) harmful, damaging, dangerous, unhealthy. 5 (*bad food/gone bad*) rotten, decayed, mouldy, tainted, putrid, (*inf*) off. 6 (*bad weather*) unpleasant, nasty, dreadful, terrible, disagreeable. 7 (*feel bad about hurting her*) sorry, regretful, apologetic, guilty, sad. 8 (*an invalid feeling bad today*) ill, unwell, sick, poorly, under the weather, (*inf*) below par.

badge n (*wear the club badge on their blazers*) crest, emblem, symbol.

badly adv 1 (*do the work badly*) poorly, unsatisfactorily, inadequately, shoddily. 2 (*Things worked out badly*) unsuccessfully, unfortunately, unfavourably, unluckily, unhappily. 3 (*want something badly*) greatly, very much, enormously, to a great degree. 4 (*behave badly*) wrongly, naughtily, improperly, wickedly, immorally, sinfully, criminally.

baffle vb (*police baffled by the crime/stu-*

dents *baffled by the exam question*)
puzzle, perplex, mystify, nonplus,
stump, flummox, bamboozle, bewilder.

baggage n (*collect one's baggage at the
airport*) luggage, bags, suitcases, things,
belongings, gear, paraphernalia.

baggy adj (*wear baggy clothes*) loose,
slack, roomy, floppy, ballooning.

bake vb 1 (*bake cakes*) cook. 2 (*earth
baked by the sun*) scorch, burn, parch,
dry, harden.

balance n 1 (*weigh the substance on a
balance*) scales, weighing machine.
2 (*trip and lose one's balance*) steadiness, stability, equilibrium. 3 (*pay the
balance of the account*) remainder,
rest, residue, difference, surplus, excess.

bald adj 1 (*men going bald*) baldheaded, hairless, (*inf*) thin on top. 2 (*a
bald statement*) direct, forthright,
blunt, plain, unadorned.

ball n 1 (*a glass ball*) sphere, globe, orb.
2 (*be invited to a ball*) dance, formal
dance.

ballot n (*choose the new leader by ballot*)
vote, poll, election.

ban vb (*ban smoking in the hall*) prohibit,
forbid, debar, bar, veto, make illegal.

ban n (*impose a ban on smoking*) prohibition, veto, embargo, interdict.

band n 1 (*the jazz band playing at the
wedding celebrations*) group, ensemble,
orchestra. 2 (*a band of thieves*) group,
troop, company, gang, pack, bunch,
mob, team. 3 (*a metal band/a rubber
band*) binding, cord, tie, link, ring,
hoop, ligature. 4 (*a band of blue on the*

white sweater) strip, stripe, steak, line,
bar. 5 (*a band round her hair*) ribbon,
braid.

bang n 1 (*a loud bang when the bomb
went off*) boom, crash, blast, explosion, report. 2 (*get a bang on the
head*) blow, knock, bump, hit, smack.

bang vb 1 (*the door banged shut*) slam,
crash. 2 (*bang the table with his fist*)
strike, hit, beat, thump, rap, whack,
(*inf*) bash.

bang adv (*bang in the middle of his
speech*) right, exactly, precisely, absolutely, directly, (*inf*) smack.

banish vb 1 (*banish them from their native land*) exile, deport, cast out, send
away, expel. 2 (*banish the child's fears*)
drive away, dispel, dismiss, get rid of,
cast out.

bank n 1 (*borrow money from the bank*)
financial institution, high-street bank.
2 (*a child's bank*) piggy bank, savings
bank, cash box. 3 (*a bank of information*) store, stock, reserve, reservoir,
repository. 4 (*children sliding down
grassy banks*) slope, rise, incline, hillock. 5 (*the river bank*) edge, side,
shore.

bankrupt adj (*bankrupt after the failure
of his business*) ruined, insolvent, penniless, impecunious, (*inf*) in the red,
(*inf*) on the rocks, (*inf*) broke.

banner n (*banners flying for the king's
coronation*) flag, standard, pennant,
streamer.

banquet n feast, dinner, dinner party,
(*inf*) spread.

baptize vb (*baptize a baby*) christen,
name.

bar n **1** (*an iron bar*) rod, pole, rail, girder. **2** (*a bar of soap*) block, cake, lump, wedge. **3** (*getting drunk in bars*) pub, public house.

bar vb **1** (*bar the door*) bolt, lock, padlock, fasten, secure. **2** (*bar them from joining the club*) debar, prohibit, forbid, preclude, ban. **3** (*fallen trees barring their way*) block, hinder, impede, obstruct.

bare adj **1** (*sunbathing bare*) nude, naked, stark naked, undressed, unclothed, without clothes, unclad. **2** (*a bare room*) empty, vacant, unfurnished, unadorned. **3** (*a bare landscape*) barren, bleak, desolate.

barely adv (*barely enough food*) hardly, scarcely, only just, just.

bargain n **1** (*make a bargain not to quarrel*) agreement, pact, contract, deal. **2** (*get a bargain at the sales*) good buy, (*inf*) snip.

barge vb **1** (*people barging into each other in the crowded shops*) bump, collide, cannon, crash. **2** (*barge into a private meeting*) interrupt, intrude on, burst in on, (*inf*) butt in on.

barn n outbuilding, outhouse, shed, byre.

barrel n (*a barrel of beer*) cask, keg, vat.

barren adj **1** (*barren fields*) infertile, unproductive, arid, desert, waste. **2** (*barren women*) infertile, sterile, childless. **3** (*barren discussions*) fruitless, worthless, useless, valueless, purposeless.

barricade n (*barricades keeping back the crowds*) barrier, blockade, obstacle, bar.

barrier n (*a barrier to keep the spectators off the football pitch*) barricade, bar, fence, railing, blockade.

base n **1** (*the base of the statue*) foundation, support, prop, foot. **2** (*paints with an oil base*) basis, essence, source. **3** (*climbers setting up a base*) headquarters, depot, centre, camp, starting-point.

base vb **1** (*base his statement on the facts available*) found, build, establish, ground. **2** (*base the novel on his childhood memories*) locate, situate, station.

bashful adj shy, reserved, diffident, retiring, modest, self-conscious.

basic adj (*the basic facts/the basic principles*) fundamental, elementary, rudimentary, primary, essential, chief.

basin n (*a pudding basin*) bowl, dish, container, receptacle.

basis n **1** (*the basis for his conclusions*) grounds, foundation, base. **2** (*issues that form the basis of the discussion*) starting-point, foundation, base.

batch n (*a batch of new pupils/a batch of old magazines*) group, quantity, collection, set.

bathe vb **1** (*bathe the wound*) clean, cleanse, wash. **2** (*bathe in the sea*) swim, go swimming, (*inf*) take a dip.

batter vb (*batter the door*) bang, beat, strike, knock, pound, thump.

battle n (*a battle to prevent the enemy army invading*) conflict, fight, clash, skirmish, engagement, encounter, struggle, contest.

bawl vb (*bawl in order to attract attention*) shout, cry out, yell, roar, bellow, scream.

bay n (*ships anchored in the bay*) inlet, cove, gulf, basin, bight.

bay vb howl, bark, yell, cry, growl.

bazaar n (*tourists at an eastern bazaar*) market, market-place, souk.

beach n (*pull the boat on to the beach*) seaside, coast, shore, sands.

beam n **1** (*roof beams*) board, timber, plank, joist, rafter, support. **2** (*a beam of light*) ray, shaft, steam, streak, flash, gleam, glint.

bear vb **1** (*bearing gifts*) carry, bring, take, convey. **2** (*bear the weight*) carry, support, hold up, sustain. **3** (*unable to bear the pain*) put up with, stand, suffer, endure, tolerate. **4** (*bear a son*) give birth to, produce. **5** (*bear a grudge*) have, hold, harbour.

bearded adj (*a bearded man*) unshaven, whiskered, stubbly, hirsute.

bearings npl (*lose our bearings on the mountain*) location, position, whereabouts, way, course, direction.

beast n **1** (*the beasts of the jungle*) animal, creature, mammal. **2** (*He was an absolute beast*) brute, monster, savage, pig, ogre.

beat vb **1** (*beat the drum*) bang, hit, strike, pound. **2** (*with hearts beating*) throb, pound, thump, pulsate, pulse, palpitate. **3** (*They beat their children*) hit, strike, batter, thump, wallop, thrash, slap. **4** (*birds with their wings beating*) flap, flutter, vibrate. **5** (*beat the butter and sugar*) mix, blend, whisk, stir. **6** (*beat the opposition*) defeat, conquer, vanquish, rout, trounce, crush, overwhelm, (*inf*) lick.

7 (*beat the record*) outdo, surpass, exceed, excel, transcend.

beat n **1** (*the beat of the music*) rhythm, time, measure, pulse, throb. **2** (*the policeman's beat*) round, circuit, course, route.

beautiful adj **1** (*a beautiful woman*) lovely, pretty, attractive, handsome, glamorous, gorgeous. **2** (*a beautiful view*) lovely, attractive, picturesque, charming, delightful, magnificent, splendid.

beauty n **1** (*a woman of great beauty*) loveliness, prettiness, attractiveness, handsomeness, glamour. **2** (*the beauty of the scheme*) advantage, benefit, asset.

becoming adj **1** (*a becoming dress*) flattering, attractive, elegant. **2** (*behaviour that was hardly becoming*) fitting, suitable, appropriate, apt, proper, seemly, decorous.

before adv (*We had met before*) previously, earlier, formerly, in the past.

beg vb **1** (*homeless people begging in the streets*) ask for money, cadge, scrounge. **2** (*beg for mercy*) ask for, require, plead for, entreat, beseech, implore.

beggar n vagrant, down-and-out, tramp, mendicant.

begin vb **1** (*begin work*) start, commence, set about, embark on. **2** (*when the trouble begins*) start, commence, get going, arise.

beginning n **1** (*the beginning of he relationship*) start, starting-point, commencement, outset, onset, inception. **2** (*the beginning of the book*) start, commencement, first part, introduction, opening, preface.

begrudge vb (begrudge him his success) grudge, envy, be envious of, resent, be jealous of.

behave vb (behave in a responsible way) act, conduct oneself.

behaviour n (criticize the behaviour of the football crowd) actions, conduct, manners.

being n 1 (the reason for our being) existence, life, living. 2 (beings from another planet) creature, living thing, individual.

belief n 1 (It is her belief that he is still alive) opinion, feeling, impression, view, viewpoint, way of thinking, theory. 2 (religious beliefs) faith, creed, doctrine, credo. 3 (have no belief in their ability) faith, trust, reliance.

belligerent adj (a belligerent fellow who started a fight) aggressive, quarrelsome, argumentative, pugnacious.

belong vb 1 (The car belongs to me) be owned by, be the property of. 2 (She belongs to the tennis club) be a member of, be associated with.

belongings npl (lose all her belongings) possessions, things, property, personal effects.

beloved adj (her beloved husband) dearest, darling, loved, adored.

beloved n (wish to marry her beloved) sweetheart, boyfriend/girlfriend, fiancé/fiancée.

belt n 1 (wear a plastic belt round her waist) girdle, sash, strap, cummerbund. 2 (a belt of green fields between the towns) area, region, tract, zone.

3 (a belt of blue across the white walls) strip, stripe, streak, line, band.

bench n 1 (pupils sitting on a bench) form, seat. 2 (a carpenter's bench) work-bench, work-table, table, counter.

bend vb 1 (try to bend the iron band) curve, flex, loop, arch, twist, contort, warp. 2 (The road bends to the left) curve, turn, twist, swerve, veer, incline. 3 (She bent down to pick up the letter) stoop, crouch down, lean down, bow down.

bend n (a bend in the road) curve, turn, twist, corner, angle.

beneficial adj (a climate beneficial to her health) of benefit, advantageous, favourable, helpful.

benefit n 1 (one of the benefits of living near the sea) advantage, gain, good point, asset, boon. 2 (things that are of benefit to all) advantage, good, profit, use, value, help, service.

benevolent adj 1 (a benevolent old man) kind, kindly, kind-hearted, generous, helpful. 2 (benevolent institutions) charitable, non-profit-making.

bent adj 1 (a bent iron rod) curved, crooked, angled, twisted, contorted, warped. 2 (with bent backs) bowed, arched, stooped, hunched.

bent n (of a musical bent) inclination, leaning, tendency, predisposition, talent, aptitude, flair.

bequest n (receive a bequest in her employer's will) legacy, inheritance.

bereavement n (Their grandfather has died—we must sympathize with them on their bereavement at this sad time) loss, death, decease.

bereft adj (bereft of speech) deprived of, robbed of, devoid of, lacking.

berserk adj (He went berserk when he saw the damage to his car) mad, insane, frenzied, out of one's mind, wild, enraged, raging, amok, (inf) ape, (inf) bananas.

besides adv (I do not want to go—besides it is too late) also, in addition, additionally, moreover, furthermore.

besides prep (four people besides us) as well as, apart from, in addition to, not counting.

besiege vb (a city besieged by the enemy) lay siege to, blockade, surround, encircle, beleaguer.

best adj 1 (the best player) top, foremost, leading, finest. 2 (the best thing to do) right, correct, most suitable, most fitting.

bet vb (bet £100 on a horse) gamble, wager, stake, risk, venture.

bet n 1 (place a bet on a horse) wager, stake. 2 (one's best bet) choice, option, alternative, course of action.

betray vb 1 (betray his friend to the police) be disloyal to, break faith with, inform on, double-cross, (inf) blow the whistle on, sell down the river. 2 (betray her secret) reveal, disclose, divulge, let slip, give away.

beware vb (advised to beware of thieves) be careful, be wary, be on one's guard, guard against, watch out.

bewilder vb (bewildered by all the traffic signs) confuse, muddle, puzzle, perplex, baffle, nonplus, bamboozle, bemuse.

bewitch vb 1 (bewitched by the pianist's performance) captivate, enchant, entrance, beguile, charm. 2 (The wizard bewitched the prince) put a spell on, cast a spell over, enchant.

biased adj (accuse the referee of being biased/a biased attitude) prejudiced, one-sided, influenced, partial, bigoted, unfair, unjust.

bid vb 1 (bid £100 for the vase at the auction) offer, tender, proffer, put forward. 2 (bid them farewell) wish, greet, tell, say.

big adj 1 (a big house/a big car) large, sizeable, great, substantial, huge, enormous, vast, colossal, gigantic. 2 (a big man) large, tall, heavy, burly, thickset. 3 (a big decision) important, significant, major, serious, grave, weighty.

bigotry n (religious bigotry) prejudice, intolerance, bias, partiality, narrow-mindedness, fanaticism.

bilious adj 1 sick, nauseated, queasy. 2 (walls of a bilious colour) garish, violent, nauseating.

bill n 1 (send them the bill for the work/pay the restaurant bill) account, invoice, (inf) tab. 2 (post bills to advertise the show) poster, advertisement, notice, circular.

bin n (a rubbish bin/a bin for corn) container, receptacle, box, can.

bind vb 1 (bind the sheaves of corn together) tie, tie up, fasten, secure, attach, truss. 2 (bind the wound) bandage, dress, cover. 3 (bind the seams) edge trim, hem, finish.

birth n 1 (present at the birth) delivery,

childbirth, confinement. **2** (*of humble birth*) origin, descent, family, parentage, extraction, ancestry. **3** (*the birth of civilization*) origin, beginning, start, creation.

bit *n* (*a bit of chocolate/a bit of cheese*) piece, section, segment, lump, chunk, scrap, sliver, morsel, grain, speck, particle.

bite *vb* **1** (*bite into the apple/biting her nails*) chew, munch, crunch, nibble at, gnaw at, eat. **2** (*The dog bit the postman*) sink one's teeth into, snap at, nip. **3** (*bitten by mosquitoes*) sting, puncture.

bite *n* **1** (*a bite of the apple/a bite of food*) mouthful, piece, morsel, bit. **2** (*The dog gave her a bite*) snap, nip. **3** (*insect bites*) sting, prick, puncture. **4** (*food with a bite*) sharpness, spiciness, piquancy, pungency.

bitter *adj* **1** (*a bitter taste*) acid, tart, sour, acrid, harsh, pungent, vinegary. **2** (*a bitter old man*) embittered, resentful, sour, acrimonious, spiteful, vindictive. **3** (*a bitter wind*) biting, sharp, raw, penetrating, stinging, freezing. **4** (*from bitter experience*) painful, distressing, unhappy, sad, tragic.

black *adj* **1** (*black clothes/black horses*) jet-black, pitch-black, inky, sable, dusky. **2** (*black nights*) dark, pitch-black, inky, murky, unlit, starless. **3** (*in a black mood*) depressed, gloomy, pessimistic, melancholy, sad.

blame *vb* **1** (*blame her for the crime*) hold responsible, hold accountable, accuse, charge, find guilty, condemn.

2 (*blame the crime on her*) attribute, ascribe, lay at the door of, (*inf*) pin on.

blame *n* (*put the blame for the crime on her*) responsibility, accountability, liability, fault, accusation, guilt, condemnation (*inf*) rap.

bland *adj* **1** (*bland food*) tasteless, flavourless, insipid, mild. **2** (*a bland manner*) smooth, suave, urbane, gracious.

blank *adj* **1** (*a blank piece of paper*) empty, unfilled, unwritten on, unmarked, bare. **2** (*a blank tape*) clean, empty, unfilled, unused. **3** (*a blank face*) expressionless, vacant, empty, deadpan, impassive.

blast *n* **1** (*hear the blast several streets away*) explosion, bang, report, eruption. **2** (*a blast of cold air*) gust, rush, draught, wind, gale. **3** (*a blast of loud music*) blare, boom, roar.

blatant *adj* (*a blatant crime*) glaring, flagrant, obvious, conspicuous, unmistakable, brazen.

blaze *n* **1** (*old people killed in the blaze*) fire, flames, conflagration, inferno. **2** (*a sudden blaze of light*) flash, flare, beam, streak.

blaze *vb* **1** (*logs blazing in the fire*) burn, be ablaze, flame. **2** (*lights blazing*) shine, beam, flash, flare.

bleak *adj* **1** (*a bleak countryside*) bare, barren, desolate, dismal, exposed. **2** (*a bleak future*) gloomy, depressing, miserable, dismal, grim, dark.

blemish *n* **1** (*blemishes on the fruit*) mark, spot, blotch, bruise, imperfection. **2** (*a blemish in his character*) flaw, fault, defect. **3** (*a blemish on her reputation*) stain, blot.

blend vb (blend the ingredients for the pudding) mix, combine, mingle.

blessing n **1** (The minister said a blessing) benediction, grace, prayer, dedication. **2** (The rain is a blessing for the dried-out gardens) boon, advantage, benefit, asset, help. **3** (give the scheme his blessing) approval, support, sanction, endorsement.

blind adj **1** (a blind person with a guide dog) unsighted, sightless, unseeing, visually impaired, visually challenged. **2** (blind to the problems) unmindful of, heedless of, oblivious to, indifferent to, unaware of, unconscious of, ignorant of.

blind n **1** (The blind kept out the sunlight) screen, shade, shutters, curtain. **2** (His shop was a blind for drug-pushing) front, screen, smoke screen, camouflage, cloak, disguise.

blink vb **1** (people blinking in the bright light) screw up one's eyes, wink, squint. **2** (with eyelids blinking) flicker, wink, bat. **3** (Christmas trees blinking) flicker, twinkle, wink, glimmer, glitter.

bliss n (the bliss of being in love) ecstasy, elation, euphoria, joy, rapture, happiness, delight.

block n **1** (a block of chocolate) bar, cake, brick, slab, chunk, lump, hunk, wedge. **2** (a block in the waste pipe) blockage, obstruction, stoppage. **3** (the science block of the university) building, complex.

block vb **1** (leaves blocking the drains) clog, choke, stop up, obstruct, (inf) bung up. **2** (fallen trees blocking the flow of traffic) bar, halt, obstruct, hinder, impede, hold back.

bloodshed n (a battle which resulted in great bloodshed) killing, murder, slaughter, massacre, carnage.

bloom vb **1** (flowers which bloom in the summer) flower, be in flower, come into flower, blossom. **2** (children blooming in their new environment) flourish, thrive, blossom, get on well, prosper, succeed.

blot n **1** (ink blots/blots of grease) blotch, spot, smudge, splodge, smear. **2** (a blot on her character) stain, blemish, flaw, fault, defect, taint.

blot vb **1** (paper blotted with ink spots) spot, smudge, blotch, smear, mark. **2** (blot their reputation) sully, blacken, stain, tarnish, besmirch. **3** (blot out memories of the past) wipe out, rub out, erase, obliterate, destroy.

blow n **1** (a blow on the head) hit, knock, bang, thump, smack, slap, rap, (inf) clout. **2** (It was a blow when her friend went away) shock, upset, jolt, setback, disappointment, misfortune, disaster, catastrophe.

blue adj **1** (blue skies) azure, indigo, sapphire, ultramarine, navy, navy blue, sky-blue, powder-blue, royal blue. **2** (feeling blue) depressed, gloomy, miserable, downcast, glum, sad, unhappy, melancholy. **3** (blue jokes) obscene, indecent, improper, dirty, smutty.

bluff vb (She believed him but he was only bluffing) pretend, sham, fake, feign, put it on, lie, deceive, fool, hoax, hoodwink.

bluff n (He said that he would report her

but it was only a bluff) pretence, sham, fake, deception, subterfuge, hoax.

bluff adj (*a bluff manner*) outspoken, plain-spoken, blunt, direct, frank, candid.

blunder n (*make a blunder in the calculations*) mistake, error, slip, inaccuracy, (*inf*) slip-up, (*inf*) boob, (*inf*) clanger.

blunder vb 1 (*discover that someone had blundered and had forgotten to book the hall*) make a mistake, err, (*inf*) slip up, screw up. 2 (*blundering about in the dark without a torch*) stumble, lurch, stagger, flounder.

blunt adj 1 (*a blunt knife*) dull, dulled, unsharpened. 2 (*a blunt statement*) abrupt, curt, brusque, outspoken, plainspoken, direct, frank, straightforward, candid.

blur vb 1 (*Tears blurred her vision*) obscure, dim, make hazy, make misty, make fuzzy, cloud. 2 (*Grease blurred the windscreen*) smear, smudge. 3 (*Time had blurred her memory*) dim, make hazy, make vague, dull, confuse.

blur n (*When she did not have her glasses on everything was just a blur*) haze, mist.

blurred adj (*blurred vision*) hazy, misty, fuzzy, indistinct, unclear.

blush vb (*She blushed with embarrassment*) redden, go red, turn red, go scarlet, go crimson, flush, colour.

board n 1 (*a bridge made of wooden boards*) plank, slat, beam. 2 (*charge her for her board*) food, meals.

board vb 1 (*board the plane*) get on, enter, go on board, mount, embark. 2 (*board up the windows*) cover up,

shut up, seal. 3 (*He boards with a friend of his mother*) lodge, live, have rooms.

boast vb (*She was always boasting about how well she could sing*) brag, crow, blow one's own trumpet, show off, swagger, (*inf*) swank.

boastful adj (*a boastful person always telling people about her fine house*) bragging, swaggering, conceited, vain, (*inf*) big-headed, (*inf*) swanking.

boat n vessel, craft, dinghy, yacht, ship, rowing-boat.

body n 1 (*healthy bodies*) physique. 2 (*pains in his body and in his limbs*) trunk, torso. 3 (*bodies in the mortuary*) dead body, corpse, carcass, cadaver. 4 (*the ruling body in the organization*) group, party, band, company, bloc. 5 (*a large body of water*) mass, expanse, extent.

bodyguard n (*the president's bodyguard*) guard, protector, defender.

bog n (*The walkers got stuck in the bog*) marsh, marshland, swamp, mire, quagmire.

bogus adj 1 (*The man in the hospital turned out to be a bogus doctor*) fraudulent, fake, sham, (*inf*) phoney. 2 (*pay for the goods with bogus £10 notes*) counterfeit, forged, fake, fraudulent, sham, (*inf*) phoney.

boil vb (*soup boiling on the stove*) bubble, cook, simmer.

boisterous adj 1 (*boisterous children*) lively, active, spirited, noisy, loud, rowdy, unruly. 2 (*a boisterous wind*) blustery, gusting, stormy, wild.

bold adj 1 (*a bold adventurer*) brave,

courageous, valiant, gallant, daring, adventurous, intrepid, fearless, heroic. **2** (*a bold young woman/so bold as to invite themselves to the party*) brazen, impudent, forward, audacious. **3** (*bold colours*) striking, bright, vivid, eye-catching, showy.

bolt n **1** (*bolts on the door*) bar, catch, latch, fastener, lock. **2** (*nuts and bolts*) rivet, pin, peg. **3** (*make a bolt for it*) dash, run, sprint, dart, rush.

bolt vb **1** (*They bolted the door*) bar, lock, fasten, secure. **2** (*bolt from the room in fear*) dash, run, sprint, dart, rush, hurtle, flee. **3** (*The children bolted their food*) gulp, gobble, wolf, guzzle.

bomb n (*a building blown up by a bomb*) incendiary device, incendiary, explosive, shell.

bombard vb **1** (*The enemy bombarded the military stores*) bomb, shell, torpedo, blitz, attack. **2** (*bombard them with questions*) assail, attack, besiege, subject to.

bond n **1** (*the bond between mother and child*) tie, link, connection, attachment. **2** (*prisoners escaping from their bonds*) chains, fetters, shackles, rope.

bonus n **1** (*The good food on holiday was a welcome bonus*) extra, addition, (*inf*) plus, benefit, gain, boon. **2** (*staff getting a Christmas bonus*) gift, tip, gratuity, (*inf*) perk, reward.

bony adj angular, scraggy, gaunt, skinny, skeletal.

book vb (*book theatre seats/book hotel rooms*) reserve, make reservations for.

book n (*borrow a book from the library*) volume, tome, publication.

bookish adj (*She is rather a bookish child*) studious, scholarly, academic, intellectual, learned, highbrow.

boom vb **1** (*hear guns booming*) bang, banging, blast, roar, rumble. **2** (*a boom in the number of tourists*) increase, growth, upsurge, upswing, upturn, boost.

boor n (*boors with bad manners*) lout, oaf, (*inf*) yob, (*inf*) yobbo.

boost vb (*boost the morale of the troops*) raise, increase, heighten, improve, encourage, help, assist.

booth n **1** (*a market booth*) stall, stand, counter. **2** (*a telephone booth*) cubicle, compartment.

booty n (*the booty hidden by the burglars*) loot, spoils, plunder, haul, (*inf*) swag.

border n **1** (*sew a colourful border on the skirt*) edging, edge, fringe, trimming. **2** (*a flower border*) bed. **3** (*the borders of the lake*) edge, verge, perimeter, margin. **4** (*show one's passport at the border*) frontier, boundary.

bore vb **1** (*bore into the wood/bore a hole in the wood*) drill, pierce, perforate, penetrate, puncture. **2** (*an audience bored by the comedian*) weary, tire, fatigue, be tedious to, bore to tears, bore to death.

boring adj (*a boring speech*) dull, tedious, monotonous, unexciting, uninteresting, wearisome, tiring.

borrow vb (*borrow money from someone/borrow someone's pen*) ask for the loan of, take as a loan, use temporarily, (*inf*) scrounge, (*inf*) cadge.

boss n (*The workers asked the boss for a wage rise*) employer, manager, director, owner, (*inf*) honcho.

bossy adj domineering, bullying, overbearing, dominating, dictatorial.

bother vb **1** (*The children were told not to bother their mother when she was resting*) disturb, trouble, worry, pester, annoy, harass, (*inf*) hassle. **2** (*Please don't bother to wait for me*) take the trouble, trouble oneself, inconvenience oneself, make the effort. **3** (*It bothers me that she is not here yet*) concern, worry, trouble, upset.

bother n **1** (*Please don't go to any bother over dinner*) trouble, inconvenience, effort, fuss. **2** (*There was a bit of bother at the football match*) trouble, disturbance, commotion, disorder, fighting.

bottle n **1** (*a bottle of milk/a bottle of wine*) container, flask, carafe. **2** (*not have the bottle to climb the high tree*) courage, bravery, daring, nerve, boldness.

bottom n **1** (*at the bottom of the hill*) foot, base. **2** (*the bottom of the sea*) floor, bed, depths. **3** (*the bottom of the garden*) the far end, the farthest point.

bound vb (*bound into the room/bound over the fence*) leap, jump, spring, vault, spring.

bound adj (*She thought that she was bound to win*) certain, sure, very likely, destined.

boundary n **1** (*the boundary between the countries*) border, frontier, dividing line. **2** (*the boundary of the estate*) bounds, border, perimeter, periphery, confines, limits, margin.

bouquet n **1** (*the bride's bouquet/a bouquet of roses*) bunch of flowers, bunch, spray, posy.

bout n **1** (*a boxing bout*) combat, contest, match, round, fight. **2** (*a bout of coughing*) fit, attack, turn, spell.

bow vb (*bow his head*) incline, bend, nod, stoop.

bowl n (*a bowl of cereal*) dish, basin, container.

bowl vb (*bowl a ball*) pitch, throw, fling, hurl, toss.

box n container, receptacle, carton, case, pack, chest, bin, crate.

box vb **1** (*He used to box for England*) fight. **2** (*box the child on the ears*) strike, hit, cuff, slap, smack, wallop, (*inf*) belt.

boy n (*when he was a boy*) youth, lad.

boycott vb **1** (*boycott goods from that country*) bar, ban, black, blacklist, embargo, place an embargo on, prohibit. **2** (*boycott their company*) shun, avoid, spurn, send to Coventry, eschew.

boyfriend n (*She has a new boyfriend*) sweetheart, young man, lover, partner.

bracing adj (*a bracing climate*) invigorating, refreshing, stimulating, exhilarating, reviving, health-giving.

brag vb (*He brags about having a lot of money*) boast, crow, blow one's own trumpet, show off, (*inf*) talk big.

brain n (*have a good brain*) intellect, mind, intelligence, powers of reasoning, head.

branch n **1** (*the branch of a tree*)

bough, limb. **2** (*the local branch of the business*) division, subdivision, section, department, part.

brand n **1** (*a brand of breakfast cereal*) make, kind, variety, type, sort, line, label, trade name, trademark. **2** (*her brand of wit*) kind, variety, type, sort, style.

brandish vb (*a criminal brandishing a knife*) wave, flourish, swing, wield, shake.

brash adj (*a brash young man*) bold, cocky, self-confident, self-assertive, insolent, impudent, cheeky, brazen.

brave adj courageous, valiant, intrepid, fearless, plucky, gallant, heroic, bold, daring.

brawl n (*a brawl in a public house*) fight, affray, wrangle, rumpus, row, quarrel, argument, squabble, free-for-all, scrap.

brawny adj (*brawny hammer-throwers*) burly, muscular, hefty, powerful, strong, strapping.

bray vb (*donkeys braying*) whinny, neigh, hee-haw.

brazen adj (*It was brazen of her to kiss a complete stranger on the lips*) bold, audacious, forward, brash, impudent, insolent, impertinent, immodest, shameless.

breach n **1** (*a breach in the sea wall*) break, split, crack, gap, hole, opening. **2** (*a breach of the legal agreement*) breaking, violation, infringement.

breadth n **1** (*measure the breadth of the room*) width, wideness, broadness, span. **2** (*discover the breadth of her knowledge of the subject*) extent, range, scope, scale, degree.

break vb **1** (*break a cup*) smash, shatter, crack. **2** (*break the handle of the bag*) snap, split, tear. **3** (*The machine broke*) break down, become damaged, stop working, cease to operate, (*inf*) go kaput. **4** (*break the law*) violate, contravene, breach, infringe, disobey, disregard, defy. **5** (*break his arm*) fracture, crack. **6** (*break the news*) tell, impart, announce, communicate, reveal, disclose.

break n **1** (*a break in the water pipe*) crack, hole, gash, split, fracture, chink, tear. **2** (*a break in her career to look after her children*) interruption, discontinuation, pause, hiatus. **3** (*have a cup of tea during her break*) rest period, interval, intermission, breathing-space. **4** (*take a weekend break*) holiday, vacation, time off.

breakthrough n (*a breakthrough in cancer research*) advance, step forward, development.

breathe vb **1** (*breathe in/breathe out*) inhale/exhale, inspire/expire, puff, pant. **2** (*as long as he breathes*) be alive, live, have life.

breathless adj (*breathless after running for the bus*) out of breath, gasping, panting, puffing.

breed n (*a breed of cattle*) variety, kind, strain.

breed vb **1** (*Rabbits breed very rapidly*) reproduce, multiply, give birth. **2** (*He breeds horses*) raise, rear. **3** (*poverty which can breed crime and violence*) cause, bring about, give rise to, create, produce, stir up.

breeze n (a cool breeze on a hot day) puff of wind, gust of wind, current of air, draught, zephyr.

bribe vb (try to bribe a member of the jury) buy off, corrupt, give an inducement to, (inf) grease the palm of, (inf) give a backhander to, (inf) give a sweetener to.

bridge n (a bridge over the motorway) overpass, flyover, viaduct, suspension bridge.

brief adj 1 (a brief statement) short, concise, succinct, to the point, compact, terse. 2 (a brief friendship) short, short-lived, fleeting, passing, transient, transitory, ephemeral.

brief vb (brief a lawyer) instruct, give instructions to, direct, give directions to, inform, give information to, prime.

bright adj 1 (a bright light) shining, brilliant, dazzling, blazing, gleaming, radiant. 2 (bright colours) vivid, brilliant, intense, glowing, bold, rich. 3 (bright children) clever, intelligent, sharp, quick, quick-witted, (inf) smart, brilliant, (inf) brainy, gifted, talented. 4 (a bright future) promising, favourable, hopeful, optimistic, encouraging, fortunate, good.

brilliant adj 1 (a brilliant light) bright, shining, dazzling, gleaming, radiant. 2 (brilliant children) bright, clever, intelligent, sharp, quick, quick-witted, (inf) smart, (inf) brainy, gifted, talented.

brim n (glasses full to the brim) rim, lip, top, edge.

brim vb (glasses brimming with wine/eyes brimming with tears) be full, be filled with, overflow, run over.

bring vb 1 (bring food home) carry, take, convey, transport, fetch. 2 (famine which brought disease) cause, produce, create, result in, give rise to.

brink n 1 (on the brink of the lake) edge, verge, boundary, border, margin. 2 (on the brink of the disaster) edge, verge, threshold, point.

brisk adj 1 (walk at a brisk speed) quick, fast, rapid, swift, speedy, energetic, lively. 2 (Business was brisk) busy, active, hectic.

brittle adj (Toffee is a brittle substance) hard, crisp, breakable, splintery.

broad adj 1 (a broad street) wide. 2 (a broad range of subjects) wide, wide-ranging, broad-ranging, general, comprehensive. 3 (a broad statement of their plans) general, non-detailed, imprecise, vague.

brochure n (an advertising brochure) booklet, leaflet, pamphlet, circular, notice, bill.

brooch n (She wears a silver brooch on her lapel) pin, clip.

brow n 1 (wipe the sweat from his brow) forehead, temple. 2 (the brow of the hill) top, summit, crown, peak.

brown adj (go brown in the summer) tanned, sun-tanned, bronze, bronzed.

brush vb 1 (brush the back yard) sweep, clean. 2 (brush her hair) groom, tidy. 3 (brush her cheek with his lips) touch, flick, glance.

brusque adj (a brusque reply) abrupt, blunt, curt, sharp, gruff, rude.

brutal adj (a brutal attack) savage, cruel, vicious, callous, ruthless.

bubble vb 1 (*champagne bubbling*) fizz, effervesce, sparkle, foam, froth. 2 (*a sauce bubbling on the stove*) boil, simmer.

bucket n (*need a bucket of water to wash the floor*) pail, container.

buckle n (*the buckle of the belt*) clasp, catch, fastener, fastening, clip.

bug n 1 (*bitten by bugs when sitting on the grass*) insect, mite, (*inf*) creepy-crawly. 2 (*He caught a bug and is off work*) infection, virus, germ, bacterium, micro-organism.

build vb 1 (*build a new school*) construct, put up, erect. 2 (*build model planes*) make, construct, assemble, put together. 3 (*build his own business*) found, set up, establish, start, begin, develop, institute.

building n (*old buildings which are tourist attractions*) edifice, structure.

bulge n (*The bag of sweets made a bulge in her pocket*) swelling, bump, lump, protuberance.

bulk n 1 (*The wardrobe was difficult to move because of its sheer bulk*) size, mass, extent, largeness, hugeness. 2 (*The bulk of the people voted against the proposal*) majority, most, preponderance, mass.

bulky adj (*bulky furniture*) large, big, massive, substantial, heavy, unwieldy, cumbersome, awkward.

bully vb (*older boys bullying the younger ones*) browbeat, domineer, intimidate, threaten, persecute, torment, tyrannize, (*inf*) push around.

bump vb (*The car that bumped into ours was not insured*) knock, hit, strike, crash into, bang, collide with, ram.

bump n 1 (*The child fell out of the tree with a bump*) thud, thump, bang, jolt, crash. 2 (*He has a bump on the head from the accident*) lump, swelling, bulge.

bumpy adj (*bumpy roads*) uneven, rough, rutted, pitted, potholed.

bunch n 1 (*a bunch of flowers*) bouquet, spray, posy, sheaf. 2 (*a bunch of grapes*) cluster, clump. 3 (*a friendly bunch of people*) group, band, crowd, gang.

bundle n (*a bundle of old clothes*) pile, heap, stack, bale.

burden n 1 (*the pony's burden*) load, pack. 2 (*the burden of being head of the family*) responsibility, obligation, onus, worry, weight, strain.

burglar n (*catch a burglar breaking into the house*) housebreaker, cat burglar, thief, robber.

burglary n (*He was sent to prison on a charge of burglary*) house-breaking, breaking and entering, forced entry, theft, robbery, larceny.

burly adj (*the burly figure of the hammer-thrower*) muscular, powerful, thickset, strapping, hefty, beefy, stout.

burn vb 1 (*The house was burning*) be on fire, be ablaze, blaze. 2 (*burn the rubbish*) set on fire, set alight, ignite. 3 (*burn the shirt with the iron*) scorch, singe, sear.

burst vb 1 (*The water pipes have burst*) crack, split, fracture, rupture. 2 (*They burst into the room*) push one's way, barge. 3 (*burst into tears*) break out, explode, erupt, begin suddenly.

bury vb 1 (bury the corpse) inter, lay to rest. 2 (bury her head in her hands) hide, conceal, cover, put, submerge.

business n 1 (She owns her own business) company, firm, concern, organization, establishment. 2 (We don't know what business he is in) occupation, line, work, profession, job, career. 3 (It was none of their business) concern, affair, problem, responsibility. 4 (an odd business) affair, situation, matter, circumstance, thing.

busy adj 1 (Don't disturb your mother—she's busy) occupied, engaged, working, at work. 2 (have a busy day) active, energetic, full, hectic.

buy vb (buy a new house) purchase, make a purchase of, pay for, invest in.

bypass n (the city bypass) ring road, detour, alternative route.

C

café n (*They stopped for a snack at a café*) coffee bar, coffee shop, cafeteria, snack bar, tea-room, tea shop, restaurant, wine bar, bistro.

cajole vb (*Try to cajole him into coming with us*) wheedle, coax, inveigle, persuade.

cagey adj (*They seemed rather cagey about where they were going*) secretive, guarded, non-committal.

cake n 1 (*have some cake and coffee*) gateau. 2 (*a cake of soap*) bar, block, slab, lump.

calculate vb (*calculate the cost*) work out, count, estimate, gauge, figure out, reckon.

call vb 1 (*She called out in fear*) cry, shout, yell, scream. 2 (*They called their son Peter*) name, christen. 3 (*The vegetables are called courgettes/That is called wind-surfing*) name, style, designate, term, describe, dub, label. 4 (*She called you from a public telephone box*) telephone, phone, ring. 5 (*He will call tomorrow to do his aunt's shopping*) pay a call, pay a visit, stop by, drop in. 6 (*If the child is ill you had better call a doctor*) send for, ask for, summon. 7 (*They called a meeting of the committee*) call together, convene, summon. 8 (*I call it shocking that he got away with the crime*) think, consider, regard, judge.

calm adj 1 (*She remains calm even in an emergency*) cool, composed, self-possessed, unruffled, tranquil, quiet. 2 (*The sea was calm when the boat set out*) still, smooth. 3 (*It was a calm day for their trip to the seaside*) still, windless, mild.

camouflage n (*The polar bear's coat is a camouflage in the snow*) protective colouring, disguise, cover, screen, concealment.

camp n 1 (*the soldier's camp*) encampment, campsite, camping ground. 2 (*He is in the left-wing camp of the party*) group, set, faction, clique.

can n (*a can of soup*) tin, container.

cancel vb 1 (*They had to cancel the meeting because of bad weather*) put off, call off. 2 (*They cancelled the order because it was late*) call off, retract, declare void, declare null and void, revoke.

candid adj (*He was quite candid with them about his reasons for leaving*) frank, open, honest, direct, forthright, blunt, plainspoken.

cap n 1 (*He wore a cap to hide his baldness*) hat, bonnet. 2 (*I can't get the cap off the bottle*) top, lid, stopper, cork.

capable adj 1 (*She is a very capable person*) able, competent, efficient, effective. 2 (*He is quite capable of cheating*) likely to, liable to.

capital n 1 (*Edinburgh is the capital of Scotland*) first city, chief city, seat of administration. 2 (*He does not have enough capital to buy the company*) money, finance, funds, cash, means, resources, wherewithal, assets. **3** (*write the title in capitals*) capital letter, upper case letter, (*inf*) cap.

capsize vb **1** (*The boat capsized in heavy seas*) overturn, turn over, up-end, keel over, turn turtle. **2** (*The child capsized the bucket of water*) upset, overturn, up-end.

captivity n (*enjoy freedom after months in captivity*) imprisonment, custody, confinement, incarceration.

capture vb (*The police have captured the escaped prisoners*) catch, take prisoner, take captive, take into custody, arrest, apprehend, seize.

card n **1** (*She sent a card to her mother on her birthday*) greetings card, postcard. **2** (*The salesman handed them his card*) business card, identification, ID. **3** (*He was asked to deal the cards*) playing card.

care n **1** (*The children were told to cross the road with care*) carefulness, caution, heed, heedfulness, wariness, attention, vigilance, prudence. **2** (*She iced the cake with care*) carefulness, conscientiousness, accuracy, meticulousness, punctiliousness. **3** (*The child is in the care of the local authorities*) protection, charge, keeping, custody, supervision. **4** (*They show no care for other people*) concern, regard, interest, solicitude, sympathy. **5** (*She looked older than she was after a life full of care*) worry, anxiety, trouble, distress, hardship, stress.

careful adj **1** (*The children were told to be careful crossing the road*) cautious,

heedful, wary, attentive, vigilant, prudent. **2** (*You must be careful of your belongings at the airport*) mindful, heedful, protective. **3** (*You must be careful what you say to the lawyer*) mindful, attentive, heedful, thoughtful. **4** (*They are all careful workers*) conscientious, painstaking, accurate, meticulous, punctilious. **5** (*They do not earn much and so they have to be very careful with money*) thrifty, economic, frugal, cautious, canny.

careless adj **1** (*a careless pedestrian who walked out in front of the moving car*) unthinking, inattentive, thoughtless, forgetful, remiss, negligent. **2** (*The pupil's exercise is very careless*) inaccurate, slapdash, disorganized, (*inf*) sloppy.

carpet n **1** (*They laid a new carpet in the hall*) rug, floor covering, mat. **2** (*a carpet of autumn leaves on the grass*) covering, layer.

carry vb **1** (*She was asked to carry the shopping home*) bring, take, transport, convey, lug. **2** (*Will the bridge carry the weight of the car?*) take, support, bear, sustain. **3** (*The shop carries a wide range of goods*) sell, stock, offer.

case n **1** (*put the cases in the boot of the car*) suitcase, brief case, piece of luggage. **2** (*a silver cigarette case*) container, box, receptacle. **3** (*a display case for ornaments*) cabinet, cupboard. **4** (*It was the case that she had been ill*) situation, position, circumstance. **5** (*They decided that it had been a case of misunderstanding*) instance, occurrence, occasion, example. **6** (*He has been accused of murder and the case comes up next week) lawsuit, trial, legal proceedings. **7** (the heart cases in the ward) patient, sufferer, victim, invalid.

cash n **1** (He earns quite a lot but he never seems to have any cash when we go out) money, wherewithal, funds, (inf) dough, (inf) the ready. **2** (They want us to pay in cash but we have only credit cards) money, ready money.

cast vb **1** (snakes casting their coats) shed, slough, discard, throw off. **2** (The street lamps cast a yellow light) give off, send out, shed, emit, radiate. **3** (The children were casting stones in the river) throw, fling, pitch, toss, hurl, heave. **4** (She cast him a glance of contempt) send, throw, bestow.

casual adj **1** (She wears casual clothes at the weekend) informal, leisure. **2** (He is a casual acquaintance not a close friend) slight, superficial. **3** (casual hotel work in the summer) irregular, temporary, part-time. **4** (He just made a casual remark about the state of the business) spontaneous, offhand, impromptu. **5** (They have a very casual attitude to the dangers of the journey) unconcerned, nonchalant, blasé, indifferent. **6** (I did not arrange to meet her—it was just a casual meeting) chance, accidental, unintentional, unforeseen, unexpected.

catch vb **1** (He failed to catch the ball) get hold of, grasp, grab, seize, snatch, grip. **2** (The police are determined to catch the escaped prisoner) capture, take captive, seize, apprehend, arrest. **3** (Did you catch what he said?) get, understand, follow, grasp, make out, comprehend, fathom. **4** (Something bright caught his attention) attract, draw, capture. **5** (The child has caught a cold) contract, develop, get, become infected with, come down with.

catch n **1** (The catch of the bag is broken) lock, fastener, fastening, clasp. **2** (There is no catch on the door) lock, snib, latch, bolt.

cause n **1** (What was the cause of the accident?) origin, source, root, agent. **2** (The patient's condition gives cause for concern) reason, justification, grounds, call. **3** (the cause of animals' rights) ideal, principle, belief.

cautious adj (be cautious about trusting strangers) careful, wary, watchful, guarded, chary, heedful, attentive, alert, vigilant.

cease vb (The firm has ceased to operate/It ceased operating) stop, halt, finish, leave off, suspend, quit, desist from.

celebrated adj (the celebrated painter) famous, renowned, well-known, notable, noted, distinguished, eminent, illustrious.

central adj **1** (occupying a central position in the town) middle. **2** (central London) middle, inner. **3** (That is the central issue of the discussion) main, chief, principal, key, core, focal.

centre n **1** (The town hall is in the centre of the town) middle, heart. **2** (at the centre of the quarrel) middle, hub, core, focus, focal point, hub, kernel.

certain adj **1** (They are certain that he will arrive) sure, positive, confident, assured. **2** (*Failure is certain*) sure, assured, inevitable, inescapable, (*inf*) in the bag. **3** (*It is certain that they have already left*) sure, definite, unquestionable, beyond question, indubitable, undeniable, incontrovertible. **4** (*There is no certain remedy for the disease*) sure, definite, definite, unfailing, dependable, reliable, foolproof, (*inf*) sure-fire. **5** (*There were certain people who did not believe him*) particular, specific.

chain *n* (*a chain of events*) series, succession, string, sequence, train, progression.

chance *n* **1** (*They took a chance when they crossed the bridge—it is very rickety*) risk, gamble, hazard. **2** (*There is a good chance that we will get there on time*) prospect, possibility, probability, likelihood. **3** (*You will not get another chance like that again*) opportunity, opening. **4** (*We haven't been in touch for years—we met again quite by chance*) accident, coincidence, luck, fortuity.

change *vb* **1** (*We have had to change the arrangements for the meeting*) alter, modify, vary, reorganize, transform. **2** (*She has changed completely since I last saw her*) alter, be transformed, metamorphose. **3** (*She has changed jobs*) switch.

character *n* **1** (*He seems to have changed in character since I first knew him/The character of the seaside village has altered*) nature, disposition, temperament, temper, personality, make-up, ethos. **2** (*We need a person of*

character in the job) strength, backbone, integrity, uprightness, honesty. **3** (*His former teacher gave him a letter saying he was of good character/The incident damaged his character*) reputation, name, standing. **4** (*one of the characters in Shakespeare's 'Hamlet'*) role, part, persona. **5** (*one of the village's characters*) eccentric, individual, (*inf*) card.

characteristic *adj* (*He treated the occasion with characteristic arrogance*) typical, distinguishing, individual, particular.

charge *vb* **1** (*The accused has been charged with murder*) accuse, indict. **2** (*The French forces charged the enemy army*) attack, rush, assault, storm. **3** (*The soldier charged the cannon*) load, fill. **4** (*What did they charge for the car?*) ask, levy. **5** (*Tell them to charge it to my account*) debit, put down to, bill.

charge *n* **1** (*The charge was one of murder*) accusation, indictment, arraignment. **2** (*He has charge of the accounts*) responsibility, care, protection, custody. **3** (*What is the charge for hiring the boat?*) cost, price, fee, rate, amount, payment.

charm *n* **1** (*She had a great deal of charm/They were taken with the charm of the village*) attractiveness, attraction, appeal, allure, fascination. **2** (*She has a tiny horseshoe as a lucky charm*) amulet, talisman. **3** (*She has a bracelet with charms on it*) trinket, ornament. **4** (*the sorcerer's charm*) spell, magic.

chart *n* (*record the information in the*

form of charts) table, graph, diagram.

chase vb 1 (*The hounds were chasing the fox*) run after, pursue, follow. 2 (*They chased away the burglar*) put to flight, drive away.

cheap adj 1 (*Fruit is very cheap in the summer there*) inexpensive, low-cost, low-priced, reasonable, economical. 2 (*She wears cheap and gaudy jewellery*) inferior, shoddy, tawdry, trashy, tatty, cheap-jack, (*inf*) tacky.

cheat vb 1 (*He cheated the old lady into giving him her savings*) deceive, trick, swindle, dupe, hoodwink. 2 (*His brother cheated him out of his inheritance*) deprive of, deny, thwart, prevent from.

check vb 1 (*The police checked the car's tyres*) examine, inspect, look at, scrutinize, test. 2 (*You must check that the door is locked*) confirm, make sure, verify. 3 (*They had to find some way to check the vehicle's progress*) stop, halt, slow down, delay, obstruct, impede.

cheeky adj (*He was scolded for being cheeky to the teacher*) impertinent, impudent, insolent, disrespectful, forward .

cheer vb 1 (*The crowds began to cheer*) applaud, shout hurrah, hurrah. 2 (*The arrival of her friends cheered her*) brighten up, buoy up, perk up, enliven, hearten, exhilarate, gladden, elate.

cheerful adj 1 (*They were in a cheerful mood when the sun shone*) happy, merry, bright, glad, light-hearted, carefree, joyful. 2 (*She was wearing a dress in cheerful colours*) bright.

cherish vb 1 (*She cherishes memories of her father*) treasure, prize, hold dear, revere. 2 (*The children cherish their pets*) look after, care for, tend, protect. 3 (*They cherish hopes of success*) have, entertain, cling to, harbour.

chest n 1 (*He was wounded in the chest*) breast, sternum. 2 (*The miser kept his treasure in a chest*) box, trunk, casket, coffer, container, receptacle.

chew vb (*children told to chew their food thoroughly*) munch, crunch, champ, masticate.

chief adj 1 (*the chief man of the tribe*) head, leading, foremost, principal. 2 (*We must discuss the chief points in the report*) main, principal, most important, essential, prime, key, central.

child n 1 (*when he was a child*) young one, little one, youngster, young person, (*inf*) kid. 2 (*parents and their child*) offspring, progeny, son/daughter.

choice n 1 (*You have some choice in the matter—the meeting is not compulsory*) option, selection, preference. 2 (*There is a wide choice of fruit and vegetables in the supermarket*) selection, range, variety. 3 (*We have little choice but to go*) option, alternative, possibility.

choke vb 1 (*The murderer choked her to death*) strangle, throttle. 2 (*He choked to death on the smoke from the fire*) suffocate, smother, stifle, asphyxiate. 3 (*The drains are choked and had to be cleared*) block, clog, obstruct.

choose vb 1 (*The child chose some sweets from the shop's selection*) pick, select, settle on, opt for, decide on. 2 (*He always does just as he chooses*) like, wish, want, prefer, fancy, desire.

chop vb **1** (*They began to chop the old trees down*) cut down, fell, hew, hack down. **2** (*They chopped up the vegetables for the soup*) cut up, dice, cube.

chronic adj **1** (*She suffers from a chronic illness*) long-standing, long-term, persistent, lingering. **2** (*They are chronic liars*) habitual, hardened, inveterate.

circle n **1** (*The children were asked to draw a circle*) ring, round, ball, globe, sphere, orb, loop, disc. **2** (*She has a large circle of friends*) group, set, crowd, ring, clique.

circuit n (*They had to run three circuits of the track*) round, lap, turn, loop, ambit.

circulate vb **1** (*They circulated information to the club members*) spread, distribute, issue, give out, disseminate, advertise. **2** (*blood constantly circulating*) flow, move round, go round, revolve, rotate.

circumstances npl (*The family lives in poverty-stricken circumstances*) state, situation, conditions.

civil adj **1** (*There had been a civil war in the country*) internal, domestic, home. **2** (*The army were in control but there is now a civil government*) civilian, non-military. **3** (*She might have asked in a more civil way/They are very civil people*) polite, courteous, mannerly, well-mannered, refined, civilized, cultured.

civilized adj **1** (*peoples of the world who were not then civilized*) enlightened, educated, socialized. **2** (*She is a very civilized person*) cultivated, cultured,

educated, sophisticated, refined, polished.

claim vb **1** (*He wrote in to claim his prize*) lay claim to, request, ask for, demand. **2** (*They claim that they had nothing to do with the crime*) assert, declare, maintain, profess, allege.

clash vb **1** (*The child clashed the cymbals*) strike, bang, clang, clatter, clank. **2** (*I have another appointment which clashes with my proposed meeting with you*) coincide, conflict. **3** (*One group of the committee clashed with the other*) be in conflict. have a disagreement, argue, quarrel, fight. **4** (*The curtains clashed horribly with the carpet*) jar, be incompatible, be discordant, (*inf*) scream.

class n **1** (*what appeals to the middle classes*) social division. **2** (*The awards are divided into four classes*) grade, rank, level, classification, category, set, group. **3** (*a lot consisting of one class of objects*) category, group, set, order, sort, type, variety, order, species, genre, genus. **4** (*The two pupils are in the same class*) study group.

clean adj **1** (*The children had no clean clothes*) unsoiled, spotless, laundered. **2** (*The village is in need of a clean water supply*) pure, clear, unpolluted, untainted, uncontaminated. **3** (*The pupil asked for a clean piece of paper*) unused, blank. **4** (*people who live clean lives*) good, virtuous, upright, honourable, righteous.

clear adj **1** (*It was clear that she was ill*) obvious, evident, plain, apparent, unmistakable. **2** (*You must try to give a* *clear account of what happened*) plain, explicit, lucid, coherent, intelligible. **3** (*We had a clear day for our flight*) bright, fair, fine, cloudless. **4** (*a door made of clear glass*) transparent. **5** (*You have to stay five clear days*) whole, complete, entire.

clever *adj* **1** (*He is a very clever pupil*) intelligent, bright, smart, gifted. **2** (*It was clever of them to open a new restaurant at that time*) smart, shrewd, astute, ingenious. **3** (*They are not very academic but they are clever with their hands*) skilful, deft, handy, dexterous.

climate *n* **1** (*a cold climate*) weather, weather pattern. **2** (*an unstable political climate*) atmosphere, feeling, mood, spirit.

climb *vb* (*The boy climbed the ladder*) go up, ascend, mount, scale, clamber up.

cling *vb* **1** (*She began to cling to her mother's hand*) hold on to, grip, clutch, grasp, clasp. **2** (*They tried to change her mind but she clings to her old beliefs*) stick to, hold to, stand by, adhere to.

clip *vb* (*She clipped her son's hair*) cut, trim, snip, crop, shear, prune.

cloak *n* **1** (*She wore a black evening cloak*) cape, mantle, shawl, wrap. **2** (*There was a cloak of secrecy surrounding the whole affair*) cover, screen, mask, mantle, veil, shield.

clog *vb* **1** (*They thought that it was leaves that were clogging up the drains*) block, obstruct, stop up. **2** (*The sheer volume of correspondence has clogged up the system*) obstruct, impede, hinder, hamper.

close *vb* **1** (*They were asked to close the gate*) shut, fasten, secure, lock, bolt. **2** (*They closed the meeting with the chairman's speech*) end, bring to an end, conclude, finish, wind up. **3** (*The gap between the two runners closed*) narrow, lessen, grow less, dwindle. **4** (*They finally closed the bargain*) conclude, complete, settle, seal, clinch.

close *adj* **1** (*The cottages were very close to each other*) near. **2** (*They have been close friends for years*) intimate, devoted, close-knit, bosom. **3** (*You must pay close attention to what she says*) careful, attentive, intense, assiduous. **4** (*She was able to give a close description of the man who attacked her*) exact, precise, accurate. **5** (*The weather was very close*) humid, muggy, stuffy, airless, oppressive. **6** (*The whole family is extremely close with money*) mean, miserly, parsimonious, stingy.

clothing *n* (*They washed all their clothing*) clothes, garments, attire, apparel.

cloudy *adj* **1** (*under cloudy skies*) overcast, hazy, grey, leaden, heavy. **2** (*The liquid in the glass was cloudy*) opaque, milky, murky, muddy. **3** (*Her vision is rather cloudy*) unclear, blurred, hazy.

clumsy *adj* **1** (*The antique wardrobe is a clumsy piece of furniture*) awkward, unwieldy, hulking, heavy, solid. **2** (*The child is clumsy and is always bumping into things*) awkward, ungainly, uncoordinated, blundering, maladroit, like a bull in a china shop.

coarse *adj* **1** (*The coat was made of a very coarse fabric*) rough, bristly, hairy, shaggy. **2** (*She prefers to bake with a coarse flour*) unrefined, unprocessed, crude. **3** (*They all have rather coarse features*) heavy, rugged. **4** (*He tells coarse jokes*) crude, vulgar, smutty, blue, dirty, bawdy, earthy, obscene, pornographic.

cold *adj* **1** (*It was a cold winter's day*) chilly, cool, freezing, icy, raw, frosty, glacial. **2** (*The children were feeling cold*) chilly, freezing, frozen, frozen to the marrow, shivery. **3** (*She seems rather a cold woman/She received them with rather a cold manner*) frigid, unresponsive, unemotional, indifferent, apathetic, distant, remote, reserved, detached.

collect *vb* **1** (*The children were collecting firewood for a bonfire*) gather, accumulate, amass, pile up, stockpile, store, hoard. **2** (*They are collecting money for a children's charity*) gather, raise. **3** (*She collected the shoes from the repair shop*) fetch, call for, go and get. **4** (*A crowd collected round the speaker*) gather, assemble, converge, congregate.

collide *vb* (*The cars collided*) crash, smash, bump.

colour *n* **1** (*She has sweaters in several colours*) shade, hue, tint, tone. **2** (*people of different colour*) skin-colouring, skin-tone, complexion, colouring. **3** (*The children were told to add a bit of colour to their stories*) vividness, life, animation.

combine *vb* **1** (*They combined the ingredients*) mix, blend, amalgamate, bind. **2** (*They have combined their resources to open a restaurant*) join, put together, unite, pool, merge. **3** (*They*

have combined to form one team*) get together, join forces, team up, club together, cooperate, associate, amalgamate, merge.

comfort *n* **1** (*They were poor but they now live in comfort*) ease, cosiness, snugness, well-being, affluence. **2** (*They tried to bring some comfort to the widow*) solace, consolation, condolence, sympathy, support. **3** (*The children were a comfort to their mother*) solace, help, support.

comic *adj* (*It was a comic situation*) funny, amusing, entertaining, diverting, droll, hilarious, farcical.

command *vb* **1** (*The king commanded them to go*) order, direct, instruct, bid. **2** (*He commands the force*) be in command of, be in charge of, control, rule, govern, direct, preside over, head, lead, manage.

comment *n* (*He passed comments on how ill she was looking*) remark, observation, statement, view.

commercial *adj* **1** (*He has undertaken a commercial training*) business, trade, marketing. **2** (*The seaside village is becoming too commercial*) money-orientated, profit-orientated, mercenary, materialistic. **3** (*His business idea was not a commercial one*) profit-making, profitable.

commitment *n* **1** (*She has a great deal of commitment to her job*) dedication, devotion, involvement. **2** (*He had many financial commitments*) responsibility, obligation, undertaking, duty, liability.

common *adj* **1** (*Fighting in the street is*

common there) usual, ordinary, everyday, regular, frequent, customary, habitual, standard, routine, commonplace, run-of-the-mill, traditional. **2** (*There is a common belief that the place is haunted*) widespread, universal, general, prevalent, popular. **3** (*things that appeal to the common people*) ordinary, normal, average, typical, run-of-the-mill. **4** (*It was a very common type of watch*) ordinary, commonplace, common-or-garden, unexceptional, undistinguished. **5** (*The politicians said that they were working for the common good*) communal, collective, public. **6** (*They regard her as a very common girl*) vulgar, coarse, uncouth, low.

communicate vb **1** (*They were unable to communicate the information back to headquarters*) pass on, convey, make known, impart, report, relay. **2** (*We do not communicate with them any more*) be in touch, be in contact, have dealings with. **3** (*In order to get a job in some industries it is important to be able to communicate*) be articulate, be fluent, be coherent, be eloquent.

compatible adj **1** (*The couple are just not compatible*) suited, well-suited, like-minded, in tune, having rapport. **2** (*The two accounts of the incident are not at all compatible*) in agreement, consistent, in keeping.

compel vb (*They plan to compel him to go*) force, make, coerce, oblige, dragoon, pressurize, pressure.

compete vb **1** (*Will they all compete in the race?*) take part, participate, go in

for, be a competitor, be a contestant. **2** (*The two brothers are competing against each other in the final*) vie, contend.

competent adj (*They are very competent workers*) capable, able, proficient, efficient, skilful.

complaint n **1** (*They made a complaint about the standard of the food*) protest, criticism, grievance. **2** (*Nothing ever pleases them—they are full of complaints*) grumble, (*inf*) grouse, (*inf*) gripe. **3** (*He has a stomach complaint*) illness, disease, disorder, ailment.

complete vb (*They failed to complete the job on time*) bring to completion, finish, conclude, accomplish, fulfil, achieve, execute, perform.

complete adj **1** (*He has the complete set of books*) whole, entire, full, total, intact, unbroken. **2** (*They think that she is a complete fool*) absolute, utter, thorough, thoroughgoing, total, out-and-out.

complicated adj (*It is a very complicated problem*) difficult, involved, complex, puzzling, perplexing.

compose vb **1** (*The children were asked to compose a poem*) make up, think up, create, concoct, invent, produce. **2** (*She was upset but tried to compose herself*) calm, calm down, quieten, control.

comprehend vb **1** (*The young students were unable to comprehend the scientific information*) understand, grasp, fathom, take in. **2** (*We cannot comprehend how they could behave like that*) understand, imagine, conceive, fathom, perceive, get to the bottom of.

comprehensive adj (His knowledge of the subject is quite comprehensive) inclusive, thorough, extensive, exhaustive, full, broad, widespread.

compulsory adj (Attendance at school assembly is compulsory) obligatory, mandatory, forced, essential, de rigueur.

conceal vb 1 (She concealed the papers under her mattress) hide, keep hidden, cover up, secrete, tuck away. 2 (They tried to conceal their fears) hide, cover up, disguise, mask.

conceited adj (She is so conceited that she spends ages looking in the mirror) vain, proud, arrogant, haughty, immodest, egotistical. (inf) big-headed.

concern n 1 (We were full of concern for the safety of the missing children) worry, anxiety, distress, apprehension. 2 (The news was of concern to all parents) interest, importance, relevance. 3 (They were told that it was none of their concern) business, affair, interest, responsibility, job, duty. 4 (They are partners in a manufacturing concern) business, firm, company, establishment.

concise adj (a concise report that gave all the main points) brief, short, succinct, terse, crisp, to the point.

conclude vb 1 (We concluded the talks at midnight) finish, end, close. 2 (We were unable to conclude an agreement with the other side) negotiate, bring about, pull off, clinch. 3 (We were forced to conclude that the witness was lying) come to the conclusion, deduce, gather, assume, suppose.

condemn vb 1 (We condemned them for injuring children) blame, censure, criticize, disapprove of, upbraid. 2 (The murderer was condemned to death) sentence.

condition n 1 (housing conditions) state, situation, circumstances, position. 2 (The horses were in good condition) form, shape, order, fitness, health. 3 (They were allowed to rent the land but with certain conditions) restriction, proviso, provision, stipulation, prerequisite, stipulation. 4 (The old lady has a heart condition) complaint, disorder, disease, illness, ailment, problem.

conduct n 1 (The teacher reported the child's conduct to his parents) behaviour, actions. 2 (Their conduct of the economy was criticized) direction, organization, management, control.

confess vb 1 (She confessed when she heard that her friend was being blamed for the crime) own up, admit guilt, plead guilty, accept blame, make a clean breast of it. 2 (I must confess that I know nothing about it) admit, acknowledge, concede, allow, grant.

confidence n 1 (The people have no confidence in the government) trust, faith, reliance. 2 (competitors full of confidence) self-confidence, self-assurance, poise, aplomb. 3 (The girls exchanged confidences) secret, private affair.

conflict n 1 (There has been conflict between the neighbours for years) disagreement, discord, dissension, friction, strife, hostility, ill will. **2** (*the conflict between love and duty*) clash, friction. **3** (*There were many killed in the military conflict*) battle, fight, war, clash.

confuse *vb* **1** (*All the questions confused the child*) bewilder, puzzle, perplex, muddle. **2** (*His remarks just confused the situation*) muddle, mix up, jumble, obscure, make unclear. **3** (*The old man became confused in old age*) muddle, disorientate, befuddle. **4** (*She confused the two books which looked alike*) mix up, mistake.

congratulate *vb* (*We congratulated them on the birth of their son*) wish joy to, offer good wishes to, compliment, felicitate.

connect *vb* **1** (*The gardener connected the garden hose to the tap*) attach, fasten, join, secure, clamp, couple. **2** (*Only a path connects the two mountain villages*) link, join, unite. **3** (*The child connects his mother with security*) associate, link, equate, identify.

connection *n* **1** (*There is no connection between the crimes*) relationship, link, association, correspondence. **2** (*They had a meeting in connection with staff redundancies*) reference, relation. **3** (*one of her husband's connections*) relative, relation, kindred.

conscientious *adj* (*conscientious workers*) careful, diligent, painstaking, hard-working, assiduous, meticulous, punctilious.

consequence *n* **1** (*unable to foresee the consequences of their actions*) result, effect, upshot, outcome, repercussion. **2** (*It was a matter of no con-*

sequence) importance, significance, note.

considerate *adj* (*She has very considerate children*) thoughtful, attentive, concerned, solicitous, obliging, kind, sympathetic.

consistent *adj* (*keep the room at a consistent temperature*) uniform, steady, constant, unchanging.

conspicuous *adj* **1** (*There had been conspicuous alterations to the city*) obvious, clear, noticeable, evident, apparent, discernible, visible. **2** (*Her clothes were conspicuous by their bright colours*) obvious, striking, obtrusive, blatant, showy.

constant *adj* **1** (*keep it at a constant temperature*) uniform, even, regular, steady, stable, unchanging, invariable. **2** (*We have had a constant stream of enquiries*) continuous, uninterrupted, unbroken. **3** (*tired of her constant complaints*) never-ending, non-stop, endless, unending, incessant, continual, perpetual, interminable. **4** (*He was constant in his love for her*) faithful, devoted, staunch, loyal, true.

contact *vb* (*They tried to contact her parents*) get in touch with, communicate with, be in communication with.

container *n* (*containers to transport the food*) receptacle, vessel.

content *adj* (*He is quite content with his life*) contented, satisfied, pleased, happy, comfortable.

contest *n* (*the competitors in the contest*) competition, tournament, match, game.

continual *adj* **1** (*tired of their continual*

questions) frequent, regular, repeated, recurrent, persistent, habitual. **2** (*There was continual noise from their flat*) continuous, endless, non-stop, incessant, constant, interminable.

continue vb **1** (*The road continues beyond the village*) go on, extend, keep on, carry on. **2** (*He may continue as chairman*) go on, carry on, stay, remain, persist. **3** (*We continued the search all night*) maintain, sustain, prolong, protract. **4** (*They continued looking for the ring*) go on, carry on, keep on, persist in, persevere in. **5** (*They stopped the search overnight but continued it at dawn*) resume, renew, recommence, carry on with.

continuous adj (*They have a continuous supply of fuel/upset by the continuous traffic noise*) constant, uninterrupted, unbroken, non-stop, endless, perpetual, incessant, unceasing, interminable, unremitting.

contract n (*a business contract*) agreement, arrangement, deal, settlement, pact, bargain, transaction.

contrast n **1** (*the contrast between the two styles of government*) difference, dissimilarity, distinction, disparity. **2** (*He is a complete contrast to his father*) opposite, antithesis.

contribute vb **1** (*They were all asked to contribute to the charity*) give, give a contribution, donate, give a donation to, subscribe to, help, give assistance to, assist, aid, support. **2** (*His leadership contributed to the success of the company*) add to, help, assist, have a hand in, be conducive to, be instrumental in.

control vb **1** (*It is she who controls the budget of the company*) be in control of, be in charge of, manage, administrate, direct, govern, head. **2** (*The fire fighters could not control the fire*) contain, keep in check, curb, limit.

convenient adj **1** (*select a time convenient for both of us*) suitable, appropriate, fitting, favourable, advantageous. **2** (*houses convenient for schools*) handy, within reach, within easy reach, accessible.

convert vb **1** (*We converted the attic into another bedroom*) alter, adapt, make into, turn into, change into, transform. **2** (*convert pounds into dollars*) change, exchange. **3** (*The missionary converted the tribesmen to Christianity*) cause to change beliefs, reform, convince of.

convict n (*The convict escaped*) prisoner, jailbird, criminal, felon, (*inf*) crook.

convincing adj **1** (*Her argument seemed very convincing*) persuasive, plausible, credible, cogent, powerful. **2** (*Our team had a convincing victory*) decisive, conclusive.

cool adj **1** (*The weather was rather cool*) cold, coldish, chilly, fresh. **2** (*They wanted a cool drink*) cold, refreshing. **3** (*people who can remain cool in an emergency*) calm, composed, self-possessed, unexcited, unruffled, unperturbed, **4** (*She was rather cool when we went to see her*) aloof, distant, remote, offhand, unfriendly, chilly, unwelcoming, unresponsive, apathetic. **5** (*They* were amazed at the cool way she stole the goods from the shop) bold, audacious, brazen, impudent.

cope vb **1** (He found it difficult to cope when his wife died) manage, carry on, get by, get along. **2** (He had to cope with the money problems) deal with, handle, contend with, manage.

copy n **1** (give out copies of the report at the meeting) duplicate, facsimile, photocopy, Xerox (trademark), Photostat (trademark). **2** (It was not the original vase but a clever copy) reproduction, replica, fake, sham, counterfeit. **3** (buy several copies of the newspaper) issue, example.

correct adj **1** (That is not the correct answer) right, accurate, true, precise, exact, (inf) spot on. **2** (What is the correct behaviour on such an occasion?) proper, suitable, fitting, seemly, appropriate, apt, accepted, usual.

cost vb **1** (How much does a car like that cost?) be priced at, sell for, come to, fetch. **2** (You should get the mechanic to cost the repairs for you) price, put a price on, estimate, evaluate.

cosy adj (a cosy room) snug, comfortable, homely, home-like, secure.

count vb **1** (pupils asked to count the row of numbers) count up, add up, total, calculate, compute. **2** (Could you count the people as they enter the hall?) keep a count of, keep a tally of, enumerate. **3** (What he thinks does not count) matter, be important, be of account, mean anything. **4** (They counted themselves fortunate to have somewhere to live) consider, deem, regard,

look upon, think, judge.

counterfeit adj (counterfeit bank notes) fake, forged, fraudulent, sham, bogus, (inf) phoney.

country n **1** (all the countries of the world) nation, state, realm. **2** (He would do anything for his country) native land, homeland, fatherland, mother country. **3** (They left the city to live in the country) countryside, rural area. **4** (The government should listen to what the country thinks) public, general public, people, nation, population. **5** (The country around there is very flat) land, terrain, territory.

courage n (the courage of the soldiers in battle) bravery, valour, gallantry, heroism, boldness, daring.

course n **1** (in the course of a varied career) progress, progression, development. **2** (The ship was a bit off course) route, way, track, direction, path, tack, orbit. **3** (You should try a different course of action) method, procedure, process, system, technique. **4** (The car disappeared in the course of a few minutes) duration, passage, lapse, period, interval, span. **5** (The race was cancelled as the course was flooded) track, circuit.

courtesy n (She showed a lack of courtesy towards elderly people) politeness, civility, good manners, respect, deference.

cover n **1** (There was a cover of snow over the ground) covering, layer, coat, blanket, carpet, mantle, film. **2** (They sought cover from the storm) shelter, protection, refuge, sanctuary. **3** (His business is just a cover for his drug-dealing) cover-up, concealment, disguise, pretext, front, camouflage, screen, mask, cloak, veil. **4** (*The insurance policy provides cover against fire and theft*) insurance, protection, compensation. **5** (*the design on the cover of the book*) jacket, dust jacket, wrapper. **6** (*pull up the covers over the sleeping child*) bedcover, bedclothes, blankets, duvet.

cowardly adj (*He is too cowardly to complain*) timid, timorous, fearful, faint-hearted, lily-livered, (*inf*) yellow, (*inf*) chicken.

crack n **1** (*There is a crack in this cup*) chip, chink. **2** (*There are several cracks in the wall*) fracture, split, crevice, slit. **3** (*The crack on the head made him pass out*) blow, knock, bump, smack, whack, thump, wallop. **3** (*They heard the crack of a pistol*) report, bang.

crash vb **1** (*The cymbals crashed*) clash, clang, clank, clatter, bang. **2** (*The car crashed into the wall*) bang into, bump into, hit, collide with. **3** (*His son crashed his car*) smash, wreck, write off. **4** (*The chimney crashed on to the pavement*) topple, fall, plunge, tumble. **5** (*They listened to the sea crashing against the ship*) dash, batter, smash, break. **6** (*Their business crashed*) fail, collapse, fold, go under, go to the wall.

credit n **1** (*He received little credit for a fine performance*) praise, commendation, acclaim, tribute, applause, recognition. **2** (*The famous artist was regarded as being a credit to the town*) honour, asset, glory. **3** (*His credit is not good*) financial standing, solvency.

creep vb **1** (*creatures that creep along the ground*) crawl, slither, wriggle. **2** (*They began creeping up on the burglar*) steal, sneak, slink, tiptoe.

crime n **1** (*He was convicted of the crime of theft*) offence, misdeed, wrong, misdemeanour, felony. **2** (*Crime is on the increase*) law-breaking, wrongdoing, felony, evil, vice.

criticize vb (*She is always criticizing him*) find fault with, blame, censure, pick holes in, (*inf*) nit-pick.

crooked adj **1** (*a crooked stick*) bent, curved, twisted. **2** (*The old man had a crooked back*) deformed, misshapen. **3** (*That picture is crooked*) tilted, at an angle, askew, slanted, sloping. **4** (*They think that he is a crooked salesman*) dishonest, dishonourable, unscrupulous, fraudulent.

cross adj **1** (*Their mother was cross at the children's naughtiness*) angry, annoyed, irritated, vexed. **2** (*She is a cross old woman who is always shouting at the neighbourhood children*) irritable, short-tempered, bad-tempered, ill-humoured, disagreeable, surly, crotchety, cantankerous.

crush vb **1** (*The workers crushed the grapes*) squash, squeeze, compress. **2** (*They crushed the stones*) break up, smash, pulverize, ground, pound. **3** (*Sitting so long had crushed her dress*) crease, crumple, rumple, wrinkle, crinkle. **3** (*The army crushed the rebellion*) quell, quash, suppress, subdue, put down, stamp out, overpower.

cry vb **1** (*The children began to cry for their mothers*) weep, shed tears, sob, wail. **2** (*She cried out in pain*) call out, shout out, yell, scream.

cure n (*trying to find a cure for cancer*) remedy, treatment, panacea.

curious adj **1** (*We are curious to hear what happens at the meeting*) interested. **2** (*She is always curious about the affairs of her neighbours*) inquisitive, prying, meddlesome, snooping, (*inf*) nosy. **3** (*It was a curious sight*) odd, strange, unusual, peculiar, queer, weird, bizarre, mysterious.

current adj **1** (*the current fashion for pale-coloured clothes*) present, present-day, contemporary, existing, modern. **2** (*Those traditions are no longer current*) around, prevalent, common, general, popular.

curved adj (*a curved stick/a curved back*) bent, arched, bowed, crooked, rounded, humped.

custom n **1** (*The local customs are dying out*) tradition, practice, convention, ritual. **2** (*It was his custom to go for a walk before breakfast*) habit, practice, routine, wont, way. **3** (*He is grateful for their custom*) trade, business, patronage.

customer n (*shops trying to attract new customers*) client, patron, buyer, shopper, consumer.

cut vb **1** (*cut the meat into cubes*) cut up, chop, divide, carve, slice. **2** (*He cut his finger with a razor blade*) wound, gash, slash, pierce. **3** (*She cut her son's hair*) trim, clip, crop, snip, prune, shear. **4** (*The firm must cut its expenditure*) cut back on, reduce, decrease, curtail, slash. **5** (*The essay is too long—you must cut it*) shorten, abridge, condense, abbreviate. **6** (*She cut some paragraphs from the article*) cut out, delete, excise. **7** (*The driver cut the engine*) switch off, turn off.

cynical adj (*She is cynical about our chances of success/They are very cynical people*) pessimistic, sceptical, doubting, distrustful, suspicious.

D

dagger n (*He killed his enemy with his dagger*) stiletto, poniard, dirk, knife.

dainty adj 1 (*a dainty little girl*) petite, neat, graceful. 2 (*dainty china cups*) delicate, fine, exquisite.

damage n 1 (*There was a great deal of damage to his car*) harm, destruction, accident, ruin, impairment. 2 (*The incident caused damage to his reputation*) harm, injury, hurt, detriment, loss, suffering.

damp adj 1 (*They hung up their damp clothes to dry*) wet, soaking, sopping. 2 (*The ground was damp*) wet, soggy. 3 (*It was a damp day*) wet, rainy, drizzly, humid, muggy.

danger n 1 (*There was an element of danger in the job*) peril, jeopardy, risk, hazard. 2 (*Pollution is a danger to lives*) risk, menace, threat, peril.

dangerous adj 1 (*They were in a dangerous situation*) risky, perilous, hazardous, precarious, insecure. 2 (*The police say that he is dangerous*) threatening, menacing, alarming, nasty.

dare vb 1 (*He did not dare climb the high tree*) have the courage, pluck up courage, have the nerve, risk, venture. 2 (*His friends dared him to jump from the high wall*) challenge, throw down the gauntlet. 3 (*They dared their father's anger to go to the nightclub*) defy, brave, face, confront.

daring adj (*a daring deed/a daring fellow*) bold, adventurous, brave, courageous, plucky, reckless, rash.

dark adj 1 (*It was a very dark night*) black, pitch-dark, pitch-black, inky, dim, murky, unlit. 2 (*She has dark hair*) dark brown, black, jet-black, sable. 3 (*They lived in the dark ages*) unenlightened, ignorant, uneducated, uncultivated, uncultured. 4 (*dark, dingy rooms*) gloomy, dismal, drab, dim, dingy, bleak, dreary, cheerless. 5 (*She was in a dark mood*) gloomy, depressed, morose.

dawdle n (*They dawdled on their way to school*) dally, loiter, linger, delay, tarry.

day n 1 (*She doesn't mind driving during the day*) daylight, daytime. 2 (*in this modern day*) time, age, era, epoch.

dead adj 1 (*Her father is dead/the dead man*) deceased, departed, lifeless, gone. 2 (*dead village traditions*) extinct, gone, perished. 3 (*dead matter*) without life, lifeless, inanimate. 4 (*Her fingers were dead with cold*) numb, benumbed, without feeling. 5 (*The small town is dead at night*) boring, dull, uneventful, unexciting.

deadly adj 1 (*He drank a deadly poison*) fatal, lethal, toxic, poisonous. 2 (*He was struck a deadly blow*) fatal, mortal, lethal, dangerous, death-dealing, terminal. 3 (*They were deadly enemies*) fierce, hostile, grim, hated.

deaf adj 1 (*The accident left him deaf*) with impaired hearing, stone deaf, as deaf as a post. 2 (*They were deaf to *her pleas*) indifferent, unmoved by, oblivious to, heedless of.

deal vb 1 (*She was unable to deal with the problem*) cope with, handle, attend to, sort out, tackle, manage. 2 (*They need a book that deals with the early history of the town*) be about, have to do with, concern, discuss. 3 (*He does not know how to deal with children*) act towards, behave towards, cope with, manage. 4 (*He was asked to deal the cards*) distribute, give out, share out, divide out, dole out. 5 (*They dealt him a fatal blow*) give, deliver, administer.

deal n 1 (*a business deal*) arrangement, agreement, transaction, contract, pact. 2 (*He did not get a fair deal*) treatment, usage.

dear adj 1 (*He lost his dear wife*) beloved, loved, darling, cherished. 2 (*She was a dear child*) sweet, adorable, lovable, darling, attractive, winning, enchanting. 3 (*It was a dear car*) expensive, costly, high-priced, valuable, exorbitant.

death n 1 (*Death was caused by strangling*) dying, demise, decease, loss of life, passing away, killing, murder, slaughter. 2 (*There were many deaths in the flu epidemic*) fatality, dead people. 3 (*The close of the firm marked the death of his hopes*) end, finish, cessation, destruction, ruin, annihilation.

decay vb 1 (*The food had begun to decay*) go bad, rot, decompose, putrefy, spoil. 2 (*The Roman empire decayed*) decline, degenerate, deteriorate, wane, ebb.

deceitful adj 1 (*She is a very deceitful child*) lying, untruthful, dishonest, false, insincere, untrustworthy, underhand. 2 (*He got into the house by deceitful means*) underhand, fraudulent, crooked, dishonest, cheating, crafty, sneaky.

deceive vb (*His friends did not realize that he was deceiving them*) delude, mislead, take in, hoodwink, pull the wool over (someone's) eyes, swindle, dupe.

decent adj 1 (*He seemed a decent enough fellow*) honest, honourable, trustworthy, worthy, civil. 2 (*Her behaviour was not considered decent*) seemly, proper, appropriate, decorous, pure. 3 (*He earns a decent salary*) reasonable, ample, good, adequate, sufficient.

decide vb 1 (*They decided to stay*) come to a decision, reach a decision, make up one's mind, resolve, commit oneself. 2 (*That decided the matter*) settle, resolve, determine. 3 (*The judge will decide the case*) judge, make a judgement on, make a ruling on, give a verdict.

decision n 1 (*They finally reached a decision*) resolution, conclusion, determination, settlement. 2 (*The judge will announce his decision*) judgement, verdict, ruling. 3 (*He is a man of decision*) decisiveness, determination, resolution, resolve, firmness.

decisive adj 1 (*Her personality was the decisive factor in her getting the job*) deciding, determining, conclusive, critical, crucial. 2 (*They need someone* _decisive in charge of the firm)_ determined, resolute, firm, forceful.

decline vb I _(They declined the invitation)_ turn down, refuse, say no to. **2** _(The influence of the leader has declined)_ get less, lessen, decrease, diminish, dwindle, fade. **3** _(The Roman empire was declining then)_ deteriorate, degenerate.

decorate vb I _(They decorated the Christmas tree)_ adorn, ornament, embellish, trim. **2** _(They have begun to decorate the house)_ paint, paper, renovate, (inf) do up. **3** _(The soldier was decorated for bravery)_ honour, give a medal to, cite.

decrease vb I _(The number of the pupils at the school is decreasing)_ grow less, lessen, diminish, dwindle, drop, fall off, decline. **2** _(They have decreased the number of places available at the school)_ reduce, lower, lessen, cut back, curtail. **3** _(The storm finally decreased)_ die down, abate, subside.

deed n I _(a dishonest deed)_ act, action, feat, exploit, undertaking, enterprise. **2** _(The deeds to the house)_ document, contract, title deed.

deep adj I _(They dug a deep hole in the garden)_ yawning, cavernous. **2** _(They have a deep affection for each other)_ intense, fervent, ardent, heart-felt. **3** _(He has a deep distrust of doctors)_ profound, extreme, intense, great. **4** _(He has a very deep voice)_ low, low-pitched, bass, booming, resonant. **5** _(She always wears clothes in deep colours)_ rich, strong, vivid, intense, dark.

defeat vb I _(The army finally defeated_

the enemy) beat, conquer, vanquish, win a victory over, get the better of, overcome, rout. **2** _(The parliamentary motion was defeated)_ reject, overthrow, throw out, outvote.

defect n I _(a defect in the material)_ fault, flaw, imperfection, blemish. **2** _(They tried to find the defects in the system)_ deficiency, weakness, shortcoming, failing, inadequacy, snag.

defence n I _(Walls built as a defence for the house)_ protection, safeguard, guard, security, cover, fortification, barricade. **2** _(a report in defence of the system)_ justification, vindication, argument, apology, exoneration.

defer vb _(They had to defer the date of the meeting)_ put off, postpone, delay, hold over, adjourn.

deficiency n I _(She suffers from vitamin deficiency)_ lack, want, shortage, dearth, insufficiency, scarcity, deficit. **2** _(It was the only deficiency in the system)_ defect, flaw, fault, imperfection, failing, shortcoming, drawback, snag.

definite adj I _(They have no definite plans)_ clear-cut, fixed, established, precise, specific, particular. **2** _(It is not definite that he is leaving)_ certain, sure, settled, decided, fixed.

defy vb I _(They decided to defy their parents and go to the cinema)_ disobey, disregard, ignore. **2** _(The army defied the enemy)_ withstand, resist, stand up to, brave, confront.

degree n I _(There was a marked degree of improvement in her work)_ extent, amount, level, measure. **2** _(The dancers reached a high degree of expertise)_ level, stage, grade, point.

dejected adj (She was feeling dejected after her friends left) miserable, wretched, downcast, depressed, sad, despondent.

delay vb 1 (We have had to delay our holiday) postpone, put off, put back, defer, adjourn, put on ice. 2 (They were delayed by heavy traffic) hold up, hold back, detain, hinder, impede, hamper, obstruct.

deliberate adj (His murder was quite deliberate) intentional, on purpose, planned, calculated, pre-arranged, premeditated.

delicate adj 1 (She was very delicate as a child) weak, frail, sickly, unwell, infirm. 2 (cups made of delicate china) fine, exquisite, fragile, thin. 3 (It was a very delicate matter) difficult, sensitive, tricky. 4 (The situation required delicate handling) careful, tactful, discreet, diplomatic.

delicious adj (They serve delicious food at the restaurant) tasty, flavoursome, appetizing, luscious, (inf) scrumptious.

delight n (She was filled with delight at seeing her friend again) joy, pleasure, gladness, happiness.

delightful adj 1 (We had a delightful evening at the theatre) pleasant, enjoyable, entertaining, amusing, diverting. 2 (She is a delightful person) charming, engaging, attractive, nice.

deliver vb 1 (He delivers morning newspapers) distribute, bring, take round. 2 (They delivered the little girl to her mother) hand over, convey, present. 3 (She delivered a moving speech/ deliver a sigh of relief) give, give voice to, utter, speak, express, pronounce. 4 (They were able to deliver the prisoners) free, set free, liberate, release.

demand vb 1 (The workers demanded a wage rise) call for, ask for, request, press for, insist on, clamour for. 2 (The work demanded patience) call for, require, need, take, involve.

demanding adj (They have very demanding jobs) difficult, taxing, exacting, hard, tough.

demolish vb (They began to demolish the old buildings) knock down, tear down, pull down, level, flatten, raze, dismantle.

demonstrate vb 1 (She demonstrated how to change an electric plug) show, illustrate, teach, explain. 2 (Her expression demonstrated how she was feeling) show, indicate, display, exhibit, manifest. 3 (The documents demonstrated that she was telling the truth) show, establish, prove, confirm, verify. 4 (They planned to demonstrate against the new road) protest, stage a protest.

dense adj 1 (They were lost in a dense forest) thick, close-packed, impenetrable. 2 (He was too dense to follow the instructions) stupid, thick, dim, slow.

deny vb 1 (He began to deny that he had said it) contradict, refute, retract, negate, disagree with. 2 (The committee might deny their request) refuse, reject, turn down, decline, dismiss.

depart vb 1 (We have to depart at dawn) leave, go, take one's leave, take oneself off, set out, start out, (*inf*) make tracks. **2** (*results that depart from the norm*) deviate, diverge, differ, vary.

depend *vb* **1** (*The firm depends on him to look after the place*) rely on, count on, bank on, lean on, put one's faith in. **2** (*The success of the business will depend on the order*) be dependent on, hinge on, turn on, hang on, rest on, revolve around.

deport *vb* (*They decided to deport the refugees*) banish, expel, exile, evict, transport, extradite, expatriate.

depreciate *vb* (*The houses have depreciated in value*) decrease, lessen, lower.

depressed *adj* (*He was feeling depressed having lost his job*) miserable, downcast, low in spirits, melancholy, gloomy, glum, dejected, sad, unhappy.

depth *n* **1** (*measure the depth of the water*) deepness. **2** (*It was a book of great depth*) profoundness, profundity, wisdom, insight, understanding, weight, importance.

deprived *adj* (*deprived children brought up in poverty*) poor, needy, in want, disadvantaged.

derelict *adj* (*derelict farmhouses*) dilapidated, tumbledown, rundown, ramshackle, broken-down, abandoned, forsaken.

descend *vb* **1** (*She descended the stairs gracefully*) come down, go down, climb down. **2** (*The hot air balloon descended*) go down, come down, drop, fall, sink, plummet. **3** (*They descended from the train with their luggage*) get off, get down, alight, dismount.

describe *vb* **1** (*He was asked to describe the incident*) give a description of, give an account of, give details of, recount, relate, report, explain, tell about, narrate. **2** (*They have described her as beautiful*) call, label, designate.

desert *vb* **1** (*a man who had deserted his family*) abandon, forsake, leave, turn one's back on, leave in the lurch, throw over. **2** (*The army are looking for the soldiers who deserted*) abscond, run away, quit, defect.

deserve *vb* (*He deserves reward*) merit, be worthy of, warrant, rate, be entitled to, have a claim on.

design *n* **1** (*The architect showed the committee the designs for the new building*) plan, blueprint, sketch, drawing, outline. **2** (*The fabric designs are very modern*) pattern, motif, style. **3** (*It was a cunning design to break into the building*) plan, scheme, plot, stratagem, aim. **4** (*They did it with the design of stealing money*) aim, intention, goal, objective, purpose.

desire *vb* **1** (*She desires some comfort in her old age*) wish, want, long for, yearn for, crave, covet, hanker after, (*inf*) have a yen for. **2** (*They desire to leave at once*) wish, want, feel like.

desolate *adj* **1** (*on the edge of a desolate moor*) bare, barren, bleak, wild. **2** (*an area full of desolate farms*) deserted, forsaken, solitary, lonely, isolated. **3** (*She was desolate when he went away*) miserable, wretched, sad, unhappy, dejected, forlorn, lonely.

despair *vb* (*He has despaired of ever*

getting a job) lose hope, give up hope, lose heart, be discouraged, give up, throw in the towel.

desperate adj 1 (It was a desperate attempt to save the town) daring, risky, hazardous, wild, reckless, rash, imprudent. 2 (Some desperate criminals have escaped) wild, violent, lawless, reckless. 3 (They are in desperate need of more food) urgent, pressing, critical, crucial, serious, dire, great. 4 (They are desperate for money) in great need of, in want of. 5 (The family is in a desperate state) dreadful, shocking, appalling, deplorable, intolerable. 6 (help required for desperate people) despairing, hopeless, despairing, distressed, wretched.

despise vb (She despises people who tell lies) scorn, look down on, shun, disdain, sneer at, mock, hate, loathe.

despondent adj (The pupil was despondent when she heard that she had failed the exam) downcast, cast down, low in spirits, disheartened, discouraged, disappointed, gloomy, melancholy, wretched, miserable.

destroy vb (The bridge was destroyed in the war) demolish, knock down, pull down, tear down, wreck, smash, shatter, blow up, wipe out.

detach vb 1 (She detached the hood from her coat) unfasten, remove, separate, uncouple, free. 2 (She detached herself from her group to join us) move away from, separate, dissociate.

detail n 1 (The police try to notice every detail at the scene of the crime) particular, point, circumstance, feature, aspect. 2 (draw up a general plan and not bother with the details) particular, fine point, minutiae.

detect vb 1 (They thought that they detected a smell of gas) notice, note, make out, spot, identify, distinguish, sense, observe. 2 (The police were detecting the crime) investigate, probe.

deter vb (They hope the stiff sentence will deter others from committing such a crime) put off, prevent, stop, discourage, restrain, scare off.

determined adj 1 (He is a very determined person and will probably win) firm, resolute, tenacious, single-minded, strong-willed, dogged, persistent, stubborn, inflexible. 2 (They are determined to leave) set on, intent on, bent on.

detest vb (The rivals detest each other) hate, loathe, abhor, feel aversion to, feel hostility to.

detrimental adj (The incident was detrimental to his reputation) injurious, harmful, damaging, hurtful, disadvantageous, destructive.

develop vb 1 (children quickly developing into adults) grow, turn, mature. 2 (modern cities developing rapidly) grow, expand, enlarge, spread, progress, evolve. 3 (They are trying to develop a scheme for expansion) originate, set in motion, establish, form, institute. 4 (They have the beginnings of a plan but they have to develop it) elaborate, work out, enlarge on, amplify, flesh out. 5 (The child has developed a cough) acquire, get, contract. 6 (A quarrel developed between the two women) begin, start, commence, happen, come about, break out.

device n 1 (a handy device for use in the kitchen) gadget, appliance, utensil, implement, tool, apparatus, contrivance, contraption. 2 (They thought of a cunning device to get into the building) ploy, ruse, trick, stratagem, scheme, dodge, plan.

devil n 1 (a story about the devil and hell) Satan, Beelzebub. 2 (She dreamt that she was being pursued by devils) demon, evil spirit, fiend. 3 (The slave's master was a devil) brute, savage, monster, beast, fiend, scoundrel, villain. 4 (The child is a little devil) scamp, rascal, rogue.

devious adj (They are very devious people/They will get what they want only by devious means) underhand, cunning, sly, crafty, wily, deceitful.

devoted adj 1 (the king's devoted followers) loyal, faithful, true, staunch, dedicated, committed, constant. 2 (time devoted to hobbies) set aside, allocated, assigned, allotted.

devout adj 1 (devout churchgoers) pious, religious, godly, holy, church-going. 2 (It was their devout hope that he would be present) sincere, deep, profound, earnest, heart-felt, fervent, genuine.

diagnose vb (The doctor diagnosed mumps) identify, recognize, distinguish, detect, pronounce.

dialogue n (a dialogue between the presidents) conversation, talk, exchange of views, discussion, conference, tête à tête.

die vb 1 (The doctors think that he is going to die) pass away, breathe one's last, lose one's life, meet one's end, (inf) give up the ghost, (inf) kick the bucket, expire. 2 (All hope died when they heard the news) end, come to an end, vanish, disappear, pass, fade. 3 (The car's engine died) stop, fail, break down, peter out.

differ vb 1 (Their tastes differ completely) be different, be dissimilar, be unlike, vary, diverge. 2 (The two sides still differ on the best course of action) disagree, dissent, be at variance, be in dispute, be in conflict, clash, argue, quarrel. 3 (The scientist's results differ from the norm) vary, diverge, deviate, depart from, contradict.

difference n 1 (There was marked difference between the two sisters) dissimilarity, distinction, variation, contrast, disparity, incongruity. 2 (They have had several differences over the years) difference of opinion, disagreement, dispute, clash, argument, quarrel, row, altercation.

different adj 1 (Their tastes in clothes are very different) dissimilar, unlike, at variance, contrasting. 2 (With her new hairstyle she looks completely different) changed, altered, transformed. 3 (She wears a different sweater every day) another, fresh. 4 (The dress is available in different colours) various, several, varied, assorted. 5 (She was looking for something a bit different to wear to the wedding) unusual, out of the ordinary, uncommon, distinctive, special, singular, extraordinary, rare.

difficult adj 1 (Working on the building site was very difficult work) hard, strenuous, arduous, demanding, taxing, laborious, tiring. 2 (It is a difficult problem to solve) hard, complicated, complex, involved, intricate, problematic, tough. 3 (I felt that we had arrived at a difficult time) inconvenient, ill-timed, unfavourable. 4 (The family has gone through a difficult period) hard, tough, distressing, grim. 5 (She has always been a difficult child) troublesome, unmanageable, recalcitrant, intractable.

dig vb 1 (dig the earth before planting potatoes) break up, work, turn over, loosen. 2 (The prisoners dug a tunnel to try to escape) dig out, excavate, hollow out, gouge out, scoop out, burrow, mine. 3 (She dug her friend in the ribs at the lecture to wake him up) prod, jab, poke, push, elbow. 4 (The newspaper reporter is trying to dig up facts about the politician's private life) search, probe, investigate, research, delve.

dignity n 1 (She was anxious not to lose her dignity in front of people) pride, self-esteem, self-respect. 2 (the dignity of the royal procession) stateliness, ceremoniousness, formality, decorum, majesty, grandeur, nobility.

dilapidated adj (an area full of dilapidated houses) run-down, tumbledown, broken-down, ramshackle, crumbling, in disrepair, decaying, neglected.

diligent adj (diligent pupils studying hard in school) conscientious, industrious, hard-working, assiduous, painstaking, studious, zealous.

dim adj 1 (The light from the street lamps was dim) faint, feeble, weak. 2 (people frightened to walk along the dim corridors) dark, gloomy, badly lit, dingy. 3 (They saw a dim shape in the mist) vague, indefinite, ill-defined, blurred, shadowy, fuzzy. 4 (They have only a dim recollection of the incident) vague, indistinct, hazy, blurred, confused. 5 (He failed to understand because he is a bit dim) stupid, dense, thick, dull, slow-witted. 6 (His prospects of getting a job are rather dim) gloomy, unpromising, depressing, discouraging.

dingy adj (They live in run-down dingy houses) dim, dark, gloomy, dull, drab, murky, dirty, discoloured, shabby.

direct adj 1 (the direct route to the city) straight, shortest, uncircuitous. 2 (a very direct manner/a direct statement) frank, straightforward, blunt, forthright, clear, plain, candid, open.

direction n 1 (They complained about his direction of the project) administration, management, government, leadership, supervision, conduct, handling, control, guidance. 2 (You must obey the teacher's directions) order, command, instruction, directive, bidding. 3 (The climbers have gone in the wrong direction) route, way, course, path.

dirt n 1 (They cleaned the dirt from their boots) grime, mud, muck, filth, dust. 2 (piles of dirt in the garden) soil, earth, loam. 3 (She complained about the dirt in some of the videos) filth, obscenity, indecency, smut, pornography, bawdiness, lewdness, ribaldry. **4** (*She is given to spreading dirt about her neighbours*) scandal, slander, gossip.

dirty adj **1** (*Their boots were dirty*) unclean, soiled, grubby, grimy, muddy, mucky, filthy, dusty, messy, stained, polluted. **2** (*He embarrassed her by telling dirty jokes*) filthy, obscene, indecent, blue, smutty, pornographic, bawdy, lewd, ribald **3** (*That was a dirty trick*) nasty, unfair, dishonest, dishonourable, deceitful, underhand, fraudulent.

disability n (*help for people with some form of disability*) incapacity, learning difficulty, learning disability, infirmity, handicap.

disadvantage n **1** (*discover the disadvantages of the system*) drawback, snag, weak spot, weakness, flaw, defect, fault, handicap, obstacle, minus. **2** (*children who suffer from financial disadvantage*) deprivation, hardship. **3** (*The incident turned out to be to their disadvantage*) detriment, disservice, harm, damage, injury, hurt, loss.

disadvantageous adj (*The circumstances were disadvantageous to them*) unfavourable, adverse, unfortunate, detrimental, prejudicial, deleterious, damaging, injurious.

disagree vb **1** (*The two sides had talks but they still disagreed*) differ, diverge, be at variance, be at odds. **2** (*The police said that the stories of the witnesses disagreed*) differ, be dissimilar, be unlike, be different, vary, clash, conflict,

diverge. **3** (*The children were always disagreeing*) argue, quarrel, bicker, wrangle.

disagreeable adj **1** (*It was a very disagreeable experience*) unpleasant, nasty, horrible, foul, dreadful, revolting. **2** (*He is a disagreeable old man*) bad-tempered, ill-natured, cross, irritable, surly, churlish, rude, nasty, unpleasant.

disappear vb **1** (*The sun disappeared behind the cloud*) vanish, recede, fade, retire, retreat. **2** (*traditions which have now disappeared*) die out, be no more, end, pass, fade, perish, become extinct.

disappoint vb **1** (*We hated to disappoint the children by cancelling the picnic*) let down, dishearten, upset, sadden. **2** (*We had to disappoint their hopes*) thwart, frustrate, baulk, foil, baffle, hinder, obstruct, hamper, impede.

disapprove vb (*She disapproves of the young people's behaviour*) find unacceptable, dislike, be against, be displeased by, frown on, blame.

disaster n **1** (*earthquakes and other natural disasters*) catastrophe, calamity, tragedy, mishap, setback, reversal. **2** (*The play was a disaster*) failure, flop.

discard vb (*discard old newspapers*) throw away, throw out, dispose of, jettison, scrap, dump.

discharge vb **1** (*The pipe was discharging a foul-smelling liquid*) give off, send out, emit, exude, excrete, ooze, leak. **2** (*Several workers were discharged*) dismiss, sack, get rid of, declare redundant, (*inf*) fire, (*inf*) axe. **3** (*She did not discharge her duties*) carry out, do, perform, execute. **4** (*He discharged a firearm*) let off, fire, shoot. **5** (*The prisoner has been discharged*) set free, free, release, let go, acquit, clear, reprieve.

disclose *vb* (*She finally disclosed her reasons for leaving*) make known, reveal, divulge, tell, communicate, impart.

discomfort *n* **1** (*She experiences some discomfort in her eye*) ache, pain, soreness, twinge, irritation, throbbing. **2** (*the discomfort of travelling long journeys in a very small car*) inconvenience, difficulty, trouble, bother, drawback.

discordant *adj* (*She has a discordant voice/discordant sounds*) harsh, strident, shrill, grating, jarring.

discourage *vb* **1** (*The young man was discouraged by failing his driving test*) dishearten, dispirit, deject, depress, disappoint, demoralize. **2** (*They tried to discourage the girl from applying for the job*) deter, dissuade, talk out of, advises against, restrain.

discover *vb* **1** (*The police discovered a new clue*) uncover, find, come across, bring to light, turn up, unearth. **2** (*The scientists have discovered a new cancer drug*) invent, devise, originate. **3** (*We discovered that he was very ill*) learn, find out, come to realize.

discreet *adj* (*behaviour that was far from being discreet/a few discreet remarks*) careful, cautious, prudent, tactful, diplomatic, wise.

discriminate *vb* **1** (*Children should be*

taught to discriminate between right and wrong*) distinguish, differentiate, separate. **2** (*She said that her employers discriminated against women*) show prejudice towards, show bias towards, be biased towards.

discuss *vb* (*The committee discussed the problem*) talk about, confer about, debate, consider, deliberate.

disease *n* (*The old man is suffering from a brain disease*) illness, disorder, complaint, condition, malady, ailment.

disgrace *n* **1** (*He found it difficult to endure the disgrace of being in prison*) shame, humiliation, dishonour, degradation, ignominy. **2** (*The pupil is in disgrace for playing truant*) disfavour, discredit, disrepute.

disgraceful *adj* **1** (*Their behaviour was disgraceful*) shameful, shameless, dishonourable, shocking, outrageous, unseemly, improper. **2** (*The pupil's work is disgraceful*) very bad, appalling, dreadful, terrible, shocking.

disguise *vb* **1** (*They disguised themselves as police officers*) dress up, camouflage. **2** (*He tried to disguise the scar on his face*) conceal, hide, cover up, mask, screen.

disgust *vb* **1** (*The thought of eating snails disgusts them*) revolt, repel, put off, sicken, nauseate, (*inf*) turn off. **2** (*They were disgusted by the behaviour of the teenagers*) scandalize, shock, appal, outrage, offend.

dishevelled *adj* (*They felt dishevelled after their long journey*) untidy, unkempt, bedraggled, messy, tousled.

disinterested *adj* **1** (*The judges of the*

competition must be disinterested) unbiased, unprejudiced, impartial, detached, objective, neutral, fair. 2 (They were completely disinterested in the subject) uninterested, bored, indifferent, apathetic.

dismal adj 1 (feeling dismal because he was ill and had to stay in bed) miserable, wretched, despondent, gloomy, sad, unhappy. 2 (They plan to redecorate the dismal room) dark, dim, dull, dingy, drab, dreary, bleak, cheerless.

dismiss vb (He was dismissed from his job) sack, give notice to, discharge, lay off, declare redundant, (inf) fire.

disobey vb (They disobeyed the rules) defy, disregard, flout, contravene, infringe, violate.

disorderly adj 1 (They tried to tidy the disorderly office) untidy, messy, cluttered, disorganized, out of order, chaotic. 2 (The police tried to control the disorderly crowds) unruly, rowdy, boisterous, rough, wild, lawless, rebellious.

display vb 1 (They displayed the goods in the shop window) exhibit, put on show, show, present, set out. 2 (The young gymnasts displayed their expertise) demonstrate, exhibit, show, show off, flaunt. 3 (The accused displayed no emotion as he was sentenced by the judge) show, exhibit, indicate, manifest, show evidence of, demonstrate.

dispose:— dispose of vb (They disposed of the rubbish by burying it) get rid of, throw away, throw out, discard, jettison, scrap, dump.

dispute n (The two friends had a dispute over money) argument, quarrel, row, wrangle, clash, altercation, feud.

disrupt n (The protesters disrupted the meeting) disturb, interrupt, interfere with, obstruct, impede, hamper.

dissolve vb 1 (Salt dissolves in water) liquefy, melt. 2 (They both dissolved in tears) break into, be overcome by. 3 (They have decided to dissolve their partnership) end, terminate, break up, discontinue, wind up. 4 (The crowds dissolved when the police arrived) break up, split up, disband, separate, go their separate ways.

distance n 1 (measure the distance between the two trees) space, gap, interval, span, stretch. 2 (They were concerned about the distance of the house from the town) remoteness.

distant adj 1 (The children like to hear stories of distant places) far-off, remote, out of the way, outlying, far-flung. 2 (in distant times) long ago, far-off. 3 (The two villages are ten miles distant from each other) away, apart, separate. 3 (I have only a distant recollection of what happened) dim, vague, faint, hazy, indistinct. 4 (She is rather a distant person) aloof, detached, remote, reserved, unfriendly, unsociable, uncommunicative, stand-offish, unapproachable.

distinct adj 1 (There was a distinct resemblance between the two crimes) clear, clear-cut, plain, obvious, marked, definite, unmistakable, manifest, patent. 2 (There are two distinct issues to be discussed) separate, individual, different, disparate.

distinguish vb **1** (*He found it difficult to distinguish some colours from others*) tell apart, tell the difference between, differentiate, discriminate. **2** (*They thought that they could distinguish a dim shape in the mist*) make out, detect, discern, notice, see, observe. **3** (*The soldier distinguished himself in the battle*) make famous, bring fame to, bestow honour on.

distress n **1** (*the child's distress on being separated from her parents*) suffering, pain, agony, misery, wretchedness, heartache, sorrow, sadness. **2** (*homeless people in distress*) hardship, adversity, misfortune, need, want, poverty, deprivation.

distribute vb **1** (*They distributed advertising leaflets on the street*) issue, pass out, pass round, circulate. **2** (*The teacher distributed books to the children*) give out, hand out. allocate, issue, allot, dispense.

district n (*They live in a district at the edge of the city*) area, region, place, locality, neighbourhood, sector.

disturb vb **1** (*They don't like being disturbed when they are at work*) interrupt, distract, bother, trouble, pester, intrude on, interfere with, harass, (*inf*) hassle. **2** (*The cleaner was asked not to disturb the documents on the desk*) disarrange, disorganize, muddle, confuse. **3** (*The news of the closure of the school disturbed them*) concern, worry, upset, fluster, perturb.

dive vb (*He dived into the water to save the drowning child*) jump, leap, dip, drop, nose-dive, submerge.

diverge vb (*The roads diverge at the end of the village*) separate, divide, split, part, fork, branch off.

divide vb **1** (*You should divide the rope in two*) sever, cut, split, separate. **2** (*The road divides suddenly*) diverge, separate, divide, split, part, fork, branch off. **3** (*They divided the cake out among the children*) distribute, deal out, share out, allocate, allot, apportion.

divine adj **1** (*divine beings*) godly, heavenly, celestial, holy. **2** (*Taking part in divine worship*) religious, holy, spiritual. **3** (*The bride looked divine*) lovely, beautiful, charming, wonderful, marvellous.

doctor n (*They called a doctor when the child was ill*) medical practitioner, general practitioner, GP, hospital doctor, consultant, specialist.

document n (*the documents relating to the business deal*) paper, official paper, certificate, record, deed.

dogged adj (*They admired her dogged determination*) determined, resolute, stubborn, obstinate, tenacious.

dominant adj **1** (*He is the dominant member of the group*) supreme, controlling, influential, authoritative, domineering. **2** (*It was the dominant issue on the agenda*) chief, main, principal, leading, predominant.

domineering adj (*He is so domineering that everyone is afraid of him*) overbearing, arrogant, dictatorial, masterful, tyrannical, bullying, (*inf*) bossy.

doom n (*people who are always pre-*

dicting doom) catastrophe, disaster, destruction, ruin, downfall.

door n (*stand at the door of the block of flats*) doorway, entrance, entry.

doting adj (*doting parents*) indulgent, adoring, devoted, fond.

double adj 1 (*They parked on a double yellow line*) duplicate, twofold, in pairs. 2 (*a double thickness of cloth*) twofold, folded, two-ply. 3 (*His words had a double meaning*) dual, ambiguous, ambivalent, two-edged.

doubt n 1 (*They are having doubts about his efficiency as a leader*) misgiving, mistrust, distrust, reservations. 2 (*They are full of doubts about what they ought to do*) uncertainty, indecision, hesitation, irresolution.

doubtful adj 1 (*It is doubtful that he will be present*) uncertain, in doubt, unsure. 2 (*The genuineness of the signature is doubtful*) open to question, questionable, uncertain, dubious, debatable, disputable, inconclusive. 3 (*The meaning of the word is doubtful*) dubious, unclear, ambiguous, obscure. 4 (*His parents thought that he was associating with doubtful people*) dubious, questionable, suspicious, suspect.

down adj 1 (*They were feeling down at the end of the holidays*) downcast, dejected, depressed, gloomy, miserable, sad, unhappy. 2 (*The computer system is down*) malfunctioning, inoperative, not working.

downright adv (*She was downright rude*) utterly, completely, totally, absolutely, thoroughly, positively.

drab adj (*They live in very drab surroundings*) dingy, dull, dismal, dreary, gloomy, cheerless, dim, dark.

drag vb 1 (*They dragged the fallen trees from the forest*) haul, pull, draw, tug, yank, tow. 2 (*Time dragged*) move slowly, crawl.

drastic adj (*a drastic remedy*) extreme, severe, rigorous, harsh, radical, dire.

draw vb 1 (*draw a house*) sketch, make a picture of, make a diagram of, portray, depict, design. 2 (*draw a chair up to the table*) pull, drag, haul, tow, tug, yank. 3 (*He drew a sword from its sheath*) take out, bring out, withdraw, extract, produce. 4 (*Her hat drew a lot of attention*) attract, catch, captivate. 5 (*draw the curtains*) pull, close, shut. 6 (*They drew level with the other car*) move, go, proceed.

dreadful adj 1 (*It was a dreadful accident*) terrible, frightful, horrible, grim, awful, shocking, appalling, ghastly, gruesome. 2 (*What a dreadful man!*) nasty, unpleasant, disagreeable, horrible, frightful, odious.

dream vb 1 (*The child seems to dream every night*) have dreams, have nightmares. 2 (*He said that he saw a ghost but he must have been dreaming*) see things, hallucinate, imagine things. 3 (*She was dreaming instead of concentrating on her work*) daydream, be in a reverie, be lost in thought, be in a brown study. 4 (*He would not dream of upsetting her*) think, consider.

dreary adj (*They live in dreary surroundings*) dismal, drab, dingy, dull, gloomy, cheerless, gloomy, dark.

dress vb 1 (*They were all dressed in black*) clothe, attire, array, garb. 2 (*She was late and had to dress quickly*) get dressed, put on clothes. 3 (*The nurse dressed the wound*) cover, bandage, bind up. 4 (*The children dressed the Christmas tree*) decorate, adorn, ornament, trim, deck.

drink vb (*She drank the water quickly*) swallow, gulp down, partake of, quaff, (*inf*) swig.

drip vb (*Water began to drip from the tap*) trickle, dribble, plop, leak, splash, ooze, exude.

drive vb 1 (*young people learning to drive a car*) operate, steer, handle, direct, manage. 2 (*They came by train but we drove here*) go by car, come by car, travel by car, motor. 3 (*They drove the cattle to the milking parlour*) press, urge, push, prod, goad, spur. 4 (*Poverty drove them to steal*) force, compel, oblige, make, pressure, coerce. 5 (*They began to drive posts into the ground to make a fence*) hammer, ram, bang, plunge, sink.

drop vb 1 (*The hot air balloon dropped out of the sky*) drop down, descend, fall, plummet, plunge. 2 (*Water dropped from the branches*) fall, drip, trickle, dribble, plop. 3 (*She dropped her luggage and fell into a chair*) let fall, let go. 4 (*He has decided to drop piano lessons*) give up, stop, abandon, discontinue, cease, end, finish. 5 (*She has dropped her latest boyfriend*) leave, forsake, abandon, jilt. 6 (*House prices have dropped*) fall, lessen, decrease, decline, dwindle, plummet, plunge.

drowsy adj (*People often feel drowsy after a heavy meal*) sleepy, tired, weary, lethargic, sluggish.

drug n 1 (*Medical scientists have discovered a new cancer drug*) medical drug, medicine, medication, medicament, cure, remedy. 2 (*concern over young people who are addicted to drugs*) addictive drug, narcotic, opiate, barbiturate, (*inf*) dope.

drunk adj (*drunk people staggering down the road*) intoxicated, inebriated, under the influence, tipsy.

dry adj 1 (*the dry regions of the world*) arid, parched, scorched, dehydrated, desiccated. 2 (*dry autumn leaves*) withered, shrivelled, wilted, desiccated. 3 (*The cheese has grown very dry*) dried out, hard, stale. 4 (*The lecture was very dry and the audience was bored*) boring, dull, uninteresting, tedious, monotonous, tiresome.

dual adj (*He plays a dual role in the firm*) double, duplicate.

dubious adj 1 (*He is dubious about going to the meeting*) doubtful, unsure, uncertain, hesitant, irresolute, wavering. 2 (*The result is still dubious*) doubtful, uncertain, unsure, unsettled, up in the air. 3 (*He seems rather a dubious character*) suspicious, suspect, questionable, untrustworthy.

dull adj 1 (*It was a dull day*) overcast, cloudy, dark, gloomy, dismal, bleak. 2 (*She always wore dull colours*) drab, dreary, dark, sombre. 3 (*We heard the dull thud of something falling*) muffled, muted, indistinct. 4 (*The lecturer gave a very dull talk*) boring, uninteresting, dry, tedious, monotonous.

dumb adj 1 (He has been dumb since birth) without speech, mute. 2 (They were struck dumb at the beauty of the view) speechless, silent, wordless, mute, inarticulate, at a loss for words. 3 (He is so dumb that he did not get the job) stupid, unintelligent, dense, thick, slow-witted.

duplicate vb 1 (She was asked to duplicate the documents) copy, photocopy, reproduce, Photostat. 2 (There does not seem to be work around and workers are duplicating tasks) repeat, do over again.

duplicity n (his duplicity in swindling the old lady) deceit, deceitfulness, double-dealing, trickery, guile, dishonesty.

durable adj 1 (the durable effects of the drug) long-lasting, lasting, persisting, permanent. 2 (The boots must be durable) long-lasting, lasting, hard-wearing, sturdy, strong, tough.

dust vb 1 (dust the furniture) wipe, brush, clean, mop. 2 (She dusted the cake with icing sugar) sprinkle, dredge, scatter.

duty n 1 (He has a sense of duty towards his parents) responsibility, obligation. 2 (He failed to carry out his duties and was sacked) job, task, chore, assignment. 3 (They had to pay duty on the goods which they brought into the country) tax, levy, tariff, excise.

dwindle vb (Their hopes are dwindling as time goes on) grow less, lessen, decrease, diminish, fade.

E

eager *adj* **1** (*eager students*) keen, enthusiastic, avid, earnest, zealous, fervent. **2** (*people eager to learn/eager for information*) avid, anxious, longing for, yearning for, desirous of.

early *adv* **1** (*get up early*) at dawn, at daybreak, with the lark, at cock-crow. **2** (*visitors who arrived early*) too soon, ahead of time, prematurely. **3** (*It is very important that you arrive early for your interview*) in good time, ahead of schedule.

early *adj* **1** (*an early reply*) prompt, speedy, quick, rapid, fast, without delay. **2** (*an early crop*) advanced, forward, premature, precocious. **3** (*early man*) primitive, prehistoric, primeval.

earn *vb* **1** (*earn an extremely high salary*) make, get, receive, obtain, draw, clear, take home. **2** (*earn the respect of his colleagues*) gain, win, attain, secure, merit, deserve.

earnest *adj* **1** (*an earnest young man who studies hard*) serious, solemn, grave, intense, staid, studious, diligent. **2** (*make an earnest plea for mercy*) fervent, ardent, passionate, intense, heartfelt, sincere, urgent.

earnest:—in earnest *adj* **1** (*They were in earnest about walking all the way home*) serious, sincere, not joking. **2** (*They set to work in earnest*) zealously, wholeheartedly, with a will, with commitment, determinedly.

earnings *npl* (*She tries to save part of her earnings*) income, salary, wages, pay.

earth *n* **1** (*earth, moon and stars*) globe, world, planet. **2** (*the earth and the sky*) land, ground. **3** (*children getting covered in earth from playing in the garden*) soil, dirt.

earthenware *n* (*a shop selling local earthenware to the tourists*) pottery, crockery, stoneware, ceramics.

earthly *adj* **1** (*a book about creatures that were not earthly*) terrestrial. **2** (*earthly pleasures*) worldly, non-spiritual, secular, temporal, material, fleshly, carnal. **3** (*They have no earthly chance of success*) feasible, possible, conceivable, likely, realistic.

earthy *adj* **1** (*the earthy smell of a newly dug garden*) soil-like, dirt-like. **2** (*tell jokes which were rather earthy*) bawdy, crude, coarse, ribald, indecent, blue.

ease *n* **1** (*wealthy people leading a life of ease*) comfort, contentment, affluence, wealth, prosperity, luxury. **2** (*do the job with ease*) effortlessness, facility, no difficulty, deftness, adroitness. **3** (*Ease of manner is important in his job*) naturalness, relaxedness, composure, affability.

ease *vb* **1** (*receive some pills to ease the pain*) lessen, reduce, diminish, relieve, soothe, alleviate, mitigate. **2** (*The storm finally eased*) lessen, grow less, abate, moderate, slacken off. **3** (*A letter would ease his mother's mind*) comfort, give comfort to, calm, soothe, give solace to. **4** (*try to ease the part of the machine into the right position*) guide, manoeuvre, inch, edge, steer, slide.

easy *adj* **1** (*an easy task*) simple, effortless, uncomplicated, straightforward, undemanding. **2** (*She had an easy mind when she knew her family were safe*) at ease, untroubled, unworried, at peace, calm, tranquil, composed. **3** (*an easy manner*) natural, relaxed, easygoing, composed, unreserved, affable, (*inf*) laid-back.

easygoing *adj* (*He is too easygoing to get upset about anything*) even-tempered, relaxed, placid, happy-go-lucky, tolerant, understanding, undemanding, patient, (*inf*) laid-back.

eat *vb* **1** (*eat sweets*) consume, devour, chew, swallow, gulp down, bolt, wolf, (*inf*) tuck into, scoff. **2** (*What time do you eat?*) have a meal, take food. **3** (*Acid had eaten away the material*) erode, corrode, wear away, rot.

eavesdrop *vb* (*The child tried to eavesdrop on her parents' conversation*) listen in on, overhear.

ebb *vb* **1** (*when the tide ebbed*) go out, flow back, retreat, draw back, recede. **2** (*The popularity of the president ebbed*) decline, lessen, decrease, dwindle, fade away, peter out.

eccentric *adj* (*The villagers think he is eccentric/She has an eccentric way of dressing*) strange, peculiar, odd, queer, weird, outlandish, bizarre, zany, freakish, unconventional, (*inf*) off-beat, (*inf*) way-out.

echo *vb* **1** (*The sound echoed round the hall*) resound, reverberate, ring. **2** (*She simply echoed what her father said*) repeat, reiterate, reproduce, copy, imitate, parrot.

economical *adj* **1** (*have to be economical with fuel so that it will last the winter*) sparing, thrifty, careful, frugal. **2** (*an economical form of transport*) inexpensive, reasonable, low-cost, low-price, cheap.

economize *vb* (*Since prices have gone up we will have to economize*) cut back, spend less, cut expenditure, tighten one's belt, draw in one's horns.

ecstasy *n* (*Her idea of ecstasy was to lie on a beach all day*) bliss, rapture, joy, elation, delight, happiness, pleasure.

ecstatic *adj* (*They were ecstatic when their team won the championship*) elated, exultant, in raptures, overjoyed, joyful, jubilant, jumping for joy, on cloud nine, in seventh heaven.

edge *n* **1** (*the edge of the road*) side, verge. **2** (*the edge of the town*) border, boundary, perimeter.

edgy *adj* (*feel edgy when her children were late home*) on edge, anxious, nervous, tense, uneasy, worried, (*inf*) nervy, (*inf*) uptight.

edible *adj* (*food that is scarcely edible*) eatable, consumable, digestible, palatable.

edict *n* (*by edict of the emperor/obey the official edicts*) order, decree, command, law, rule, act, statute.

edit *vb* **1** (*They edited the manuscript which he had written*) revise, correct, alter, adapt, emend. **2** (*He edits the* *daily newspaper*) be the editor of, be in charge of, direct.

edition n (*last week's edition of the magazine*) issue, number, publication.

educate vb (*children who were educated at the little local school*) teach, instruct, school, train.

educated adj (*the kind of books that educated people might read*) well-read, knowledgeable, literate, cultivated, cultured.

education n (*receive a good education*) schooling, teaching, instruction, training, tuition.

eerie adj (*hear an eerie noise in the middle of the night*) strange, unnatural, uncanny, ghostly, frightening, (*inf*) scary.

effect n 1 (*It is difficult to say what the effect of the changes will be*) result, consequences, outcome, influence, impact. 2 (*I like the general effect of the colour scheme*) impression, impact.

effect, take effect vb 1 (*new regulations taking effect from next week*) come into force, come into operation, begin, become law, become valid. 2 (*when the sleeping pills take effect*) work, be effective.

effective adj 1 (*an effective government*) successful, competent, capable, efficient, productive. 2 (*an effective colour scheme*) striking, impressive, attractive. 3 (*rules which will be effective from next year*) valid, in force, in operation, operative.

effects npl (*her personal effects*) belongings, possessions, goods, things, luggage.

effervescent adj (*effervescent soft*

drinks) sparkling, fizzy, bubbly, carbonated.

efficient adj 1 (*a very efficient worker*) capable, competent, able, effective, productive, skilful, organized. 2 (*an efficient system*) effective, well-organized, well-run, streamlined.

effigy n (*effigies of ancient kings*) likeness, image, statue, bust.

effort n 1 (*work requiring a great deal of effort*) exertion, power, energy, work, force, application, struggle, strain, (*inf*) elbow grease. 2 (*She passed the driving test at her second effort*) attempt, try, endeavour, (*inf*) shot, (*inf*) go.

effortless adj (*He made lifting the heavy weights seem effortless*) easy, simple, uncomplicated, trouble-free, unexacting, undemanding.

effrontery n (*She had the effrontery to go straight to the top of the queue*) impudence, impertinence, cheek, audacity, temerity, (*inf*)nerve, (*inf*) brass neck.

effusive adj (*When she pays people compliments she is so effusive*) gushing, fulsome, demonstrative, extravagant, lavish, (*inf*) over the top.

egg, egg on vb (*His friends egged him on to steal the apples*) encourage, urge, spur, goad, prod, prompt.

eject vb 1 (*He was ejected from the club for trying to start a fight*) throw out, remove, banish, evict, (*inf*) kick out, (*inf*) turf out, (*inf*) chuck out. 2 (*She was ejected from the plane*) thrust out, throw out, propel.

eke:—eke out vb 1 (*eke out the lamb*

stew by adding a lot of vegetables) stretch out, increase, supplement. **2** (We must try to eke out our fuel supplies) be economical with, be sparing with, economize on. **3** (The poor peasants eke out a living from the soil) scrape, scratch.

elaborate adj **1** (elaborate carvings/ elaborate patterns) detailed, intricate, complex, ornate, fancy, showy, fussy, (inf) flashy. **2** (draw up an elaborate plan) complicated, detailed, complex, involved, intricate.

elaborate vb (asked to elaborate on his suggestion) expand, enlarge, amplify, flesh out.

elapse vb (A long time elapsed before they met again) pass, go by, roll by, slip by.

elastic adj **1** (elastic materials) stretchy, springy, pliant, flexible, rubbery. **2** (Our holiday plans are elastic) flexible, fluid, adaptable, adjustable.

elated adj (They were elated at their victory) overjoyed, jubilant, jumping for joy, joyful, delighted, gleeful, ecstatic, euphoric, over the moon, on cloud nine, in seventh heaven.

elation n (their elation at their victory) jubilation, joy, joyfulness, delight, glee, ecstasy.

elbow vb (elbow him out of the way to get to the front of the crowd) push, jostle, shoulder, knock, bump.

elderly adj (the elderly couple next door) oldish, old, advanced in years.

elderly:—the elderly npl elderly people, older people, senior citizens, old-age pensioners, pensioners, OAPs,

retired people (be kind to the elderly).

elect vb **1** (elect a team captain) choose, select, pick, opt for, appoint, decide on. **2** (elect an MP) vote for, choose.

election n (vote in an election for a new leader) ballot, poll.

electrify vb (He electrified the audience with his performance) excite, thrill, rouse, stir, move, fire.

elegance n (admire the elegance of the model) stylishness, style, grace, gracefulness, fashion, fashionableness.

elegant adj (the elegant women at the wedding reception) stylish, graceful, fashionable, tasteful, artistic.

elegy n (an elegy for his friend's death) funeral poem, funeral song, lament, dirge, requiem.

element n **1** (the main elements of the project) component, ingredient, constituent, factor, feature, detail. **2** (the natural element of the lion) environment, habitat, milieu, sphere.

elementary adj **1** (He said that the problem was elementary) easy, simple, uncomplicated, straightforward. **2** (students taking a course in elementary mathematics) basic, fundamental, rudimentary, primary.

elements npl (climbers braving the elements) weather, climate, atmospheric conditions.

elicit vb (try to elicit the information from them) draw out, extract, obtain, get.

eligible adj (not eligible for the post/not eligible to take part in the race) qualified, suitable, acceptable, authorized.

eliminate vb **1** (She was eliminated

from the team) drop, leave out, exclude, omit, reject. **2** (*a gunman hired to eliminate the members of the other gang*) get rid of, dispose of, destroy, put an end to, kill.

elocution *n* (*take lessons in elocution*) speech, diction, enunciation, articulation, voice production, delivery.

eloquent *adj* (*an eloquent speech*) articulate, expressive, fluent, persuasive, forceful.

elude *vb* (*try to elude the police*) avoid, dodge, evade, escape from, get away from.

emaciated *adj* (*emaciated children in the famine region*) skeletal, gaunt, wasted, scrawny, skinny, scraggy, thin as a rake.

embargo *n* (*place an embargo on trade with that country*) ban, bar, prohibition, interdict.

embark *vb* **1** (*Passengers were asked to embark early*) board ship, board a plane, go on board. **2** (*someone embarking on a new career*) set out on, begin, start, commence, enter on, set about.

embarrassed *adj* (*feel embarrassed when she forgot the words of her speech*) awkward, uncomfortable, self-conscious, upset, disconcerted, discomfited, flustered, confused, abashed, ashamed, mortified.

embarrassment *n* (*overcome with embarrassment when she forgot the words of her speech*) awkwardness, discomfort, self-consciousness, discomfiture, confusion, shame, mortification.

embezzle *vb* (*embezzle money from his*

company) steal, rob, thieve, pilfer, filch, appropriate, (*inf*) nick.

emblem *n* (*the emblem of the society*) crest, badge, symbol, sign, device.

embrace *vb* (*He embraced his daughter as she got on the train*) hug, cuddle, clasp, cling to, squeeze.

emerge *vb* **1** (*They stood around the pool as the swimmers emerged*) come out, come into view, appear, surface, become visible. **2** (*waiting for the facts to emerge*) come out, become known, come to the fore.

emergency *n* (*emergencies such as fires*) crisis, danger, accident, extremity.

emigrate *vb* (*people emigrating to find work*) move overseas, move abroad, migrate, relocate.

eminent *adj* (*an eminent writer*) famous, well-known, distinguished, renowned, notable, noteworthy, great, important, prominent.

emit *vb* **1** (*chimneys emitting smoke*) give out, pour out, issue, send forth, discharge, issue. **2** (*emit a scream for help*) utter, express, voice.

emotion *n* (*in a voice in which there was no emotion*) feeling, sentiment, passion.

emotional *adj* **1** (*an emotional person*) passionate, ardent, demonstrative, excitable. **2** (*an emotional moment*) moving, touching, affecting, poignant, emotive.

emphasis *n* **1** (*As far as the interviews were concerned the emphasis was on qualifications*) stress, priority, importance, weight, urgency. **2** (*put the* *emphasis on the first syllable*) stress, accent, accentuation.

emphasize vb **1** (*emphasize the importance of working hard*) stress, accentuate, underline, highlight, spotlight, point up. **2** (*emphasize the first syllable*) stress, put the stress on, accentuate.

emphatic adj (*He issued an emphatic denial*) definite, decided, firm, positive, absolute.

employ vb **1** (*He wishes to employ three more people in his office*) engage, hire, take on, sign on. **2** (*His work employs all his time*) take up, occupy, fill, use up. **3** (*employ modern methods in their factory*) use, make use of, apply.

employment n (*He is looking for employment in the computing industry*) work, occupation, job.

empty adj **1** (*an empty house*) vacant, unoccupied, uninhabited, unfilled. **2** (*an empty page*) blank, unused, clean. **3** (*empty threats*) meaningless, futile, ineffective, idle, insubstantial.

enchant vb (*The children were enchanted by the ballet*) captivate, fascinate, entrance, bewitch, charm, delight.

enclosure n (*the enclosure for the animals at the dog show*) compound, ring, arena, paddock, fold.

encounter vb **1** (*She encountered an old friend in the shopping centre*) meet, run into, run across, come upon, (*inf*) bump into. **2** (*encounter problems*) meet, be faced with, face, confront.

encourage vb **1** (*encourage those who had given up hope*) inspire, hearten,

stimulate, motivate, incite, prompt. **2** (*a plan to encourage exports*) boost, promote, help, assist, aid.

end n **1** (*the far end of the lake*) edge, border, boundary, extremity, tip. **2** (*the end of the film*) ending, conclusion, close, finish, culmination, denouement. **3** (*the end of the train*) rear, back. **4** (*their end in mind*) aim, objective, intention, purpose. **5** (*meet a peaceful end*) death, demise.

end vb **1** (*when his membership of the club ends*) come to an end, finish, come to a stop, stop, cease, conclude. **2** (*The incident ended their friendship*) bring to an end, bring to a close, finish, stop, discontinue, wind up.

endanger vb (*things which endanger the species*) put in danger, expose to danger, put at risk, risk, jeopardize.

endearing adj (*one of her endearing features*) charming, attractive, loveable, adorable, engaging, sweet.

endeavour vb (*endeavour to do better*) attempt, try, exert oneself, make an effort, strive.

ending n (*a happy ending to the novel*) end, finish, close, conclusion.

endless adj **1** (*endless patience*) unending, without end, unlimited, infinite, everlasting, boundless. **2** (*an endless chain*) continuous, unbroken, uninterrupted, unbroken.

endorse vb (*endorse their course of action*) approve, support, back, champion, uphold, subscribe to.

endow vb (*She was endowed with good looks*) give, provide, supply, gift, confer.

endure vb **1** (*unable to endure the traffic noise any longer*) put up with, stand, bear, tolerate, abide. **2** (*hope that their love would endure*) last, continue, remain, live on, persist.

enemy n (*the army of the enemy/regard his former friend as an enemy*) foe, opponent, adversary, rival.

energetic adj (*not feeling energetic enough to go for a walk*) active, lively, sprightly, vigorous, animated, enthusiastic.

energy n (*lacking in energy after her illness*) strength, stamina, vigour, power, force, liveliness, vitality, animation.

enforce vb **1** (*enforce the law*) apply, carry out, administer, implement, impose. **2** (*enforce silence on the group*) force, compel, insist on.

engage vb **1** (*engage a new nanny*) employ, hire, appoint, take on. **2** (*engage in a game of chess/ be engaged in a bitter argument*) take part in, join in, participate in, enter into. **3** (*an attempt to engage their attention*) attract, catch, draw, gain, capture.

engaged adj **1** (*The manager is engaged*) busy, occupied, unavailable, (*inf*) tied up. **2** (*The toilet is engaged*) occupied, in use. **3** (*engaged couples*) going to be married, betrothed, affianced.

engaging n (*an engaging smile*) charming, attractive, appealing, winning, pleasing, sweet.

engineer vb (*engineer a secret meeting between them*) bring about, cause, contrive, devise, (*inf*) wangle.

engrave vb **1** (*engrave their initials on the tree*) carve, etch, inscribe, cut. **2** (*Her words are engraved on his heart*) fix, set, imprint, stamp.

engross vb (*The book engrossed me*) occupy, absorb, preoccupy, engage, rivet.

engulf vb (*a town engulfed by a tidal wave*) flood, inundate, swamp, swallow, swamp, submerge.

enjoy vb (*enjoy a trip to the seaside*) like, love, be entertained by, take pleasure in, delight in.

enjoy:—enjoy oneself vb have a good time, have fun, (*inf*) have a ball (*The children are enjoying themselves at the funfair*).

enjoyable adj (*an enjoyable occasion*) entertaining, amusing, delightful, pleasant, nice.

enlarge vb (*enlarge the garden*) expand, extend, add to, amplify.

enormous adj (*an enormous creature/ an enormous load*) huge, immense, massive, vast, colossal, gigantic, mammoth.

enough adj (*We have enough food*) sufficient, adequate, ample, abundant.

enrol vb **1** (*enrol for a French course*) register, sign up, enter, volunteer. **2** (*We enrolled several new recruits in the society*) register, sign up, take on, admit, accept.

ensue vb (*the argument and the fight that ensued*) follow, come after, result, arise.

ensure vb (*You must try to ensure that he will be present*) make sure, make certain, guarantee, certify.

enter vb **1** (*enter the hall*) come into, go

into, pass into, move into. **2** (*a bullet entered his chest*) go into, pierce, penetrate. **3** (*enter a competition*) go in for, take part in, participate in. **4** (*enter one's name on the form*) put down, register, record, mark down, note.

enterprise *n* **1** (*The festival is an annual enterprise*) project, undertaking, operation, venture. **2** (*The wool firm is a private enterprise*) business, industry, firm, establishment. **3** (*young people showing some enterprise*) resourcefulness, initiative, drive, imagination, spirit, enthusiasm, boldness, (*inf*) get-up-and-go.

enterprising *adj* (*an enterprising member of staff*) resourceful, go-ahead, imaginative, spirited, enthusiastic.

entertain *vb* (*He entertained the children with conjuring tricks*) amuse, divert, please, delight, interest.

entertainment *n* **1** (*several forms of entertainment for non-working hours*) amusement, fun, recreation, diversion, distraction. **2** (*sing for the entertainment of the children*) amusement, enjoyment, diversion, pleasure, delight, interest. **3** (*the entertainment at the club that evening*) show, performance.

enthralling *adj* (*The acrobats gave an enthralling performance*) fascinating, gripping, riveting, spellbinding, enchanting, captivating, entrancing.

enthusiastic *adj* (*enthusiastic members of the flying club*) eager, keen, ardent, zealous, passionate, wholehearted, devoted, earnest, fanatical.

entice *vb* (*try to entice customers into his shop*) lure, tempt, attract, coax, decoy.

entire *adj* **1** (*his entire collection of records*) whole, total, complete, full. **2** (*not an entire success*) total, absolute, unqualified, thorough, outright.

entirely *adv* (*not entirely true*) absolutely, completely, totally, wholly, altogether.

entitle *vb* **1** (*Your pass entitles you to go to three matches*) allow, permit, enable, qualify, give the right to. **2** (*His novel is entitled "Lost Dreams"*) call, name.

entrance *n* **1** (*the entrance to the office block*) way in, entry, doorway, gateway, lobby, porch, foyer. **2** (*gain entrance to the building*) entry, access, admission, admittance. **3** (*the entrance of the headmaster*) entry, arrival, appearance.

entrance *vb* (*We were entranced by their graceful dancing*) hold spellbound, fascinate, captivate, enchant, enthral.

entrant *n* (*count the number of entrants for the competition*) competitor, contestant, participant, candidate, applicant.

entreat *vb* (*She entreated us to go with her*) beg, implore, beseech, plead with, appeal to.

entrenched *adj* (*entrenched political ideas*) deep-rooted, well-established, fixed, set, firm, unshakeable, dyed-in-the wool.

entry *n* **1** (*the entry to the block of flats*) entrance, doorway, gateway, lobby, porch, foyer. **2** (*gain entry to the office building*) entrance, access, admission, admittance. **3** (*the entry of the ballet dancers*) entrance, arrival, appearance. **4** (*an entry in her diary*) statement, item, record, note, listing.

envelop vb (*mountain tops enveloped in mist*) cover, blanket, surround, engulf, swathe.

enviable adj (*He has an enviable collection of CDs*) desirable, tempting, impressive, excellent.

envious adj (*She was envious when she saw her friend's new car*) jealous, covetous, green, begrudging, resentful.

environment n (*Children need a loving environment/the ideal environment for tigers*) surroundings, habitat, background, situation, conditions, circumstances, atmosphere, milieu.

envy n (*her envy of her neighbour's garden*) enviousness, covetousness, jealousy, resentment.

envy vb (*She envies her friend her new car*) be envious of, be jealous of, covet, be covetous, begrudge, grudge, resent.

ephemeral adj (*the ephemeral life of the mayfly*) short-lived, fleeting, transitory, brief, passing, temporary.

episode n **1** (*the second episode of the TV serial*) part, instalment, section. **2** (*an unhappy episode in their lives*) incident, event, occurrence, happening, experience.

equal adj **1** (*children of equal ability*) the same, identical, like, comparable. **2** (*an equal contest*) even, evenly matched, level. **3** (*not feeling equal to the task*) up to, fit for, ready for, capable of.

equal vb **1** (*six plus six equals twelve*) be equal to, come to, amount to, add up to, make, total. **2** (*The runner equalled the record for the race*) match, be level with, reach.

equate vb (*They equate money with happiness*) associate, bracket, link, connect.

equip vb **1** (*equip the children for their skiing trip*) fit out, kit out, rig out, dress. **2** (*equip the hall with gymnastic apparatus*) fit out, furnish, supply, stock.

equipment n (*the equipment needed to do the job*) tools, gear, apparatus, materials, things, paraphernalia.

equivalent adj (*ask the shop to exchange the item for something of equivalent value*) equal, the same, identical, similar, like, comparable, corresponding, matching.

equivalent n (*the equivalent of our Chancellor of the Exchequer in their country*) counterpart, opposite number, equal.

era n (*furniture from the Jacobean era*) age, period, time, days, aeon, epoch.

eradicate vb (*try to eradicate the weed from his garden/A government tries to eradicate tax avoidance*) get rid of, do away with, root out, wipe out, eliminate, extirpate.

erase vb (*erase the incorrect passage from the report*) remove, rub out, wipe out, delete, cancel, expunge.

erect adj (*Human beings stand erect*) upright, vertical, straight.

erect vb **1** (*erect a tent*) put up, set up, set upright, pitch, assemble. **2** (*erect a* block of flats) build, construct, put up, raise.

erode vb (cliffs eroded by the sea) wear away, wear down, eat away, corrode.

err vb 1 (They erred when they accused him of theft) be in error, be wrong, be incorrect, make a mistake, be mistaken, get it wrong, miscalculate, (inf) slip up. 2 (ministers who urge the members of their congregation not to err) do wrong, sin, behave badly, misbehave, transgress.

errand n task, job, chore, assignment, mission.

erratic adj 1 (worried about her erratic behaviour) inconsistent, irregular, variable, unstable, unpredictable, unreliable, capricious. 2 (a driver steering an erratic course) wandering, meandering, wavering.

erroneous adj (an erroneous statement) wrong, incorrect, inaccurate, untrue, false, mistaken.

error n 1 (an error in their calculation of the building costs) mistake, inaccuracy, miscalculation, blunder, fault, oversight, (inf) slip-up. 2 (see the error of his ways) wrongdoing, sin, evil, misbehaviour, misconduct.

erupt vb 1 (A flow of lava erupted from the volcano) to be discharged, gush, pour out, issue, belch. 2 (violence erupted between the two gangs of football supporters) break out, flare up, blow up, burst forth.

eruption n 1 (an eruption of violence) outburst, outbreak, flare-up. 2 (an eruption on her face) rash, inflammation, outbreak.

escalate vb 1 (The violence has escalated/The war escalated) increase, intensify, heighten, accelerate, be stepped up, mushroom. 2 (Prices have escalated) go up, mount, climb, soar.

escapade n (The children were punished for their escapades) adventure, prank, stunt, trick, (inf) lark.

escape vb 1 (The prisoners escaped from the jail) get away, run away, abscond, bolt, break free, make one's getaway, (inf) do a runner, (inf) do a bunk. 2 (succeed in escaping punishment) avoid, evade, dodge, elude, steer clear of, side-step. 3 (gas escaping) leak, seep out, discharge, spurt, gush.

escort n (require an escort for the dance) partner, companion, attendant, (inf) date.

especially adv 1 (The products sell well, especially in the summer) particularly, above all, chiefly, mainly, principally. 2 (designed especially for her) specially, specifically, expressly, particularly, exclusively.

espionage n (a novel about espionage) spying, intelligence, undercover work.

essay n (asked to write an essay on a favourite author) composition, dissertation, paper, article, thesis, discourse.

essence n 1 (the essence of good speech) essential part, main ingredient, nature, kernel, quintessence. 2 (vanilla essence) extract, concentrate, distillate.

essential adj 1 (essential equipment/It is essential to arrive early) necessary, vital, indispensable, crucial, important.

2 (*the essential theme of the novel*) basic, fundamental, inherent, principal.

establish vb **1** (*establish a computing firm*) set up, form, found, institute, create, inaugurate. **2** (*try to establish his innocence*) prove, show, demonstrate, verify, certify.

estate n **1** (*He owns a town house and a country estate*) property, land property, lands, land-holding. **2** (*His estate at his death amounted to nearly a million pounds*) assets, resources, effects, possessions, belongings, wealth. **3** (*a housing estate*) area, development.

esteem n (*hold the writer in great esteem*) regard, respect, admiration, honour, reverence, appreciation.

estimate vb (*estimate the cost of repairs*) work out, calculate, assess, gauge, reckon, guess, (*inf*) guesstimate.

estimation n **1** (*In our estimation he is the best player*) opinion, view, judgement, consideration, way of thinking, feeling. **2** (*When she lied she went down in our estimation*) good opinion, regard, respect, admiration, approval, favour.

estuary n (*boats in the estuary*) river mouth, inlet, cove, bay.

eternal adj **1** (*life eternal*) everlasting, endless, without end, never-ending, perpetual, immortal, infinite. **2** (*We are tired of their eternal quarrelling*) endless, never-ending, incessant, ceaseless, non-stop, constant, continuous, continual, interminable, unremitting.

ethical adj (*not an ethical thing to do*) moral, honourable, virtuous, good, decent, honest.

ethnic adj (*ethnic restaurants/ethnic customs*) racial, cultural, national.

etiquette n (*wedding etiquette*) rules of conduct, accepted behaviour, protocol, custom, convention.

eulogy n (*a eulogy about their team's performance*) praise, accolade, acclamation, applause, tribute, paean, panegyric.

evacuate vb **1** (*people asked to evacuate areas likely to be bombed by the enemy*) leave, vacate, quit, abandon, retreat from, (*inf*) pull out. **2** (*The police evacuated everyone from the area*) move out, clear.

evade vb **1** (*try to evade her responsibilities*) avoid, escape from, dodge, shirk, side-step, (*inf*) duck. **2** (*succeed in evading the enemy*) avoid, escape from, elude, shake off, give the slip to, keep out of the way of, steer clear of.

even adj **1** (*even ground*) level, flat, smooth, uniform. **2** (*The temperature of the room must remain even*) constant, uniform, steady, stable, unchanging. **3** (*We gave the children even amounts of money*) equal, the same, identical, like, similar, comparable. **4** (*The score was even at half-time*) level, equal, all square, tied, drawn, (*inf*) even steven. **5** (*people of an even disposition*) even-tempered, calm, placid, serene, composed, unexcitable, unperturbable.

event n **1** (*The sad and happy events in their lives*) happening, occurrence, occasion, episode, incident, experience.

2 (*the track events in the Olympic Games*) contest, competition, match.

eventually adv (*She took her driving test several times and eventually passed*) in the end, finally, at last, ultimately.

everlasting adj **1** (*everlasting life*) eternal, endless, without end, never-ending, perpetual, abiding, immortal, infinite. **2** (*their everlasting complaints*) endless, never-ending, non-stop, incessant, ceaseless, continuous, continual.

evict adj (*get evicted from their house for not paying the rent/get evicted from the club for being under age*) throw out, put out, turn out, eject, remove, oust, (*inf*) chuck out, kick out, turf out.

evidence n **1** (*They will have to produce evidence of his guilt*) proof, confirmation, verification, corroboration. **2** (*There was evidence of a struggle at the scene of the murder*) sign, indication, mark.

evident adj (*It was evident that he was unwell/an evident improvement*) obvious, clear, apparent, plain, noticeable, conspicuous, perceptible, visible.

evil adj (*appalled at his evil deeds*) wicked, bad, wrong, sinful, immoral, villainous.

exacerbate vb (*His remarks exacerbated the situation*) make worse, worsen, aggravate, intensify, add fuel to the fire.

exact adj **1** (*an exact description*) precise, accurate, close, faithful, true. **2** (*the exact time*) precise, accurate, right.

exacting adj (*an exacting task*) demanding, difficult, hard, arduous, tough, laborious, taxing, onerous.

exactly adv **1** (*His estimate was exactly right*) precisely, absolutely, just, quite, (*inf*) on the nail, (*inf*) bang on, (*inf*) spot on. **2** (*repeat the information exactly*) word for word, verbatim, literally, to the letter, closely, faithfully.

exaggerate vb **1** (*exaggerate the length of time the journey took*) overstate, overemphasize, overstress, overestimate. **2** (*It's not that expensive—you're exaggerating*) overstate, embroider, embellish, overdraw, add colour, over-elaborate, make a mountain out of a molehill, (*inf*) lay it on with a trowel, (*inf*) lay it on thick.

examine vb **1** (*It is necessary to examine the facts*) look at, study, inspect, survey, analyse, review, observe, check out, weigh up. **2** (*examine a patient*) look at, check over, give a check-up, assess.

example n **1** (*buy an example of the artist's early work*) sample, specimen, instance, illustration. **2** (*follow his brother's example*) model, pattern, standard. **3** (*punish some pupils as an example to the others*) warning, caution, lesson.

exasperate vb (*She was exasperated by their objections*) annoy, irritate, anger, infuriate, incense, enrage.

excavate vb **1** (*excavate a trench*) dig, dig out, hollow out, scoop out. **2** (*excavate an ancient Roman settlement*) unearth, dig up, uncover, disinter.

exceed vb **1** (*His talent as a musician exceeds that of his brother*) be greater than, be more than, be superior to, surpass, outstrip, outshine, overshadow, top, cap. **2** (*exceed the speed limit*) go beyond, go over, do more than, overstep. **3** (*at a price not exceeding £5000*) be greater than, be more than, go beyond, top.

exceedingly adv (*She was exceedingly beautiful*) extremely, exceptionally, extraordinarily, tremendously, enormously, vastly, greatly, highly, hugely.

excellent adj (*an excellent player*) very good, first-rate, first-class, great, fine, distinguished, superb, outstanding, marvellous, brilliant, (*inf*) A1, (*inf*) top-notch.

exception n **1** (*the whole school will go with the exception of the first class*) exclusion, omission. **2** (*Their case is an exception*) special case, anomaly, deviation, irregularity, oddity, freak.

exceptional adj **1** (*exceptional weather for the time of year*) unusual, uncommon, abnormal, out of the ordinary, extraordinary, atypical, rare. **2** (*people of exceptional talent*) excellent, extraordinary, remarkable, outstanding, phenomenal.

excerpt n (*read an excerpt from one of Shakespeare's plays*) extract, passage, quotation, quote, piece, section.

excessive n **1** (*an excessive amount of water*) too much, extravagant, immoderate, undue, inordinate, (*inf*) over the top. **2** (*The prices seem excessive*) exorbitant, outrageous, unreasonable.

exchange vb (*The children agreed to exchange toys*) swap, trade, barter.

excite vb **1** (*the thought of the party excited the children*) thrill, stimulate, rouse, animate, (*inf*) turn on. **2** (*excite feelings of anger in the crowd*) cause, bring about, rouse, arouse, incite, provoke, kindle, stir up.

exclamation n (*He gave an exclamation of surprise*) cry, call, shout, yell, shriek.

exclude vb **1** (*She was excluded from their talks*) leave out, keep out, debar, bar, ban. **2** (*They cannot exclude the possibility of murder*) rule out, set aside, preclude, eliminate.

exclusive adj **1** (*an exclusive club*) select, private, fashionable, chic. **2** (*gave them her exclusive attention*) complete, undivided, full, absolute, entire, total. **3** (*the price exclusive of drinks*) excluding, not including, omitting, not counting, excepting.

excruciating adj (*an excruciating pain in her stomach*) agonizing, acute, severe, intense, extreme.

excursion n (*go on an excursion to the seaside*) trip, expedition, jaunt, outing, journey.

excuse vb **1** (*impossible to excuse their crime*) forgive, pardon, condone, justify, defend. **2** (*ask to be excused from the gymnastics class*) let off, exempt, release.

excuse n **1** (*their excuse for not arriving on time*) defence, justification, reason, grounds, vindication. **2** (*His supposed illness was just an excuse for staying off school*) pretext, cover-up, front, pretence.

execute vb **1** (*Murderers used to be*

executed) put to death, kill, hang. **2** (*execute a plan*), carry out, perform, accomplish, fulfil, put into effect, implement.

exercise vb **1** (*The women were exercising in order to keep fit*) do exercises, work out, train. **2** (*try to exercise a little patience*) use, employ, apply, exert.

exercise n **1** (*do exercises every morning to keep fit*) physical training, work-out, drill. **2** (*Some exercise is necessary to keep healthy*) activity, physical exertion, physical effort. **3** (*pupils given an English exercise*) task, piece of work, problem.

exert vb **1** (*They could finish the job in time if they exerted themselves*) make an effort, spare no effort, put oneself out, try hard, do one's best, strive, struggle, strain, labour. **2** (*It was necessary to exercise some pressure*) employ, use, apply, wield.

exhaust vb **1** (*The long walk exhausted her*) tire, tire out, wear out, fatigue, weary, (*inf*) poop, (*inf*) knacker. **2** (*We have exhausted our supplies of food*) use up, consume, finish, deplete, expend.

exhaustive adj (*The police made an exhaustive search*) intensive, all-out, comprehensive, thorough.

exhibit vb **1** (*The firm exhibited their latest works*) put on show, show, put on display, display, put on view, demonstrate, present. **2** (*exhibit patience/exhibit signs of improvement*) show, indicate, reveal, demonstrate, express.

exhibition n **1** (*a book exhibition*) show, display, demonstration, presentation,

fair, exposition. **2** (*an exhibition of bad temper*) display, show, expression, indication, demonstration.

exile vb (*exiled from their native land*) banish, expatriate, deport, expel, outlaw.

exile n **1** (*sent into exile*) banishment, expatriation, deportation. **2** (*exiles from their native land*) expatriate, deportee, outlaw, refugee, displaced person.

exist vb **1** (*children believing that fairies exist*) be, have being, have existence, live, be living. **2** (*difficult to exist on such a low income*) live, stay alive, survive.

exit n (*the exit from the cinema*) way out, egress.

expand vb **1** (*substances that expand when heated*) grow larger, get larger, increase in size, swell, distend. **2** (*expand the business*) make larger, make bigger, increase, amplify, add to, extend.

expanse n (*an expanse of blue water*) stretch, area, extent, tract, sweep.

expect vb **1** (*I expect that they will arrive soon*) believe, think, assume, suppose, imagine, presume, surmise. **2** (*I am expecting a parcel from them*) await, wait for, look for, anticipate, hope for.

expedite vb (*try to expedite the process*) speed up, hasten, hurry, accelerate, step up.

expedition n **1** (*an expedition to the centre of the jungle*) journey, exploration, safari, undertaking, quest. **2** (*a shopping expedition*) trip, outing, excursion, jaunt. **3** (*the members of the* *expedition to climb Everest)* group, team, party, company.

expel vb 1 *(expel him from school/expel him from the club)* throw out, oust, drum out, bar, ban, blackball. 2 *(expel them from their native land)* banish, exile, drive out, cast out, expatriate, deport.

expense n 1 *(victory in the war at the expense of many lives)* cost, sacrifice. 2 *(go to a great deal of expense to buy her a present)* outlay, cost, spending.

expensive adj *(expensive clothes)* costly, high-priced, dear, overpriced, exorbitant, extortionate, *(inf)* steep.

experience n 1 *(a terrifying experience)* event, incident, occurrence, happening, affair, episode. 2 *(a job requiring experience as well as a university degree)* practical knowledge, skill, practice, training, *(inf)* know-how, *(inf)* hands-on experience.

experiment n *(medical experiments to find new drugs)* test, trial, investigation, research, pilot study.

expert n *(an expert on local history)* authority, specialist, professional, pundit, *(inf)* buff.

expert adj *(an expert chess player)* knowledgeable, specialist, experienced, professional, skilful, proficient, adept, *(inf)* crack.

expire vb 1 *(Her membership of the club has expired)* run out, be no longer valid, end, come to an end, finish, stop, cease, lapse. 2 *(people expiring from lack of food)* die, pass away, breathe one's last, decease.

explain vb 1 *(explain how to work the*

machine) give an explanation of, describe, define, make clear, spell out, throw light on. 2 *(called upon to explain their actions)* give an explanation of, account for, give a reason for, justify, defend, vindicate.

explanation n 1 *(a clear explanation as to how the machine works)* description, definition, clarification, interpretation. 2 *(unable to accept their explanation for their absence)* account, reason, grounds, excuse, justification, defence, vindication

explode vb 1 *(The bomb exploded)* blow up, go of, detonate, burst. 2 *(The gas boiler exploded)* blow up, burst open, fly into pieces, erupt. 3 *(explode his theory)* disprove, discredit, refute, invalidate, debunk.

exploit n *(a book about the exploits of the knights of old)* deed, feat, adventure, stunt.

exploit vb 1 *(exploit the resources which they have)* make use of, use, utilize, put to good use, turn to one's advantage, profit by, make capital out of. 2 *(a mill-owner who exploited the workers/a man who exploited his friends)* make use of, take advantage of, abuse, impose upon.

explore vb 1 *(explore areas of jungle)* travel in, survey, reconnoitre. 2 *(explore every possibility)* examine, look into, investigate, inquire into, consider, research.

explosion n 1 *(There was a loud explosion and we discovered the boiler had blown up)* bang, blast, boom, rumble, crash, crack, report. 2 *(an explosion in* the population figures) increase, escalation, mushrooming, rocketing.

expose vb 1 (expose her skin to the sun) bare, lay bare, uncover. 2 (newspapers exposing the details of the scandal) reveal, disclose, divulge, make known, uncover, unveil. 3 (expose the baby to harsh weather) lay open to, leave unprotected by, put at risk from.

express vb 1 (express their gratitude in a short speech) voice, state, put into words, articulate, utter, make known, communicate. 2 (express their appreciation with a gift of money) show, demonstrate, indicate, convey. 3 (express juice from the oranges) press, squeeze, force out, extract.

expression n 1 (We could tell from her expression that she was angry) face, countenance, look, appearance, air. 2 (find the right expression to say what she means) word, words, phrase, term, wording, language, turn of phrase, phraseology. 3 (play the violin piece with expression) feeling, emotion, passion, intensity, vividness.

extant adj (a species of bird that is still extant) still existing, in existence, living, alive, existent, surviving, remaining.

extend vb 1 (extend the territory which he rules over) expand, increase, enlarge, lengthen. 2 (extend the ladder to its full length) stretch out, draw out, lengthen, elongate. 3 (extend the period of his employment) increase, prolong, lengthen, stretch out, protract. 4 (The lake extends for many miles) continue, stretch, stretch out, carry

on, run on. 5 (extend a warm welcome to the guests) offer, give, proffer, hold out.

extensive adj 1 (a house with extensive grounds) large, large-scale, sizeable, substantial, vast, immense. 2 (have extensive knowledge of the Bible) comprehensive, thorough, wide-ranging, wide, broad. 3 (The storm caused extensive damage to the crops) great, widespread, wholesale, universal.

extent n 1 (the extent of her knowledge/ the extent of the damage) scope, range, coverage, degree. 2 (the extent of the land around the house) area, expanse, length, stretch.

exterior adj (the exterior surface) outside, outer, outermost, outward, external, surface.

extinct adj 1 (a species of bird now extinct) died out, wiped out, gone, defunct. 2 (an extinct volcano) inactive, extinguished, burnt out.

extinguish vb (extinguish the candles) put out, blow out, quench, snuff out.

extra adj 1 (They need extra help to finish the job) more, additional, added, further, supplementary, auxiliary, subsidiary. 2 (We have extra food in our picnic—would you like some?) surplus, spare, left over, superfluous, excess, reserve.

extract vb (extract a tooth) pull out, draw out, take out, remove.

extract n (read extracts from her novel on the radio) excerpt, passage, selection, quotation, citation.

extraordinary adj 1 (have an extraordinary memory) exceptional, unusual, uncommon, rare, striking, remarkable. phenomenal. **2** (*It was extraordinary that she survived*) amazing, astonishing, remarkable, astounding, surprising, strange.

extravagant *adj* **1** (*an extravagant way of life*/*It was extravagant to buy such an expensive dress*) spendthrift, thriftless, improvident, profligate, wasteful. **2** (*He tried to flatter her by paying her extravagant compliments*) exaggerated, excessive, outrageous, absurd, (*inf*) over the top.

extreme *adj* **1** (*in the extreme north of the country*) farthest, furthest, outermost, most remote. **2** (*in extreme danger*) very great, greatest, maximum, utmost, severe. **3** (*people who hold extreme political views*) immoderate, fanatical, exaggerated, intemperate.

extremely *adv* (*She is extremely beautiful*) very, exceedingly, exceptionally, extraordinarily, markedly, uncommonly.

eye *n* **1** (*have sharp eyes*) eyesight, sight, vision. **2** (*The police are keeping an eye on her*/*She is under the eagle eye of the head teacher*) watch, observation, notice, surveillance.

F

fabric n 1 (*curtains made of a brightly coloured fabric*) cloth, material, textile, stuff. 2 (*the fabric of the building/the fabric of society*) framework, frame, structure, constitution.

fabulous adj 1 (*stories about fabulous creatures such as dragons*) mythical, imaginary, fictitious, fictional, legendary. 2 (*an emperor of fabulous wealth*) incredible, unbelievable, unimaginable, inconceivable, astonishing. 3 (*They had a fabulous time on holiday*) marvellous, wonderful, superb, great, (*inf*) fab, (*inf*) super.

face n 1 (*She had a beautiful face*) countenance, features. 2 (*She came rushing out with an angry face*) expression, look, air. 3 (*the faces of a cube*) front, side, surface. 4 (*She was afraid of losing face in the firm*) prestige, status, standing, dignity. 5 (*She had the face to call us liars*) impudence, impertinence, audacity, effrontery, cheek, (*inf*) nerve, (*inf*) brass neck.

face vb 1 (*a block of flats facing the sea*) look on to, overlook, be opposite to, front on to. 2 (*They are facing many difficulties*) meet, encounter, confront.

facetious adj (*Please don't make facetious remarks—it is a serious situation*) flippant, frivolous, light-hearted, joking, jocular, funny, amusing.

fact n 1 (*difficult to separate fact from fiction*) reality, actuality, truth. 2 (*wish to have all the facts of the case*) detail, particular, factor, piece of information, piece of data, circumstance.

factor n (*consider all the factors connected with the situation*) element, point, detail, feature, item, circumstance.

fade vb 1 (*The curtains had faded in the sunlight*) lose colour, become bleached, become pale, become washed out, dull, dim. 2 (*fresh flowers that had faded*) wilt, wither, droop, die. 3 (*Hope had faded/Memories of the occasion had faded*) dim, grow less, die away, dwindle, grow faint, vanish, die.

fail vb 1 (*Their attempt to climb the mountain failed*) be unsuccessful, fall through, be in vain, come to nothing, come to grief, (*inf*) flop. 2 (*They failed the exam*) not pass, fail, (*inf*) flunk. 3 (*The engine failed*) break down, stop working, cut out, (*inf*) conk out. 4 (*He failed to keep us informed*) omit, neglect, forget. 5 (*Her health is failing*) decline, deteriorate, diminish, dwindle, wane. 6 (*His business has failed*) collapse, crash, go under, go bankrupt, go to the wall, fold, (*inf*) go bust, (*inf*) flop.

failing n (*Untidiness is his main failing*) fault, shortcoming, weakness, flaw, imperfection, defect, foible.

failure n (*Our attempt was a complete failure*) non-success, disaster, fiasco, (*inf*) flop.

faint adj 1 (faint traces of paint on the table) indistinct, unclear, dim, faded, obscure. 2 (hear a faint sound of laughter) indistinct, soft, low, muted, feeble. 3 (a faint smell of violets) slight, indistinct, delicate. 4 (have a faint chance of winning the match) slight, small, remote, vague. 5 (feel faint) dizzy, giddy, light-headed, (inf) muzzy.

faint vb (She fainted in the heat) pass out, collapse, black out, lose consciousness, swoon, (inf) conk out.

fair adj 1 (She had fair hair) blond, yellow, flaxen, pale, light brown. 2 (the accused was given a fair trial) just, impartial, unprejudiced, unbiased, objective. 3 (a fair judge) fair-minded, just, impartial, unprejudiced, unbiased, open-minded, honest. 4 (the weather was fair for the picnic) fine, dry, bright. 5 (The standard of his work is just fair) satisfactory, all right, middling, so-so, average, adequate.

fairly adv (She was fairly good at playing the piano) quite, rather, somewhat, reasonably, passably, tolerably, (inf) pretty.

faith n 1 (they have faith in their doctor) trust, confidence, belief, reliance. 2 (they are of the Christian faith) religion, creed, belief, persuasion.

faithful adj 1 (the leader's faithful followers) loyal, constant, true, devoted, dependable, reliable, trustworthy, staunch. 2 (a faithful account of the event/a faithful copy of the picture) accurate, true, exact, precise, close.

fake adj 1 (fake ten pound notes) counterfeit, forged, fraudulent, false, imitation, (inf) phoney. 2 (wearing a string of fake pearls) imitation, artificial, synthetic, simulated, mock, sham, ersatz.

fall vb 1 (The leaves fall in autumn) drop, descend. 2 (The child fell as she left the bus) fall down, trip over, stumble, topple over, go head over heels, (inf) take a spill. 3 (The level of the water in the river was falling in the drought) sink, subside, abate. 4 (The price of houses has fallen) decrease, decline, go down, grow less, plummet, slump. 5 (a memorial to the soldiers who fell in battle) die, be killed, be slain, perish, be a fatality, be a casualty. 6 (Her birthday falls on a Monday this year) be, take place, occur, happen.

false adj 1 (They gave a false account of their movements to the police) untrue, wrong, incorrect, inaccurate, erroneous. 2 (He gave a false name) assumed, made-up, invented, fictitious, (inf) phoney. 3 (false friends) disloyal, unfaithful, faithless, treacherous, untrustworthy.

falsehood n (accuse him of telling falsehoods) lie, untruth, fib, story, (inf) porky.

falter vb 1 (The young boxer faltered when he saw the size of his opponent) hesitate, waver, flinch, stumble. 2 (The speaker was nervous and faltered over his speech) stumble, stutter, stammer.

fame n (His fame as an artist has spread/seek fame in Hollywood) renown, eminence, distinction, notability, greatness, glory, honour.

familiar adj 1 (*The old man was a familiar sight in the village shop*) well-known, common, customary, accustomed, regular, commonplace, everyday. 2 (*workers who were familiar with the computing system*) acquainted with, conversant with, versed in, experienced in, with knowledge of.

family n 1 (*people of noble family*) ancestry, parentage, descent, extraction, blood, line. 2 (*The poor old woman has no family*) relatives, relations, people, one's own flesh and blood, next of kin. 3 (*The couple have no family*) children, offspring, progeny, (*inf*) kids.

fan n (*a football fan/a fan of the pop star*) admirer, follower, enthusiast, devotee, fanatic, addict, aficionado, (*inf*) buff, (*inf*) freak.

fancy n 1 (*the fancy of the poet*) imagination, creativity. 2 (*The person from Mars was just a fancy on the child's part*) figment of the imagination, hallucination, illusion, delusion, fantasy. 3 (*have a fancy for some chocolate*) desire, urge, notion, wish, want, hankering, longing, yearning, (*inf*) yen.

fancy vb 1 (*He fancied he saw a ghostly figure*) imagine, think, believe. 2 (*He said that he fancied a drink*) would like, wish, want, desire, hanker after, long for, yearn for, (*inf*) have a yen for.

fancy adj (*fancy patterns/fancy decorations*) ornate, elaborate, ornamental, decorated, adorned, embellished, showy, (*inf*) jazzy.

fantastic adj 1 (*He had fantastic notions about seeing aliens from Mars*) fanciful, imaginary, wild, strange. 2 (*fantastic figures and shapes in his painting*) strange, weird, bizarre, outlandish, fanciful, whimsical. 3 (*He earns a fantastic amount of money*) huge, enormous, tremendous. 4 (*He thought the concert was fantastic*) marvellous, wonderful, sensational, superb, excellent.

fantasy n 1 (*a children's book which is full of fantasy*) fancy, imagination, creativity, originality, vision. 2 (*She is always having fantasies about winning a lot of money*) flight of fancy, dream, daydream, pipe-dream, reverie, illusion.

far adv 1 (*it is not far to the next village*) a long way, a great distance. 2 (*It is far too soon to know*) by a long way, to a great extent, very much.

far adj (*the far places of the world*) faraway, far-off, distant, remote, far-flung.

fare n (*Train fares have gone up*) ticket, charge, cost, price.

far-fetched adj (*They found his story rather far-fetched*) unlikely, improbable, implausible, incredible, unbelievable, unconvincing .

farm vb (*farm land in the north*) cultivate, till, work.

fascinate vb (*The children were fascinated by the mime artist*) captivate, enchant, enthral, entrance, hold spellbound, charm, absorb, engross.

fashion n 1 (*the fashions of the nineteenth century*) style, trend, taste, craze, vogue. 2 (*She has a job in fashion*) clothes, the clothes industry, couture, (*inf*) the rag trade. **3** (*She arranged things in an organized fashion*) way, manner, method, style, system.

fashionable *adj* (*fashionable clothes/furniture that is no longer fashionable*) in fashion, stylish, up-to-date, in vogue, modern, contemporary, (*inf*) trendy.

fast *adj* **1** (*at a fast pace*) quick, rapid, swift, brisk, speedy, hurried. **2** (*fast colours*) fixed, indelible, permanent.

fast *adv* **1** (*walk fast*) quickly, rapidly, swiftly, briskly, speedily, hurriedly, like the wind. **2** (*a lorry stuck fast in the mud*) firmly, tightly, securely, immovably. **3** (*children who were fast asleep*) sound, deeply.

fast *vb* (*people who fast during certain religious holidays/fasting in aid of a famine charity*) go without food, eat nothing, go hungry, starve oneself, deny oneself food.

fasten *vb* **1** (*She fastened a brooch to her dress*) attach, fix, clip, pin. **2** (*fasten the dog to the gatepost*) attach, tie, bind, tether. **3** (*The links of the chain are fastened to each other*) join, connect, couple, unite, link.

fat *adj* **1** (*fat people trying to lose weight*) plump, obese, stout, overweight, portly, chubby, tubby, podgy, flabby. **2** (*fat reference books*) thick, big, substantial. **3** (*people told to avoid fat substances for the sake of their health*) fatty, greasy, oily.

fat *n* **1** (*require some form of fat to make a cake*) animal fat, vegetable fat, lard, butter, margarine. **2** (*She was embarrassed by her fat*) fatness, plumpness, obesity, stoutness, portliness,

chubbiness, tubbiness, flab.

fatal *adj* (*a fatal blow/a fatal illness*) mortal, deadly, lethal, killing, terminal.

fatality *n* (*There were several fatalities in the motorway crash*) death, dead, casualty, mortality.

fate *n* (*She wondered what fate had in store for him*) destiny, providence, chance, luck, fortune, the stars, nemesis.

fateful *adj* (*a fateful meeting*) critical, crucial, decisive, momentous, important.

father *n* **1** (*Her father left her a lot of money*) male parent, (*inf*) dad, (*inf*) daddy, (*inf*) pa, (*inf*) old man. **2** (*the father of modern medicine*) founder, originator, initiator, creator, architect.

fatigue *n* (*He was suffering from fatigue after climbing the mountain*) tiredness, overtiredness, weariness, exhaustion.

fatty *adj* (*fatty foods*) fat, greasy, oily.

fault *n* **1** (*discover a fault in the material*) flaw, defect, imperfection. **2** (*one of the main faults in her character*) flaw, defect, failing, shortcoming, weakness, weak point, deficiency. **3** (*The accident was her fault*) blame, responsibility.

faulty *adj* **1** (*a faulty lock*) broken, damaged, defective, unsound. **2** (*take the faulty goods back to the shop*) flawed, defective, imperfect.

favour *n* **1** (*He did her a favour by giving her a lift*) good turn, good deed, service, kindness. **2** (*He looked on the new scheme with favour*) approval, approbation, goodwill, friendliness.

favourable *adj* **1** (*in less favourable cir-*

cumstances/favourable winds) advantageous, beneficial, helpful, promising, auspicious. **2** (She hoped to make a favourable impression on her friend's parents) good, pleasing, agreeable. **3** (He received a favourable report from his teacher) good, approving, praising, commendatory, enthusiastic.

favourite adj (the child's favourite toy) best-loved, dearest, favoured, chosen, preferred.

favourite n (The youngest child is her grandfather's favourite) pet, darling, idol, (inf) blue-eyed boy/girl.

fear n (filled with fear at the sight of the strange man) fright, terror, alarm, panic, apprehensiveness, dread, horror, nervousness.

fear vb **1** (They fear their grandfather) be afraid of, be scared of, be apprehensive of, dread. **2** (We fear for their safety) worry, be anxious, feel concerned. **3** (We fear that they could be right) be afraid, suspect, have a suspicion.

fearful adj **1** (They were fearful of disturbing the guard dogs) afraid, frightened, terrified, alarmed, apprehensive. **2** (The smashed cars were a fearful sight) terrible, frightful, appalling, ghastly, horrific, horrible, shocking. **3** (The house was in a fearful mess) terrible, frightful, appalling, very great.

fearless adj (fearless soldiers fighting the enemy/fearless explorers) brave, courageous, gallant, valiant, intrepid, bold, heroic.

feasible adj (It was not feasible to leave earlier) possible, practicable, work-able, reasonable, realistic, within reason.

feat n (read about the daring feats of the knights of old) deed, act, action, exploit, achievement.

feather n (the bird's feathers) plumage, plumes, down.

feature n (the feature of the burglary that confused the police) aspect, characteristic, side, detail, quality, peculiarity.

features npl (She had very regular features) face, countenance.

fee n (the fee for membership of the club) charge, price, cost, payment, subscription.

feeble adj **1** (people who have grown feeble with age) weak, weakly, frail, infirm, delicate, failing, helpless, debilitated. **2** (They made a feeble attempt to get there on time) ineffective, ineffectual, weak, futile, inadequate.

feed vb (not make enough money to feed the family) give food to, nourish, provide for, cater for.

feel vb **1** (feel faint at her father's words) experience, undergo, know, be conscious of, be aware of, notice. **2** (feel the silky cloth) touch, stroke, caress, finger, handle, fondle. **3** (He tried to feel his way to the house in the dark) grope, fumble. **4** (The weather feels warmer today) seem, appear. **5** (feel the temperature of the water before bathing the baby) test, try out. **6** (We feel that we ought to go) believe, think, consider, be of the opinion, judge.

feeling n **1** (Blind people are able to identify objects by feeling) feel, touch, sense of touch, **2** (*He could not describe his feelings when he lost his job*) emotion, sentiment, sensation. **3** (*There was a feeling of unhappiness about the place*) feel, atmosphere, mood, impression, air, aura. **4** (*My feeling is that we should go*) thoughts, opinion, view, way of thinking, instinct. **5** (*I had a feeling that he would win*) idea, suspicion, funny feeling, hunch.

feign *vb* **1** (*feign illness*) pretend, fake, simulate, sham, affect, give the appearance of. **2** (*We thought that he was sleeping but he was only feigning*) pretend, put on an act, put it on, fake, sham, act, play-act.

fellow *n* (*a suspicious-looking fellow over there*) man, boy, individual, (*inf*) chap, (*inf*) bloke, (*inf*) guy, (*inf*) character.

fellowship *n* (*Now that she has retired she misses the fellowship of her workmates*) companionship, company, friendship, comradeship.

female *n* (*a club just for females*) woman, lady, girl.

feminine *adj* **1** (*a very feminine young woman/feminine clothes*) womanly, ladylike, soft, delicate. **2** (*a rather feminine man*) effeminate, womanish, unmanly, (*inf*) sissyish, (*inf*).

fence *n* (*build a fence round the garden*) barrier, barricade, railing, paling, hedge, wall.

fence *vb* **1** (*fence the garden*) enclose, surround, encircle. **2** (*fence in the cows*) shut in, confine, pen.

fend *vb* (*He tried to fend off his attacker's blows with his arm/a speaker trying to fend off questions*) ward off, turn aside, deflect, avert, keep off.

ferment *vb* **1** (*beer fermenting in vats*) foam, froth, bubble, effervesce. **2** (*He set out to ferment trouble in the crowd*) cause, incite, excite, provoke, stir up, foment.

ferocious *adj* **1** (*ferocious animals*) fierce, savage, wild. **2** (*He was injured in a ferocious attack*) fierce, savage, brutal, vicious, violent, murderous, barbaric.

fertile *adj* **1** (*fertile soil*) fruitful, productive, rich, fecund. **2** (*a fertile imagination*) inventive, creative, resourceful, ingenious.

fertilizer *n* (*put fertilizer on the garden*) plant food, manure, compost.

fervent *adj* (*his fervent enthusiasm for football/a fervent supporter of animal rights*) passionate, ardent, zealous, devout, vehement, eager, earnest.

festival *n* (*the village's annual festival*) fête, carnival, gala day.

fetch *vb* **1** (*fetch the milk from the shop*) get, go for, bring, carry, collect, transport. **2** (*an antique table that fetched thousands of pounds at the auction*) sell for, go for, realize.

feud *n* (*There had been a bitter feud between the families for generations*) vendetta, quarrel, dispute, conflict.

fiasco *n* (*The picnic was a fiasco because of the weather*) disaster, catastrophe, failure, (*inf*) flop.

fickle *adj* (*so fickle that she is always changing boyfriends/fickle weather*) capricious, changeable, variable, unpredictable, unstable, unreliable.

fictitious adj 1 (*not a real person but a fictitious character*) fictional, made up, invented, imaginary, unreal, mythical. 2 (*He gave a fictitious address to the police*) false, invented, bogus, fake, sham.

fiddle vb 1 (*fiddling with his pencil instead of writing his essay*) play, fidget, toy, twiddle. 2 (*fiddle his accounts*) falsify, forge, (*inf*) cook.

fidelity n (*a leader who looked for fidelity in his followers*) faithfulness, loyalty, devotion, allegiance, constancy, trustworthiness.

fidget vb (*children fidgeting with boredom*) to be restless, wriggle, squirm. 2 (*pupils fidgeting with their pencils*) fiddle, play, toy, twiddle.

field n 1 (*look at the cows in the field*) pasture, meadow, paddock. 2 (*working in the field of computing*) area, sphere, line, speciality. 3 (*the school games field*) ground, pitch, arena, stadium.

fierce adj 1 (*a fierce animal*) ferocious, savage, wild. 2 (*a fierce attack*) ferocious, savage, brutal, vicious, violent, murderous. 3 (*her fierce love of liberty*) passionate, ardent, intense, fervent. 4 (*a fierce wind*) strong, violent, stormy, blustery. 5 (*face fierce competition in the race*) keen, intense, strong, competitive.

fight vb 1 (*enemy armies fighting*) do battle, wage war, take up arms, meet in combat. 2 (*armies fighting a battle*) wage, carry on, be engaged in. 3 (*two men fighting in the street*) exchange blows, hit each other, punch each other, brawl. 4 (*The two sisters are always fighting with each other*) quarrel, argue, bicker, squabble, disagree, (*inf*) fall out, feud. 5 (*decide to fight the council's plans for a new road*) contest, take a stand against, oppose, object to, protest against.

fight n 1 (*Our army lost the fight*) battle, encounter, engagement. 2 (*The champion lost the fight*) boxing match. 3 (*two men in a fight outside the pub*) brawl, fisticuffs, (*inf*) scrap, (*inf*) punch-up. 4 (*She has had a fight with her sister*) quarrel, argument, disagreement, difference of opinion, squabble, dispute, feud.

figure n 1 (*write down the figures from 1 to 10*) number, numeral, digit. 2 (*What figure did you have in mind as a salary?*) amount, sum. 3 (*fail to recognize the figures disappearing into the mist*) shape, form, outline, silhouette. 4 (*have rather a plump figure*) body, shape, build, physique. 5 (*a bronze figure of the saint*) likeness, image, statue, carving. 6 (*the figures in the text*) diagram, illustration, drawing, chart.

figure vb 1 (*figure out the cost of the holiday*) calculate, count, work out, reckon, add up. 2 (*try to figure out why he did it*) work out, make out, understand, comprehend, fathom. 3 (*His mother figures in his novel*) appear, feature, play a part, be mentioned.

fill vb 1 (*fill the supermarket shelves*) load, stock, supply. 2 (*food that will fill the children*) make full, satisfy, stuff. 3 (*The perfume of roses filled the air*) pervade, permeate, spread through. **4** (*They filled the hole with sand*) stop up, block up, bung up, plug. **5** (*fill in the form*) fill up, answer.

film n **1** (*a film of oil on the road*) layer, coat, coating, covering, sheet. **2** (*see it through a film of tears*) haze, mist, blur. **3** (*a Walt Disney film*) movie, picture.

film vb (*film the wedding ceremony*) photograph, take photographs of, take pictures of, shoot, video, make a film of, televise.

filter vb (*filter the coffee*) strain, sieve, sift.

filth n **1** (*an old basement covered in filth*) dirt, grime, muck, mud, squalor, (*inf*) crud. **2** (*complaining about the filth in some magazines*) pornography, obscenity, smut, bawdiness.

filthy adj **1** (*filthy houses/filthy hands*) dirty, grimy, grubby, mucky, muddy, squalid, unwashed, unclean. **2** (*filthy literature*) pornographic, obscene, indecent, smutty, bawdy, (*inf*) blue.

final adj **1** (*the final minutes of the football match*) last, closing, concluding, finishing, terminal. **2** (*The decision of the judges is final*) conclusive, decisive, unalterable, indisputable, definitive, absolute.

finalize vb (*finalize our arrangements*) complete, conclude, settle, put the finishing touches to.

finance n **1** (*look for a job relating to finance*) money matters, money management, economics. **2** (*Our finances are low at this time of year*) money, cash, capital, funds, assets, resources.

finance vb (*look for someone to finance*) pay for, fund, provide capital for, provide backing for, subsidize.

find vb **1** (*We found a wallet in the street*) come across, stumble on, discover. **2** (*She lost her handbag and never found it*) get back, recover, retrieve. **3** (*doctors trying to find a cure for cancer*) discover, come upon, bring to light, uncover, unearth, hit upon. **4** (*He is trying to find a new job*) get, obtain, acquire, procure. **5** (*She found that the food did not agree with her*) discover, realize, become aware, learn.

fine adj **1** (*hope for a fine day for their picnic*) dry, fair, clear, sunny. **2** (*ornaments made of fine china*) delicate, fragile, dainty. **3** (*summer dresses made of fine material*) light, lightweight, thin, delicate, filmy, flimsy. **4** (*a beach with fine sand*) powdery, fine-grained. **5** (*There is only a fine distinction between the two schemes*) tiny, minute, subtle. **6** (*The musician gave a fine performance*) splendid, excellent, first-class, first-rate, outstanding. **7** (*a wedding party wearing fine clothes*) elegant, stylish, expensive. **8** (*He was ill but he is fine now*) all right, well. **9** (*If you want to leave early that is fine with us*) all right, acceptable, suitable, (*inf*) OK.

fine n (*a fine for speeding*) penalty, forfeit.

finger vb (*children told not to finger the fruit before buying it*) touch, handle, feel, fiddle with.

finish vb **1** (*workmen who did not finish the job in time*) complete, accomplish, carry out, get done, fulfil. **2** (*when the* concert finished/when the work finished) end, come to an end, conclude, cease, stop, terminate. **3** (We finished the bread at breakfast) use, use up, consume, exhaust, (inf) polish off. **4** (They finish work at five o'clock) stop, cease, end, discontinue, halt.

fire n **1** (modern homes that do not have a fire) fireplace, hearth, grate. **2** (Fortunately no one was hurt in the fire) blaze, flames, conflagration, inferno. **3** (make a fire to burn the rubbish) bonfire. **4** (Her playing of the piece was without fire) passion, ardour, inspiration.

fire vb **1** (He fired the gun) shoot, let off, discharge. **2** (They were found guilty of firing the farm buildings) set fire to, set on fire, set alight, ignite. **3** (His performance fired them with enthusiasm) inspire, rouse, arouse, stir up, stimulate. **4** (He was fired for always being late) sack, dismiss, declare redundant, (inf) axe.

firm adj **1** (The ice was not firm enough to skate on) hard, hardened, solid, set, rigid. **2** (The poles for the fence must be firm in the ground) fixed, secure, fast, stable, set, tight. **3** (We have no firm plans/make a firm arrangement) fixed, settled, agreed, definite, decided, established. **4** (They were quite firm about refusing the invitation) determined, resolute, resolved, decided, adamant, unwavering, obstinate, stubborn. **5** (They have become firm friends) devoted, faithful, loyal, dependable.

firm n (he started his own publishing firm) business, company, organization, establishment, concern.

first adj **1** (the first stages of the manufacturing process) early, earliest, opening, introductory. **2** (the first aeroplane) earliest, original. **3** (the first people to arrive) earliest, soonest.

first n (We knew from the first that he was not suitable) beginning, start, outset, commencement, (inf) the word go.

fit adj **1** (Is the water fit to drink?) suitable, good enough, satisfactory, appropriate. **2** (She was not fit for the job) suitable, good enough, satisfactory, able, capable, competent, adequate, trained, qualified. **3** (The football player was injured but he is fit now) well, healthy, in good health, strong, in good condition, in good shape.

fit vb **1** (The shoes do not fit) be the right size, be the correct size. **2** (fit the parts of the doll's house together) assemble, put together, join, connect. **3** (fit the tiles to the floor) lay, fix, put in place, put in position, position. **4** (clothes that do not fit the occasion) suit, be suitable for, be appropriate for, be apt for. **5** (His account of the accident does not fit with hers) agree, be in agreement, match, accord, concur, tally.

fit n **1** (She had a coughing fit) bout, attack, spell. **2** (an epileptic fit) convulsion, seizure, spasm, paroxysm.

fitting adj **1** (The criminal should receive a fitting punishment) suitable, appropriate, due, apt. **2** (It was not fitting for her to wear those clothes to a funeral) proper, right, seemly, decent, decorous, suitable, appropriate.

fix vb 1 (*fix the bookshelves to the study wall*) attach, fasten, secure, stick, screw, nail. 2 (*fix a date for the party*) set, decide on, settle, arrange, agree on, name. 3 (*He is trying to fix the car*) repair, mend, sort, put right, put to rights.

fizzy adj (*fizzy drinks*) sparkling, bubbly, effervescent.

flabbergasted adj (*He was flabbergasted at how much the new car was going to cost*) astounded, amazed, dumbfounded, stunned, staggered, nonplussed.

flag n (*decorate the streets with flags for the coronation*) banner, pennant, streamer, standard.

flag vb 1 (*Their interest in the subject matter is flagging*) fade, fail, decrease, decline, diminish. 2 (*The speeding motorist was flagged down by the police*) wave down, signal to stop.

flair n (*have a flair for languages*) talent, gift, ability, aptitude, bent, genius.

flake n (*flakes of paint*) n chip, shaving, sliver, fragment, bit.

flame n (*burn with a bright flame*) fire, glow, gleam, brightness.

flame vb (*The dry wood flamed up*) burn, blaze, burst into flames, catch fire.

flap vb 1 (*The flags were flapping in the wind*) flutter, wave, swing. 2 (*birds with wings flapping*) beat, flail, vibrate, thresh. 3 (*The hostess started to flap when the oven broke down*) panic, go into a panic, become flustered, be-

come agitated, (*inf*) be in a state.

flare vb 1 (*The fire suddenly flared up*) blaze, flame. 2 (*Trouble flared up when the army left*) break out, burst out, recur. 3 (*She flares up whenever anyone disagrees with her*) lose one's temper, go into a rage, get angry, fly off the handle.

flash n (*a flash of light*) blaze, burst, flare, gleam, beam, streak. 2 (*She was there in a flash*) instant, moment, second, trice, twinkling of an eye.

flashy adj (*wear flashy clothes*) showy, gaudy, ostentatious, flamboyant, loud, garish, tawdry, (*inf*) jazzy, (*inf*) tacky.

flat adj 1 (*flat surfaces*) level, horizontal, even, smooth. 2 (*lying in a flat position*) spread out, stretched out, prone, supine, prostrate. 3 (*a flat tyre*) deflated, collapsed, burst, punctured. 4 (*The party was rather flat after she had left*) boring, dull, tedious, unexciting, lifeless, uninspired.

flat n (*She left home and rented a flat*) apartment, rooms.

flatten vb 1 (*flatten the surface to make the new road*) make flat, level, even out, smooth out, plane. 2 (*flatten the old buildings to make way for a new housing development*) pull down, knock down, tear down, demolish, raze to the ground. 3 (*gales which flattened the crops*) crush, squash, compress.

flatter vb 1 (*He flatters her whenever he wants to borrow her car*) pay compliments to, compliment, praise, sing the praises of, humour, (*inf*) sweet-talk. 2 (*The dress flatters her*) suit, become, show to advantage.

flavour n 1 (*people who dislike the flavour of garlic*) taste, savour. 2 (*a sauce in need of flavour*) flavouring, seasoning, spiciness, piquancy. 3 (*a book that captured the flavour of the times*) spirit, character, feel, feeling, tone, nature, essence, ambience.

flaw n 1 (*a flaw in the dress material*) defect, imperfection, fault. 2 (*a flaw in the china*) defect, imperfection, fault, crack, chip.

flee vb (*The villagers fled as the enemy army approached*) run away, run off, escape, take flight, make off, abscond, (*inf*) do a bunk, retreat.

fleeting adj (*a fleeting feeling of regret*) brief, short-lived, momentary, transient, transitory, ephemeral.

flesh n 1 (*the flesh and bones of the animals*) meat, brawn, muscle. 2 (*prefer the pleasures of the flesh to those of the spirit*) body, human body, physical nature.

flexible adj 1 (*flexible materials*) pliable, pliant, elastic, springy, bendable. 2 (*Our holiday plans are flexible at the moment*) adaptable, adjustable, variable, changeable, open to change.

flight n 1 (*the flight of the refugees from the war zone*) fleeing, running away, escape, absconding, retreat. 2 (*write a book on the history of flight*) flying, aviation. 3 (*The flight to Australia from London is very long*) plane journey, plane trip.

flimsy adj 1 (*a summer dress made of a flimsy material*) thin, light-weight, light, delicate, sheer. 2 (*a flimsy hut to shelter the refugees*) insubstantial, frail, rickety, ramshackle, makeshift. 3 (*a flimsy excuse for being absent*) feeble, weak, poor, thin, inadequate, unconvincing.

flinch vb 1 (*The boy flinched as his father raised his fist*) draw back, recoil, shrink, quail, wince. 2 (*soldiers who do not flinch from their duty*) shrink from, shy away from, shirk, dodge, duck.

fling vb (*fling the rubbish into the tip*) throw, toss, hurl, cast, pitch, lob, heave, (*inf*) chuck.

flippant adj (*She gave a flippant reply to his serious question*) frivolous, shallow, glib, offhand, carefree.

float vb 1 (*things which can float on water*) stay afloat, be buoyant. 2 (*marker buoys floating along*) bob, drift. 3 (*balloons floating in the air*) drift, hover, hang.

flog vb (*people who think that wrongdoers should be flogged*) whip, lash, flay, birch, scourge, beat, thrash, cane.

flood n 1 (*property damaged in the flood*) deluge, torrent, spate, inundation. 2 (*After the article in the newspaper there was a flood of correspondence*) abundance, overabundance, profusion.

flood vb 1 (*houses damaged by rivers flooding*) overflow, break its banks. 2 (*water which flooded the town*) pour over, inundate, submerge, immerse.

floor n (*a house on three floors*) storey, level.

flop vb 1 (*His head flopped to one side and he fell asleep*) droop, sag, dangle. 2 (*She flopped into a chair after a hard* *day's work*) slump, drop, collapse, fall. **3** (*His first play flopped*) fail, be unsuccessful, be a disaster, (*inf*) bomb.

flourish vb **1** (*plants which flourish in a dry climate*) thrive, bloom, grow, do well, develop. **2** (*The company is flourishing now*) be in good condition, thrive, be successful, succeed, make progress. **3** (*He flourished the trophy which he had won*) brandish, wave, wield, swing, shake, twirl, hold aloft.

flow vb **1** (*rivers flowing*) run, glide, course, stream, ripple, surge. **2** (*a serious wound with blood flowing from it*) gush, well, spurt, spill, ooze.

flower n (*put the flowers in a vase*) bloom, blossom.

flowery adj **1** (*curtains with a flowery pattern*) floral, flower-covered. **2** (*dislike the flowery language of his writing*) high-flown, ornate, elaborate, bombastic.

fluent adj **1** (*a fluent lecturer*) eloquent, articulate, smooth-spoken. **2** (*We admired his fluent French*) smooth, flowing, effortless, unhesitating.

flurry n **1** (*a sudden flurry of snow*) shower, gust, squall. **2** (*in a flurry of excitement waiting for the visitors to arrive*) fluster, bustle, whirl, fuss, flap.

flush vb **1** (*flush the toilet*) rinse out, wash out, cleanse. **2** (*She flushed with embarrassment*) blush, redden, go red, turn red, crimson, colour.

fluster vb (*The guests flustered her by arriving early*) agitate, unsettle, upset, ruffle, panic, confuse, disconcert, (*inf*) rattle.

flutter vb **1** (*birds fluttering their wings*) flap, beat, quiver, vibrate. **2** (*streamers fluttering in the wind*) flap, wave, fly, ripple.

fly vb **1** (*We decided to fly to Paris rather than go by train*) go by air, go by plane. **2** (*He was flying the plane*) pilot, control, operate. **3** (*watch the birds flying overhead*) hover, flutter, soar. **4** (*flags flying to celebrate the victory*) wave, flap, flutter. **5** (*She flew to the window when she heard the car*) rush, race, run, dash, dart. **6** (*They decided to fly as the enemy army approached*) flee, run away, take flight, make one's escape, escape, retreat.

foam n **1** (*the foam on the beer*) froth, head. **2** (*the foam on the soapy water*) froth, bubbles, lather, suds, spume.

foe n (*They easily defeated their foes*) enemy, opponent, adversary, rival, antagonist.

fog n (*The fog was making it difficult for motorists to see*) mist, haze, smog.

foil vb (*The police foiled the thief's attempt to rob the bank*) thwart, frustrate, stop.

foist vb (*He tried to foist some of his work on to the junior employees*) force, unload, thrust, impose.

fold vb **1** (*fold the sheets*) double over, overlap, crease. **2** (*The firm lost money and folded*) fail, collapse, shut down, go bankrupt, (*inf*) go bust.

folder n (*The documents for the meeting were in a folder*) file, binder, cover.

follow vb **1** (*She followed her brother into the house*) walk behind, go behind, go after. **2** (*We asked the taxi to follow the car with the thieves in it*) go after, pursue, chase, (*inf*) tail. **3** (*He followed his father as king*) come after, succeed, replace, take the place of. **4** (*They were told to follow the instructions*) obey, observe, keep to, comply with, heed, take notice of. **5** (*The students could not follow what the lecturer was saying*) understand, comprehend, grasp, fathom. **6** (*He follows the local football team*) be a follower of, be a fan of, be an admirer of, be a supporter of.

fond *adj* (*He is very fond of his grandchildren/She is fond of spicy food*) having love for, having a liking for, keen on, attached to, having a soft spot for.

food *n* **1** (*children with not enough food to survive on*) sustenance, nourishment, provisions. **2** (*The hostess served delicious food*) refreshment, fare, diet, (*inf*) grub, (*inf*) nosh.

foolish *adj* **1** (*It was a foolish idea/They thought it was a foolish thing to do*) silly, absurd, senseless, unintelligent, unwise, ill-considered. **2** (*He is a foolish fellow*) stupid, silly, unintelligent, brainless, dense, ignorant, dull-witted, (*inf*) dumb.

foot *n* **1** (*the foot of the pillar*) base, bottom. **2** (*We met at the foot of the road*) bottom, end.

forbid *vb* (*They were forbidden to go on the farmer's land*) prohibit, ban, bar, debar, preclude.

force *n* **1** (*It required a great deal of force to open the door*) strength, power, might, energy, effort, exertion, pressure, vigour. **2** (*They were accused of using force to get him to con-*

fess) pressure, compulsion, coercion, duress, constraint, violence. **3** (*recognize the force of his arguments*) persuasiveness, effectiveness, strength, power, cogency.

force *vb* **1** (*You cannot force them to go with you*) use force on, make, compel, coerce, bring pressure to bear on, pressurize. **2** (*We lost the key and had to force the drawer*) break open, burst open.

forecast *vb* (*We could have forecast that they would win*) predict, foretell, prophesy, foresee, speculate.

foreign *adj* (*customs that were foreign to them*) alien, unfamiliar, strange, unknown, unfamiliar, exotic.

foresee *vb* (*We could not have foreseen those problems*) anticipate, envisage, predict, foretell, forecast, prophesy.

forfeit *vb* (*She had to forfeit her pocket money to pay for the damage*) give up, hand over, relinquish, surrender.

forge *vb* (*He forged his father's signature on the cheque*) falsify, fake, counterfeit, imitate, copy.

forget *vb* **1** (*I forget their address*) be unable to remember, be unable to recall. **2** (*He tried to forget the terrible event*) put out of one's mind, ignore, disregard. **3** (*She forgot her husband's birthday*) overlook, neglect, disregard. **4** (*She forgot her gloves*) leave behind, omit to take.

forgive *vb* (*Their mother forgave them for being late*) excuse, pardon, let off.

form *n* **1** (*describe the form of the crystals*) shape, formation, structure. **2** (*the human form*) body, figure, shape, build, frame, physique, anatomy **3** (*a form of entertainment*) kind, type, sort, variety. **4** (*She is in the fourth form at our school*) class, year. **5** (*fill in a form to apply for the job*) document, paper, application.

form *vb* **1** (*form clay into animal shapes*) shape, mould, fashion, model, make. **2** (*They formed a committee to raise money for charity*) set up, establish, found, institute. **3** (*begin to form plans to solve the problem*) put together, draw up, think up, devise, frame. **4** (*icicles began to form in the cold weather*) take shape, develop, appear, materialize.

forthcoming *adj* **1** (*forthcoming events in the town*) future, coming, approaching, imminent. **2** (*The children were not very forthcoming about where they had been*) communicative, talkative, informative, open.

forthright *adj* (*a very forthright person who told them the truth*) direct, frank, candid, blunt, plain-speaking.

fortunate *adj* **1** (*He was fortunate to survive the accident*) in luck. **2** (*They are in a fortunate position to have been offered jobs*) favourable, lucky, advantageous.

fortune *n* **1** (*It was only by good fortune that he found the book*) chance, luck, accident. **2** (*He amassed a great fortune*) wealth, riches, assets, possessions.

forward *adj* **1** (*the forward part of the army*) front, foremost, leading **2** (*They were annoyed at her forward behaviour*) bold, brash, brazen, impudent, impertinent, (*inf*) pushy.

foul *adj* **1** (*The rotting meat was a foul sight*) disgusting, revolting, repulsive, nauseating, nasty, dirty. **2** (*The air was foul/foul water*) polluted, contaminated, impure, dirty. **3** (*foul weather*) rainy, stormy, wild, rainy, wet, nasty, disagreeable. **4** (*foul language*) profane, blasphemous, vulgar, crude, coarse, rude, filthy. **5** (*What a foul thing to do*) horrible, nasty, hateful, disgraceful, low, wicked, evil.

found *vb* (*found a new company*) set up, establish, institute, start, create.

fracture *n* (*fractures in the outer wall*) break, crack, split.

fragile *adj* (*china that is very fragile*) delicate, fine, breakable, brittle, frail.

fragment *n* (*fragments of glass*) piece, bit, chip, sliver, splinter, particle.

frail *adj* **1** (*frail old ladies*) delicate, infirm, weak, slight. **2** (*frail model aeroplanes*) fragile, breakable, flimsy, insubstantial.

frame *n* **1** (*ships built on a frame of steel*) framework, foundation, shell, skeleton. **2** (*a photograph frame*) mounting, mount. **3** (*wrestlers with huge frames*) body, physique, figure.

frank *adj* (*He answered in a frank manner*) direct, candid, forthright, plain, open, outspoken, blunt.

fraud *n* **1** (*He was accused of fraud*) swindling, sharp practice, dishonesty, crookedness, deceit, deception. **2** (*The magician's act was a fraud*) swindle, hoax, deception, (*inf*) con, (*inf*) rip-off. **3** (*The bank-note was a fraud*) fake, counterfeit, sham, (*inf*) phoney.

frayed adj (frayed shirt cuffs) ragged, tattered, worn.

freak adj (a freak storm) abnormal, unusual, atypical, exceptional, odd, strange, bizarre.

free adj 1 (We got free tickets for the concert) free of charge, for nothing, without charge, at no cost, complimentary, gratis. 2 (They were free of any worries) without, devoid of, unaffected by, clear of. 3 (We were free to go anywhere we wanted) allowed, permitted, able. 4 (They asked us to the party but we were not free) available, unoccupied, not busy, at leisure. 5 (We looked for a free table in the cafe) unoccupied, empty, vacant, spare. 6 (nations that wanted to be free) independent, self-governing, emancipated, autonomous.

freedom n 1 (prisoners longing for their freedom) liberty, release. 2 (nations seeking freedom) independence, self-government, sovereignty.

freezing adj 1 (freezing weather) icy, frosty, chilly, arctic, wintry. 2 (We were freezing waiting for the bus) chilled through, chilled to the marrow, numb with cold.

frequent adj 1 (They have frequent storms in that area) many, numerous, repeated, recurrent, persistent. 2 (a frequent visitor) regular, habitual, common, usual, constant.

fresh adj 1 (serve fresh fruit for dessert) raw, unpreserved, unprocessed. 2 (a supply of fresh water) pure, unpolluted, uncontaminated, clean. 3 (They are hoping for some fresh ideas) new, modern, original. 4 (We felt fresh after our holiday) energetic, invigorated, lively, refreshed, revived.

friend n (The children invited their friends to a party) companions, (inf) pal, (inf) chum, (inf) mate.

friendly adj (friendly neighbours) amiable, affable, sociable, hospitable, approachable, good-natured, kindly.

frighten vb (The children were frightened when they heard the noise) scare, alarm, startle, terrify.

front n 1 (the front of the queue) head, top, beginning. 2 (They painted the front of the building red) frontage, façade, face. 3 (His business is just a front for drug-dealing) cover, cover-up, disguise, blind, mask.

froth n 1 (froth on the soapy water) bubbles, lather, suds, spume. 2 (froth on the beer) bubbles, effervescence, head.

frown vb 1 (She frowned in anger) scowl, glower, glare. 2 (They frowned upon casual clothes at the club) disapprove of, take a dim view of, dislike.

fulfil vb 1 (He failed to fulfil the tasks given to him) carry out, perform, discharge, accomplish, complete, execute. 2 (He was the only person who fulfilled the job requirements) satisfy, meet, answer, obey.

full adj 1 (Their glasses were full) filled, brimming, brimful. 2 (All the hotel rooms are full) occupied, taken, in use. 3 (The supermarket was full on Saturdays) crowded, packed, crammed, chock-a-block. 4 (She gave us a full list of the names of people present) complete, whole, entire, comprehensive, detailed, thorough.

fumble vb **1** (*fumble for his keys in the dark*) grope, feel for. **2** (*fumble a catch at cricket*) miss, mishandle.

fumes npl (*the fumes from the car's exhaust pipe*) gases, smoke, vapour, smell.

fun n (*The children had fun at the party*) entertainment, amusement, enjoyment, pleasure, a good time.

function n **1** (*his function in the firm*) role, job, duty, task, responsibility. **2** (*the function of the machine*) use, purpose. **3** (*invited to the firm's annual function*) party, reception, gathering, social occasion, social event.

fundamental adj (*learn fundamental cooking skills*) basic, rudimentary, elementary, essential, primary.

funny adj **1** (*They laughed at his funny stories*) amusing, comic, comical, humorous, hilarious, laughable, riotous. **2** (*There was something funny about the way he was behaving*) odd, peculiar, strange, queer, weird, bizarre, suspicious.

furious adj (*They were furious at being treated rudely*) enraged, infuriated, indignant, angry, wrathful.

furnish vb **1** (*furnish the room with modern furniture*) equip, fit out. **2** (*furnish the committee with the required information*) provide, supply, equip, present.

furniture n (*buy antique furniture for the house*) furnishings, appointments, effects.

further adj (*require further supplies*) additional, more, extra.

furtive adj (*The police were suspicious of his furtive behaviour*) secretive, stealthy, sneaky, surreptitious, sly.

fury n (*her parent's fury at the damage caused during the party*) anger, rage, wrath, ire.

future n **1** (*hope for better things in the future*) time to come, time ahead, time hereafter. **2** (*There is little future for that industry*) prospects, expectations, outlook, likely success.

future adj (*an advertisement for future events*) coming, approaching, to come.

G

gadget n (a kitchen with a lot of labour-saving gadgets) appliance, device, piece of apparatus, implement.

gag n (The comedian told a series of old gags) joke, jest, quip, witticism, wisecrack.

gain vb (They tried to gain an advantage over the opposition) get, obtain, acquire, procure, secure, achieve.

gain n (their gains from the sale of the company) profit, return, yield, proceeds, earnings, reward, benefit, (inf) pickings.

gale n (ships damaged at sea in a gale) storm, hurricane, squall, tempest, tornado, cyclone.

gallant adj (gallant soldiers who died in battle) brave, courageous, valiant, heroic, plucky, fearless, intrepid, stout-hearted.

gallop vb 1 (horses galloping around the field) canter, prance, frisk. 2 (The children always gallop home for tea) rush, run, dash, race, sprint, hurry.

gamble vb 1 (He loves to gamble and loses a lot of money) bet, place a bet, wager, lay a wager, (inf) punt. 2 (He gambled when he invested in the company) take a risk, take a chance, speculate, venture.

game n 1 (the children's games) amusement, entertainment, diversion, sport, pastime, hobby. 2 (We are all going to the game tomorrow) match, competition, contest, tournament, athletics event, sports meeting.

gang n 1 (A gang of people had gathered to listen to the speaker) group, band, crowd, mob, horde. 2 (The boys formed a gang) club, clique, circle, set. 3 (a gang of workmen) squad, team, troop.

gap n 1 (crawl through a gap in the wall) opening, hole, aperture, space, chink. 2 (The police are trying to fill in a few gaps in the account of the accident) omission, blank, void, lacuna.

gape vb 1 (They gaped at the sheer size of the huge man) stare, goggle, gaze. 2 (The caves gaped before them) open wide, yawn.

garden n (He grows vegetables in his garden) allotment, plot.

garish adj (The holidaymakers were wearing garish clothes) flashy, loud, gaudy, bold, flamboyant.

garland n (wearing garlands of flowers round their necks) wreath, festoon.

garment n (wearing a strange black garment) piece of clothing, item of clothing, article of clothing.

garments npl (wearing mourning garments) clothes, clothing, dress, attire, apparel, outfit, garb.

gash n (He gashed his hand when carving the meat) cut, slash, lacerate, wound, nick.

gasp vb (He was gasping as he reached the top of the mountain) pant, puff, puff and pant, blow, choke, wheeze.

gate n (*the gate at the end of the driveway to the house*) gateway, barrier, entrance.

gather vb 1 (*A crowd gathered to hear the speaker*) collect, come together, assemble, congregate, meet. 2 (*gather food for the fire*) collect, get together, accumulate, heap up, store, stockpile, hoard. 3 (*gather blackberries*) pick, pluck, harvest, collect. 4 (*We gather that she is ill*) understand, believe, be led to believe, hear, learn.

gathering n (*be invited to the firm's annual gathering*) party, function, get-together, social.

gaudy adj garish, bold, over-bright, loud, glaring, flashy, showy, lurid.

gauge vb 1 (*He was asked to gauge the length of the garden*) measure, calculate, determine, estimate. 2 (*It is difficult to gauge the extent of his interest in the project*) assess, estimate, judge, guess.

gaunt adj (*He looked gaunt after his long illness*) haggard, drawn, emaciated, skinny, bony, scrawny, scraggy, skeletal, cadaverous.

gay adj 1 (*people feeling gay on holiday*) merry, jolly, light-hearted, glad, happy, cheerful, in good spirits. 2 (*girls wearing summer dresses in gay colours*) bright, brightly coloured, vivid, brilliant, flamboyant. 3 (*a gay club*) homosexual, (*inf*) queer.

gaze vb (*tourists gazing at the beauty of the sunset*) stare, eye, contemplate, look fixedly.

gear n 1 (*the mountaineers and all their gear*) equipment, apparatus, kit, implements, tackle, things, possessions, belongings, (*inf*) stuff, paraphernalia. 2 (*young people who like to be dressed in the latest gear*) clothes, clothing, dress, garments, attire, apparel, (*inf*) togs.

gem n (*an engagement ring with sparkling gems*) jewel, precious stone, stone.

general adj 1 (*The general feeling is that he is guilty*) common, widespread, broad, wide, accepted, prevalent, universal. 2 (*The general rule is that people have to have three years' experience before getting a job there*) usual, customary, common, normal, standard, ordinary, typical. 3 (*He gave them a general idea of his plans for the business*) broad, non-detailed, vague, indefinite, inexact, rough.

generous adj 1 (*he was a generous contributor to the charity*) kind, liberal, magnanimous, benevolent, lavish, open-handed. 2 (*there was a generous supply of food and drinks at the party*) abundant, liberal, plentiful, ample, copious, rich.

genius n 1 (*He is a genius at mathematics*) master-mind, prodigy, intellectual, expert, (*inf*) Einstein. 2 (*people of genius*) brilliance, brains, intellect, intelligence. 3 (*have a genius for making delicious low-cost meals*) gift, talent, flair, bent, knack, aptitude, ability, forte.

gentle adj 1 (*She remembered with love her gentle mother*) kind, kindly, lenient, tender-hearted, sweet-tempered, mild, soft, peaceful. 2 (*her gentle* *touch*) soft, light, smooth, soothing. **3** (*a gentle breeze*) mild, light, soft, moderate, temperate. **4** (*children learning to ski on gentle slopes*) gradual, slight. **5** (*The dog was a very gentle animal*) tame. placid, docile. **6** (*She tried to give him a gentle hint about his bad manners*) indirect, subtle.

genuine adj **1** (*His excuse for being absent turned out to be genuine*) real, true, authentic, sound, legitimate, valid, (*inf*) kosher, (*inf*) the real McCoy. **2** (*They doubted if his feelings were genuine*) real, sincere, honest, truthful, true, unaffected.

gesture n (*He made a gesture to indicate that he agreed*) signal, sign, motion.

get vb **1** (*She wondered where she could get a book on antiques*) obtain, acquire, get hold of, come by, procure, buy, purchase. **2** (*He went upstairs to get a book for his mother*) fetch, bring, carry, go for, retrieve. **3** (*They get a high salary*) earn, be paid, bring in, make, clear, take home. **4** (*She got flu last winter*) catch, become infected by, contract. **5** (*The children were getting tired*) become, grow. **6** (*When do you expect to get there?*) arrive at, reach. **7** (*I didn't get what he was talking about*) understand, comprehend, follow, grasp. **8** (*We eventually got her to agree*) persuade, coax, induce, talk (someone) into.

ghastly adj **1** (*There has been a ghastly motorway accident*) terrible, horrible, dreadful, frightful, shocking, grim, horrifying. **2** (*She looked ghastly when she went to hospital*) white, white as a sheet, pale, pallid, wan, colourless, drawn, ashen. **3** (*He is an absolutely ghastly man*) dreadful, nasty, unpleasant, disagreeable, hateful, loathsome, foul, contemptible.

ghost n (*She imagined that she saw a ghost in the graveyard*) apparition, spectre, phantom, spirit, wraith, (*inf*) spook.

gibberish n (*They accused him of talking gibberish*) nonsense, rubbish, twaddle, drivel, balderdash, (*inf*) poppycock, (*inf*) piffle.

gibe n (*She was upset at the gibes of her classmates*) sneer, jeer, taunt, mocking, scorn.

giddy adj **1** (*feel giddy at the top of the ladder*) dizzy, light-headed, faint, (*inf*) woozy. **2** (*giddy girls who had no interest in having a career*) silly, flighty, frivolous, irresponsible, thoughtless, unstable.

gift n **1** (*birthday gifts*) present. **2** (*He was thanked for his gift to the charity*) present, donation, contribution, offering. **3** (*The pupil has a gift for foreign languages*) talent, flair, aptitude, knack, ability, expertise, genius.

gigantic adj (*They caught sight of a gigantic mountain through the mist*) huge, enormous, colossal, immense, vast, mammoth, gargantuan.

giggle vb (*pupils giggling at the back of the class*) titter, snigger, snicker, laugh, (*inf*) tee-hee.

girl n **1** (*She lived in the village as a girl*) young woman, (*inf*) lass. **2** (*The couple have a boy and a girl*) daughter.

3 (*He went to the pictures with his girl*) girlfriend, sweetheart, fiancée.

gist n (*Some of his lecture was a bit difficult for the audience but most of them got the gist of it*) drift, substance, essence, sense.

give vb **1** (*She lifted the book and gave it to him*) hand, hand over, pass. **2** (*The old lady gave a very large sum of money to the local hospital*) donate, contribute, present, bestow, make over. **3** (*The charity worker was giving out soup and bread to homeless people*) hand out, distribute, allot, allocate, dole out. **4** (*They were given some bad advice*) provide, supply, furnish, offer. **5** (*She gives the impression of being very efficient*) show, display, demonstrate, manifest, indicate. **6** (*The chair gave and the child fell to the floor*) give way, collapse, break, come apart, fall apart.

giver n (*the giver of the money to the hospital*) donor, contributor.

glad adj **1** (*We were very glad to see our visitors*) happy, pleased, delighted, (*inf*) chuffed. **2** (*hear the glad news*) happy, delightful, joyful, welcome, cheerful.

glamorous adj **1** (*glamorous filmstars*) beautiful, lovely, attractive, elegant, smart, dazzling, alluring. **2** (*She has a glamorous career in advertising*) exciting, fascinating, dazzling, high-profile, (*inf*) glitzy.

glance vb **1** (*He only glanced at the stranger*) take a quick look at, look briefly at, glimpse, peep. **2** (*glance through the newspapers at breakfast*) skim through, leaf through, flick through, flip through, thumb through, scan. **3** (*The bullet glanced off the tree*) bounce, rebound, ricochet. **4** (*The car glanced the wall as he drove it into the garage*) graze, brush, touch, skim.

glare n **1** (*He was unaware of her angry glares*) scowl, frown, glower, black look, (*inf*) dirty look. **2** (*the glare from the headlights of oncoming cars*) flare, blaze, dazzle.

glass n (*a glass of cold water*) tumbler, beaker, goblet.

gleam n **1** (*a gleam of light*) beam, glow, ray, shimmer, sparkle. **2** (*the gleam of the polished tables*) glow, shine, gloss, sheen, lustre. **3** (*There is still a gleam of hope*) glimmer, ray, trace, suggestion, hint, flicker.

glib adj (*She was persuaded into buying the goods by a glib salesman*) smooth, plausible, smooth-talking, fluent, suave.

glide vb (*They watched the yachts gliding by*) sail, slide, slip, skim, float, drift.

glimpse n (*She thought that she glimpsed a stranger through the trees*) catch sight of, spot, make out, notice, espy.

glitter vb (*The diamonds glittered in the candlelight*) sparkle, flash, twinkle, flicker, blink, wink, shimmer, gleam, glint.

gloat vb (*She was gloating over her rival's misfortunes*) relish, delight in, take pleasure in, revel in, rejoice in, glory in, crow about.

global adj **1** (*the possibility of global war*) world, world-wide, universal, international. **2** (*The government tried to impose a global wage settlement on all public service employees) general, universal, across-the-board, comprehensive.

gloomy adj **1** (a gloomy November day) dark, overcast, cloudy, dull, dismal, dreary. **2** (an old house full of gloomy rooms) dark, sombre, dingy, dismal, dreary, depressing. **3** (He is in a gloomy mood today) in low spirits, depressed, sad, unhappy, miserable, dejected, downcast, down-hearted, glum, melancholy.

glorious adj **1** (It was a glorious day) bright, beautiful, lovely, sunny. **2** (The royal procession was a glorious sight) splendid, magnificent, wonderful, marvellous. **3** (celebrate a glorious victory) famous, celebrated, renowned, noble, distinguished.

glossy adj (the glossy surfaces of the polished tables) gleaming, shining, shiny, bright, sparkling, shimmering, polished, burnished.

glow vb (The lights glowed) gleam, shine, glimmer.

glow n **1** (the glow from the table lights) gleam, brightness, glimmer, luminosity. **2** (the glow from the fire) warmth, heat, redness. **3** (She felt a warm glow when she thought of her friends) warmth, happiness, contentment, satisfaction.

glower vb (She glowered at her rival) scowl, frown, look daggers at.

glue vb (glue the broken pieces together) stick, gum, paste, cement.

glum adj (in a glum mood) gloomy, depressed, sad, unhappy, miserable, dejected, downcast, down-hearted, melancholy.

glut n (a glut of soft fruit on the market) surplus, excess, surfeit, superfluity, overabundance, oversupply.

gnaw vb **1** (The dog was gnawing on a bone) chew, munch, crunch, bite, nibble, worry. **2** (The metal had been gnawed away by rust) erode, corrode, wear away, eat away.

go vb **1** (go carefully on the icy roads) move, proceed, walk, travel. **2** (It is time to go) go away, leave, depart, withdraw, set off, set out. **3** (The pain has gone) stop, cease, vanish, disappear, fade, be no more. **4** (The machine has stopped going) work, be in working order, function, operate, run. **5** (His beard has gone white) become, grow, turn, get, come to be. **6** (This road goes to the next town) extend, stretch, reach, lead to. **7** (Time went slowly while they were waiting for the train) pass, elapse, slip by. **8** (How did the party go?) turn out, work out, progress, fare. **9** (curtains and carpets that don't go) go together, match, blend, harmonize.

goal n (Making a lot of money was his one goal in life/He read out a statement of the goals of the organization) aim, objective, end, purpose, object, target, ambition.

gobble vb (children told not to gobble their food) wolf, bolt, gulp, guzzle, (inf) scoff.

god n (the gods of ancient Greece) deity, divinity, divine being, idol.

God n (the biblical story about God and

Moses) God Almighty, the Almighty, God the Father, Our Maker.

golden adj **1** (girls with golden hair) gold-coloured, blond, yellow, fair, flaxen. **2** (a golden opportunity) splendid, superb, excellent, favourable, fortunate, advantageous, profitable.

good adj **1** (The children were told to be good) well-behaved, well-mannered, obedient, manageable. **2** (She is such a good person who never treats anyone badly) honourable, virtuous, righteous, upright, honest, decent, moral, ethical. **3** (She is noted for her good deeds) helpful, kind, thoughtful, virtuous, admirable, creditable. **4** (He is not a very good driver) competent, capable, able, skilful, adept, proficient, expert, first-class, (inf) A1. **5** (The car does not have very good brakes) efficient, reliable, dependable, trustworthy. **6** (athletes in good condition) fine, healthy, sound, strong, robust, vigorous. **7** (The party was very good) enjoyable, agreeable, entertaining, pleasant, lovely, nice. **8** (We had good weather on holiday) fine, sunny, pleasant.

gossip n **1** (I heard that he had been in prison but it turned out to be just gossip) rumour, tittle-tattle, scandal, hearsay, (inf) mud-slinging. **2** (She was having a good gossip with her neighbour) chat, blether, tête à tête, (inf) chin-wag.

govern vb (the party that is governing the country) rule, manage, lead, be in power over, be in charge of, preside over, control.

government n (He is a member of the government) administration, parliament, congress, ministry, council, (inf) the powers that be.

grab vb **1** (He was told to grab the end of the rope) catch hold of, take hold of, grasp, clutch, grip. **2** (He grabbed the money and ran) seize, snatch.

grace n **1** (admire the grace of the dancers) gracefulness, elegance. **2** (He did not to have the grace to apologize) manners, courtesy, decency, decorum. **3** (He was at one time the king's favourite courtier but he fell from grace) favour, goodwill. **4** (pray for God's grace) forgiveness, mercy, pardon, clemency. **5** (say grace before dinner) blessing, benediction, thanksgiving.

graceful adj **1** (They admired the gymnasts' graceful movements) smooth, flowing, supple, agile, easy, elegant. **2** (He gave a graceful speech of thanks) elegant, polished, suave, refined.

gracious adj **1** (The old duchess was a very gracious lady) kind, kindly, benevolent, friendly, amiable, pleasant, cordial, courteous, polite, civil. **2** (their gracious lifestyle) elegant, tasteful, comfortable, luxurious. **3** (believe in a gracious God) merciful, compassionate, lenient, gentle.

grade n **1** (What grade has he reached in the firm?) level, stage, position, rank, standard. **2** (grades of eggs) category, class, classification.

gradual adj (There has been a gradual improvement) slow, steady, gentle, moderate, step-by-step, systematic.

grain n **1** (have grains of sand in her

shoes) particle, granule, bit, piece, fragment, speck. **2** (the farmer grows grain) cereal crop, corn. **3** (We found that there was not a grain of truth in his statement) particle, scrap, iota, trace, hint, suggestion. **4** (the grain of the wood) texture, surface.

grand adj **1** (the grand houses of the rich) great, impressive, magnificent, splendid, imposing, majestic, stately, palatial. **2** (a grand occasion) important, great, splendid, magnificent, (inf) posh.

grant vb **1** (The president granted the journalist an interview) agree to, consent to, give one's assent to, allow, permit. **2** (I grant that you may be right) acknowledge, admit, concede, allow.

grant n (get a grant to study at college) allowance, award, subsidy, bursary.

grapple vb **1** (The policeman grappled with the burglar) struggle, wrestle, fight, tussle, clash. **2** (He is still grappling with the problem of how to get there) struggle, tackle, handle, deal with, cope with, attend to.

grasp vb **1** (He grasped the handrail to prevent himself from falling) grip, clutch, grab, take hold of, hold on to, clench. **2** (He seemed unable to grasp the situation) understand, follow, comprehend, take in, get the drift of.

grateful adj **1** (They were grateful to him for his help) thankful, filled with gratitude, indebted, obliged, appreciative. **2** (We received a grateful letter for our contribution) appreciative, thankful.

grave n (the grave of the unknown soldier) burial place, tomb, sepulchre.

grave adj **1** (He was in a grave mood when he came back from the hospital) solemn, serious, earnest, sober, sombre, grim, severe, unsmiling. **2** (There were grave matters to discuss at the meeting) serious, important, significant, weighty, pressing, urgent, vital, crucial.

graveyard n (The funeral procession arrived at the graveyard) cemetery, burial ground, churchyard.

graze vb **1** (He grazed his knee) scrape, skin, scratch, wound, bruise, abrade. **2** (The car grazed the garage wall) brush, touch, glance off, shave, skim.

greasy adj **1** (dislike greasy foods) fatty, fat, oily. **2** (The car skidded on the greasy roads) slippery, slippy, slimy.

great adj **1** (a great stretch of water) large, big, extensive, vast, immense, huge. **2** (The invalid was in great pain) extreme, severe, intense, acute. **3** (They have travelled to all the great cities of the world) major, main, chief, principal, leading. **4** (the great people of the country) important, prominent, leading, top, eminent, distinguished, notable, famous. **5** (He was a great tennis player) expert, skilful, adept, proficient, masterly, (inf) ace, (inf) crack. **6** (They had a great time at the party) enjoyable, splendid, wonderful, marvellous, (inf) fabulous.

greedy adj **1** (greedy children who ate all the cakes before some people arrived) gluttonous, gannet-like, (inf) gutsy. **2** (people greedy for information) avid, eager, hungry, desirous of, craving. **3** (*a greedy miser hoarding gold*) grasping, avaricious, acquisitive, miserly, tight-fisted.

greet vb **1** (*He greeted his neighbour as he walked down the street*) say 'hello' to, address, hail. **2** (*The hostess greeted her guests*) receive, welcome, meet.

grief n (*her grief at the death of her husband*) sorrow, sadness, misery, distress, heartbreak, dejection, mourning.

grievance n (*Management refused to listen to the workers' grievances*) complaint, protest, charge, grumble, (*inf*) gripe, (*inf*) grouse.

grieve vb **1** (*The widow is still grieving*) mourn, be in mourning, lament, be sorrowful, sorrow, be sad, be distressed, fret. **2** (*She was grieved by her son's behaviour*) hurt, upset, distress, sadden, wound.

grim adj **1** (*She held on with grim determination*) determined, resolute, obstinate, unwavering, relentless. **2** (*The teacher was wearing a grim expression*) stern, severe, fierce, forbidding, formidable, sombre. **3** (*The murdered corpse was a grim sight*) horrible, dreadful, terrible, frightful, shocking, ghastly, gruesome.

grime n (*trying to clean the grime from the old house*) dirt, filth, dust, (*inf*) muck, (*inf*) grunge, (*inf*) crud.

grin vb smile, smile broadly, smile from ear to ear.

grind vb **1** (*grind coffee beans*) crush, pound, pulverize, powder, mill.

2 (*grind knives*) sharpen, whet, file, polish. **3** (*She had a habit of grinding her teeth*) gnash, grate, rasp.

grip vb **1** (*She gripped the handrail of the ship*) grasp, clutch, clasp, clench, grab, take hold of, seize. **2** (*The audience was gripped by the exciting play*) absorb, rivet, engross, fascinate, enthral, hold spellbound.

grit n **1** (*put grit on icy roads*) gravel, pebbles, dirt, sand, dust. **2** (*He did not have the grit to tell her himself that he was breaking off the engagement*) courage, bravery, pluck, nerve, backbone.

groan vb **1** (*The accident victim groaned in pain*) moan, whimper, wail, cry. **2** (*The workers were groaning about their low wages*) grumble, complain, moan, (*inf*) grouse, (*inf*) gripe.

grope vb **1** (*They had to grope their way in the pitch dark*) fumble, feel. **2** (*She groped for her keys in her handbag*) fumble, feel for, fish for, scrabble for.

ground n **1** (*The ground is very wet after all the rain*) earth, soil, dirt, land, loam. **2** (*She became ill and fell to the ground*) earth, floor, (*inf*) deck. **3** (*They would like a new sports ground*) stadium, pitch, field, arena, park.

grounds npl **1** (*They have grounds for concern about their missing son*) reason, cause, basis, foundation, justification. **2** (*The house was set in beautiful grounds*) land, surroundings, property, estate, lawns, gardens, park. **3** (*coffee grounds*) dregs, lees, deposit, sediment.

group n **1** (*We divided the books into*

groups) category, class, set, lot, batch. **2** (*She has joined a cookery group*) society, association, club, circle. **3** (*A group of people gathered to watch the fight*) band, gathering, cluster, crowd, flock, bunch.

grow *vb* **1** (*The farmers grow wheat*) cultivate, produce, raise, farm. **2** (*The plants will not grow in this very dry soil*) shoot up, spring up, sprout, germinate, thrive, flourish. **3** (*The boy is growing rapidly*) become taller, get bigger, grow larger, stretch, lengthen, expand, fill out. **4** (*The situation is growing serious*) become, come to be, get, get to be, turn, turn out to be.

grudge *vb* (*She grudges them their success*) begrudge, resent, be jealous of, envy, mind.

grumble *vb* (*The passengers were grumbling about the train being late*) complain, protest, object, moan, (*inf*) grouse, (*inf*) gripe, (*inf*) beef.

guarantee *vb* **1** (*He guaranteed that he would attend the meeting*) promise, pledge, give one's word, give an assurance, vow, swear. **2** (*This ticket guarantees you a seat at the match*) ensure, secure. **3** (*He guaranteed his daughter's car loan*) act as guarantor, provide security for, provide surety for, underwrite, vouch for.

guard *n* **1** (*prison guards*) warder, jailer, gaoler, keeper, (*inf*) screw. **2** (*the castle guards*) sentry, sentinel, custodian, watchman, look-out, garrison. **3** (*put a new guard on the machine*) safety guard, safety device, shield.

guard *vb* **1** (*the people who were guarding the jewels*) stand guard over, watch over, protect, safeguard, defend, shield, look after, preserve. **2** (*the people guarding the prisoners*) keep under guard, keep watch over, keep under surveillance, mind, supervise. **3** (*Tourists are asked to guard against thieves*) beware of, be on the alert for, be on the look-out for, keep an eye out for.

guess *vb* **1** (*We were asked to guess the weight of the cake*) estimate, predict, (*inf*) guesstimate. **2** (*We guessed that they would take the shortest route*) surmise, conjecture, suppose, assume, reckon.

guest *n* (*The hostess welcomed her guests*) visitor, company, caller.

guide *vb* **1** (*He guided them down the mountain*) lead, conduct, show, usher, direct, show the way to, escort. **2** (*They asked for someone to guide them in their choice of career*) advise, give advice to, counsel, direct.

guide *n* **1** (*They hired a guide to show them round the city sights*) escort, leader, advisor. **2** (*buy a guide to Rome*) guidebook, handbook, directory, manual. **3** (*The lights acted as a guide to shipping*) landmark, marker, signal, beacon. **4** (*The pupils were given an essay as a guide*) model, pattern, standard, example, yardstick.

guilt *n* **1** (*It was impossible to prove his guilt*) guiltiness, blame, blameworthiness, culpability, fault, responsibility. **2** (*feelings of guilt at their treatment of her*) guiltiness, guilty conscience, remorse, penitence, shame.

guilty adj 1 (*He was tried and found guilty*) to blame, blameworthy, culpable, at fault, responsible. 2 (*they felt guilty about not inviting her*) conscience-stricken, remorseful, repentant, penitent, ashamed, shamefaced, sheepish.

gulf n 1 (*They were asked to find the Gulf of Mexico on the map*) bay, cove, inlet. 2 (*They had a quarrel and there is now a gulf between the two families*) chasm, rift, split, division, divide.

gullible adj (*The old lady was not gullible enough to be taken in by his story*) naive, ingenuous, overtrustful, foolish, credulous.

gulp vb 1 (*The children were told not to gulp their food*) bolt, wolf, gobble, devour. 2 (*She tried to gulp back her tears*) fight back, choke back, suppress, stifle, smother.

gush vb 1 (*Water gushed from the burst pipe*) pour, steam, rush, spout, spurt, flood, cascade. 2 (*She embarrassed the little girls by gushing about their prettiness*) enthuse, be effusive, babble, fuss.

gust n (*a gust of wind*) puff, rush, flurry, blast, squall.

gutter n (*flood water running down the gutter*) drain, sewer, sluice, ditch.

H

habit n 1 (It was their habit to eat late in the evening) custom, practice, routine, convention. 2 (smoking and other harmful habits) addiction, dependence, compulsion, obsession.

habitat n (the animal's usual habitat) environment, background, home.

habitual n 1 (They went home by their habitual route) usual, customary, accustomed, regular, routine. 2 (He is a habitual smoker) addicted, confirmed, hardened.

hack vb (They hacked down the trees) chop down, cut down, fell, hew.

hackneyed adj (The writer is too apt to use hackneyed phrases) overused, stale, stereotyped, unoriginal, run-of-the-mill, stock.

haggard adj (She looked haggard with tiredness) drawn, gaunt, hollow-cheeked.

haggle vb (haggle over the price of a shawl in the market) bargain.

hail vb (She hailed her friend in the street) greet, salute, wave to, say 'hello' to.

hair n 1 (She has beautiful hair) locks, tresses. 2 (the animal's hair) fur, coat.

half-hearted adj (They made a half-hearted attempt at saving the business) lukewarm, unenthusiastic, apathetic, indifferent.

hall n 1 (The guests left their coats in the hall) entrance hall, hallway, lobby, vestibule. 2 (The crowds surged into the hall) concert hall, auditorium, theatre.

hallucination n (She thought that she had seen a ghost but it was only a hallucination) illusion, figment of the imagination, vision, fantasy, apparition.

halt vb 1 (The traffic has to halt at the end of the road) come to a halt, stop, come to a stop, pull up, draw up. 2 (Work halted when the heating system broke down) stop, finish, end, break off, discontinue. 3 (The strike halted progress on the export order) stop, put a stop to, put an end to, arrest, interrupt, obstruct, impede.

halve vb (halve the orange for the two children) cut in half, divide in two.

hamper vb (The bad weather hampered progress on the building) hinder, impede, obstruct, hold up.

hand n 1 (the hand of a clock) pointer, indicator, needle. 2 (They had to sack some of the hands) worker, employee, helper.

hand vb (hand the prize to the winner) hand over, give, pass, transfer, transmit.

handbook n (read the instructions in the handbook) manual, directions, instructions, guide, guidebook.

handicap vb (Her lack of qualifications was a handicap to her in her career) disadvantage, impediment, obstruction, hindrance, block.

handle vb (the handle of the tool/the handle of the pan) shaft, grip, hilt.

handle vb 1 (They were asked not to

handle the goods before they bought them) touch, finger, feel, pick up, lift. **2** (He cannot handle the more difficult pupils) cope with, deal with, manage, control.

handsome n **1** (Her husband is a very handsome man) attractive, good-looking. **2** (The antique table was a handsome piece of furniture) attractive, fine, elegant, tasteful. **3** (Her parents gave them a handsome gift as a wedding present) generous, magnanimous, lavish, sizeable.

handy adj **1** (Do you have the book handy?) to hand, available, within reach, accessible, nearby. **2** (That is a handy kitchen utensil) useful, helpful, convenient, practical. **3** (It is useful to have someone handy to do repairs around the house) good with one's hands, practical, capable.

hang vb **1** (There were mobiles hanging from the ceiling in the nursery) hang down, be suspended, dangle, swing. **2** (She hung the picture from the picture rail) suspend, put up. **3** (She employed him to hang wallpaper) put up, stick on. **4** (They used to hang murderers in Britain) send to the gallows, put a noose on, send to the gibbet, execute, (inf) string up.

hanker vb (She hankers after a cottage in the country) desire, long for, yearn for, crave, covet, fancy, (inf) have a yen for.

haphazard adj (The books were arranged in a haphazard way) random, unsystematic, unmethodical, disorganized, slapdash, careless.

happen vb **1** (The accident happened on icy roads) occur, take place, come about. **2** (We happened to meet her in the supermarket) chance. **3** (Whatever happened to them?) become of, befall. **4** (They happened upon some valuable old books) find, come upon, chance upon, stumble upon.

happening n (There has been a series of sad happenings in her life) event, incident, occurrence, experience.

happy adj **1** (The children were happy playing in the sunshine) cheerful, merry, light-hearted, joyful, carefree. **2** (They were happy to see their grandparents) pleased, glad, delighted. **3** (By a happy chance we found the lost necklace) fortunate, lucky.

harass vb (The children were bored and were harassing their mother) pester, disturb, bother, annoy, badger, torment, (inf) hassle.

harbour n (The ships were tied up in the harbour) quay, jetty, pier, wharf, dock.

harbour vb **1** (She was accused of harbouring an escaped prisoner) shelter, give protection to, give asylum to. **2** (They still harbour resentment against their mother for abandoning them) nurse, retain, maintain, cling to.

hard adj **1** (The ground was hard) solid, solidified, stony, rocky. **2** (a hard substance) solid, rigid, stiff, inflexible, tough. **3** (The work was very hard) arduous, strenuous, heavy, laborious, tiring, demanding, taxing, exacting. **4** (The problem was a hard one) difficult, complicated, complex, involved, intricate. **5** (They are hard workers) industrious, diligent, energetic, keen. **6** (*Their father was a hard man*) harsh, stern, severe, ruthless. **7** (*He was wounded by a hard blow to the head*) strong, forceful, powerful, violent. **8** (*She had a hard life*) difficult, uncomfortable, harsh, grim, unpleasant, distressing.

hardship n (*The refugees are suffering hardship*) adversity, deprivation, want, need, distress.

harm n vb **1** (*The kidnappers did not harm the child*) hurt, injure, wound, abuse, maltreat. **2** (*The incident harmed his reputation*) damage, mar, spoil.

harm n **1** (*No harm came to the child*) injury, hurt, pain, suffering, abuse. **2** (*Some harm was done to his reputation*) damage, detriment, loss.

harmful adj (*The drug is not thought to have any harmful effects*) hurtful, injurious, disadvantageous, detrimental, deleterious.

harmless adj **1** (*a weed-killer that is thought to be harmless to pets*) safe, innocuous, non-toxic. **2** (*He was just a harmless old man*) innocuous, inoffensive, blameless, innocent.

harmony n (*The different nationalities lived in harmony in the country*) peace, peacefulness, agreement, accord, concord, friendship.

harsh adj **1** (*The harsh noise grated on their ears*) grating, jarring, rasping, strident, discordant. **2** (*The colours of the walls were a bit harsh*) gaudy, garish, loud, bold. **3** (*It had been a harsh winter*) hard, severe, cold. **4** (*She had*

been brought up under harsh conditions) severe, grim, rough, austere. **5** (*He was a harsh ruler*) cruel, brutal, merciless, ruthless, tyrannical. **6** (*The school rules used to be very harsh*) severe, stern, stringent, inflexible.

haste n (*Haste is required to get the order delivered on time*) speed, swiftness, rapidity, fastness.

hasty adj **1** (*You should avoid making hasty decisions*) hurried, rushed, impetuous, impulsive. **2** (*She gave a hasty look at her notes before she spoke*) quick, rapid, swift, brief, fleeting, cursory, superficial. **3** (*She has a hasty temper*) hot, fiery, quick, irritable.

hat n (*He wore a hat to protect his head from the sun*) cap, bonnet.

hate vb **1** (*He hates his rival/She hates football*) loathe, detest, dislike, abhor, have an aversion to. **2** (*I would hate to upset her*) be reluctant, be loath, be unwilling.

hateful adj (*She thinks that he is a hateful person*) loathsome, detestable, abhorrent, revolting, offensive, horrible, nasty.

hatred n (*He is full of hatred towards his rivals*) hate, loathing, abhorrence, dislike, aversion, ill-will.

haughty adj (*She looks at everyone in a very haughty way*) arrogant, proud, disdainful, condescending, snobbish.

haul vb (*They hauled the dead body from the river*) pull, tug, drag, draw, heave.

have vb **1** (*They have two cats*) own, possess, keep. **2** (*The house has five rooms*) contain, comprise, include. **3** (*She had a lot of trouble with her* eldest son) experience, undergo, go through, endure. **4** (She will not have such behaviour in her house) permit, allow, tolerate, stand for.

hay n (They gave hay to the horses) fodder, straw.

hazard n (one of the hazards of being a soldier) danger, risk, peril, menace.

hazy adj **1** (It was rather a hazy day) misty, foggy. **2** (Her memory of the event is a bit hazy) unclear, vague, blurred, fuzzy, muddled.

head n **1** (He has a good head for business) mind, brain, intellect. **2** (He was the head of the whole organization) chief, leader, director, manager, principal, boss. **3** (She is at the head of the company) top, control, command, charge, leadership. **4** (at the head of the hill) top, summit, crest, brow, apex. **5** (She was at the head of the queue) top, front.

head vb **1** (He was heading the expedition) be in charge of, lead, be in control of, direct. **2** (They headed for town) make for, set out for, go to.

heal vb **1** (The ointment will heal the wound) cure, make better, remedy, treat. **2** (The wound began to heal) get better, mend, improve.

health n (The children are full of health) healthiness, fitness, strength, vigour.

healthy adj **1** (healthy young men playing football) well, fit, robust, strong, vigorous. **2** (They live in a healthy climate) health-giving, invigorating, bracing. **3** (They eat a healthy diet) health-giving, healthful, nutritious, nourishing, wholesome.

heap n (heaps of leaves in the garden) pile, mound, stack, mass, stockpile.

heap vb (The children heaped up the leaves in the garden) pile, stack, stockpile, accumulate.

hear vb **1** (I could not hear what she said) catch, take in. **2** (We heard that they had gone abroad) find out, discover, gather, learn.

heart n **1** (He loves her with all his heart) love, passion, affection, emotion. **2** (She thinks he has no heart) tenderness, compassion, sympathy, humanity, kindness. **3** (The discussion did not get to the heart of the matter) centre, core, nucleus, hub, crux.

hearten vb (The team were heartened by their success) cheer, cheer up, uplift, encourage, elate, buoy up.

hearty adj **1** (They were given a hearty welcome) enthusiastic, eager, warm, friendly. **2** (He has a hearty dislike of deceit) wholehearted, great, complete, thorough. **3** (They ate a hearty breakfast) substantial, solid, filling, ample.

heat n (The heat melted the ice) hotness, warmth.

heave vb **1** (He hurt his back heaving heavy weights) lift, raise, haul, pull, tug. **2** (They heaved a sigh of relief) utter, give, let out.

heaven n **1** (Bible stories about heaven) paradise. **2** (She thought that lying on a beach in the sun was heaven) bliss, ecstasy, rapture, supreme happiness.

heavy adj **1** (He had to carry heavy weights in his job) weighty, hefty, substantial, burdensome. **2** (It proved a *heavy task*) hard, difficult, arduous, laborious, demanding, exacting. **3** (*He received a heavy blow to the head*) hard, strong, powerful, forceful, violent. **4** (*He was a heavy man*) large, bulky, hefty, stout, overweight, fat, obese. **5** (*a heavy mist*) dense, thick, solid. **6** (*with heavy heart*) depressed, gloomy, downcast, despondent.

hectic *adj* (*They had a hectic day at the office*) busy, frantic, bustling, frenzied.

hedge *vb* **1** (*The trees hedged in the garden*) surround, enclose, encircle, fence in. **2** (*She simply hedged when they asked her a direct question*) prevaricate, equivocate, hum and haw, beat about the bush.

heed *n* (*They pay no heed to what anyone says*) attention, notice, note, consideration.

hefty *adj* (*He is a hefty young man*) heavy, bulky, stout, brawny, muscular, powerfully built.

height *n* **1** (*measure the height*) tallness, altitude. **2** (*He died at the height of his career*) culmination, peak, zenith.

heir/heiress *ns* (*He was heir to his father's estate*) inheritor, beneficiary, legate.

help *vb* **1** (*She did it to help her parents*) assist, aid, support, lend a hand to. **2** (*They gave her something to help the pain*) ease, soothe, relieve, alleviate, cure.

help *n* **1** (*The old lady is in need of some help*) assistance, aid, support. **2** (*There was no help for the condition*) ease, relief, alleviation, cure.

helpful *adj* **1** (*He made some helpful suggestions*) useful, of use, beneficial, advantageous, valuable. **2** (*Their neighbours are very helpful people*) supportive, obliging, cooperative, caring, charitable, friendly.

hereditary *adj* **1** (*The disease is hereditary*) inherited, genetic, congenital. **2** (*hereditary property*) inherited, bequeathed.

hero *n* **1** (*He was the hero of the battle*) victor, champion, celebrity. **2** (*The pop singer is the girl's hero*) idol, ideal. **3** (*the hero in the play*) male lead.

heroic *adj* (*It was a heroic act to try and save his friend's life*) brave, courageous, valiant, gallant, intrepid, fearless, bold.

hesitate *vb* **1** (*She hesitated before making such an important decision*) pause, delay, hang back, wait, vacillate, waver, shilly-shally. **2** (*They hesitate to interfere in their daughter's life*) be reluctant, be unwilling, be disinclined, shrink from. **3** (*He hesitates a bit when he gets nervous*) stammer, stutter, stumble, falter.

hide *vb* **1** (*The thieves hid the jewels in the garden*) conceal, secrete. **2** (*The escaped prisoners were hiding in the cellar*) take cover, lie low, conceal oneself, go to ground. **3** (*clouds hiding the sun*) obscure, block, eclipse, obstruct. **4** (*She tried to hide her motives*) conceal, keep secret, suppress, hush up.

hide *n* (*the animal's hide*) skin, pelt, coat, fur.

hideous *adj* **1** (*The new curtains are hideous*) ugly, unsightly, gruesome, grim, repulsive, revolting. **2** (*It was a hideous* crime) horrible, horrific, shocking, outrageous, dreadful, appalling.

high adj 1 (a street with high buildings) tall, lofty, towering. 2 (He has a high rank in the organization) top, leading, prominent, important, powerful. 3 (They have a high opinion of his work) favourable, good, approving, admiring. 4 (She has a very high voice) high-pitched, shrill, sharp, piercing. 5 (The ship was in difficulties in the high winds) strong, intense, forceful, violent.

highbrow adj (Her taste in books is rather highbrow) intellectual, scholarly, educated, bookish.

highlight n (The trip to the theatre was one of the highlights of our trip) high spot, feature, peak, climax.

hijack vb (The thieves hijacked the lorry) seize, take over, commandeer, expropriate.

hike vb (They hiked over the hills) tramp, march, walk, ramble, trek, trudge.

hilarious adj (The comedian's jokes were hilarious) uproarious, hysterical, side-splitting, funny, amusing, humorous, comic, entertaining.

hill n 1 (The hills behind the town) heights, highland, rising ground, mountain, peak. 2 (The cars went slowly up the steep hill) slope, rise, incline, gradient.

hinder vb (The bad weather hindered their efforts to get the bridge built) hamper, impede, hold up, obstruct, delay, curb, block.

hindrance n (Their long tight skirts were a hindrance to them when they tried to hurry) impediment, obstacle,

obstruction, handicap, drawback.

hint n 1 (She gave no hint that she was planning to leave) inkling, clue, suggestion, indication, mention. 2 (He writes a column in the newspaper giving gardening hints) tip, suggestion, pointer. 3 (There was just a hint of ginger in the sauce) trace, touch, dash, suggestion, soupçon.

hire vb 1 (They hired a boat) rent, lease, charter. 2 (The firm is hiring more staff) engage, take on, sign on, appoint, employ.

hiss vb 1 (The kettle was hissing) whistle, wheeze. 2 (The audience hissed at the comic's bad jokes) boo, jeer.

historic n (It was a historic battle/It was a historic event when the country gained its independence) famous, notable, celebrated, memorable, important, significant, outstanding.

hit vb 1 (The bully hit the little boy) strike, slap, smack, punch, bang, thump. 2 (The car was out of control and hit the lorry) bang into, crash into, knock into, smash into.

hitch n (Our travel arrangements were going well but then there was a sudden hitch) snag, hindrance, hold-up, obstacle, difficulty, stumbling-block.

hoard vb (They hoarded food in the summer in case of bad weather in the winter/misers hoarding gold) store, stock up, save, accumulate, pile up, gather, collect.

hoarse adj (She had a cold and her voice was hoarse) harsh, gruff, husky, croaking, grating, rasping, raucous.

hoax n (The bomb threat was a hoax)

practical joke, joke, prank, trick, (*inf*) spoof.

hobble vb (*Her feet were sore and she had to hobble down to the shops*) limp, shuffle, totter.

hobby n (*They work so hard that they have little time for hobbies*) pastime, diversion, amusement, sport.

hold vb 1 (*They held their luggage tightly*) hold on to, clutch, grip, grasp, cling to. 2 (*They held each other close*) embrace, cuddle, hug, clasp. 3 (*The bank holds all their private documents*) have, keep, retain, own, possess. 4 (*He holds a position of responsibility*) hold down, have, be in, occupy, fill. 5 (*One suitcase will not hold all these clothes*) contain, take, carry, include. 6 (*The bridge will not hold his weight*) bear, carry, support, sustain. 7 (*Police are holding him to help with their inquiries*) detain, hold in custody, confine, keep, imprison. 8 (*It is difficult to hold the interest of the children*) keep, retain, occupy, engage. 9 (*I wonder if the warm weather will hold*) last, continue, go on, remain, stay. 10 (*The old rule does not hold anymore*) be valid, be in force, apply. 11 (*They hold him responsible for the accident*) consider, think, regard, view. 12 (*The club holds meetings every month*) have, conduct, run.

hole n 1 (*There was a hole in the hedge/ The material was full of holes*) opening, aperture, gap, breach, break, crack, rent, slit, perforation, orifice. 2 (*There was a huge hole in the ground after the explosion*) crater, cavity, chasm, hollow, depression, dip. 3 (*the animal's hole*) lair, burrow, earth.

holiday n (*Today is a school holiday/They usually take their holidays in the late spring*) vacation, time off, day off, leave.

hollow adj 1 (*a hollow space*) hollowed out, empty, vacant. 2 (*She has hollow cheeks*) sunken, concave. 3 (*We heard a hollow sound*) dull, low, muffled, deep.

hollow vb (*They hollowed out a tree trunk to make a canoe*) scoop out, gouge out, excavate.

holy adj 1 (*The saint's grave was a holy place*) blessed, consecrated, sacred, hallowed. 2 (*They are holy people*) God-fearing, religious, pious, devout.

home n 1 (*I know where he works but not where his home is*) house, residence, abode, domicile, dwelling place. 2 (*the home of the chimpanzee*) habitat, environment, abode. 3 (*The old lady is in a home*) residential home, institution.

honest adj 1 (*honest people who do not steal other people's goods*) honourable, upright, good, decent, righteous, moral, virtuous, trustworthy, law-abiding. 2 (*She gave honest replies to the questions*) true, truthful, sincere, genuine, direct, frank, candid. 3 (*He gave an honest judgement*) fair, just, impartial, objective, unbiased.

honour n 1 (*He was a man of honour and handed in the money which he had found*) honesty, integrity, uprightness, decency, principle, righteousness, morals, virtue. 2 (*His honour was at stake*) reputation, good name. 3 (*He*

*did not care about the honour of win-
ning*) glory, prestige, fame, renown,
distinction.

honourable adj **1** (*honourable people
who tell the truth*) honest, upright,
good, decent, righteous, moral, virtuous, trustworthy, admirable. **2** (*It was
an honourable victory for the army*) famous, renowned, prestigious, notable, distinguished.

hook n **1** (*a hook used for cutting corn*)
scythe, sickle. **2** (*hooks for the children's coats*) peg. **3** (*the hook of the
dress*) fastener, catch.

hook vb **1** (*They hooked a fish*) catch,
take. **2** (*hook the trailer on to the car*)
fasten, secure.

hooked adj **1** (*She has a hooked nose*)
hook-shaped, aquiline, curved, bent.
2 (*He is hooked on cigarettes*) addicted,
dependent, obsessed by.

hooligan n (*The police are looking for
the hooligans who damaged the cars*)
ruffian, thug, vandal, (*inf*) yobbo.

hoop n (*hoops of steel*) ring, band, circle, circlet.

hop vb (*The frogs were hopping everywhere*) jump, leap, bound, spring, skip.

hope n **1** (*We were full of hope for a victory*) hopefulness, optimism, confidence, expectation, faith. **2** (*Is there
any hope of success?*) likelihood, prospect.

hope vb (*We are hoping for victory*) have
hopes of, be hopeful of, expect, anticipate, look forward to, have confidence in.

hopeful adj **1** (*We are hopeful of winning*) expectant, optimistic, confident.

2 (*The news is hopeful*) optimistic,
promising, encouraging, favourable.

horde n (*hordes of Christmas shoppers*)
crowd, swarm, mob, throng, multitude, host.

horizontal adj (*both the horizontal and
vertical supports of the frame/an invalid
lying horizontal*) flat, level, prone, supine.

horrible adj **1** (*It was a horrible sight*)
dreadful, awful, horrid, terrible,
frightful, shocking, appalling, grim,
hideous, ghastly, gruesome, disgusting, revolting. **2** (*She was a horrible old
woman*) disagreeable, nasty, unpleasant, mean, obnoxious.

horrify vb (*We were horrified at her behaviour*) shock, appall, outrage, scandalize, disgust.

horror n (*They looked at the dead body
with horror*) terror, fear, alarm, shock.

horse n (*She rode a brown horse*)
mount, hack, pony, steed, stallion,
mare, racehorse.

hospitable adj (*The people we stayed
with were most hospitable*) generous,
kind, cordial, sociable, friendly.

hostage n (*They kept the child hostage*)
captive, prisoner, pawn, surety.

hostile adj **1** (*The crowd grew hostile*)
belligerent, aggressive, antagonistic,
angry, unfriendly. **2** (*They were quite
hostile to the idea*) opposed, averse,
antagonistic.

hot adj **1** (*There was no hot food left in
the restaurant/hot food straight from the
oven*) warm, piping hot, boiling, siz-
zling, scalding. **2** (*It was a very hot day*)
boiling, sweltering, scorching, baking,

blistering, sultry, torrid. **3** (*The sauce was too hot for their taste*) spicy, peppery, pungent, sharp. **4** (*She had a hot temper*) fiery, fierce, furious, violent.

hotel n (*book in at the local hotel*) inn, tavern, guest-house, boarding house.

house n **1** (*The house they live in is very old*) abode, residence, dwelling, home. **2** (*They own a publishing house*) firm, company, business, establishment, concern.

house vb (*The flats house about thirty people*) accommodate, lodge, have room for.

hover vb **1** (*children's kites hovering in the air*) hang, flutter, fly, drift, float. **2** (*She was hovering behind them hoping to hear what they were talking about*) linger, hang about, wait.

howl vb **1** (*hear the dogs howling*) bay, yowl, yelp. **2** (*children howling for their mothers*) cry, weep, scream, bawl, wail.

huddle vb **1** (*The children huddled together to keep warm*) cuddle up, snuggle, nestle, curl up. **2** (*The sheep huddled in the corner of the field*) crowd, cluster, squeeze, pack.

hue n (*ribbons of many hues*) colour, shade, tone, tint.

hug vb (*The children hugged their mother*) embrace, cuddle, hold close.

huge adj (*a story about huge monsters*) enormous, massive, vast, immense, colossal, gigantic.

hum vb **1** (*machines humming in the factory*) drone, vibrate, throb, whirr, buzz. **2** (*She was humming a happy tune*) croon, murmur, mumble, sing.

human n (*animals and humans/fairies and humans*) human being, mortal.

humane adj (*It is humane to put animals down when they are in pain*) kind, compassionate, sympathetic, merciful, charitable.

humble adj **1** (*He has achieved much fame but is very humble*) modest, unassuming, self-effacing, unpretentious. **2** (*The humble people of the village*) common, ordinary, low-born, lowly, poor, unimportant. **3** (*She hates his humble attitude to his employer*) servile, subservient, submissive, obsequious, sycophantic.

humid adj (*a humid atmosphere*) damp, moist, muggy, sticky, steamy, clammy.

humiliate vb (*She humiliated her husband by criticizing him in public*) mortify, make ashamed, humble, disgrace, embarrass.

humility n (*He showed humility even when he won*) humbleness, modesty, self-effacement.

humorous adj (*He told a very humorous story*) funny, amusing, comic, hilarious, facetious, entertaining.

humour n **1** (*He could not see the humour in the situation*) funny side, comedy, farce, absurdity. **2** (*his own particular brand of humour*) comedy, jokes, jests, wit. **3** (*He is not in a very good humour*) mood, temper, temperament, frame of mind, disposition.

hunch n **1** (*He has a hunch on his back*) hump, swelling, bump, bulge. **2** (*The police have a hunch that he is guilty*) feeling, intuition, sixth sense, inkling, suspicion.

hunger n **1** (*The children died of hunger*) starvation, famine. **2** (*He has a hunger for knowledge*) desire, longing, yearning, craving, thirst.

hungry adj **1** (*hungry children with nothing to eat*) starving, famished, ravenous. **2** (*They are hungry for knowledge*) eager, anxious, avid, craving, longing for.

hunk n (*a hunk of cheese*) lump, block, chunk, wedge, mass.

hunt vb **1** (*They are hunting stags*) chase, pursue, stalk, track. **2** (*She was hunting for her glasses*) look for, search for, seek, rummage for, scrabble for.

hurdle n **1** (*The runner failed to clear the first hurdle*) fence, rail, railing, barrier. **2** (*There were several hurdles in the way of progress*) obstacle, obstruction, impediment, barrier, stumbling block.

hurl vb (*The crowd hurled stones at the police*) throw, fling, cast, pitch, toss.

hurricane n (*lives lost in the hurricane*) tornado, cyclone, typhoon, storm, tempest.

hurry vb (*You must hurry if you want to catch the train*) hurry up, hasten, make haste, speed up, run, dash, (*inf*) get a move on.

hurt vb **1** (*His leg was hurt in the accident*) injure, wound, bruise, maim. **2** (*Her leg hurts*) be sore, be painful, ache, throb. **3** (*She was hurt by his unkind remarks*) upset, wound, grieve, sadden, offend.

hurtle vb (*The runner hurtled towards the finishing post*) race, dash, sprint, rush.

hush vb **1** (*Try to hush the children*) quieten, silence, (*inf*) shut up. **2** (*The crowd suddenly hushed*) fall silent, quieten down, (*inf*) shut up. **3** (*They tried to hush up the scandal but the press found out*) conceal, suppress, cover up.

hut n (*a garden hut*) shed, lean-to, shack, cabin.

hygienic adj (*Hospitals must be hygienic*) sanitary, clean, sterile, germ-free.

hymn n (*sing hymns in church*) psalm, religious song.

hypnotic adj (*hypnotic effects*) mesmerizing, mesmeric.

hypocritical adj (*It is hypocritical of him to go to church as he is a very evil person*) insincere, false, deceitful, dishonest, dissembling.

hypothetical adj (*Let us take a hypothetical case*) supposed, assumed, theoretical, imagined.

hysterical adj **1** (*She became hysterical at the news of his death*) frantic, frenzied, in a frenzy, out of control, berserk, beside oneself, distracted, overwrought, demented, crazed. **2** (*She told us a hysterical story about her travels*) hilarious, uproarious, side-splitting, comical, funny, amusing.

I

idea n **1** (*The idea of death terrifies him*) concept, notion. **2** (*We asked for their ideas on the subject*) thought, view, opinion, feeling. **3** (*I had an idea that he was dead*) thought, impression, belief, suspicion. **4** (*Their idea is to sail round the world*) plan, aim, intention, objective. **5** (*We need some idea of the cost*) estimation, approximation, guess.

ideal adj (*The conditions were ideal*) perfect, faultless, excellent.

identify vb **1** (*She was able to identify her attacker*) recognize, name, distinguish, pinpoint. **2** (*They were able to identify the cause of the problem*) establish, find out, ascertain, diagnose. **3** (*She identifies her mother with security*) associate, connect. **4** (*She identifies with homeless people*) empathize, relate.

identical adj **1** (*The twins wear identical clothes*) like, similar, matching. **2** (*That is the identical dress that her sister wore last week*) same.

idiot n (*He was an idiot to behave in that way*) fool, dolt, ass, dunce.

idiotic adj (*It was an idiotic thing to do*) stupid, foolish, senseless.

idle adj **1** (*He was an idle fellow who did not want to work*) lazy, indolent, slothful. **2** (*The workers are idle through no fault of their own*) unemployed, jobless.

idol n **1** (*The heathens were worshipping idols*) god, icon, image, effigy. **2** (*He is a pop idol to the teenagers*) hero/heroine, favourite, darling.

idolize vb (*The children idolize their grandfather*) adore, love, worship.

ignite vb **1** (*ignite the fire*) set alight, set fire to, kindle. **2** (*The dry material ignited easily*) catch fire, burn, burst into flames.

ignorant adj **1** (*They had never gone to school and were quite ignorant*) uneducated, illiterate. **2** (*They were ignorant of the legal facts*) unaware, unconscious, uninformed.

ignore vb **1** (*The child was told to ignore their insulting remarks*) disregard, take no notice of. **2** (*The pupils were told to ignore the last question in the exam paper*) disregard, omit, (*inf*) skip.

ill adj **1** (*She has been ill and off work for some time*) unwell, sick, poorly, indisposed, unhealthy, (*inf*) under the weather. **2** (*The medicine has no ill effects*) harmful, detrimental. **3** (*There is ill feeling between the two families*) hostile, antagonistic, unfriendly.

illegal adj (*They were imprisoned for their illegal deeds*) unlawful, illicit, criminal.

illegible adj (*Her handwriting was illegible*) unreadable, indecipherable, unintelligible.

illiterate adj (*people who never went to school and so are illiterate*) uneducated, unschooled, ignorant.

illness n (*She is suffering from a mysterious illness*) complaint, ailment, disease, disorder, affliction, (*inf*) bug.

illogical vb (*His behaviour was illogical*) irrational, unreasonable, unsound.

illusion n 1 (*The magician did not really do that—it was just an illusion*) deception. 2 (*The supposed ghost was just an illusion*) hallucination, dream, fantasy 3 (*She was under the illusion the he was unmarried*) delusion, misapprehension, misconception.

illustrate vb 1 (*She illustrated the children's book*) decorate, ornament. 2 (*He illustrated his theory with examples*) demonstrate, exemplify.

illustration n 1 (*the coloured illustrations in the book*) picture, drawing, sketch, diagram. 2 (*the illustrations which he used to prove his point*) example, case, instance.

image adj 1 (*There were images of famous saints in the churchyard*) likeness, effigy, statue, figure, representation. 2 (*You can see your image in the mirror*) reflection, likeness.

imaginary adj (*The child has an imaginary friend*) fictitious, invented, made up, legendary, mythical, unreal, fanciful.

imagination n 1 (*The poem shows imagination*) creativity, vision, inspiration, fancifulness .2 (*She thought she saw her father but it was only her imagination*) illusion, fancy, hallucination, dream, figment of the imagination.

imagine vb 1 (*Can you imagine what life will be like in fifty years?*) picture, visualize, envisage, conceive. 2 (*He imag-* ined that the meeting would last an hour) presume, assume, suppose, think, believe.

imitate vb 1 (*She imitated the style used by the writer*) copy, emulate, follow. 2 (*The cruel children imitated the boy with the limp*) mimic, impersonate, mock, parody.

imitation n (*The portrait is not genuine but an imitation*) copy, reproduction, counterfeit, forgery, fake.

immature adj 1 (*It was immature of the young man to behave like that*) childish, juvenile, infantile. 2 (*The fruit was picked when it was immature*) unripe, green.

immediate adj 1 (*There was an immediate reaction to his speech*) instant, instantaneous, prompt, swift, sudden. 2 (*He turned to his immediate neighbour in the hall*) next, near, nearest, adjacent. 3 (*We have no immediate plans to go*) existing, current.

immediately adv 1 (*He plans to leave immediately*) right away, straight away, at once, without delay. 2 (*They were sitting immediately behind us*) directly, right.

immense adj 1 (*an immense figure of a man*) huge, enormous, vast, colossal, gigantic, giant. 2 (*There has been an immense improvement*) huge, immense, vast.

immerse vb 1 (*She immersed the dress in the soapy water*) submerge, plunge, dip, lower. 2 (*They immersed themselves in their work before the exam*) absorb, engross, occupy, preoccupy.

immoral adj (*Everyone disapproved of*

his immoral acts) bad, wrong, evil, wicked, sinful, unethical.

immortal adj (*Human beings are not immortal*) everlasting, endless, eternal, undying.

impact n 1 (*Both cars were damaged in the impact*) collision, crash, bump, smash, clash. 2 (*His speech had a powerful impact on the crowd*) effect, influence, impression. 3 (*His nose took the full impact of the blow*) force, shock, impetus, brunt.

impartial adj (*We had to make sure that the judge was impartial*) unbiased, unprejudiced, disinterested, objective, detached.

impatient adj 1 (*The children were impatient to get out to play*) eager, anxious, keen, avid. 2 (*The show was late starting and the audience was growing impatient*) restless, restive, agitated, edgy, fidgety.

impeccable adj (*His performance was impeccable*) faultless, flawless, perfect, exemplary.

impede vb (*The weather impeded their progress*) hinder, obstruct, hamper, block, check, delay, deter.

impediment n 1 (*The weather was an impediment to their plans*) hindrance, obstruction, obstacle, handicap, block, check, bar, barrier. 2 (*She has an impediment and has to speak slowly*) stammer, stutter.

imperative adj (*It is imperative that we leave now*) essential, necessary, urgent, vital, important, crucial.

imperceptible adj (*The difference between the two vases was imperceptible*) undetectable, unnoticeable, slight, small, minute.

impersonal adj (*The nurse had a very impersonal manner*) cold, cool, aloof, distant, stiff, formal, detached.

impersonate vb (*The pupil began to impersonate the teacher*) imitate, copy, mimic, mock, ape.

impertinent adj (*It was impertinent to speak to the old lady like that*) insolent, impudent, cheeky, rude, impolite, ill-mannered.

imperturbable adj (*She is imperturbable even in an emergency*) calm, cool, composed, unruffled.

impetuous adj (*He is given to impetuous actions*) hasty, impulsive, spontaneous, rash, foolhardy.

implement n (*The garden implements have been stolen/buy new kitchen implements*) tool, utensil, appliance, instrument, device, gadget.

implore vb (*She implored him to help*) beg, plead with, appeal to, entreat, beseech.

imply vb (*He implied that she was not telling the truth*) insinuate, hint, suggest, indicate.

important adj 1 (*It is important to arrive on time*) necessary, essential, vital, crucial, urgent. 2 (*The two countries are having important talks*) significant, critical, crucial, serious, momentous, of great import. 3 (*She noted the important points in the lecture*) chief, main, principal, salient, significant. 4 (*All the important people in the town were invited to the reception*) prominent, notable, foremost, leading, distinguished, eminent, influential.

impose vb 1 (*The judge imposed a heavy fine on him*) exact, charge, levy, inflict, enforce. 2 (*She tries to impose her views on all her colleagues*) force, foist, inflict, thrust. 3 (*They felt she was imposing on their mother's generosity*) take advantage, exploit, abuse.

impossible adj 1 (*It was obviously an impossible task*) unimaginable, inconceivable, impracticable, impractical, hopeless. 2 (*Life became impossible for them in the damp conditions*) unbearable, intolerable.

impostor, imposter ns (*They thought that he was a doctor but he was an impostor*) fake, fraud, charlatan, swindler, cheat, (*inf*) con man.

impotent adj (*The small army was impotent in the face of the enemy*) powerless, helpless, weak, feeble.

impoverished adj (*impoverished people with no homes*) poor, poverty-stricken, penniless, impecunious, destitute, indigent.

impracticable adj (*The task was totally impracticable*) impossible, out of the question.

impractical adj 1 (*The proposed solution was totally impractical*) impossible, non-viable, hopeless, ineffective, useless. 2 (*They are impractical people*) unrealistic, idealistic.

impress vb 1 (*The crowd was impressed by his speech*) make an impression on, affect, influence, sway, move, stir. 2 (*You must impress on them the need for silence*) stress, emphasize, inculcate.

impression n 1 (*His speech made a powerful impression on his audience*) effect, influence, impact. 2 (*We had the impression that he disliked us*) feeling, idea, notion, sensation, suspicion, hunch. 3 (*He does impressions of the prime minister*) impersonation, imitation, mimicry, parody, (*inf*) send-up.

impressive adj 1 (*It was an impressive building*) imposing, grand, splendid, magnificent. 2 (*He made an impressive speech*) moving, stirring, powerful.

imprison vb (*The criminals were imprisoned*) put in prison, jail, lock up, take into custody, incarcerate, confine, detain.

impromptu adj (*He made an impromptu speech at the wedding reception*) unrehearsed, unprepared, spontaneous, improvised, extempore, off the cuff, ad lib.

improve vb 1 (*They tried to improve conditions for the poor*) better, make better. 2 (*The standard of her work has improved*) get better, advance, progress, move on.

improvise vb 1 (*They had to improvise a shelter when they lost their tent*) put together, devise, rig up, concoct. 2 (*He has not prepared a speech and so he will have to improvise*) make do, extemporise, ad lib.

impudent adj (*The girl was impudent enough to swear at the teacher*) impertinent, insolent, cheeky, bold, forward, brazen, presumptuous.

impulsive adj (*He was given to impulsive decisions*) impetuous, impromptu, spontaneous, hasty, rash, thoughtless.

in adj 1 (*Short skirts are in*) fashionable, stylish, (*inf*) trendy. 2 (*She is in with the boss*) in favour, favoured.

inadequate adj 1 (*Their supplies of fuel are inadequate*) insufficient, deficient, scanty, meagre. 2 (*She feels that she is an inadequate mother*) incompetent, inefficient, inept.

inadvertent adj (*There were a few inadvertent omissions from the list of guests*) accidental, unintentional.

inane adj (*It was an inane thing to do*) foolish, stupid, idiotic, absurd, ridiculous.

inanimate adj (*inanimate objects*) lifeless, without life.

inapt adj (*her inapt remarks*) inappropriate, unsuitable, inapposite.

inaugurate vb (*They are inaugurating a new club*) launch, initiate, begin, commence, found, establish.

inborn adj (*his inborn pessimism*) inherent, innate, inbred, inherited.

incense vb (*He was incensed at the children's behaviour*) enrage, annoy, anger, infuriate, exasperate.

incentive n (*They gave the workers more money as an incentive*) inducement, incitement, encouragement, motivation, spur.

inception n (*She has been a member of the club since its inception*) start, beginning, launch, opening.

incessant adj (*They were tired of their neighbour's incessant noise*) never-ending, unending, endless, unceasing, continuous, continual, unremitting.

incident n (*There were various sad incidents in her life*) event, happening, occurrence, episode, occasion.

incite vb 1 (*The speaker tried to incite the crowd to rebellion*) egg on, urge, goad, spur on, excite, rouse, stimulate. 2 (*They incited a rebellion*) provoke, instigate, stir up.

inclination n 1 (*He has an inclination to put on weight*) tendency, propensity, predisposition, habit. 2 (*flat ground with a slight inclination*) slope, gradient, rise. 3 (*with a slight inclination of his head*) bow, bending, nod.

incline vb 1 (*The land inclines towards the shore*) slope, slant, tilt, bend. 2 (*He inclines towards the left on politics*) tend, lean, veer.

incline, be inclined to vbs (*They are inclined to tell lies*) be apt to, have a tendency to, have a habit of, be liable to, be likely to.

include vb 1 (*The menu includes all their favourite dishes*) contain, take in, incorporate, comprise. 2 (*Remember to include their names on the list*) put in, add, insert, enter.

inclusive adj 1 (*The hotel quoted an inclusive price*) all-in. 2 (*the total bill inclusive of service charge*) including.

incognito adj/adv (*He travelled incognito*) in disguise, disguised.

incoherent adj (*She was badly shaken and gave a very incoherent account of the accident*) confused, muddled, jumbled, disjointed, garbled.

income n (*his income after tax*) salary, wages, pay, earnings, profits.

incompatible adj 1 (*Their two statements are incompatible*) conflicting, contradictory, inconsistent. 2 (*It was* *obvious before they married that they were incompatible)* unsuited, mismatched, ill-assorted.

incongruous adj *(The modern steel furniture looked incongruous with the old style of decoration)* out of keeping, unsuitable, unsuited, inappropriate, discordant, strange, odd.

increase vb **1** *(Demand for the product has increased)* grow, go up, rise, multiply, mushroom, escalate. **2** *(They have increased the number of college places)* add to, augment, enlarge, extend, expand, raise, *(inf)* step up.

incredible adj **1** *(His story seemed quite incredible)* unbelievable, far-fetched, unconvincing, unlikely. **2** *(The gymnast's performance was quite incredible)* extraordinary, marvellous, amazing.

incriminate vb *(He was found guilty of the crime and tried to incriminate his friend)* accuse, charge, blame, implicate, involve.

indecent adj *(The comic told indecent jokes)* vulgar, crude, coarse, rude, bawdy, smutty, dirty, blue.

indefinite adj **1** *(He gave us rather an indefinite answer)* vague, unclear, confused, ambiguous. **2** *(She was rather indefinite about whether to go or not)* undecided, indecisive, uncertain, irresolute. **3** *(The date for the meeting is indefinite as yet)* undecided, unsettled, uncertain. **4** *(an indefinite shape in the mist)* indistinct, blurred, vague, dim.

indent vb *(They have indented for more textbooks)* order, request, ask for.

independent adj **1** *(It is an independent state)* self-governing, autonomous, free. **2** *(The children are grown up and independent)* self-supporting, self-sufficient. **3** *(The firms are independent of each other)* unattached, unconnected, unrelated, separate.

indicate vb **1** *(His ragged clothes indicated his poverty)* show, demonstrate, point to, be a sign of, suggest, mean. **2** *(He indicated which direction he was turning)* show, point out, make known.

indication n **1** *(Her paleness is an indication of her illness)* sign, symptom, mark, signal. **2** *(He frowned as an indication of his anger)* demonstration, display, show.

indifferent adj **1** *(He seemed indifferent about the result of his trial)* apathetic, unconcerned, detached, unemotional. **2** *(He gave an indifferent performance)* mediocre, run-of-the-mill, commonplace, uninspired, undistinguished.

indignant adj *(They were indignant at being ignored)* angry, annoyed, irate, furious.

indispensable adj *(employees who were considered indispensable)* essential, necessary, crucial, imperative.

indisposed adj ill, unwell, poorly, *(inf)* under the weather.

indistinct adj **1** *(indistinct noises)* muffled, low. **2** *(The picture was rather indistinct)* blurred, fuzzy, hazy, misty.

individual adj **1** *(the individual petals of the flower)* single, separate, particular, specific. **2** *(The writer has a very individual style)* characteristic, distinctive, peculiar, original, idiosyncratic.

indolent vb (He was too indolent to look for a job) lazy, idle, slothful.

induce vb 1 (The salesman tried to induce them to buy a new car) persuade, prevail upon, get, press. 2 (The drug induced a skin reaction) produce, cause, give rise to, bring about.

indulgent adj (The children's grandparents are too indulgent) permissive, easygoing, doting.

industrial adj (an industrial area of the country) manufacturing.

industrious adj (industrious pupils) hard-working, diligent, conscientious, assiduous.

inert adj (people lying inert after the previous night's party) inactive, motionless, still.

inevitable adj (A guilty verdict seemed inevitable) unavoidable, unpreventable, inescapable, irrevocable.

infallible adj (She claims that it is an infallible cure) unfailing, foolproof, reliable, sure, certain.

infamous adj 1 (He is an infamous criminal) notorious, villainous, wicked. 2 (It was an infamous crime) notorious, scandalous, disgraceful, shocking, outrageous.

infant n (She was very ill as an infant) baby, young child.

infatuation n (his infatuation with one of his female colleagues) love, fancy, obsession, fixation, (inf) crush.

infect vb 1 (waste material that infected the town's water supply) contaminate, pollute, taint. 2 (The wound was infected) poison, make septic. 3 (He infected others with his enthusiasm) influence, affect.

infectious adj (an infectious disease), communicable, transmittable, catching.

infer vb (From the evidence the jury inferred that he was guilty) deduce, reason, conclude, gather.

inferior adj 1 (She occupies an inferior position in the firm) subordinate, lower, lesser, junior, minor, low, humble. 2 (The firm produces inferior goods) imperfect, faulty, defective, substandard, shoddy. 3 (They do not employ inferior workers) incompetent, second-rate.

infest vb (houses infested with rats) overrun, pervade, invade, plague.

infidelity n 1 (accused of infidelity to their king) disloyalty, unfaithfulness, treachery, perfidy. 2 (his wife's infidelity) unfaithfulness, adultery.

infinite adj 1 (Space is infinite) boundless, unbounded, limitless, unlimited, endless. 2 (She has infinite patience) unlimited, endless, unending, inexhaustible.

infirm adj (The old people are becoming infirm) frail, failing, feeble, weak.

inflamed adj 1 (a badly inflamed arm) red, reddened, sore, infected, festering, septic. 2 (inflamed passions) aroused, roused, excited.

inflammable adj (nightdresses made of inflammable material) flammable, combustible.

inflammation n (He was given some ointment to cure the inflammation) redness, sore, swelling.

inflate vb 1 (He had to stop and inflate

his bicycle tyres) blow up, pump up. **2** (*a decision that might inflate prices*) increase, raise, boost, escalate.

inflexible adj **1** (*inflexible substances*) rigid, stiff, hard. **2** (*an inflexible work schedule*) fixed, rigid, unalterable. **3** (*their inflexible attitudes*) stubborn, obstinate, adamant, firm, unaccommodating, unbending.

inflict vb (*inflict distress on his parents*) administer, deal out, mete out, impose, give.

influence vb **1** (*Her state of health influenced her decision*) affect, have an effect on, have an impact on, sway, control, determine. **2** (*They would like to influence the jury*) sway, bias, prejudice, bribe.

influence n **1** (*She had a great deal of influence on her colleagues*) effect, impact, sway, control, power. **2** (*He was under the influence of alcohol*) effect.

influential adj (*He is an influential figure in the government*) powerful, important, leading.

inform vb **1** (*We had to inform her that he was dead*) tell, advise, notify, communicate to, impart to. **2** (*He informed on his friends to the police*) betray, (*inf*) grass on, (*inf*) blow the whistle on.

informal adj **1** (*wear informal clothes at weekends*) casual, comfortable. **2** (*an informal party*) casual, unceremonious, unofficial, simple, relaxed.

information n **1** (*collect information on all of the countries of the world*) data, facts, statistics. **2** (*When will we receive information about the next meeting?*)

news, word, communication, advice, instruction.

infringe vb **1** (*infringe the rules*) break, disobey, violate, contravene, disregard. **2** (*He infringed on his neighbour's land*) encroach, intrude, trespass.

infuriate vb (*They were infuriated at being overcharged in the restaurant*) enrage, incense, annoy, anger, exasperate.

ingenious adj (*They thought up an ingenious plan*) clever, shrewd, cunning, inventive, resourceful.

ingenuous adj (*She was too ingenuous to try to deceive them*) open, sincere, honest, frank, artless, simple, guileless.

inhabit vb (*They inhabit a remote area of the country*) live in, dwell in, reside in, occupy.

inherent adj **1** (*There is an inherent tendency to heart disease in the family*) inborn, inbred, hereditary, congenital. **2** (*It was an inherent part of the design of the building*) intrinsic, innate, essential, basic, fundamental.

inherit vb **1** (*She inherited a great deal of money from her grandmother*) be left, be bequeathed. **2** (*He inherited the title on his father's death*) succeed to, accede to, assume.

inheritance n (*He has already spent his inheritance from his father*) legacy, bequest, estate.

inhibited adj (*She feels inhibited in the presence of her parents*) shy, reticent, reserved, self-conscious, subdued.

initial adj (*He was involved right from the initial stages of the company*) first, beginning, commencing, opening, early, introductory.

initiate vb 1 (*They asked him to initiate the proceedings*) begin, start off, commence, open, institute, launch. 2 (*The boys initiated a new member into their gang*) admit, introduce, induct, install, enrol.

initiative n 1 (*He took the initiative and made the opening speech*) first move, first step, lead, start, beginning. 2 (*There will be promotion prospects for workers with initiative*) enterprise, resourcefulness, inventiveness, drive.

injection n (*He was given an injection against tetanus*) inoculation, vaccination, shot, (*inf*) jab.

injure vb 1 (*He injured his leg in the accident*) hurt, damage, wound. 2 (*His behaviour has injured his reputation*) damage, ruin, spoil, mar.

inkling n (*The workers had no inkling that the firm was going to shut down*) hint, clue, indication, suspicion.

inlet n (*They tied the boat up in a sandy inlet*) cove, bay.

inn n (*They had a meal at the local inn*) pub, tavern.

inner adj (*the inner layer*) inside, interior.

innocent adj 1 (*The accused was found innocent*) not guilty, guiltless, blameless. 2 (*innocent young girls*) simple, naive, artless, trusting, inexperienced, gullible, virtuous, pure. 3 (*It was just innocent fun*) harmless, safe, inoffensive.

innocuous adj (*The substance was found to be innocuous*) harmless, safe,

non-toxic, non-poisonous.

innovation n (*The new owner introduced some innovations*) new measure, change, alteration.

innuendo n (*She made an innuendo about his lack of honesty*) insinuation, suggestion, hint.

innumerable adj (*He has been late on innumerable occasions*) numerous, countless, many.

inordinate n (*They caused an inordinate amount of trouble*) excessive, undue, unreasonable, uncalled-for.

inquire vb 1 (*The police are inquiring into the cause of the fire*) make inquiries, investigate, look into, probe, query. 2 (*We inquired about her mother's health*) ask, make inquiries.

inquiry n 1 (*The police are conducting a murder inquiry*) investigation, inquest, interrogation, examination. 2 (*She is employed to answer customers' inquiries*) query, question.

inquisitive adj (*She is inquisitive about other people's business*) curious, prying, snooping, (*inf*) nosy.

insane adj 1 (*The murderer has been declared insane*) mad, deranged, demented, unhinged, out of one's mind. 2 (*It was insane to take such risks*) mad, crazy, idiotic, foolish, stupid, absurd.

insanitary adj (*The toilet facilities are insanitary*) dirty, filthy, unhygienic, unhealthy, contaminated, polluted.

insatiable adj (*He has an insatiable appetite/insatiable for knowledge*) hungry, greedy, voracious.

inscription n 1 (*the inscription on the gravestone*) writing, engraving, epitaph. **2** (*the inscription in the front of the book*) dedication, message.

insert vb **1** (*She inserted the letter in the envelope*) put in, push in, thrust in, slip in. **2** (*He decided to insert a few more lines into his report*) put in, introduce, enter, interpolate.

inside adv (*She decided to stay inside in the cold weather*) indoors.

insignificant adj (*concentrate on the main points in the report and ignore the insignificant details*) unimportant, minor, trivial, trifling, negligible.

insinuate vb **1** (*She insinuated that she did not trust him*) hint, suggest, imply, indicate. **2** (*She succeeded in insinuating herself into the old lady's affections*) worm one's way, work one's way, ingratiate oneself.

insipid adj (*She is a very insipid person*) colourless, dull, drab, vapid, uninteresting.

insist vb **1** (*At first they refused to go but their parents insisted*) stand firm, be firm, stand one's ground, be determined, not to take no for an answer. **2** (*She insisted that they go immediately*) demand, command, urge. **3** (*He insists that he is innocent*) maintain, assert, declare, swear.

insolent adj (*The pupil was accused of being insolent*) impertinent, impudent, cheeky, rude.

inspect vb (*The police inspected the stolen car*) examine, check, scrutinize, study.

inspiration n **1** (*His wife acts as an inspiration to the artist*) stimulus, stimulation, encouragement, motivation,

spur. **2** (*His poetry lacks inspiration*) creativity, originality, inventiveness, imagination. **3** (*They were completely puzzled but then he had a sudden inspiration*) bright idea.

install vb **1** (*They have installed a new bathroom*) put in, insert, fix, establish. **2** (*They installed themselves in comfortable chairs*) settle.

instalment n **1** (*They are paying for the goods by instalment*) part payment, hire purchase, HP. **2** (*They published the novel in instalments*) part, portion, section.

instance n (*That was just one instance of his impertinence*) case, example, illustration.

instant adj (*She demanded an instant reply*) instantaneous, immediate, on-the-spot, rapid, prompt.

instant n (*He was gone in an instant*) moment, minute, second, trice, (*inf*) jiffy.

instinct n **1** (*Some birds migrate by instinct*) intuition, sixth sense. **2** (*She has an instinct for doing the right thing*) ability, knack, aptitude, gift, talent.

institution n **1** (*He has been living in an institution since he was very young*) home, hospital, detention centre. **2** (*It was one of the village's institutions*) custom, tradition, practice.

instruct vb **1** (*He instructs the pupils in gymnastics*) teach, train, coach, educate. **2** (*She instructed the bank to close her account*) tell, order, command, direct, bid.

instructor n (*a sports instructor*) teacher, coach, trainer, tutor.

instrument n 1 (*instruments used by dentists*) implement, tool, appliance, apparatus, utensil, gadget. 2 (*She plays several instruments*) musical instrument.

insult n (*His insults were quite unjustified*) slur, abuse, affront, slight, gibe.

insult vb (*She was deeply insulted by his accusations*) affront, give offence to, abuse, slight, hurt.

intact adj (*They were pleased to find all their furniture intact after they moved house*) whole, in one piece, sound, unbroken, complete, undamaged.

integrate vb (*They integrated the various parts into a whole*) combine, unite, join, amalgamate, merge, fuse.

integrity n (*No person of integrity would have got involved in the scheme*) honour, honesty, uprightness, righteousness. decency.

intellect n (*people of limited intellect*) brain, mind, intelligence.

intellectual adj (*They are an intellectual family*) academic. well-educated, well-read, scholarly, bookish, clever.

intelligent adj (*the more intelligent pupils*) clever, bright, sharp, quick, smart, (*inf*) brainy.

intend vb (*She intends to leave soon*) aim, mean, plan.

intense adj 1 (*She could not stand the intense heat*) severe, acute, fierce, extreme, strong, powerful. 2 (*She has an intense desire to travel*) deep, profound, passionate, fervent, burning, eager, ardent.

intent adj 1 (*They were intent on getting there on time*) set on, bent on, determined to. 2 (*The child wore an intent expression as he worked*) absorbed, engrossed, attentive, concentrating.

intention n (*It is his intention to go to university*) aim, purpose, intent, goal, objective, design.

intentional adj (*It was not an accident that he hurt her—it was intentional*) deliberate, meant, purposeful, planned, calculated.

interest n 1 (*He showed no interest in the project*) concern, heed, regard, notice, attention, curiosity. 2 (*Stamp-collecting is one of his interests*) hobby, pastime, diversion. 3 (*This is a matter of interest to us all*) concern, importance, import, consequence.

interested adj 1 (*The children were not interested*) attentive, absorbed, curious. 2 (*the interested parties*) concerned, involved. 3 (*No interested person is allowed to be a judge in the competition*) involved, biased, prejudiced, partial, partisan.

interesting adj (*It was an interesting book*) absorbing, engrossing, fascinating, riveting, gripping, amusing, entertaining.

interfere vb 1 (*He is always interfering in other people's business*) meddle with, pry into, intrude into, (*inf*) poke one's nose into, (*inf*) stick one's oar into. 2 (*He lets his sports training interfere with his school work*) hinder, impede, hamper, obstruct, get in the way of.

interior n 1 (*They are painting the interior of the building*) inside. 2 (*They travelled to the interior of the country*) centre, middle, heart.

interlude n (*during the interlude at the theatre*) interval, intermission, break, lull, pause.

intermediate adj (*The team is in an intermediate position in the league*) middle, midway, halfway.

interminable adj 1 (*The journey seemed interminable*) endless, never-ending, everlasting 2 (*She was tired of his interminable questions*) endless, everlasting, ceaseless, incessant, continuous, continual, constant, persistent.

intermittent adj (*Their telephone has an intermittent fault*) occasional, irregular, sporadic, fitful, recurrent.

internal adj 1 (*They knocked down an internal wall*) interior, inside, inner, inward. 2 (*the country's internal affairs*) home, domestic,.

international adj (*international issues*) global, universal, worldwide.

interpret vb 1 (*The pupils need someone to interpret the difficult text*) explain, clarify, expound, elucidate. 2 (*They interpreted her silence as agreement*) take, construe, read, understand. 3 (*She is employed to interpret for foreign businessmen*) translate.

interrogate vb (*The police are interrogating the accused*) question, ask questions, examine, cross-examine, quiz, give the third degree to, (*inf*) grill.

interrupt vb 1 (*People in the audience kept interrupting the politician's speech*) cut in on, break in on, butt in on, intrude on, disturb. 2 (*They interrupted the meeting to make an important announcement*) discontinue, break off,

suspend, leave off, delay.

intersection n (*There was a bad road accident at the intersection*) junction, interchange, crossroads, roundabout.

interval n 1 (*There was quite an interval between the two meetings*) gap, wait, space, period. 2 (*during the interval in the theatre*) intermission, interlude, break, pause, lull.

intervene n 1 (*The quarrel between the children was so bad that their parents had to intervene*) intercede, mediate, step in, interfere. 2 (*A period of several years intervened before they met again*) occur, pass, happen, take place, ensue.

interview n 1 (*The candidates for the job had to attend an interview*) meeting, discussion, dialogue, evaluation. 2 (*The president was giving an interview to the press*) audience, press conference, dialogue, question and answer session.

intimate adj 1 (*They were intimate friends*) close, dear, near, loving, friendly, amicable. 2 (*the intimate details of her life as noted in her diary*) personal, private, confidential, secret.

intimidate vb (*They felt intimidated by the three huge men*) frighten, scare, alarm, terrify, terrorize, threaten.

intolerable adj (*an intolerable level of pain*) unbearable, unendurable, insufferable, insupportable.

intolerant adj (*intolerant members of the community who objected to the activities of young people*) bigoted, illiberal, narrow-minded, biased, prejudiced, provincial, parochial.

intoxicated adj (They were so intoxicated that they could not walk straight) drunk, tipsy, under the influence, (inf) one over the eight, (inf) tight.

intrepid adj (intrepid explorers who went into the heart of the jungle) fearless, bold, daring, brave, courageous.

intricate adj 1 (an intricate pattern) elaborate, fancy, ornate. 2 (intricate problems) complex, complicated, involved, difficult.

intriguing adj (an intriguing story) fascinating, riveting, absorbing, interesting, captivating.

introduce vb 1 (She introduced the speaker) present, announce. 2 (She introduced her friends to each other) present, make known. 3 (They introduced new business methods) bring in, initiate, launch, institute, establish, start.

introduction n (the introduction to the book) preface, foreword, front matter, prologue.

introverted adj (Her sister is very outgoing but she is introverted) inward-looking, introspective, withdrawn.

intrude vb (Although they had been invited to the party they felt as though they were intruding) interrupt, barge in, interfere, butt in.

intruder n (The police arrested the intruder) burglar, housebreaker, thief.

intuition n (She seemed to know by intuition where her child was) instinct, sixth sense.

inundate vb 1 (The river burst its banks and inundated the town) flood, overflow, swamp, deluge, engulf. 2 (They were inundated with complaints) overwhelm, swamp, bog down.

invade vb (The enemy army invaded the city) overrun, storm, take over, attack, raid.

invalid adj (The doctor visited their invalid mother) ill, sick, ailing, unwell, infirm.

invaluable adj (We thanked them for their invaluable help) useful, helpful, precious, inestimable.

invariable adj (an invariable temperature/Her style of dress was quite invariable) unchanging, constant, unvarying, fixed, regular, uniform.

invasion n (the enemy's invasion of the city) attack, assault, raid, onslaught.

invent n 1 (the person who invented television) originate, create, discover, design, devise, think up. 2 (He invented an excuse for not being present) make up, concoct, fabricate, hatch, (inf) cook up.

investigate vb (investigate a murder case) research, examine, explore, inquire into, study.

invincible adj 1 (Their army seemed invincible) unbeatable, unconquerable. 2 (The obstacles to progress seem invincible) insuperable, insurmountable, overwhelming.

invisible adj 1 (The high hedge made the cottage invisible to passers-by) unseen, unnoticed, out of sight, hidden, concealed. 2 (an invisible repair) inconspicuous, unnoticeable, imperceptible.

invite vb 1 (We invited them to dinner) ask, send an invitation to. 2 (The company is inviting applications for sales *assistants*) ask, request, seek, call for.

involuntary adj (*Blinking is usually an involuntary reaction*) reflex, automatic, instinctive, unthinking, mechanical.

involve vb 1 (*His new job involves working with computers*) entail, include, necessitate, require. 2 (*They hoped to involve all the children in the scheme*) include, take in, incorporate, concern, interest. 3 (*He tried to involve his friends in his plans for the robbery*) implicate, associate, mix up. 4 (*find a hobby that involves them*) interest, absorb, occupy, grip, engross.

involved adj (*Her excuse seemed very involved*) complicated, complex, intricate, elaborate, confused, muddled.

irate adj (*They tried to calm the irate old man*) angry, furious, indignant, infuriated.

iron vb (*They had to iron their creased shirts*) press, smooth.

iron, iron out vbs (*They had talks to try to iron out their problems*) sort out, clear up, straighten out, settle, solve.

ironic adj (*He has a tendency to make ironic remarks*) satirical, mocking, scoffing, scornful, sneering, sarcastic.

irritable adj (*He gets irritable when he is tired*) bad-tempered, ill-tempered, cross, touchy, crabbed, grumpy, cantankerous.

irritate vb 1 (*His constant stream of jokes irritates her*) annoy, get on one's nerves, try one's patience, exasperate, infuriate. 2 (*The material irritated her skin*) inflame, redden, chafe, cause discomfort to.

isolated adj 1 (*They live in an isolated place*) remote, out-of-the way, outlying, secluded, desolate, inaccessible. 2 (*She felt isolated living far away from her family and friends*) lonely, solitary, alone, forsaken 3 (*The doctors do not think it is an epidemic but just an isolated example of the disease*) single, solitary, abnormal, unusual, atypical.

issue vb 1 (*Smoke issued from the factory chimney*) pour forth, discharge. 2 (*A steady stream of people issued from the building*) come out, emerge, leave, appear from. 3 (*New stamps have been issued to mark the occasion/ They issued a press release*) put out, distribute, circulate, release, disseminate.

issue n 1 (*They argue over political issues*) matter, subject, topic, affair, problem. 2 (*They plan to buy the next issue of the magazine*) edition, number, instalment. 3 (*They have been having talks about peace but the issue is still in doubt*) result, outcome, decision, conclusion.

itch n 1 (*She has an itch in her head*) tingling, prickling, irritation. 2 (*She has an itch to travel*) desire, longing, yearning, craving, hankering, (*inf*) yen.

item n 1 (*make a list of items for sale*) object, article, thing. 2 (*There are several items to be discussed at the meeting*) point, matter, issue, thing.

itinerant adj (*an itinerant salesman*) travelling, peripatetic.

itinerary n (*Our itinerary takes us through Belgium*) route, journey, travels.

J

jab vb (She jabbed him in the ribs to wake him) prod, poke, nudge, dig.

jagged adj (the jagged edge of the bread knife) rough, uneven, pointed, notched, serrated.

jail n (The prisoners have escaped from jail) gaol, prison, lock-up, (inf) nick, (inf) clink, (inf) slammer, (inf) cooler, (inf) jug.

jail vb (The judge jailed him for life) gaol, imprison, send to prison, lock up, put away, confine, incarcerate.

jam vb 1 (They tried to jam too many people into the hall) crowd, pack, cram, squeeze, crush. 2 (roads jammed by the sheer volume of traffic) block, obstruct, congest, clog. 3 (They jammed a piece of paper under the door to keep it open) wedge, stick, force, push, stuff.

jam n (bread, butter and jam) preserves, jelly.

jar vb 1 (The knife jarred against the metal surface of the box) grate, rasp, scratch, squeak. 2 (He jarred his shoulder in the car crash) jolt, jerk, shake.

jealous adj 1 (She was jealous because her sister won the race) envious, grudging, resentful, covetous, green with envy. 2 (He had a jealous wife) suspicious, distrustful, mistrustful, possessive.

jeer vb (When the politician tried to speak the crowd jeered) mock, scoff, ridicule, taunt, sneer.

jerk vb 1 (His leg was jerking uncontrollably) twitch, shake, tremble. 2 (She jerked the child out of his seat) pull, yank, tug, wrench. 3 (The old bus jerked along the country roads) jolt, bump, lurch, jar.

jewel n (She kept her jewels in a safe) gem, precious stone.

jewellery n (She wore silver jewellery on her black dress) jewels, gems, trinkets, ornament.

jittery adj (He was jittery before the exam) nervous, nervy, jumpy, uneasy, anxious.

job n 1 (He took days to finish a simple job) task, piece of work, chore, assignment, undertaking. 2 (What is her job?) occupation, profession, employment, career, trade. 3 (It was his job to look after the garden) task, chore, responsibility, concern, function, role.

jog vb 1 (They jogged round the park) go jogging, run, trot, lope. 2 (We tried to jog her memory but she had forgotten all about the incident) prompt, stir, stimulate, refresh.

join vb 1 (We had to join the two pieces of string) fasten, attach, put together, link, connect, tie. 2 (We joined in the search party to look for the dog) take part in, participate in, contribute to. 3 (We were asked to join the tennis club) become a member of, take up membership of, enrol in, sign up for. 4 (The two clubs have joined together) join forces, amalgamate, merge, combine, ally. **5** (*Their garden joins ours*) adjoin, abut on, border, border on, meet.

joint n (*the joints in the water pipes*) join, junction, coupling, seam.

joint adj (*The organization of the party was a joint effort*) common, shared, mutual, combined, collective, cooperative, united.

joke n **1** (*Her uncle tells very funny jokes*) jest, gag, witticism, (*inf*) funny. **2** (*We took his bike for a joke*) practical joke, prank, hoax, piece of fun, trick, (*inf*) lark.

joke vb **1** (*She was hurt by his remark but he was only joking*) tease, fool, pull (*someone's*) leg. **2** (*He can be rather annoying as he jokes all the time*) tell jokes, crack jokes, jest.

jolly adj (*The party was a very jolly occasion*) merry, happy, gay, joyful, cheerful, light-hearted.

jolt vb **1** (*The old car jolted along the bumpy roads*) jerk, lurch, bump, bounce. **2** (*The little boy kept getting jolted in the crowd*) bump, jostle, push, shove, nudge. **3** (*His unexpected failure in the exam jolted him*) upset, disturb, perturb, shake, disconcert, stun.

jostle vb (*people in the crowd jostling each other to the front*) push, shove, elbow, nudge, bump, knock, jolt.

jot vb (*jot down the names of the pupil*) note, make a note of, take down, write down, mark down, list.

journalist n (*The local artist was interviewed by a journalist after the exhibition*) reporter, newsman/newswoman, member of the press.

journey n (*They were tired after their long train journey*) trip, excursion, expedition, travels.

joy n (*their joy at the birth of their daughter*) delight, pleasure, happiness, gladness, rapture.

joyful adj (*It was a joyful occasion*) happy, cheerful, merry, gay, jolly, light-hearted.

judge vb **1** (*A senior member of the legal profession judged the case*) try, pronounce a verdict. **2** (*The local mayor judged the pets' competition*) adjudicate, arbitrate, evaluate, assess. **3** (*He is too ready to judge others*) pass judgement on, criticize, find fault with. **4** (*We judge that the meat would take an hour to cook*) estimate, guess, surmise, reckon, suppose, consider, think, believe.

judgement n **1** (*The magistrate will give his judgement tomorrow*) verdict, ruling, decision, finding, conclusion. **2** (*He is not a good businessman as he is lacking in judgement*) good sense, sense, shrewdness, wisdom, judiciousness, acumen.

juicy adj (*juicy fruit*) succulent, moist, ripe.

jump vb **1** (*The dog escaped by jumping over the fence*) leap over, vault, clear, hurdle. **2** (*The game involved the children jumping*) leap, spring, bound, bounce. **3** (*The sudden noise made everyone jump*) start, flinch, jerk.

jumper n (*wear a warm jumper*) sweater, jersey, pullover, knit, top.

junction n (*The cars collided at the*

junction) intersection, interchange, cross-roads.

jungle n (*wild animals in the jungle*) forest, tropical forest, undergrowth.

junior adj 1 (*the junior members of the family*) younger. 2 (*the junior posts in the company*) subordinate, lower, lesser, minor.

just adj (*We felt it was a just decision*) fair, honest, impartial, unprejudiced, unbiased, objective.

just adv 1 (*He's just a boy*) only, merely. 2 (*I just met them*) now, a moment ago, recently. 3 (*we just caught the bus*) only just, barely, scarcely, (*inf*) by the skin of our teeth. 4 (*The house was just right for them*) exactly, absolutely, precisely, entirely.

justice n (*He expects justice from the British courts*) justness, fairness, fairmindedness, impartiality, lack of bias, objectivity.

justify vb 1 (*He was asked to justify his absence*) account for, give reasons for, give grounds for, explain, defend, excuse. 2 (*His behaviour justified our concern for his health*) support, warrant, bear out, confirm.

jut vb (*The cliff juts out over the road*) stick out, project, protrude, overhang.

juvenile adj 1 (*the juvenile section of the musical competition*) junior, young, youthful. 2 (*We were amazed at their juvenile attitude to losing the game*) childish, immature, infantile.

K

keen adj 1 (*The keen pupils asked for extra practice*) enthusiastic, eager, willing, avid, zealous, conscientious. 2 (*people who are keen on football*) fond of, devoted to, having a liking for, being a fan of. 3 (*people who are keen to get more education*) eager, anxious, avid. 4 (*a keen edge on the sword*) sharp, sharp-edged. 5 (*a keen sense of smell*) sharp, acute, sensitive. 6 (*admire her keen mind*) sharp, astute, shrewd, quick, clever, bright, intelligent. 7 (*a keen frost*) intense, extreme, severe.

keep vb 1 (*She kept the ring which he had given her*) hold on to, retain, (*inf*) hang on to. 2 (*The child keeps all his old magazines*) save up, store, accumulate, hoard, collect. 3 (*The firm tried to keep going*) continue, carry on, persist, persevere. 4 (*The local shop keeps a wide range of goods*) stock, sell, stock, carry. 5 (*He does not earn enough to keep a wife and children*) provide, support, maintain, feed. 6 (*Everyone should keep to the rules*) obey, comply with, observe, abide by, carry out. 7 (*Try to keep the news of his accident from his mother*) keep back, keep secret, hide, conceal, withhold, suppress. 8 (*He is late—something must have kept him*) keep back, delay, hold back, detain, hinder.

keep n (*She pays for her own keep*) board, food, maintenance, support.

keepsake n (*be given a keepsake of her holiday*) memento, souvenir, reminder, remembrance.

keg n (*kegs of beer*) barrel, cask, vat, tun, butt.

kernel n 1 (*hazelnut kernels*) nut, stone, seed. 2 (*try to get to the kernel of the problem*) nub, core, centre, heart, (*inf*) nitty-gritty.

key n 1 (*musical keys*) tone, pitch, timbre. 2 (*find the key to the problem*) clue, guide, pointer, answer, solution, explanation.

kick vb 1 (*kick the ball*) boot, punt. 2 (*kick the man lying on the ground*) boot, take one's boot to, take one's feet to. 3 (*try to kick the smoking habit*) give up, stop, abandon, quit.

kidnap vb (*The president's son has been kidnapped*) abduct, snatch, seize, hold to ransom, take hostage.

kill vb 1 (*He was killed by a member of a rival gang*) take (someone's) life, slay, murder, do to death, put to death, execute, assassinate, (*inf*) bump off. 2 (*The news of his death killed all our hopes*) destroy, put an end to, ruin, extinguish, scotch.

kind adj (*Kind people helped him/They appreciated his kind action*) kind-hearted, kindly, generous, charitable, benevolent, helpful, considerate, obliging, thoughtful, friendly, amiable, courteous.

kind n (*a kind of dog/a kind of car*) type,

sort, variety, class, category, brand, make, species.

king n (*He was crowned king of Denmark*) monarch, ruler, sovereign.

kingdom n (*The ruler's kingdom extended to the sea*) realm, domain, land, country, territory.

kink n 1 (*There were some kinks in the rope*) twist, bend, coil, loop, tangle. 2 (*the kinks in her character*) quirk, eccentricity, idiosyncrasy.

kiosk n 1 (*buy a newspaper from a kiosk*) stall, stand, booth. 2 (*a telephone kiosk*) booth, box.

kit n (*He forgot his football kit*) equipment, gear, tackle, stuff, things, paraphernalia.

knack n (*He has the knack of getting people to tell him things*) talent, gift, aptitude, flair, ability, skill, expertise.

kneel vb (*He knelt to pick out some weeds*) get down on one's knees, bend, stoop, crouch.

knife vb (*He was knifed to death*) stab, pierce, run through, impale.

knob n 1 (*turn the knob of the door*) handle. 2 (*turn the knob of the radio*) switch. 3 (*trees with knobs on the bark*) bump, bulge, lump, swelling, knot, nodule. 4 (*a knob of butter*) lump, piece, bit.

knock vb 1 (*They knocked at the door*) tap, rap, bang. 2 (*The child knocked into the table and hurt his head*) bang, bump, collide with, crash into. 3 (*He knocked his son on the head for being naughty*) strike, hit, slap, smack, box, thump, (*inf*) wallop.

know vb 1 (*We don't really know the other people in the street*) be acquainted with, have dealings with, socialize with. 2 (*We knew what they were saying about us*) realize, be aware of, be conscious of, notice, recognize. 3 (*He does not know any Spanish*) have knowledge of, understand, comprehend. 4 (*She has known great misfortune*) experience, go through, be familiar with. 5 (*He does not know one of the twins from the other*) distinguish, differentiate, tell.

knowledge n 1 (*He showed his knowledge by doing well in the exam*) learning, education, scholarship, erudition. 2 (*admire the taxi driver's knowledge of the area*) familiarity, acquaintanceship. 3 (*He has little knowledge of the subject*) understanding, grasp, comprehension, expertise, skill, know-how.

knowledgeable adj (*She is very knowledgeable about local history*) informed, well-informed, educated, learned.

kudos n (*the kudos of being a famous writer*) prestige, fame, honour, glory, praise.

L

label n (*put a label on the luggage/the label on the article*) tag, tab, sticker, ticket.

laborious adj (*undertake a laborious task*) hard, difficult, arduous, strenuous, tiring.

labour n 1 (*They did not receive much money for their labour*) work, toil, effort, exertion, drudgery. 2 (*employ local labour in the new factory*) workers, employees, work force.

laboured adj 1 (*the laboured breathing of the invalid*) heavy, strained, forced, difficult. 2 (*He has a laboured style of writing*) stilted, strained, stiff, unnatural.

labourer n (*labourers on the building site*) workman, worker, navvy.

labyrinth n 1 (*a labyrinth in the grounds of the stately home*) maze. 2 (*a labyrinth of cellars under the house/try to make their way through the labyrinth of rules and regulations*) maze, network, tangle, jungle.

lace n (*lose a lace from her shoe*) shoelace, cord, string.

lacerate vb (*He lacerated his hand on the cut glass*) cut, tear, gash, slash, rip.

lack n (*There is a lack of fresh water in the area*) shortage, dearth, insufficiency, scarcity, paucity, want.

lack vb (*She lacks training for the job*) be lacking, be without, have need of, be short of, be deficient in.

laconic adj (*She gave a laconic reply*) brief, concise, terse, succinct.

lad n (*They hired a lad to deliver the newspapers*) boy, youth, young man.

ladder n (*stand on a ladder to paint the ceiling*) stepladder, steps.

laden adj (*people laden with shopping*) loaded, burdened, weighed down, encumbered.

lag vb 1 (*He lagged behind the rest of the runners in the race*) fall behind, ail, linger, dawdle, dally. 2 (*They lagged their hot-water tank*) wrap up, insulate.

lair n (*the fox's lair*) den.

lake n (*The children paddled in the lake*) reservoir, loch.

lame adj 1 (*He has been lame since the accident*) limping, crippled. 2 (*She has a lame leg*) crippled, game, (*inf*) gammy. 3 (*He gave a lame excuse for being late*) weak, feeble, flimsy, inadequate.

lamp n (*The lamps were still burning*) light.

land n 1 (*He went to live in a foreign land*) country, nation, state. 2 (*The land there will not grow much*) soil, earth, ground. 3 (*a large house with a great deal of land round it*) ground, estate, property. 4 (*prefer travelling on land to travelling by sea*) dry land, terra firma.

land vb 1 (*the plane landed*) touch down, come down, alight. 2 (*They met us as we landed at the dock*) dock, disembark.

landscape n (a country with a flat landscape) countryside.

lane n 1 (take a walk down a country lane) path, track. 2 (motorway lanes) track, course.

language n 1 (the Spanish language) tongue, speech, mother tongue. 2 (Children acquire language at different rates) speech, speaking, talking, words, vocabulary, communication.

lap n 1 (The cat was sitting in its owner's lap) knee, knees. 2 (We are on our last lap of the journey) round, section, stage. 3 (The runners ran several laps of the track) circuit, course.

lap vb 1 (The cats lapped up the milk) drink, lick up. 2 (The water lapped against the rocks) wash, beat.

lapse n (We saw him again after a lapse of time) interval, break, gap, pause, passage.

large adj 1 (They have a large garden/ They are putting up large buildings) big, sizeable, substantial, tall, high, huge, immense, enormous. 2 (He is a very large man) big, burly, heavy, strapping, hulking, hefty, fat. 3 (We have large supplies of fuel) big, ample, abundant, copious, liberal, plentiful.

lash vb 1 (The master lashed the slave with a whip) whip, flog, flail, birch, trash, beat. 2 (They lashed the boat to the side of the ship) tie, bind, fasten, tether, strap.

last adj 1 (The last words of the speaker) final, closing, concluding. 2 (The last runners arrived exhausted) hindmost, rearmost, final.

last vb 1 (How long is the meeting likely to last?) continue, go on, carry on, remain, persist. 2 (The climbers cannot last on the mountains in these blizzard conditions) survive, live, endure. 3 (People said that their marriage would not last) survive, be permanent, hold out, last long. 4 (buy shoes that will last) wear well, last long, be durable.

late adj 1 (Don't wait for her. She is always late) unpunctual, overdue, behind schedule, slow. 2 (She still misses her late husband) dead, deceased. 3 (Some late news has just arrived) recent, new, fresh, up-to-the-minute.

lather n (The soap made a lot of lather) suds, soapsuds, bubbles.

latter adj (The latter is the more expensive) last-named, second, the second of two.

laugh vb 1 (The children laughed heartily at the antics of the clown) chuckle, chortle, (inf) split one's sides, (inf) fall about, (inf) be rolling in the aisles. 2 (The children laughed at the old-fashioned clothes which the little girl was wearing) jeer, mock, ridicule, sneer, make fun of, poke fun at.

launch vb 1 (They launched the ship) float, set afloat. 2 (They launched a missile) fire, discharge, send forth. 3 (We launch our new business tomorrow) begin, start, embark upon, set up, establish.

laundry n (She does the laundry on Mondays) washing, wash.

lavatory n (There is a bathroom and a separate lavatory in the flat) toilet, WC, (inf) loo.

lavish adj (a lavish supply of food) generous, liberal, abundant, copious, plentiful.

law n 1 (*It was a new law issued by Parliament*) rule, regulation, statute, act, decree, edict. 2 (*All players must obey the laws of the game*) rule, regulation, instruction, guideline.

lawful adj 1 (*They are looking for the lawful owner of the car*) legal, legitimate, rightful. 2 (*It is not lawful to play football on the grass in the park*) legal, permitted, permissible, allowed, authorized.

lawyer n (*He hired a lawyer to sue his neighbour for damage to his property*) solicitor, legal practitioner, legal adviser.

lay vb 1 (*We were asked to lay our books on the table*) put down, set down, place, deposit. 2 (*lay the blame on his friend*) place, put, attribute, assign.

layer n (*a layer of ice on the road*) coat, sheet, skin, film.

lazy adj (*He is very lazy and does not want to work*) idle, indolent, slothful, inactive, work-shy.

lead n 1 (*They need a strong man to lead the country*) be in charge of, direct, govern, be in command of, manage, head. 2 (*The horse was leading but fell just before the finish*) be in the lead, be in front, be first, be winning. 3 (*He was asked to lead the visitors to their seats*) conduct, guide, direct, escort, usher. 4 (*We hope that they will lead a happy life*) have, live, pass, experience.

lead n 1 (*the runners in the lead*) first place, leading position, forefront, vanguard. 2 (*She has the lead in the new play*) leading part, leading role, starring role, principal part. 3 (*We lost the dog's lead*) leash, chain, tether.

leader n 1 (*the leader of the team of climbers*) head, captain. 2 (*the leader of the country*) head, ruler, commander, chief. 3 (*a leader in the field of fashion/a leader in medical research*) front runner, trend-setter, pioneer, trail-blazer.

leading adj 1 (*They played a leading role in the peace talks*) chief, principal, foremost, important. 2 (*He was one of the leading artists of his day*) foremost, chief, most important, celebrated, eminent, outstanding.

leaf vb (*He leafed through the book to see if it was what he was looking for*) flick, skim, browse, glance.

leaflet n (*an advertising leaflet*) pamphlet, booklet, brochure, circular handbill.

league n (*clubs forming a football league*) alliance, federation, association, union, group, society.

leak vb 1 (*Water was leaking from the hole in the pipe*) escape, ooze, drip, seep, discharge, issue. 2 (*A member of the department leaked information to the press*) reveal, divulge, disclose, make known, pass on.

lean vb 1 (*lean the ladder against the wall*) rest, prop, support. 2 (*The ship leaned to one side*) incline, bend, slant, tilt, slope.

lean adj 1 (*He was tall and lean*) thin, slender, slim, spare, skinny 2 (*lean meat*) non-fat, low-fat.

leaning n (*He has a leaning towards*

scientific subjects) tendency, inclination, bent, propensity.

leap vb 1 (*The dog leapt over the fence*) jump, spring, bound, vault. 2 (*The children were leaping around excitedly before the party*) jump, bound, bounce, skip, hop, dance. 3 (*House prices have leapt*) soar, rocket, mount, shoot up.

learn vb 1 (*They had to learn a new method*) grasp, master, take in, pick up. 2 (*We go to school to learn*) be educated. 3 (*How did you learn that they had gone?*) find out, discover, gather, hear.

learned adj (*the learned men of the community*) erudite, educated, well-educated, well-read, scholarly, clever, intellectual.

learner n (*drivers who were learners*) trainee, pupil, apprentice.

lease vb (*They leased a car from an agency*) hire, rent, charter.

leash n (*a dog's leash*) lead, chain, cord.

leather n (*jackets made of leather*) skin, hide.

leave vb 1 (*The guests left hurriedly*) depart, go away, take one's leave, set off. 2 (*He left his job and emigrated*) give up, quit, move from. 3 (*He left his wife and children*) abandon, desert, forsake, turn one's back on. 4 (*He left his gloves in the bus*) leave behind, forget, mislay. 5 (*They were asked to leave their boots by the front door*) place, put, deposit. 6 (*She plans to leave all her money to her nephew*) bequeath, will.

leave n 1 (*The soldiers are taking some leave*) holiday, vacation, time off. 2 (*They were given leave to take some time off*) permission, consent, authorization. 3 (*They took their leave at midnight*) departure, leave-taking, farewell, goodbye.

lecture n (*The students attended a lecture on local history*) talk, speech, address.

leg n 1 (*She broke her leg*) lower limb. 2 (*The legs of the tripod for the telescope*) support, upright. 3 (*on the second leg of their journey*) stage, round, stretch, lap, part, portion.

legacy n (*He received a legacy in his aunt's will*) bequest, inheritance.

legal adj (*His action was not quite legal*) lawful, legitimate, law-abiding, permissible.

legend n (*legends about giants*) myth, saga, epic, folk-tale.

legendary adj 1 (*giants and other legendary figures*) mythical, fictitious, fictional, fabled. 2 (*legendary Hollywood actors*) famous, renowned, celebrated, illustrious.

legible adj (*writing that was scarcely legible*) readable, decipherable, clear.

leisure n (*hobbies he pursued in periods of leisure*) free time, spare time.

lend vb 1 (*She lent him a book on gardening*) loan, give (someone) a loan of, let (someone) have the use of. 2 (*The flowers lend a freshness to the room*) add, give, impart, supply.

length n 1 (*What length is the room?*) distance. 2 (*The audience were bored by the sheer length of the speech*) longness, lengthiness, extensiveness, long-windedness.

lengthen vb 1 (*They lengthened the*

skirts) make longer, elongate, let down **2** (*It will lengthen the time the job takes*) make longer, draw out, prolong, extend, protract. **3** (*It is early spring and the days are lengthening*) become longer, draw out.

lengthy adj **1** (*He gave a lengthy speech/The meeting was a lengthy affair*) long, long-lasting, prolonged, protracted, too long.

lenient adj **1** (*a lenient judge*) merciful, clement, forgiving, compassionate, tolerant, gentle. **2** (*The accused was given a lenient sentence*) mild, moderate.

lessen vb **1** (*They hoped that the storm would lessen*) grow less, get less, abate, subside, ease off, let up, dwindle, decrease. **2** (*He was given pills to lessen the pain*) reduce, decrease, ease, relieve, soothe, assuage.

lesson n **1** (*The children are having a French lesson*) class. **2** (*The Bible story is meant to teach a lesson*) moral, message, example, warning.

let vb **1** (*They let the children play in the garden*) allow, permit, give permission to, authorize. **2** (*He lets his flat to students*) let out, rent, rent out, lease, hire.

lethal adj (*The blow to his head proved lethal*) fatal, deadly, mortal, terminal, destructive.

lethargic adj (*They felt lethargic after a heavy lunch*) sluggish, inactive, listless, sleepy, lazy, languid.

letter n **1** (*the letters of the alphabet*) character, symbol. **2** (*We sent a letter of thanks*) message, note, epistle.

level adj **1** (*We need a level surface to build it on*) even, flat, smooth, flush, horizontal. **2** (*The scores were level at half-time*) equal, even, neck and neck. **3** (*We need to keep the room at a level temperature*) even, uniform, regular, consistent, stable, constant.

level n **1** (*At eye-level*) height, altitude. **2** (*The lift will take you to the second level*) floor, storey. **3** (*The two gymnasts are at about the same level of competence*) stage, standard, grade.

liable adj **1** (*The hotel is not liable for customers' lost goods*) responsible, accountable, answerable, at fault. **2** (*People who climb high buildings are liable to injury*) exposed, open to, in danger of, at risk of, subject to, vulnerable. **3** (*She is liable to burst into tears if you criticize her*) likely, apt, inclined, prone.

liberal adj **1** (*a liberal supply of food*) abundant, copious, ample, plentiful, generous, lavish. **2** (*Her parents have very liberal ideas*) tolerant, broadminded, unprejudiced, enlightened.

liberty n **1** (*a country that values its liberty*) freedom, independence. **2** (*The prisoners were suddenly given their liberty*) freedom, release, discharge, emancipation.

licence n (*He showed his driving licence as proof of identity*) permit, certificate, document, documentation.

license vb (*The shop is licensed to sell alcohol*) authorize, permit, allow.

lid vb (*He removed the lid from the jar*) cover, top, cork, stopper.

lie n (*It was obvious that he was telling a*

lie) untruth, falsehood, fib, white lie.

lie vb **I** (*The jury felt that the witness was lying*) tell a lie, tell a falsehood, fib, dissemble. **2** (*The doctor asked him to lie on the sofa*) recline, stretch out, be supine, be prone, be prostrate, be horizontal. **3** (*The village lies at the foot of a hill*) be situated, be located, be. **4** (*The volcano lies dormant*) be, continue, remain.

life n **I** (*when life began on earth*) existence, being. **2** (*They worked hard all their lives*) lifetime, life span, existence. **3** (*The children were full of life*) liveliness, animation, vitality, vivacity. **4** (*He was the life of the party*) spirit, vital spark, moving force. **5** (*They published a life of Winston Churchill*) biography, autobiography.

lifeless adj **I** (*A lifeless figure lay on the shore*) dead, deceased. **2** (*He seems to prefer lifeless objects to people*) inanimate, without life. **3** (*lifeless stretches of the world*) infertile, barren, sterile, bare, desolate. **4** (*The actor gave rather a lifeless performance*) spiritless, colourless, uninspired, flat, lacklustre.

lift vb **I** (*They lifted the sacks on to the lorry*) hoist, pick up, raise, carry. **2** (*They lifted the ban*) raise, remove, withdraw, revoke, relax, end. **3** (*The mist soon lifted*) rise, disperse, disappear.

light n **I** (*By the light of the candles*) illumination, brightness, brilliance, shining. **2** (*They carried a light to the window*) lamp, torch, flashlight. **3** (*They struck a light*) flame, spark. **4** (*We would prefer to arrive in the light*) day-

light, daytime, day. **5** (*He began to see things in a different light*) aspect, angle, slant, approach, viewpoint, point of view.

light adj **I** (*a light, airy room*) bright, well-lit **2** (*wearing light clothes*) light-coloured, pale, pastel. **3** (*She had very light hair*) light-coloured, fair, blond, pale. **4** (*The suitcases are quite light*) easy to carry, portable. **5** (*A suit of a light material*) lightweight, thin, flimsy, delicate. **6** (*The child is very light for her age*) slight, small, thin. **7** (*He is able to do only light tasks*) easy, simple, effortless, undemanding, unexacting. **8** (*She woke up with a light heart*) happy, merry, carefree, cheerful. **9** (*They were told that it was not a light matter*) frivolous, unimportant, insignificant, trivial, trifling. **10** (*There was a light wind blowing*) gentle, soft, slight.

light vb **I** (*They light the fire in the evenings*) ignite, kindle, set fire to, set alight. **2** (*The fireworks lit up the sky*) illuminate, brighten, lighten.

lighten vb **I** (*The sky lightened*) grow light, grow bright, grow brighter, brighten. **2** (*We had to lighten the donkey's load*) make lighter, lessen, reduce.

lightweight adj **I** (*wearing a lightweight suit in the heat*) light, thin, flimsy. **2** (*He is rather a lightweight writer*) insignificant, unimportant, trivial.

like prep **I** (*It was like her to lose her temper*) typical, characteristic, in keeping with. **2** (*She writes rather like Jane Austen*) in the manner of, in the same way as, resembling.

like adj (They have like tastes) similar, identical, corresponding, compatible.

like vb 1 (They seemed to like each other right away) have a liking for, be fond of, be attracted to, be keen on, love, admire, appreciate, approve of. 2 (She does not like pop music) enjoy, delight in, relish, be partial to, have a preference for. 3 (We would like to go to the party but we have another engagement) wish, want, desire, prefer.

likelihood n (There is no likelihood of our arriving on time) possibility, probability, chance, prospect.

likely adj 1 (It is likely that she will fail) probable, to be expected, possible. 2 (It is likely to be wet there at that time of year) liable, apt, inclined. 3 (They gave a likely enough reason for being absent) plausible, feasible, reasonable, credible. 4 (She found a likely place to build a house) suitable, appropriate, fitting, acceptable, reasonable.

likeness n (There is a distinct likeness between the two faces) similarity, resemblance, sameness.

limb n 1 (He injured his limbs in the accident) arm, leg, extremity. 2 (They cut a limb from the tree because it was keeping out the light from the house) branch, bough.

limelight n (She was a film actress who enjoyed the limelight) public eye, public notice.

limit n 1 (They were fishing outside the agreed limits) boundary, border, extremity, cut-off point. 2 (They tried to impose some kind of limit on their expenditure) limitation, ceiling, maximum,

restriction, restraint. 3 (The climb up the mountain pushed their powers of endurance to the limit) utmost, maximum, extremity, end.

limit vb 1 (They tried to limit their expenditure) restrict, restrain, curb, hold in check. 2 (She felt that having children would limit her freedom) restrict, restrain, curb, impede, hinder, hamper.

limp vb (He still limps after the accident to his leg) be lame, hobble.

limp adj 1 (a salad consisting of tomatoes and a few limp lettuce leaves) drooping, floppy, wilting, sagging. 2 (They felt limp in the heat) drooping, wilting, lethargic, exhausted.

line n 1 (The pupils were asked to draw a line) stroke. 2 (There was dirty line along the bath) band, strip, stripe, seam. 3 (The old woman had a face full of lines) wrinkle, furrow, crease, groove. 3 (A line of police kept back the crowd) row, column, chain, cordon, procession, queue, file. 4 (She is hanging the washing on a line in the back garden) rope, string, cable, wire. 5 (The police are taking a tough line against the wrongdoers) course of action, policy, approach, position, procedure. 6 (What line is he in?) line of work, work, business, employment, job, occupation, profession, trade.

line vb 1 (Age had lined her face) wrinkle, furrow, crease. 2 (Beech trees lined the avenue) border, edge. 3 (The children were asked to line up outside their classroom) form a line, queue up.

linger n 1 (The smell of fried fish lingered in the hall) stay, remain, persist, hang around. **2** (*Some of the students lingered to ask the lecturer questions*) stay behind, wait behind, hang around, loiter, delay, stay, remain.

link n **1** (*A link has been established between smoking and certain illnesses*) connection, association, relationship, tie-up. **2** (*They have strong family links*) bond, attachment, tie, **3** (*the links of the chain*) loop, ring, coupling.

link vb **1** (*Shex has lost the piece that links the two parts together*) join, connect, fasten together, attach, couple. **2** (*The police are linking the murder with a previous one*) connect, associate, relate, bracket together.

lip n (*the lip of the cup*) edge, rim, brim, border, brink.

liquid adj (*a liquid substance*) fluid, flowing, runny, watery.

liquidize vb (*She liquidized the mixture*) blend, crush, purée.

liquor n (*He drinks only fruit juice, not liquor*) spirits, alcohol, alcoholic drink, strong drink, (*inf*) the hard stuff.

list n (*make a list of the titles of the books*) record, catalogue, register, inventory, table.

list vb **1** (*Please list the articles which you bought*) make a list of, note down, write down, itemize, enumerate, enter, record, register. **2** (*The ship listed in the storm*) lean, tilt, tip, heel over.

listen vb (*They listened carefully to what the teacher was saying*) pay attention to, take heed, heed, take notice of, hear.

listless adj (*The tourists were feeling listless in the heat*) lethargic, sluggish, weak, exhausted, inactive.

litter n **1** (*with litter lying all over the park*) rubbish, debris, refuse, waste, junk, (*Amer*) trash, (*Amer*) garbage. **2** (*a litter of pups*) family.

little adj **1** (*a little man/a little object*) small, slight, short, tiny, minute, diminutive, mini, infinitesimal, microscopic. **2** (*a little book*) small, concise, compact. **3** (*You will gain little advantage from doing that*) hardly any, scant, slight, negligible. **4** (*They had a little argument about which of them should pay the bill*) small, minor, petty, trivial, trifling, unimportant, insignificant. **5** (*They have nasty little minds*) mean, narrow, small, shallow.

little n **1** (*He will take a little of the milk*) touch, trace, bit, dash, spot. **2** (*You will see him in a little*) short time, little while, minute, moment.

live adj (*live animals/live bodies*) alive, living, breathing, existing, animate.

live vb **1** (*in the days when dinosaurs lived*) be alive, exist, have life, be. **2** (*The casualty was not expected to live*) survive, last, endure. **3** (*old customs that live on*) survive, stay, remain, continue, abide. **4** (*They live on fruit and vegetables*) eat, feed on. **5** (*They live by begging*) make a living, subsist, support oneself, maintain oneself. **6** (*They live in a flat in town*) dwell, inhabit, reside, lodge, occupy.

lively adj **1** (*They are very lively children*) active, energetic, spirited, sprightly, perky. **2** (*They had a lively discussion on local politics*) animated, spirited, stimulating, enthusiastic.

livid adj 1 (*Their father was livid when he saw the damage which they had done to the car*) furious, enraged, infuriated, fuming. 2 (*He had a livid mark on his forehead*) bruised, discoloured, black-and-white, purplish, bluish. 3 (*the livid faces of the dead*) ashen, pale, pallid, ghastly.

load n 1 (*The donkey had a heavy load*) burden, weight. 2 (*the lorry's load*) cargo, freight, contents.

load vb 1 (*They helped to load the lorry*) fill, fill up, pack, stack. 2 (*He loaded the gun*) prime, charge, fill.

loaf vb (*loafing around the house instead of working*) laze, idle, lounge.

loan vb (*They loaned him money*) lend, give on loan.

loathe vb (*They used to be friends but now they loathe each other*) hate, detest, abhor, have an aversion to.

local adj (*They attend the local school*) nearby, near, neighbourhood.

locality n (*There are several hotels in the locality*) area, district, region, neighbourhood, vicinity.

locate vb 1 (*They plan to locate the hotel on the outside of the village*) place, position, situate, site, build, establish. 2 (*We finally located the cause of the trouble with the engine*) find, discover, detect, identify, pinpoint.

lock vb 1 (*They locked the door*) bolt, bar, fasten, secure. 2 (*The guards locked the prisoners up*) shut up, confine, imprison.

logical adj 1 (*His argument was not at all logical*) reasoned, rational, sound, coherent. 2 (*It seemed the logical thing to do*) rational, reasonable, sensible, intelligent.

loiter vb 1 (*There were gangs of youths loitering the street corners*) hang around, hang about, wait, skulk, lounge, loaf, idle. 2 (*They loitered along the road to school*) dawdle, dally, saunter, dilly-dally.

lone adj (*The sailors saw a lone yachtsman*) solitary, single, sole, unaccompanied, by oneself.

lonely adj 1 (*She lived by herself and sometime felt lonely*) friendless, lonesome, forlorn, neglected, desolate, isolated, unhappy, sad. 2 (*a lonely landscape*) desolate, isolated, remote, out-of-the-way, deserted.

long adj (*a piece of wood three metres long*) in length, lengthways, lengthwise. 2 (*It was a long journey*) lengthy, extended, slow, prolonged. 3 (*He gave a long speech*) lengthy, prolonged, protracted, long-drawn-out, wordy, long-winded.

long vb (*They longed for a long cool drink*) yearn for, wish for, desire, crave, pine for, hanker after.

longing n (*They had a longing for some sunshine*) yearning, wish, desire, craving.

long-winded adj (*a long-winded speech*) wordy, verbose, rambling, lengthy, long-drawn-out, prolonged, protracted.

look vb 1 (*We looked and saw a beautiful painting*) take a look, observe, view, contemplate, gaze, stare, examine, study. 2 (*She looks ill*) appear, seem. 3 (*The dining room of the hotel* *looks south*) face, overlook.

loom vb **1** (*A dark figure loomed out of the shadows*) appear, emerge, materialise. **2** (*The exams are looming*) be imminent, be close, be ominously close.

loop n (*loops of ribbon*) coil, hoop, circle, curl.

loose adj **1** (*They wore loose clothes*) loose-fitting, slack, wide, baggy. **2** (*The table leg is loose*) not secure, insecure, movable, wobbly, unsteady, shaky. **3** (*The rope was loose*) slack, untied, unfastened. **4** (*The pigs were loose in the village street*) at large, at liberty, free, unconfined.

loose vb (*She loosed the dogs when she saw the strange man in the garden*) let loose, set free, release, unleash, untie.

loosen vb **1** (*He loosened his belt*) slacken, let out, undo, unfasten, unhook. **2** (*He loosened his grip on the rail*) relax, slacken, weaken.

loot n (*The police found the burglar's loot*) booty, haul, plunder, spoils.

loot vb (*Gangs looted the shops after the fire in the city centre*) plunder, pillage, ransack, rob, burgle.

lorry n (*They loaded the lorry*) truck, van, juggernaut.

lose vb **1** (*We lost our keys*) mislay, misplace, forget. **2** (*They lost their way in the dark*) stray from, wander from. **3** (*She lost a lot of blood*) be deprived of. **4** (*They lost several opportunities*) miss, pass, neglect, waste. **5** (*Our team lost*) be defeated, suffer defeat, be conquered.

loss n (*The firm made a loss in that finan-* *cial year*) deficit, non-profit.

lost adj **1** (*They eventually found the lost gloves*) missing, misplaced, mislaid, forgotten. **2** (*lost opportunities*) missed, passed, neglected, wasted.

lot n **1** (*A lot of people were present*) a great many, many, a good deal, a great deal, numerous, an abundance, plenty, masses. **2** (*She weeps a lot*) a good deal, much, many times. **3** (*The furniture was sold at auction as one lot*) collection, set, batch, quantity.

lotion n (*a lotion to soothe his sunburned skin*) cream, salve, ointment.

lottery n (*He hoped to gain a lot of money in the lottery*) draw, sweepstake, drawing of lots.

loud adj **1** (*The children were frightened by the loud noise*) noisy, blaring, booming, deafening, ear-splitting. **2** (*She disliked the loud colours in the restaurant*) garish, gaudy, flamboyant, flashy, vulgar. **3** (*She disapproved of their loud behaviour*) noisy, rowdy, boisterous, rough.

loutish adj (*Because of their loutish behaviour he was asked to leave the bar*) boorish, oafish, doltish, churlish.

love n **1** (*He showed his love by sending her red roses*) affection, fondness, care, concern, attachment, devotion, adoration, passion. **2** (*The child has a great love of chocolates*) liking, weakness, partiality, relish.

love vb **1** (*It was obvious that she loved him*) be in love with, care for, be fond of, adore, (*inf*) have a crush on. **2** (*She loves fresh peaches*) like, have a weakness for, be partial to, enjoy.

lovely adj 1 (She is a lovely girl) beautiful, pretty, attractive, good-looking, charming, enchanting. 2 (We had a lovely time at the party) delightful, pleasant, nice, marvellous, wonderful.

low adj 1 (a low table) short. 2 (a low position in the firm) inferior, humble, subordinate, junior. 3 (She spoke in a low voice) soft, quiet, whispered, hushed. 4 (She was feeling low after her defeat) in low spirits, down, downhearted, dejected, depressed, despondent. 5 (They have a low opinion of him) unfavourable, poor, bad, adverse, negative, hostile. 6 (Our supplies of food are low) sparse, meagre, scarce, scant, scanty, paltry, inadequate. 7 (It was a low thing to do) nasty, mean, foul, vile, base, dishonourable, despicable, wicked, evil.

lower vb 1 (They lowered the flag) let down, take down, haul down. 2 (They have lowered the prices) reduce, decrease, bring down, cut, slash. 3 (She was asked to lower her voice/They lowered the volume of the radio) quieten, soften, hush, turn down.

loyal adj (They were loyal subjects of the king) faithful, true, trusted, trustworthy, trusty, reliable, dependable, devoted, constant.

loyalty n (They showed their loyalty to the king) faith, faithfulness, fidelity, allegiance, trustworthiness, reliability, dependability, devotion, constancy.

lucid adj 1 (Her explanation was extremely lucid) clear, crystal clear, plain, intelligible, graphic. 2 (an old man who was scarcely lucid) sane, in one's right mind, rational, compos mentis, (inf) all there.

luck n 1 (She found the perfect flat just by luck) chance, fortune, destiny, fate, accident, serendipity. 2 (We wished them luck) good luck, good fortune, success, prosperity.

lucky adj 1 (She seemed a very lucky person who always got what she wanted) fortunate, favoured, advantaged. 2 (She didn't know the answer—it was just a lucky guess) fortunate, providential, opportune, timely, auspicious.

lucrative adj (His firm is very lucrative) profitable, profit-making, money-making, remunerative.

ludicrous adj (It was a really ludicrous suggestion) absurd, ridiculous, laughable, foolish, silly, crazy, preposterous.

luggage n (They carried her luggage to the train) bags, baggage, suitcases, things, belongings, gear.

lull vb 1 (They lulled the child to sleep) soothe, hush, quieten. 2 (Their fears were lulled) soothe, quieten, silence, calm, allay, ease.

lull n (They left while there was a lull in the storm) pause, respite, interval, break, let-up.

lumbering adj (He was a great lumbering creature) awkward, clumsy, bumbling, blundering, hulking, ungainly.

luminous adj (a clock with a luminous dial) lighted, lit, shining, phosphorescent.

lump n 1 (She bought a lump of cheese) chunk, hunk, wedge, piece, mass, (inf) wodge. **2** (*He got a lump on the head when he fell*) bump, swelling, bulge, knob, bruise.

lunatic *adj* (*It was a lunatic thing to do*) mad, insane, foolish, stupid, idiotic, senseless, absurd, ludicrous.

lunge *vb* **1** (*She lunged at her attacker with a knife*) stab, jab, thrust, poke. **2** (*He lunged towards the door when he saw his attacker*) charge, dive, spring, leap, bound.

lurch *vb* (*drunk men lurching home*) stagger, sway, reel, roll, weave, stumble, totter.

lure *vb* (*The evil men lured the children into their car*) entice, attract, induce, inveigle, decoy, tempt, cajole.

lurid *adj* **1** (*She hated the lurid colours on the walls of the restaurant*) overbright, gaudy, garish, flamboyant, loud. **2** (*The newspaper published the lurid details of the murder*) gory, gruesome, macabre, sensational, melodramatic, explicit.

lurk *vb* (*She saw a figure lurking in the shadows*) skulk, lie in wait, crouch, slink, prowl.

luscious *adj* (*luscious peaches*) juicy, delicious, succulent, mouth-watering.

lust *n* (*They needed to satisfy their lust for power*) greed, craving, desire, yearning, hunger.

luxurious *adj* (*They live in luxurious surroundings*) opulent, affluent, sumptuous, splendid, magnificent, wealthy, expensive, rich, costly, lavish, de luxe.

luxury *n* (*After they won the lottery they lived in luxury*) opulence, affluence, splendour, magnificence, wealth, ease.

lynch *vb* (*The townspeople lynched the man who had murdered the child*) put to death, execute, hang, kill, murder.

lyrics *npl* (*He wrote the lyrics of the pop songs*) words, libretto, book, text.

M

machine n apparatus, appliance, instrument, device, mechanism.

machinery n 1 (*the machinery in the factory*) apparatus, equipment, gear, plant. 2 (*the machinery of government*) workings, organization, system, agency.

mad adj 1 (*She went mad with grief*) insane, demented, deranged, of unsound mind, crazed, crazy, unbalanced, unhinged. 2 (*mothers who were mad with their children*) annoyed, angry, furious, enraged. (*He is always engaging in mad schemes*) insane, crazy, idiotic, foolish, absurd, foolhardy, rash. 4 (*They are mad about jazz*) passionate, enthusiastic, keen, fervent, fanatical.

magazine n (*She was looking for a gardening magazine*) periodical, journal, paper, (*inf*) glossy.

magic adj 1 (*people who believe in magic*) witchcraft, sorcery, wizardry, enchantment, the occult, voodoo. 2 (*the magic performed by the entertainer*) conjuring tricks, illusion, sleight of hand.

magician n 1 (*rather a frightening story about a magician*) sorcerer, witch, wizard, warlock, enchanter. 2 (*They hired a magician for the children's party*) conjuror, illusionist.

magnificent adj 1 (*a magnificent royal procession/a magnificent feast*) splendid, grand, impressive, superb, glorious. 2 (*It was a magnificent game of tennis*) excellent, skilful, fine, impressive, outstanding.

magnitude vb 1 (*try to estimate the magnitude of the explosion*) extent, size, dimensions, volume, bulk. 2 (*We were surprised at the magnitude of the flu epidemic*) size, extent, vastness, extensiveness. 3 (*fail to appreciate the magnitude of the problem*) scale, importance, significance.

maid n (*the hotel maids*) domestic worker, domestic, servant.

mail n 1 (*The postman delivered the morning mail*) post, letters. 2 (*She sent the package by mail*) post, postal service. 3 (*The knights of old wore mail*) chain, coat of mail, armour.

main adj (*the main points in the discussion/the main cities in the world*) chief, principal, leading, foremost, major, important.

mainly adv (*They mainly lived on fruit and vegetables*) for the most part, mostly, on the whole, largely.

maintain vb 1 (*He has always maintained that he is innocent*) declare, insist, assert, state, proclaim, claim. 2 (*He has a family to maintain*) keep, support, provide for, take care of, look after. 3 (*He maintained a steady speed throughout the journey*) keep, keep up, continue, sustain.

major adj 1 (*play a major part in the victory*) important, leading, principal, great, crucial. **2** (*the major part of his fortune*) larger, greater, bigger, main. **3** (*one of our major artists*) leading, chief, foremost, greatest, main, outstanding, notable, eminent.

majority *n* (*the majority of the people*) most, bulk, mass, main body.

make *vb* **1** (*make furniture at his woodwork class*) build, construct, assemble, fabricate, form, fashion. **2** (*try not to make a noise*) create, produce, bring about. **3** (*He made a bow to the queen*) perform, execute, carry out, effect. **4** (*They made him apologize*) force, compel. **5** (*The bride's father made a speech*) give, deliver, utter. **6** (*He made a fortune before he was thirty-five*) earn, gain, acquire, obtain, get. **7** (*She will make a wonderful mother*) become, grow into, turn into. **8** (*We made an appointment to see him*) arrange, fix, agree on, settle on, decide on. **9** (*6 and 2 make 8*) add up to, amount to, come to, total. **10** (*He made the v into a y by mistake*) alter, change, turn, transform. **11** (*He hoped to make his destination by nightfall*) reach, arrive at, get to, achieve. **12** (*We could not make out what he was saying*) understand, follow, work out, hear. **13** (*He made up an excuse for not being present*) invent, think up, concoct, fabricate.

make *n* (*various makes of car*) brand, kind, variety, sort, type.

make-believe *n* (*She said that she saw a fairy but it was only make-believe*) fantasy, pretence, imagination.

make-believe *adj* (*the child's make-believe friend*) fantasy, made-up, pre-

tended, feigned, imaginary, fictitious, unreal.

make-up *n* (*She put on her make-up in the cloakroom*) cosmetics.

male *adj* (*male creatures*) masculine, manly, virile.

male *n* (*two males and a female*) man, boy, gentleman.

malicious *adj* (*She received an anonymous malicious letter*) spiteful, vindictive, vicious, venomous, nasty, bitter, evil.

malignant *adj* **1** (*The doctor discovered that she had a malignant growth*) cancerous. **2** (*a malignant disease/a malignant influence*) dangerous, destructive, fatal, deadly, harmful.

maltreat *vb* (*Her parents were accused of maltreating her*) abuse, ill-treat, harm, injure, molest.

mammoth *adj* (*They faced a mammoth task/a mammoth serving of ice cream*) huge, enormous, gigantic, vast, colossal, massive.

man *n* **1** (*three men and a woman*) male, gentleman, (*inf*) chap, (*inf*) guy, (*inf*) bloke. **2** (*man and animals*) mankind, humankind, the human race, humans.

manage *vb* **1** (*He manages the whole firm*) run, be in charge of, be head of, control, preside over, administer. **2** (*We don't know how they managed to survive/manage the work*) succeed in, contrive, achieve, accomplish, effect. **3** (*It is going to be a large dinner party. Will you manage?*) cope, get by. **4** (*She really cannot manage such a lively horse*) handle, cope with, deal with, control.

manager vb (the workers and the departmental manager) head, superintendent, supervisor, boss, chief, administrator.

mandatory adj (Taking part in the conference was not mandatory) compulsory, obligatory, imperative, essential.

manful adj (make a manful attempt to get to the summit of the mountain) brave, courageous, gallant, heroic, bold, determined.

manhandle vb 1 (The removal men had to manhandle the piano upstairs) manoeuvre, haul, heave, push. 2 (The police were accused of manhandling the protesters) knock about, maul, mistreat, ill-treat, abuse, (inf) beat up.

mania n 1 (Sometimes he suffers from depression and sometimes from mania) frenzy, hysteria, wildness, derangement, madness, insanity. 2 (They have a mania for attending auction sales) fixation, obsession, compulsion, fascination, passion, enthusiasm, fad.

manipulate vb 1 (manipulate the controls of the aircraft) handle, operate, use, manage, manoeuvre. 2 (A clever lawyer can manipulate a jury) influence, control, guide, exploit.

mankind n (the history of mankind) man, humankind, the human race, Homo sapiens.

manly adj 1 (a manly figure) masculine, virile. 2 (showing manly characteristics) manful, brave, courageous, gallant.

manner n 1 (She does the work in an efficient manner) way, means, fashion, style, method, system. 2 (They dislike their employer's manner) attitude, behaviour, conduct, bearing, look.

manners npl (The children should be taught manners) polite behaviour, politeness, courtesy, social graces, etiquette.

mannish adj (rather a mannish voice) masculine, unfeminine, unwomanly, (inf) butch.

manoeuvre vb (He manoeuvred the piece of metal into position) guide, steer, ease, move, negotiate, manipulate.

manoeuvre vb 1 (army manoeuvres) movement, operation, exercise. 2 (It was a clever manoeuvre to try and obtain promotion) move, tactic, trick, stratagem, scheme, ploy, ruse.

mansion n (The rich family live in a huge mansion) manor house, stately home.

manual adj 1 (a manual gear change) by hand, hand-operated. 2 (manual workers rather than desk workers) physical, labouring.

manual n (an instruction manual with the washing machine) handbook, instructions, guide, guidebook.

manufacture vb (a factory manufacturing computer parts) make, produce, build, construct, turn out.

manure n (farmers spreading manure on the ground) dung, fertilizer.

many adj (many people did not turn up) numerous, a large number, innumerable, countless, (inf) a lot of, (inf) lots of, (inf) oodles of.

map n (a map of the city centre) chart, plan, diagram, guide.

march vb 1 (The soldiers marched along) walk, stride, tramp, parade, file.

2 (*Time marches on*) progress, advance, go on, continue.

margin n **1** (*They won by a narrow margin*) amount, difference. **2** (*We have so little money that there is little margin for error*) scope, room, allowance, latitude, leeway. **3** (*the margin of the lake*) edge, side, border, verge, boundary.

marginal adj (*There has been only a marginal improvement*) slight, minimal, small, tiny, minor, insignificant.

mark n **1** (*the dirty marks on the table-cloth*) stain, spot, speck, smear, streak, blotch, smudge. **2** (*a mark of respect*) sign, symbol, indication, token. **3** (*His war experiences had left their mark on him*) impression, effect, impact, influence, imprint.

mark vb **1** (*The hot teacups marked the table*) stain, smear, streak, blotch, smudge. **2** (*mark the battle sites on the map*) indicate, label, flag, tag. **3** (*teachers marking exam papers*) correct, assess, evaluate, appraise. **4** (*They marked his birthday with a huge party*) celebrate, commemorate, observe. **5** (*You should mark what the headmaster says*) pay attention to, take heed of, heed, note, take notice of, mind.

market n (*tourists buying souvenirs in the market*) market place, bazaar. **2** (*There is no market for such expensive goods in this part of the city*) demand, call, need.

maroon vb (*He was marooned on a desert island*) abandon, forsake, desert, strand.

marriage n **1** (*the marriage of their daughter to the son of their best friends*) wedding. **2** (*Their marriage lasted twenty years*) matrimony, union.

marry vb **1** (*The couple will marry later in the year*) be married, wed, be wed, become man and wife, (*inf*) tie the knot, (*inf*) get hitched. **2** (*They decided to marry their skills and set up business together*) join, unite, combine, merge.

marsh n (*plants that grow in marshes*) marshland, bog, swamp, mire, quagmire.

martial adj **1** (*the martial arts*) warlike, militant, combative, belligerent, pugnacious. **2** (*martial law*) military, army.

martyr n (*early martyrs killed because of their Christian faith*) victim, sufferer.

marvel n (*The pyramids are one of the marvels of the world*) wonder, sensation, phenomenon, miracle.

marvel vb (*We marvelled at the exploits of the acrobats*) be amazed, be astonished, stare, gape, wonder at.

marvellous adj **1** (*admire the marvellous exploits of the acrobats*) amazing, astonishing, astounding, sensational, breathtaking, spectacular, remarkable, extraordinary. **2** (*We had a marvellous evening at the theatre*) splendid, wonderful, glorious, excellent, enjoyable.

masculine adj **1** (*That tends to be a masculine habit*) male, manlike. **2** (*She says she likes really masculine men*) manly, virile, (*inf*) macho.

mash vb (*mash the potatoes*) pulp, purée, crush, pound.

mask vb (*We planted trees at the bottom of the garden to mask the view of the factory*) screen, camouflage, hide, conceal, cover up, blot out.

mass n 1 (*a mass of wood*) block, lump, hunk, chunk, piece, (*inf*) wodge. 2 (*measure the mass of the body*) size, dimension, bulk, capacity. 3 (*A mass of people attended the meeting*) many, crowd, throng, multiplexity, mob, crowd, host.

massacre vb (*The world was shocked at the massacre of civilians*) slaughter, carnage, mass murder, butchery, pogrom.

massage vb (*She massaged their stiff limbs*) knead, rub, pummel.

masses npl (*The leader did not care what the masses thought*) the people, the common people, the public, the populace, the mob.

massive adj (*They built a massive wall round their estate*) huge, enormous, immense, vast, colossal, gigantic, mammoth.

master n 1 (*In earlier time a master would have many servants*) lord, owner, employer. 2 (*He likes to think that he is master in the household*) chief, head, boss. 3 (*He is master of the ship*) captain, skipper. 4 (*Several golf masters took part in the tournament*) expert, professional, virtuoso, genius, (*inf*) ace. 5 (*pupils being taught by the French master*) schoolmaster, schoolteacher, tutor.

master vb 1 (*unable to master his horse/He must try to master his emotions*) control, subdue, check, curb, quell. 2 (*She seems unable to master the techniques of driving*) learn, grasp, understand, (*inf*) get the hang of.

match n 1 (*Take bets on who will win the football match*) contest, competition, game, tournament, trial, bout. 2 (*She was no match for the stronger player*) equal, equivalent, counterpart, rival. 3 (*Their parents tried to arrange a match*) marriage, union.

mate n 1 (*He goes to the pub with his mates every week*) friend, companion, comrade, workman, classmate, (*inf*) chum, (*inf*) pal, (*inf*) buddy. 2 (*a plumber's mate*) apprentice, assistant. 3 (*the mate of this glove*) fellow, pair, match. 4 (*Her friends think she is looking for a mate*) spouse, partner, husband/wife.

material n 1 (*dresses made of a silky material*) cloth, fabric, stuff, textile. 2 (*organic material*) matter, substance, stuff. 3 (*research material for his novel*) information, facts, details, data, (*inf*) gen.

materialize vb 1 (*We had very elaborate plans but they did not materialize*) happen, come into being, come about, occur. 2 (*Suddenly figures materialized out of the fog*) appear, come into view, become visible, emerge.

maternal adj (*maternal feelings*) motherly.

matrimony adj (*She feels she is not ready for matrimony*) marriage, wedlock.

matted adj (*The child's hair was dirty and matted*) tangled, knotted, tousled, unkempt.

matter n 1 (*There are important matters to discuss*) topic, issue, subject. 2 (*It was no laughing matter*) affair, business, situation, circumstance.

3 (*waste matter*) material, substance, stuff. **4** (*What is the matter with the car?*) problem, trouble, difficulty. **5** (*matter oozing from the wound*) pus, discharge.

matter vb (*Will it matter if we arrive a bit late?*) be of importance, be important, make any difference, count, be relevant.

mature adj **1** (*mature human beings*) adult, grown-up, grown, fully grown. **2** (*mature fruit/mature cheese*) ripe, ripened, ready, mellow.

maul vb **1** (*The zoo keeper was mauled by a lion*) tear to pieces, lacerate, mutilate, mangle. **2** (*He was accused of mauling the female employees*) paw, molest.

maximum adj (*the maximum number*) highest, greatest, utmost.

maybe perhaps, possibly.

maze n (*get lost in the maze of corridors in the hospital*) labyrinth, network, mesh, confusion.

meadow n (*cows grazing in the meadow*) field, grassland, pasture.

meagre adj (*unable to feed themselves on their meagre supply of money*) sparse, scarce, scanty, paltry, inadequate, insufficient, (*inf*) measly.

mean vb **1** (*What did his words mean?*) signify, indicate, convey, denote, stand for, suggest, imply. **2** (*We did not mean to hurt her*) intend, plan, set out, aim, propose. **3** (*I am afraid that this will mean war*) lead to, involve, result in, give rise to.

mean adj **1** (*He's too mean to buy anyone a Christmas present*) miserly,

niggardly, parsimonious, penny-pinching, grasping, greedy. **2** (*It was a mean thing to take the child's sweets*) nasty, disagreeable, foul, vile, contemptible, hateful, cruel.

meaning n **1** (*He does not know the meaning of the word*) sense, significance, drift, gist, implication. **2** (*His life seems to have no meaning anymore*) point, value, worth. **3** (*She gave him a look full of meaning*) significance, eloquence.

means n **1** (*We have no means of getting there*) way, method, manner, course. **2** (*His father is a man of means*) wealth, riches, money, property, substance. **3** (*They have not the means to buy the car*) money, capital, finance, funds, resources.

measure n **1** (*use a linear measure*) standard, scale, system. **2** (*They had to take drastic measures to stop the truancy in the school*) action, act, course of action, step, means.

measure vb (*measure the length of the room*) calculate, estimate, compute.

measurement n (*take the measurements of the room*) size, dimensions, proportions, extent, capacity.

mechanism n (*the mechanism that drives the machine*) machinery, workings, apparatus, device.

meddle vb (*His neighbours tried to meddle in his affairs*) interfere, intrude, pry, butt in.

media npl (*The politician blamed his unpopularity on the media*) the press, journalists, radio and television.

medicine n (*The doctor gave the patient*

some *medicine*) medication, drug, medicament.

mediocre adj (*She used to be at the top of the class but her work this term has been mediocre*) average, ordinary, indifferent, middling, passable, adequate, uninspired.

meditate vb (*take time to meditate on the gravity of the matter*) think about, contemplate, reflect on, consider, deliberate on.

medium adj (*of medium height*) average, middling.

meek adj (*meek people being bullied by the others*) docile, gentle, humble, patient, long-suffering.

meet vb 1 (*I met an old friend by chance in the high street*) encounter, come across, run into, bump into. 2 (*The committee meet on Thursday afternoons*) gather, assemble, congregate. 3 (*They met the demands of the job*) satisfy, fulfil, comply with. 4 (*meet one's responsibilities*) carry out, perform, execute. 5 (*He met death bravely*) face, encounter, confront. 6 (*where the two roads meet*) join, connect, unite, adjoin.

meeting n 1 (*A politician addressed the meeting*) gathering, assembly, conference. 2 (*a happy meeting between the two old friends*) encounter.

melancholy adj (*in a melancholy mood*) depressed, dejected, gloomy.

melancholy n depression, gloom, blues, low spirits.

mellow adj 1 (*mellow fruit*) ripe, mature, juicy, luscious. 2 (*She spoke in mellow tones*) sweet, tuneful, melodious,

dulcet. 3 (*in a mellow mood after a good dinner*) cheerful, happy, genial, jovial.

melodious adj (*melodious sounds*) tuneful, musical, harmonious, dulcet.

melodramatic adj (*Her reaction to the news was rather melodramatic*) theatrical, overdone, extravagant.

melt vb 1 (*The sun had melted the snow*) thaw, soften. 2 (*solids melting rapidly*) dissolve, thaw, defrost, soften.

memento n (*He gave her a memento of their holiday*) souvenir, keepsake, token, remembrance.

memorable adj (*a memorable occasion*) unforgettable, momentous, significant, notable,.

memory n 1 (*Her memory of the event is rather hazy*) recollection, recall. 2 (*They built a statue in memory of the soldiers killed in the war*) remembrance, commemoration, honour.

menacing adj (*He gave them a menacing look*) threatening, ominous, frightening, sinister.

mend vb 1 (*He mended the broken table*) repair, fix, renovate, restore. 2 (*She mended the children's socks*) darn, sew, patch.

mention vb 1 (*She mentioned your name as someone who might be interested in the job*) refer to, allude to, touch on. 2 (*She did mention that she was thinking of leaving*) remark, comment, observe.

mercenary adj (*She is very mercenary and wants to marry a rich man*) grasping, greedy, avaricious, (inf) gold-digging.

merciful adj (a merciful judge) lenient, compassionate, forgiving, sympathetic, humane.

mercy n (The judge showed mercy to the man who had stolen money to feed his children) leniency, clemency, pity, compassion, forgiveness.

merge vb 1 (The two firms have merged and staff have been made redundant) amalgamate, combine, unite, join forces. 2 (The colours in the picture seemed to merge) blend, fuse, mingle.

merit n 1 (He put forward the merits of the scheme) advantage, asset, plus, good point. 2 (She received a certificate of merit) distinction, credit. 3 (The artist's work is thought to have little merit) worth, value.

merry adj (merry children) cheerful, gay, happy, light-hearted, joyful.

mess n 1 (their mother asked them to clear up the mess in the kitchen) clutter, litter, shambles, disorder, untidiness.

message n (They were out and so we left a message for them) note, memo, word, information, news, communication.

method n (teaching methods) system, technique, procedure, routine.

microscopic adj (microscopic insects) tiny, minute, minuscule.

middle n (The children formed a circle and the little girl was in the middle/right in the middle of the city) centre, heart.

might n (unable to overcome the might of the enemy) power, force, strength.

mighty n 1 (a mighty blow) powerful, strong, forceful, hefty. 2 (mighty mountains) huge, massive, vast, enormous, colossal.

migrate vb (swallow migrating to the south in the summer/people migrating to find work) move, relocate.

mild adj 1 (mild climate/mild weather) moderate, warm, soft, balmy. 2 (She is usually of a mild disposition but she really lost her temper at the children) gentle, tender, soft-hearted, warm-hearted, compassionate, lenient, calm. 3 (a mild sauce) subtle, bland, non-spicy.

militant adj (in a militant mood) belligerent, aggressive, pugnacious, combative, warlike.

mimic vb (The pupil was caught mimicking the teacher) impersonate, give an impersonation of, imitate, copy, parody, (inf) take off.

mind vb 1 (Tell him to mind the low ceiling—he might bump his head) be careful of, watch out for, look out for, beware of. 2 (I am sure that they won't mind if you use the phone) object, care, bother, be upset, complain, disapprove. 3 (You should mind your own business) attend to, pay attention to, concentrate on.

mind n 1 (She failed her exams although she has a good mind) brain, intellect, powers of reasoning. 2 (It brought thoughts of her father to mind) memory, recollection, remembrance.

mingle vb 1 (the colours mingled) mix, blend. 2 (She was too shy to mingle with the other guests at the party) mix, socialize, circulate.

miniature adj (a miniature railway) small-scale, mini, diminutive, minute, tiny.

minimum adj (the minimum price) lowest, smallest, least, bottom.

minute adj 1 (insects which are minute creatures) tiny, diminutive, microscopic, minuscule. 2 (There is just a minute difference between the two) tiny, insignificant, infinitesimal, negligible.

miracle n (miracles described in the Bible) wonder, marvel.

miraculous adj (She made a miraculous recovery from the accident) amazing, remarkable, extraordinary, incredible.

mirage n (The travellers thought they saw an oasis in the desert but it was a mirage) hallucination, illusion, vision.

mirror n (She looked in the mirror to apply her make-up) looking-glass, glass.

mirth n (There was a lot of mirth at the party) laughter, merriment, hilarity, revelry.

misadventure n (The verdict was death by misadventure) accident, misfortune, mischance.

misbehave vb (The children misbehaved when their mother was away) behave badly, be naughty, be disobedient, (inf) act up.

miscellaneous adj (a miscellaneous collection of old clothes for the jumble sale) assorted, mixed, varied, motley.

mischief n (children who are bored and getting up to mischief) mischievousness, naughtiness, bad behaviour, misbehaviour, misconduct, wrongdoing, trouble.

mischievous adj 1 (mischievous children) naughty, badly behaved, disobedient, rascally, roguish. 2 (They were

upset by the mischievous rumours their neighbours spread about them) malicious, spiteful.

miser n (The old miser would not give any money to charity) Scrooge, skinflint, niggard, (inf) cheapskate.

miserly adj (They were too miserly to give any money to charity) mean, niggardly, parsimonious, tight-fisted, Scrooge-like, (inf) stingy.

misery n (the misery of being homeless and hungry) wretchedness, hardship, suffering, unhappiness, distress, sorrow.

misfortune n 1 (He endured many misfortunes before becoming a successful businessman) trouble, setback, adversity, calamity, disaster. 2 (By misfortune we missed the last bus) bad luck, ill luck, accident.

misgiving n (We had misgivings about lending them the car) qualm, doubt, reservation, suspicion.

mislay n (Grandfather has mislaid his glasses again) lose, misplace.

mislead vb (She deliberately tried to mislead her parents) misinform, deceive, hoodwink.

miss vb 1 (He missed a great opportunity) pass up, let go, 2 (The children are missing their mother) long for, pine for. 3 (He missed the shot) bungle, botch, muff. 4 (We tried to miss heavy traffic by leaving early) avoid, evade, escape, dodge. 5 (Try not to miss anything out when you give an account of the accident) leave out, omit, forget, overlook.

missile n (The army invested in guided

missiles) projectile, rocket.

mist n (*There was a morning mist but it soon lifted*) haze, fog.

mistake n 1 (*His homework was full of mistakes*) error, inaccuracy, fault, blunder, (inf) slip-up, (inf) howler.

misty adj 1 (*a misty morning*) hazy, foggy. 2 (*only a misty idea of what we are supposed to be doing*) vague, hazy, nebulous. 3 (*My eyesight is a bit misty just now*) blurred, fuzzy.

mix vb (*mix the ingredients for the cake*) blend, combine, put together. 2 (*She never mixes with the rest of the people in the street*) socialize, associate with, have dealings with. 3 (*The demands of her job and looking after children just don't mix*) be compatible. 4 (*She mixed up the two parcels and sent us the wrong one*) muddle, jumble, confuse. 5 (*I think that he is mixed up in the crime*) involve, implicate.

mixed adj (*a mixed lot of old clothes for the jumble sale*) miscellaneous, assorted, varied, motley.

mixture n 1 (*Pour the cake mixture into a bowl*) mix, blend, compound, concoction. 2 (*There was quite a mixture of people on the jury*) miscellany, assortment, variety, mix, collection.

moan vb 1 (*The injured woman moaned in pain*) groan. 2 (*She was always moaning about how poor she was although she spent a lot of money on clothes*) complain, grumble, whinge, (inf) grouse, (inf) gripe.

mob n 1 (*an angry mob of protesters*) crowd, horde, throng, multitude. 2 (*She thinks she is too aristocratic to mix with the mob*) the common people, the masses, the populace, the rabble.

mobile adj 1 (*a mobile caravan/a mobile shop*) movable, transportable, travelling. 2 (*The patients are mobile*) moving, walking.

mock vb (*The children mocked the new girl because she was wearing very thick glasses*) ridicule, jeer at, sneer at, laugh at, tease, mimic.

model n 1 (*a model of an old aeroplane*) replica, copy, imitation. 2 (*What model of car would you like?*) design, style, variety, type. 3 (*The architects showed us the model of the new housing estate*) prototype, design, pattern. 4 (*She wants to be a model*) fashion model, mannequin. 5 (*The art teacher used one of the pupils as a model*) artist's model, subject, sitter.

moderate adj 1 (*moderate winds*) mild, gentle, light. 2 (*We had moderate success*) reasonable, acceptable, tolerable, adequate, middling, average. 3 (*The prisoners' demands seemed moderate*) reasonable, within reason, fair. 4 (*a moderate lifestyle*) restrained, controlled, sober, steady.

modern adj 1 (*politicians in modern times*) present-day, present, contemporary, current. 2 (*Her ideas on education are very modern/modern styles of clothes*) up to date, new, advanced, progressive, fashionable, (inf) trendy.

modest adj 1 (*He had accomplished a great deal in life but was very modest*) unassuming, self-effacing, humble. 2 (*She was asked to wear modest* *clothes for the occasion*) demure, seemly, decent, decorous. **3** (*They are rich but live in a modest house*) humble, plain, simple, inexpensive. **4** (*Their demands seemed very modest*) small, slight, limited, reasonable, moderate.

modify vb (*They may have to modify the design of the new plane slightly*) alter, change, adjust, vary.

moist adj **1** (*moist weather*) wet, damp, dank, rainy, humid, clammy. **2** (*soil moist after the rain*) wet, damp. **3** (*a moist fruit cake*) juicy, soft.

moisture n (*moisture running down the walls of the damp house*) water, liquid, wetness, wet, dampness.

mole n (*a small mole on her back*) blemish, blotch, discoloration.

moment n **1** (*The peculiar noise lasted only a moment*) short time, instant, second, flash, (*inf*) jiffy. **2** (*It was a moment of great importance when the leaders first met*) time, occasion, point in time. **3** (*discuss matters of great moment*) importance, significance, note, seriousness.

momentous adj (*a momentous event in history*) crucial, important, significant, serious.

monarch n (*French monarchs*) ruler, sovereign, king/queen.

money n (*They have enough money to buy a new car*) cash, capital, finance, (*inf*) wherewithal.

monitor vb (*doctors monitoring the patient's condition*) watch, observe, check, keep an eye on.

monotonous adj **1** (*people who have to do monotonous jobs*) without variety,

repetitious, routine, humdrum, boring, dull, tedious. **2** (*He has a very monotonous job*) flat, droning.

monstrous adj **1** (*They serve monstrous helpings of food/monstrous lorries speeding down the motorways*) huge, immense, vast, colossal. **2** (*Sacking them for asking for more money was a monstrous thing to do*) shocking, outrageous, disgraceful, scandalous, terrible, dreadful, foul, vile, despicable.

monument n (*a monument to soldiers who died in the war*) memorial, statue, shrine.

mood n **1** (*They were in a happy mood*) humour, temper, state of mind, disposition. **2** (*She is in a mood*) bad mood, bad temper, sulks.

moody adj (*Teenagers are often accused of being moody*) temperamental, unpredictable, irritable, short-tempered, bad-tempered, touchy, sulky.

moon vb (*mooning around complaining of boredom*) mope, idle, languish.

moor vb (*moor the boat in the harbour*) secure, tie up, fasten, anchor.

mope vb (*Since her boyfriend went away she has been moping around the house*) be miserable, be unhappy, brood, fret, sulk, idle, languish.

moral adj (*They are far too moral to break the law*) upright, honourable, virtuous, righteous, law-abiding, pure.

morale n (*The team's morale was low after their third defeat in a row*) spirit, confidence, self-confidence, heart.

morsel n (*a morsel of cheese*) mouthful, bite, piece, bit, crumb, little.

mortal adj **1** (*a mortal blow*) deadly, fatal,

lethal, destructive. **2** (*All of us are mortal*) human, earthly.

mostly adv (*The people in the group were mostly quite young*) for the most part, mainly, in the main, on the whole, largely, chiefly.

mother n (*her mother and father*) female parent, (*inf*) mum, (*inf*) mummy.

motherly adj (*The school matron is a very motherly person*) maternal, kind, loving, warm.

motion adj (*sickness caused by the motion of the boat*) movement, moving.

motivate vb (*trying to motivate the children into reading novels*) stimulate, inspire, stir, persuade.

motive n (*She seems to have had no motive for the murder*) reason, cause, grounds, basis.

mottled adj (*skin with rather a mottled appearance*) blotchy, speckled, flecked, spotted, marbled.

motto n (*'Service with a smile' is the shop's motto*) slogan, saying, watchword.

mould n **1** (*cheese covered in mould/old wood with a layer of mould*) fungus, mildew, must. **2** (*put the jelly in a mould to set/hot metal left to set in a mould*) shape, cast.

mouldy adj (*food having gone mouldy in the cupboard*) mildewed, musty.

mound n (*mounds of leaves in the garden*) heap, pile, stack, bank.

mount vb **1** (*mount the stairs to go to bed*) climb, ascend, go up. **2** (*mount the bus*) get on, board. **3** (*He mounted the picture*) frame. **4** (*mount a book exhibition*) put on, set up, stage, organize,

arrange. **5** (*If you save a little each week your savings will soon mount up*) grow, increase, accumulate, pile up. **6** (*House prices are mounting*) rise, go up, increase, soar, escalate.

mountain n **1** (*A climber was injured on the mountain*) peak, hill. **2** (*They received mountains of mail complaining about the programme*) pile, mound, heap, stack.

mourn vb (*She is still mourning after the death of her husband last year*) grieve, sorrow, be sad.

mournful adj (*wearing a mournful expression*) sad, sorrowful, dejected, gloomy.

mouth n **1** (*the mouth of the river*) outlet, estuary. **2** (*the mouth of the cave*) opening, entry, entrance.

move vb **1** (*They moved slowly round the room*) walk, go, proceed, progress. **2** (*We moved the furniture from one room to another*) carry, transport, transfer, convey, shift. **3** (*He is moving because he has a new job*) move house, relocate, leave, go away. **4** (*She was moved by the sight of the orphan children*) affect, touch, upset, disturb. **5** (*The sight moved her to tears/They finally felt moved to act*) rouse, stir, influence, induce, prompt. **6** (*At the meeting she moved that the chairman resign*) propose, put forward, suggest.

move n (*It is difficult to predict what our opponent's next move will be*) act, action, step, deed.

moving adj **1** (*the moving parts of the machinery*) movable, mobile. **2** (*the moving force behind the scheme*) driving, stimulating, dynamic. **3** (*a moving story about two orphans*) touching, affecting, emotional, emotive.

mow vb (*mow the grass*) cut, clip, trim.

mud n dirt, slime, sludge, (*inf*) muck.

muddle vb **1** (*She accidentally muddled the books in the library*) confuse, mix up, jumble up, disorganize, mess up. **2** (*New faces tend to muddle the old woman*) confuse, bewilder, perplex, puzzle.

muffle vb **1** (*You must muffle yourself up against the cold*) wrap up, cover up. **2** (*try to muffle the loud noise*) stifle, suppress, deaden, quieten.

mug n (*a mug of cocoa*) beaker, cup.

mug vb (*They mugged an old man to get his wallet*) attack, assault, rob, (*inf*) beat up.

muggy adj (*muggy weather*) close, stuffy, sultry, oppressive, humid, clammy.

multiple adj (*She received multiple fractures in the accident*) many, several, numerous, various.

multiply vb **1** (*mice multiplying rapidly*) reproduce, breed. **2** (*Their troubles seem to be multiplying*) increase, grow, spread, accumulate.

multitude n (*They were surprised at the multitude of people who turned up for the meeting*) crowd, horde, mob.

mumble vb (*mumbling a few words*) mutter, whisper, murmur.

munch vb (*munching an apple*) chew, bite, gnaw.

mundane adj (*a meeting supposedly designed to discuss important church issues but ending up discussing mundane matters*) commonplace, common, ordinary, everyday, routine, normal, typical.

murder n (*charged with murder*) killing, slaying, homicide, slaughter.

murder vb (*convicted of murdering his father*) kill, slay, put to death, (*inf*) do in, (*inf*) bump off.

murky adj **1** (*murky water*) muddy, dirty, cloudy, opaque. **2** (*a murky time of day*) dark, dim, gloomy.

murmur vb (*She murmured that she wanted to leave*) whisper, mutter, mumble.

muscle n (*He strained the muscle while high-jumping*) tendon, sinew, ligament.

muscular adj (*muscular young men involved in body-building*) brawny, strapping, hefty, burly.

muse vb (*He mused over the situation*) think about, consider, contemplate, meditate on, reflect on.

mushroom vb (*housing estates mushrooming everywhere*) spring up, shoot up, sprout, boom, thrive.

music n (*people enjoying the music*) melody, tune, air, rhythm.

musical adj (*a musical sound*) tuneful, melodic, melodious, sweet-sounding, dulcet.

muss vb (*Climbing through the hedge had mussed her hair*) disarrange, tousle, dishevel, make untidy.

muster vb (*The general mustered the troops/He had to muster all his energy to climb the stairs*) gather, summon, rally.

musty adj (*a musty smell in the old house*) mouldy, stale, fusty, stuffy, airless, damp.

mute adj (animals making a mute appeal for help) silent, speechless, unspoken, dumb, wordless.

muted adj (muted colours) soft, subtle, subdued, discreet, understated.

mutilate vb (soldiers horribly mutilated in the war) cripple, maim, mangle, disfigure, dismember.

mutinous adj (a mutinous crew on board ship) rebellious, revolutionary, insubordinate, disobedient, unruly.

mutiny n (mutiny on board ship) rebellion, revolt, insurrection, revolution, riot.

mutter vb (She muttered that she did not want to go) mumble, murmur, whisper, complain.

mutual adj (They have mutual friends) common, shared, joint.

mysterious adj 1 (There were mysterious noises coming from the room where they were getting ready for the party) peculiar, strange, odd, weird, curious, puzzling. 2 (They were being very mysterious about where they were going) secretive, reticent, evasive.

mythical adj 1 (The dragon is a mythical creature) legendary, mythological, fabulous, imaginary, fictitious. 2 (She is always talking about her rich uncle but we think that he is a mythical figure) imaginary, fantasy, make-believe, invented, made up, (inf) pretend.

N

nag vb 1 (She is always nagging her husband) scold, carp at, find fault with, bully. 2 (children nagging their mother to buy them sweets) pester, badger, harass, (inf) hassle.

nail n (the joiner's wood and nails) pin, tack.

naive adj (She was so naive that she believed every word he said) gullible, trusting, innocent.

naked adj 1 (She could not answer the door as she was naked after her shower) nude, in the nude, undressed, unclothed, bare, stark naked. 2 (a naked flame) unprotected, uncovered, exposed. 3 (the naked truth) undisguised, unadorned, stark, plain, simple.

name n 1 (We don't know the name of the book) title. 2 (He made his name in the theatre) reputation, fame, renown, distinction.

nap n catnap, sleep, doze, (inf) snooze, (inf) forty winks.

narrate vb (The old man narrated the story of his life) tell, relate, recount, describe.

narrow adj 1 (They have very narrow wrists) slender, slim, thin. 2 (They stock only a narrow range of goods) limited, restricted, small.

narrow-minded adj (She was too narrow-minded to listen to other people's points of view) intolerant, prejudiced, bigoted, biased.

nasty n 1 (The rotting meat was a nasty sight) unpleasant, disagreeable, horrible, foul. 2 (a nasty old woman) disagreeable, bad-tempered, spiteful, mean.

nation n (an organization consisting of the nations of the world) country, land, state.

nationalistic adj (He is nationalistic and does not like foreigners) patriotic, chauvinistic.

native adj 1 (the native plants of the region) indigenous, original, local. 2 (their native instincts) natural, inborn.

natural adj 1 (a shop selling natural produce) organic, pure. 2 (natural behaviour) unaffected, simple, genuine, spontaneous. 3 (their natural instincts) inborn, native, instinctive. 4 (The illness took its natural course) usual, normal, regular, ordinary, common.

nature n 1 (The children are interested in nature) environment, Mother Nature, creation. 2 (He has a warm nature) temperament, disposition, character, personality.

naughty adj (The children were being naughty) badly behaved, bad, mischievous, misbehaving, disobedient.

nauseate vb (The sight of the rotting meat nauseated her) sicken, make sick, turn one's stomach, disgust, revolt.

navigate vb (He navigated the ship through the narrow straits) steer, pilot, direct, guide, manoeuvre, drive.

near adj (The station is very near) nearby, close, at hand, handy.

nearly adv 1 (We nearly drowned) almost, all but, as good as, practically. 2 (They collected nearly £500) almost, roughly, approximately.

neat adj 1 (children looking neat going to school) tidy, smart, spruce. 2 (They made a mess of the neat room) tidy, orderly.

necessary adj (They took the necessary action in time) essential, needful, indispensable, required, vital.

need n 1 (There is no need to shout) necessity, requirement, obligation, call. 2 (Their needs are very few) want, wish, demand, requirement. 3 (The charity helps people in need) want, poverty, deprivation.

neglect vb (She went to the cinema and neglected her work) pay no attention to, disregard, ignore, overlook, skip, shirk.

negligent adj (He was found negligent for falling asleep on duty) neglectful, careless, inattentive, sloppy.

negotiate vb 1 (The two sides succeeded in negotiating a settlement) work out, arrange, agree on. 2 (The two sides are negotiating about a financial settlement) bargain, hold talks, discuss.

neighbourhood n (They are moving to a new neighbourhood) district, area, region, locality.

nerve n 1 (Climbing the outside of the tower requires nerve) courage, bravery, daring, pluck, (inf) guts. 2 (They had

the nerve to ask us to pay more) impertinence, impudence, cheek, brazenness, effrontery, temerity.

nervous adj 1 (He was feeling nervous about his visit to the doctor) edgy, on edge, tense, anxious, agitated. 2 (They are very nervous people) timid, anxious, edgy, tense, apprehensive.

network n 1 (The pattern consisted of a network of lines) latticework, mesh. 2 (When looking for work she contacted her network of old friends) system, organization.

neutral n 1 (It is essential for referees to be neutral) impartial, unbiased, unprejudiced, open-minded, detached, disinterested. 2 (She was looking for curtains in neutral colours) indefinite, colourless, beige, stone.

never adv (She never lies) not ever, not at all, under no circumstances.

new adj 1 (They are buying a new car) brand new, unused. 2 (We need some new ideas) fresh, original, imaginative. 3 (They have introduced a new system of cataloguing books) different, modern, up-to-date.

news npl (There has been no news of the missing climbers) information, facts, communication, word, data.

next adj 1 (the next bus/the next prime minister) following, subsequent, succeeding. 2 (the next house in the avenue) neighbouring, adjacent, adjoining, closest, nearest.

nibble vb (mice nibbling on a piece of cheese) bite, gnaw, munch.

nice adj 1 (His father is a nice person) pleasant, friendly, kind, agreeable, charming. **2** (*We had a nice time at the theatre*) pleasant, enjoyable, delightful. **3** (*It was a nice day for the wedding*) fine, sunny, dry. **4** (*There is a nice distinction in meaning between the two words*) fine, subtle, minute, precise.

night n (*when night fell*) night-time, darkness, dark.

nimble adj **1** (*The old lady was still very nimble*) agile, lithe, quick-moving, spry. **2** (*The knitters had very nimble fingers*) supple, deft.

nip vb **1** (*The little boy cried out when his friend nipped him*) pinch, tweak, squeeze. **2** (*The dog nipped her ankle*) bite, snap at. **3** (*He's just nipped out to the bank*) dash, rush, dart, hurry.

noble adj **1** (*the king and the noble people of the land*) aristocratic, high-born, titled, blue-blooded. **2** (*a knight noted for his noble deeds*) brave, courageous, gallant, heroic, honourable, chivalrous. **3** (*The tourists admired the city's noble buildings*) impressive, imposing, magnificent, stately, grand.

nod vb **1** (*He nodded his head in agreement*) bow, incline, bob. **2** (*The audience began to nod*) nod off, drop off, fall asleep, doze.

noise n (*They were kept awake by the noise of traffic*) sound, loud sound, din, racket, clamour, row, commotion, hubbub, bedlam, pandemonium.

noisy adj **1** (*The teacher tried to quieten the noisy children*) rowdy, boisterous, loud. **2** (*noisy music*) loud, blaring, deafening, ear-splitting.

nondescript adj (*She was wearing nondescript clothes*) unremarkable, un-

distinguished, commonplace, ordinary.

nonsense n (*They told her that she was talking absolute nonsense*) rubbish, drivel, twaddle, gibberish, balderdash.

normal adj **1** (*temperatures that were normal for the time of year*) average, usual, common, standard, ordinary, typical. **2** (*He is of more than normal size*) average, standard.

nosey, nosy adjs (*They have nosey neighbours*) inquisitive, prying, curious, interfering, (*inf*) snooping.

notable adj **1** (*the notable achievements of the politician*) noteworthy, outstanding, remarkable, memorable, important, significant. **2** (*All the notable people in the town were present at the reception*) noted, of note, distinguished, well-known, eminent, prominent.

notch n (*make notches in the stick*) nick, dent, cut, indentation.

note n **1** (*It is wise to keep a note of how much you spend*) record, account. **2** (*I wrote her a note thanking her*) letter, line, message. **3** (*His advice is worthy of note*) notice, attention, heed, observation. **4** (*people of note in the community*) distinction, eminence, prestige, fame. **5** (*There was a note of sadness in her voice*) tone, sound. **6** (*He changed his notes into coins*) banknote, paper money.

note vb **1** (*She noted the details in her diary*) write down, jot down, put down, enter. **2** (*The police noted that he seemed frightened*) notice, observe, perceive, detect.

notice n 1 (*Very little escapes the head-master's notice*) attention, observation, heed. 2 (*We have received notice of a meeting to be held next week*) notification, information, news, announcement. 3 (*a notice on the board giving details of the meeting*) poster, handbill, information sheet, bulletin, circular. 4 (*Several workers have received their notice*) notice to quit, redundancy notice, the sack, (*inf*) marching orders.

notice vb (*We could not help noticing the bruise on her face*) see, observe, note, detect, spot, perceive, discern.

noticeable adj 1 (*The scar on her cheek was quite noticeable*) visible, obvious, plain, plain to see. 2 (*There had been a noticeable improvement in the pupil's work*) marked, obvious, evident, conspicuous, distinct.

notify vb (*They notified the police about the stranger in the garden*) inform, tell, advise, acquaint.

notion n (*They have some peculiar notions*) idea, belief, opinion, conviction, theory, thought.

notorious adj (*He is a notorious criminal*) infamous, well-known, scandalous.

nourishing adj (*give the children nourishing food*) nutritious, healthy, wholesome, beneficial.

novel adj (*He had a novel approach to the teaching of history*) new, fresh, different, original, unusual.

novelty n (*a stall at the seaside selling novelties*) knick-knack, trinket, bauble, souvenir, memento, gimmick.

novice n (*They are complete novices at the game*) beginner, learner, trainee, apprentice, newcomer, recruit.

nude adj (*They were sunbathing nude*) in the nude, naked, stark naked, bare, undressed, unclothed.

nudge vb (*She nudged him in the ribs to tell him to keep quiet*) prod, jab, poke, dig, elbow, push.

nuisance n (*She regards the cat next door as a nuisance*) pest, bother, irritant, problem, trial, bore.

numb adj (*Her fingers were numb with cold*) without feeling, immobilized, frozen, paralysed.

number n 1 (*write down all the numbers*) figure, numeral, digit. 2 (*A large number of people attended*) quantity, amount, collection. 3 (*This is last week's number of the magazine*) issue, edition, copy.

numerous adj (*He has numerous reasons for leaving*) many, very many, innumerable, several.

nurse vb 1 (*She nursed the sick child*) take care of, look after, tend, treat. 2 (*They still nurse feelings of resentment against their parents*) have, hold, harbour, entertain.

nutritious adj (*get the children to eat nutritious food instead of junk food*) nourishing, healthy, health-giving, wholesome, beneficial.

O

oath n 1 (*take an oath of loyalty to the king*) vow, promise, pledge, word. 2 (*She was offended by the oaths used by the drunk man*) swear word, curse, obscenity.

obedient adj (*obedient children/obedient dogs*) biddable, well-behaved, well-trained, docile.

obey vb 1 (*obey the school rules*) observe, abide by, comply with, keep to. 2 (*soldiers obeying orders*) carry out, perform, fulfil, execute. 3 (*children taught to obey their parents*) be dutiful to, follow the orders of.

object n 1 (*pick up a wooden object lying on the pavement*) thing, article, item. 2 (*The object of the exercise was to collect money for charity*) aim, goal, purpose, point, objective. 3 (*the object of their abuse*) target, focus, recipient.

object vb (*We objected to the way they handled the situation*) raise objections to, protest against, complain, take exception to, grumble.

objection n (*There were several objections to the scheme*) protest, complaint, grumble.

objectionable adj (*He is a most objectionable young man/We found her manner objectionable*) offensive, obnoxious, unpleasant, disagreeable, nasty.

objective adj (*Referees have to be objective*) impartial, unbiased, unprejudiced, neutral, disinterested, detached.

objective n (*Our objective was to get there before nightfall*) object, aim, goal, target, intention.

obliged adj (*You are not obliged to say anything at this stage*) bound, compelled, forced, required.

obliging adj (*We have very obliging neighbours*) helpful, accommodating, willing, generous, cooperative.

oblivious adj (*They were oblivious to the danger they were in*) unaware, heedless, unheeding, unmindful, unconscious, ignorant.

obnoxious adj (*a most obnoxious sales assistant*) offensive, objectionable, unpleasant, disagreeable, nasty, horrible, odious.

obscene adj (*obscene videos*) pornographic, indecent, blue, bawdy, smutty, dirty.

obscure adj 1 (*For some obscure reason they suddenly decided to leave*) unclear, hidden, concealed, puzzling, mysterious. 2 (*a book by some obscure poet*) unheard of, unknown, little known, insignificant.

obscure vb 1 (*The new block of flats obscures our view of the lake*) hide, conceal, screen, block out. 2 (*His remarks simply obscured the issue*) confuse, muddle, complicate, cloud.

observant adj (*The observant lad was able to get the car's registration number*) sharp-eyed, eagle-eyed, attentive, heedful, vigilant.

observe vb 1 (He observed a man watching his neighbour's house) see, catch sight of, notice, perceive, witness. 2 (All players must observe the rules of the game) obey, keep, abide by, adhere to, comply with, follow, heed. 3 (She observed that it was going to rain) remark, comment, state, announce.

obsession n (She has an obsession about having a spotlessly clean house) fixation, preoccupation, compulsion, mania.

obsolete adj (The factory uses obsolete machinery/The book has a great many obsolete words) outworn, outmoded, antiquated, out of date, old-fashioned, archaic.

obstacle n (the obstacles in the way of progress) hindrance, impediment, obstruction, barrier, bar, hurdle.

obstinate adj (The two sisters had a quarrel and were too obstinate to apologize) stubborn, pig-headed, mulish, headstrong, unyielding.

obstreperous adj (The police tried to control the obstreperous football crowd) unruly, disorderly, rowdy, boisterous, rough, wild, turbulent, riotous.

obstruct vb 1 (fallen trees obstructing the flow of traffic) block, bar, check, halt. 2 (The protesters tried to obstruct progress on the building of the new motorway) hinder, delay, impede, hamper, block, interrupt, hold up.

obstruction n (obstructions to progress) obstacle, impediment, hindrance, hurdle, barrier, bar.

obtain vb (We tried to obtain a copy of the book) get, get hold of, acquire, come by, procure, gain.

obvious adj (It was obvious that she was crying/The bruise on his face was very obvious) clear, clear-cut, plain, noticeable, evident, apparent.

occasion n 1 (They met on several occasions) time, point. 2 (The leaving party was a sad occasion) event, incident, occurrence, happening. 3 (She will go abroad if the occasion arises) opportunity, chance, opening. 4 (They met at a festive occasion) function, gathering, party, (inf) do.

occasional adj (It will be a fine day with occasional showers) infrequent, irregular, sporadic, rare, odd.

occupation n (write down your occupation on the application form) job, employment, profession, business, trade, career.

occupied adj 1 (All the hotel rooms are occupied) full, in use, engaged, taken. 2 (The houses in the new estate are all occupied already) inhabited. 3 (The manager is occupied just now and cannot speak to you) busy, engaged, (inf) tied up.

occupy vb 1 (How many people occupy this flat?) inhabit, live in, reside in, dwell in. 2 (The enemy army occupied the city) take possession of, seize, invade, capture. 3 (How does she occupy her leisure hours?) fill, use, utilize, take up. 4 (They occupy junior posts) hold, have, fill.

occur vb 1 (The police think the murder occurred last night) take place, happen, come about. 2 (The same mistakes *occur throughout the piece of work)* arise, be found, appear, be present. **3** (*It occurred to me that I had seen her before*) come to, enter one's head, strike.

occurrence n (*Car theft is a common occurrence these days*) event, incident, happening.

odd adj **1** (*We thought her behaviour was odd*) strange, peculiar, queer, weird, bizarre, outlandish, abnormal, curious. **2** (*She thinks of him at odd moments*) occasional, random, irregular. **3** (*He found an odd sock*) spare, left over, single, unmatched.

odious adj (*Our new neighbours are odious people*) horrible, nasty, loathsome, detestable, hateful, objectionable, offensive.

odour n (*the odour of frying onions*) smell, aroma, scent, fragrance, stink, stench.

offence n **1** (*They were punished for the offence which they committed*) crime, misdeed, wrong. **2** (*His ungrateful behaviour caused offence*) upset, displeasure, annoyance, disapproval.

offend vb (*He offended her parents by not thanking them for the meal*) hurt, upset, displease, annoy.

offensive adj **1** (*He was forced to apologize for his offensive remarks*) hurtful, upsetting, distressful, abusive. **2** (*He is an offensive person/We noticed an offensive smell*) unpleasant, nasty, horrible, foul, vile, objectionable, odious.

offer vb **1** (*He offered several suggestions*) put forward, propose, submit, suggest. **2** (*We offered to babysit for them*) volunteer. **3** (*The job offers good career prospects*) give, present, afford, supply, furnish.

office n **1** (*His office is on the top floor*) place of business, workplace, room. **2** (*He has the office of company secretary*) post, position, appointment, job.

official adj **1** (*receive official permission/the official documents*) authorized, formal, licensed, certified, legal. **2** (*She had to wear evening dress to the official function*) formal, ceremonial.

officious adj (*the officious man at the counter in the unemployment office*) interfering, meddlesome, bumptious, self-important.

offspring n (*a couple with no offspring*) children, family, young.

oil n **1** (*fry the food in oil, not lard*) cooking oil. **2** (*oil to lubricate the hinges of the gate*) grease, lubrication.

oil vb (*oil the rusty hinges of the gate*) grease, lubricate.

oily adj (*She dislikes oily food*) greasy, fat, fatty.

ointment n (*put ointment on his wound*) medication, cream, lotion.

old adj **1** (*a ward in the hospital full of old people*) elderly, aged, (*inf*) long in the tooth. **2** (*She was wearing old clothes to garden in*) worn, shabby. **3** (*tired of his old ideas*) old-fashioned, outdated, out-of-date, outmoded, antiquated. **4** (*the old ruins in the centre of town*) dilapidated, run-down, ramshackle, crumbling. **5** (*He collects old cars*) antique, veteran, vintage. **6** (*in the old days*) past, bygone, earlier. **7** (*an old girlfriend*) former, ex-, previous.

old-fashioned adj (old-fashioned clothes/old-fashioned ideas) out of date, outdated, out of date, unfashionable, outmoded.

omen n (They were superstitious and thought that walking under a ladder was a bad omen) sign, portent forewarning, prophesy.

ominous adj (We heard the ominous sound of gunfire) threatening, menacing.

omit vb (We omitted his name from the invitation list in error) leave out, exclude, miss out, delete, eliminate.

onlooker n (The police tried to move on the onlookers at the accident scene) observer, witness, eyewitness, spectator, bystander.

ooze vb (Pus was oozing from the wound) flow, discharge, seep, exude, leak, drip.

opaque adj 1 (opaque glass) non-transparent, cloudy. 2 (The waters were opaque with mud) cloudy, dark, murky, hazy.

open adj 1 (The door was open) ajar, unlocked, unbolted, unfastened. 2 (open boxes) uncovered, unsealed. 3 (find some open spaces for the children to run around in) unfenced, unenclosed, extensive, broad, spacious. 4 (maps lying open on the table) spread out, unfolded. 5 (She was quite open about her hatred of them) frank, candid, forthright, honest, blunt, plain-spoken. 6 (There was open hostility between them) obvious, evident, visible, unconcealed.

opening n 1 (an opening in the hedge/an opening in the wall) gap, space, aperture, hole, breach. 2 (at the opening of the meeting) beginning, start, commencement, outset. 3 (There is an opening in the firm for a receptionist) vacancy, position, post, place.

operate vb 1 (The machine suddenly ceased to operate) work, function, go, run. 2 (Can you operate this machine?) work, use, handle. 3 (The surgeon had to operate on her leg) perform surgery on.

operation n 1 (She had to have an operation on her leg) surgery. 2 (The troops took part in a military operation) manoeuvre, campaign, action.

opinion n (We were asked to give our opinions on the state of the company) view, point of view, viewpoint, thought, belief, idea.

opponent n (his opponent in the snooker game) rival, adversary, opposition, enemy, foe.

opportunity n 1 (You should go abroad if the opportunity arises) chance, occasion. 2 (It was a good opportunity to spend some time with her family) chance, occasion, time, moment.

oppose vb (Some of the committee opposed the company's plans for expansion) contest, take a stand against, argue against.

opposite adj 1 (rows of houses opposite each other) facing, face-to-face. 2 (The two brothers were on opposite sides in the dispute) opposing, rival, competitive, warring. 3 (They hold opposite views) differing, different, contrary, conflicting, contradictory, incompatible.

oppress vb (The cruel tyrant oppressed the poor people of the villages) crush, abuse, maltreat, persecute.

oppressive adj 1 (the oppressive regimes in the world) tyrannical, despotic, repressive, undemocratic, harsh, severe, brutal. 2 (They were unable to sleep in that oppressive weather) close, stifling, stuffy, suffocating, sultry.

opt vb (He opted for a red car) choose, select, pick, settle on, decide on.

optimistic adj 1 (We were optimistic about our chances of success) hopeful, confident. 2 (He was in an optimistic mood) hopeful, confident, cheerful, positive.

option adj (We had only two options—to accept his offer or resign) choice, alternative.

optional adj (Attendance at the meeting is optional) voluntary, non-compulsory, discretionary.

oral adj (He was asked to give an oral report of the events) spoken, verbal, by word of mouth.

orator n (The crowds gathered to hear the orator) speaker, public speaker.

orbit n (The spacecraft made an orbit of the earth) revolution, circle.

ordeal n (The climb up the mountain in blizzard conditions was a real ordeal) test, trial, tribulation, suffering, torment, torture, nightmare.

order n 1 (Soldiers must obey orders) command, direction, instruction, decree. 2 (The teacher restored order in the rowdy class) calm, peace, control, discipline, good behaviour. 3 (They restored the room to order after the party) orderliness, neatness, tidiness. 4 (Is the machine in working order?) condition, state, shape. 5 (arrange the words in alphabetical order) arrangement, grouping, sequence, series, system, categorization. 6 (place an order for his new novel) request, booking, reservation.

order vb 1 (the general ordered the soldiers to shoot) command, direct, instruct, bid. 2 (The shop did not have the book and so we ordered it) place an order for, book, reserve.

orderly adj 1 (an orderly piece of work) organized, methodical, systematic. 2 (an orderly crowd) well-behaved, disciplined, quiet, peaceful, restrained.

ordinary adj 1 (We followed our ordinary procedure) usual, normal, standard, common, customary, regular, routine, typical. 2 (lead ordinary lives/ordinary people) unremarkable, unexceptional, average, run-of-the-mill, commonplace, humdrum.

organization n (He is head of the organization) company, firm, corporation, association, society, club, group.

organize vb 1 (organize the books in alphabetical order by the name of the author) arrange, group, sort, classify, categorize. 2 (We organized a Christmas party for the children) arrange, co-ordinate, set up, put together, run, see to.

origin n 1 (discuss the origin of life) source, basis, creation, start, commencement. 2 (the origin of the word) derivation, etymology, root.

original adj 1 (the original owners of the house) first, earliest, initial. 2 (The judges are looking for original work) innovative, inventive, creative, new, fresh, novel, unusual.

ornament n 1 (There was a row of ornaments on the mantelpiece) knick-knack, trinket, bauble, whatnot. 2 (an outfit entirely without ornament) decoration, adornment.

ornate adj 1 (an ornate style of architecture) decorated, elaborate, fancy, fussy, showy. 2 (her ornate writing style) elaborate, flowery, high-flown, pompous, pretentious.

orthodox adj (people who question orthodox ideas) conventional, accepted, established, traditional, standard.

ostentatious adj (She was wearing a very ostentatious dress) showy, conspicuous, obtrusive, loud, pretentious, over-elaborate.

other adj 1 (We shall have to use other methods) different, alternative. 2 (give some other examples) more, additional, further.

outbreak n (an outbreak of measles) epidemic, flare-up.

outcast n (He was an outcast from his native land) exile, refugee, outlaw.

outcome n (The outcome of the talks was that the workers went on strike) result, consequence, upshot, conclusion, effect.

outcry n (the outcry when the village post office was threatened with closure) protest, commotion, outburst, uproar, clamour, hullabaloo.

outer adj (the outer layer) outside, exterior, external, surface.

outfit n 1 (her wedding outfit) clothes, ensemble, costume, clothes, (inf) gear, (inf) rig-out. 2 (a bicycle repair outfit) kit, equipment, gear, apparatus.

outing n (The children went on an outing to the seaside) trip, excursion, jaunt, expedition.

outlaw n (a book about outlaws who escaped from prison) criminal, fugitive, outcast, bandit.

outlet n 1 (water pouring through the outlet) way out, exit, vent, opening. 2 (an outlet for their farm produce) market.

outline n 1 (They saw the outline of someone against the wall) silhouette, shadow, profile, shape. 2 (They gave an outline of their plans) summary, synopsis, rough idea.

outline vb (We outlined our plans to the planning committee) sketch out, rough out, summarize.

outlook n 1 (The attic bedroom has a wonderful outlook) view, prospect, aspect. 2 (She is quite ill but the outlook is good) future, prediction, forecast. 3 (He has a depressed outlook on life) view, opinion, attitude.

outlying adj (outlying areas of the country) remote, distant, far-flung.

outrageous adj 1 (They objected to the drunk's outrageous behaviour) disgraceful, shocking, scandalous, offensive, intolerable. 2 (The invading army committed outrageous acts) terrible, dreadful, abominable, foul, vile. 3 (The prices in that restaurant are outrageous) exorbitant, excessive, preposterous.

outside n **1** (*They painted the outside of the building white*) exterior, surface. **2** (*The fruit is dark green on the outside*) exterior, surface, skin, shell.

outskirts npl (*a shopping complex on the outskirts of the town*) suburbs, outlying area.

outstanding adj **1** (*He is an outstanding artist*) excellent, exceptional, remarkable, eminent, noted, well-known. **2** (*His bill is still outstanding*) unpaid, owing, due.

outward adj **1** (*the outward layers*) outer, outside, external, exterior. **2** (*His outward cheerfulness hid his grief*) external, superficial, visible, discernible.

outwit vb (*He tried to cheat in order to win but the other player outwitted him*) outsmart, trick, fool, dupe.

oval adj (*an oval face*) egg-shaped, ovoid.

overcome vb **1** (*Our army succeeded in overcoming the enemy*) defeat, conquer, beat, vanquish, overthrow, crush. **2** (*He tried to overcome his disability*) conquer, master, triumph over.

overdue adj (*The train is overdue*) late, behind-hand, delayed, unpunctual.

overheads npl (*try to reduce the firm's overheads*) expenses, expenditure, outlay, running costs.

overjoyed adj (*They were overjoyed when their baby was born*) elated, thrilled, delighted, ecstatic.

overlook vb **1** (*Her bedroom window overlooks the lake*) face, have a view of, look out on. **2** (*He said he would overlook the error just this once*) disregard, ignore, pay no attention to, let pass, turn a blind eye to, condone. **3** (*He overlooked a note at the foot of the contract*) miss, fail to notice.

oversight n (*Omitting your name from the list was an oversight*) mistake, error, blunder, slip-up.

overtake vb (*The car overtook us on the motorway*) pass, overhaul, outdistance, catch up with.

overthrow vb (*overthrow the invading army*) overcome, defeat, conquer, vanquish, beat, overwhelm.

overwhelm vb **1** (*A tidal wave overwhelmed the village*) flood, swamp, inundate, deluge, engulf. **2** (*They overwhelmed the invading army*) overcome, defeat, conquer, vanquish, crush.

owing adj (*We had to pay the money owing right away*) outstanding, unpaid, due.

own adj (*Each of the girls had her own car*) individual, personal, particular, private.

own vb **1** (*They own two cars*) have, possess, keep. **2** (*You have to own that he may be right*) admit, acknowledge, allow, concede. **3** (*The boy finally owned up to his crime*) confess, admit, acknowledge, (*inf*) come clean.

owner n **1** (*the owner of the car*) possessor, keeper, holder. **2** (*the owner of the business*) proprietor, boss.

P

pack *vb* **1** (*They packed their suitcases*) fill, load, stuff, cram. **2** (*They packed their old clothes in a trunk*) place, put, store, stow. **3** (*Protesters packed the hall*) fill, crowd, throng, mob, cram, jam, press into, squeeze into.

packet *n* **1** (*a packet of soap powder*) carton, pack, package, container. **2** (*The postman tried to deliver a packet*) package, parcel.

painful *adj* (*The leg that she injured is still very painful*) sore, hurting, aching, throbbing, smarting, agonizing, excruciating.

paint *vb* **1** (*They are painting the walls*) apply paint to, decorate. **2** (*He painted the view from his bedroom window*) portray, depict, draw, sketch.

painting *n* (*the paintings hanging in the gallery*) picture, portrait, sketch, drawing.

pale *adj* **1** (*She looks pale after her illness*) white, whitish, white-faced, colourless, wan, drained, pallid, pasty, peaky, ashen, as white as a sheet, as white as a ghost. **2** (*She always wears pale colours*) light, light-coloured, muted, subdued, pastel.

pan *n* (*the pans on the stove*) saucepan, pot, frying pan.

panic *n* (*They were filled with panic at the sight of the flames*) alarm, agitation, hysteria, fear, fright, terror, trepidation.

paper *n* **1** (*the paper that they take on a Sunday*) newspaper. **2** (*chose a paper for the living room*) wallpaper, wall-covering. **3** (*The students have to write a paper on Shakespeare's 'Hamlet'*) essay, report, dissertation, article, treatise, thesis. **4** (*get a photocopy of all the papers for today's meeting*) document, legal paper.

paralyse *vb* **1** (*His legs were paralysed in the accident*) immobilize, make powerless, numb, deaden, cripple, disable. **2** (*The traffic system was paralysed in the snow storm*) immobilize, bring to a halt, bring to a stop, bring to a standstill.

parcel *n* (*The postman tried to deliver a parcel*) package, packet.

parcel *vb* (*parcel the Christmas presents*) parcel up, wrap, wrap up, pack, tie up.

pardon *vb* **1** (*The prisoner was pardoned by the king*) reprieve, let off, release, absolve, acquit, exonerate. **2** (*He asked her to pardon him for being so ill-tempered*) excuse, forgive, let off, condone.

part *n* **1** (*the last part of the book*) section, portion, segment, bit. **2** (*the parts of the machine*) component, bit, constituent. **3** (*She went to the northern part of the island*) section, area, district, quarter, sector. **4** (*Originally the book was issued in several parts*) section, bit, episode, volume. **5** (*He apologized for the part which he played in the hoax*) role, function, responsibility, job. **6** (*She plays the part of Joan of Arc in the play*) role, character.

part *vb* **1** (*They had to part when he went back to his own country*) separate, say 'goodbye'. **2** (*After three years of marriage they have decided to part*) separate, leave each other, split up, break up, divorce, go their separate ways. **3** (*The police parted the crowd to reach the troublemakers at the front*) divide, separate, break up.

partial *adj* **1** (*There was only a partial improvement in his work*) part, in part, incomplete, limited, imperfect. **2** (*The referee was accused of being partial*) biased, prejudiced, partisan, discriminatory, unfair, unjust.

partial:—be partial to *adj* (*She is partial to seafood*) like, have a liking for, love, be fond of, have a weakness for.

particular *adj* **1** (*You must pay particular attention to what he says*) special, exceptional, unusual. **2** (*In this particular case I think we should be generous*) specific, individual, single. **3** (*She is particular about who cuts her hair*) fussy, fastidious, selective, discriminating, (*inf*) pernickety, (*inf*) choosy.

partner *n* **1** (*They are business partners*) associate, colleague, co-owner. **2** (*the burglar and his partner in crime*) ally, confederate, accomplice. **3** (*All her friends and their partners were invited to the wedding*) husband/wife, spouse, boyfriend/girlfriend.

party *n* **1** (*It was he who was host at the party*) social gathering, social function, function, reception, (*inf*) do, (*inf*) get-together **2** (*They were part of the hunting party*) group, band, company, contingent. **3** (*a certain party who shall remain nameless*) person, individual.

pass *vb* **1** (*The car passed us on a dangerous stretch of road*) overtake. **2** (*Lorries passed along the road all night*) go, proceed, drive, run, travel. **3** (*Time passed quickly*) go past, advance, roll by, flow by, slip by. **4** (*How does he pass the time now he has retired?*) spend, fill, occupy, take up, use, while away. **5** (*He passed her the papers for the meeting*) hand over, give, reach. **6** (*The estate passes to his eldest son on his death*) be passed on, be transferred, be signed over to. **7** (*All the students have passed the exams*) be successful, get through, gain a pass. **8** (*Parliament passed the new bill*) vote for, accept, prove, adopt, sanction. **9** (*The judge passed sentence*) pronounce, utter, deliver, declare. **10** (*Eventually the hurricane passed*) run its course, die out, fade, finish. **11** (*They were still friends after everything that had passed between them*) occur, happen, take place.

past *adj* **1** (*They were congratulated on their past successes*) former, previous, prior, foregoing. **2** (*He has become very ill in the past few days*) recent, preceding, last. **3** (*the history of past ages*) gone by, bygone, former.

pastime *n* (*He is going to have to take up a pastime in his retirement*) hobby, recreation, diversion, distraction, leisure activity, amusement, entertainment.

path *n* **1** (*a winding path up the moun-*

tain) pathway, trail, track, way. **2** (*They are studying the moon's path*) course, route, circuit, orbit.

pathetic *adj* **1** (*The starving children were a pathetic sight*) pitiful, pitiable, moving, touching, affecting, poignant, distressing, heart-breaking. **2** (*He could not play cricket and made only a few pathetic attempts to hit the ball*) feeble, inadequate, unsatisfactory, poor.

patient *adj* (*There is nothing to be done about the delayed flight—we shall have to be patient*) calm, composed, even-tempered, restrained, tolerant, forbearing, resigned, stoical, uncomplaining.

pause *n* (*There was a pause in the music while he changed the tape*) interval, lull, break, halt, gap.

pay *vb* **1** (*They had to pay a huge amount for that house*) pay out, spend, lay out, part with, (*inf*) shell out, (*inf*) fork out. **2** (*He will get paid at the end of the job*) give payment to, remunerate. **3** (*He enjoys the work but it doesn't really pay*) be profitable, make money, be remunerative. **4** (*He pays his bills right away*) settle, defray. **5** (*He likes to pay compliments to women*) bestow, offer, extend.

peaceful *adj* **1** (*They were at war but conditions between the countries are now peaceful*) peaceable, at peace, friendly, amicable. **2** (*The old man looked peaceful lying asleep in his chair*) at peace, tranquil, serene, calm, composed, placid, undisturbed. **3** (*They longed for a house in a peaceful country*

setting) quiet, restful, tranquil, calm, still.

peculiar *adj* **1** (*She wears such peculiar hats*) strange, odd, queer, funny, weird, bizarre, eccentric, outlandish, unconventional, offbeat. **2** (*There was a peculiar smell in the hall*) odd, unusual, strange, curious, abnormal. **3** (*a manner of walking that is peculiar to her*) characteristic, typical, individualistic, special, unique.

peel *vb* **1** (*peel the skin from the fruit*) pare, remove. **2** (*peel the fruit*) pare, skin. **3** (*Her skin was peeling after sunbathing*) flake off, scale off.

peg *n* (*They fastened the pieces of wood with a peg*) pin, nail, screw, bolt, spike, skewer.

penetrate *vb* **1** (*The knife of the attacker did not penetrate the skin*) pierce, bore, perforate, stab. **2** (*unable to penetrate the dense jungle*) go through, get through, enter, infiltrate.

people *npl* **1** (*an issue that should be decided by the people*) the public, the general public, the common people, the populace, the electorate. **2** (*an area inhabited by a nomadic people*) population, tribe, race, nation. **3** (*A lot of people were expected to attend*) individuals, persons. **4** (*Her people should be looking after her*) relatives, relations, family, folk.

perfect *adj* **1** (*Her performance on the piano is perfect*) flawless, faultless, impeccable, consummate, ideal, supreme, excellent, marvellous. **2** (*a perfect set of the encyclopedia*) complete, full, whole, entire. **3** (*The boy is* *a perfect fool*) absolute, utter, complete, out-and-out, thoroughgoing.

perform *vb* (*They performed all the tasks which they were given*) carry out, do, execute, discharge, effect, fulfil.

perfume *n* (*a garden full of the perfume of roses*) scent, fragrance, aroma, smell, bouquet.

peril *n* (*animals in peril*) danger, risk, jeopardy, menace, threat.

period *n* 1 (*during the Tudor period of English history*) time, age, era, epoch. 2 (*Her condition worsened over a period of years*) time, space, interval, spell, stretch, span.

perish *vb* 1 (*The food perished in the heat*) go bad, go off, decay, rot, decompose. 2 (*villagers who perished in the earthquake*) die, be killed, lose one's life.

permanent *adj* (*The accident left him with a permanent limp*) lasting, perpetual, persistent, enduring, abiding, eternal, endless, never-ending, unending.

permission *n* (*He took his father's car without permission*) authorization, leave, sanction, consent, assent, agreement, approval.

permit *vb* (*Her parents would not permit her to stay out late*) give permission to, allow, let, give leave, authorize, action, consent to, assent to, agree to,.

persecute *vb* (*people who were persecuted for their religious beliefs*) oppress, abuse, maltreat, torment, torture, victimize.

persevere *vb* (*You must persevere in your attempts to get a job*) persist, keep at, keep on, continue, carry on, be resolute, be determined, be insistent.

persistent *adj* 1 (*their persistent attempts to get planning permission*) determined, relentless, unrelenting, constant, continual, incessant, endless. 2 (*persistent people who will not give up trying*) persevering, determined, resolute, insistent, obstinate, tenacious.

personal *adj* 1 (*His reasons for being off work are purely personal*) private, confidential, individual, secret. 2 (*her personal interpretation of the piece of music*) individual, individualistic, idiosyncratic, peculiar.

personality *n* 1 (*She has a very pleasant personality*) nature, disposition, temperament, character. 2 (*It is a job for someone with personality*) character, charisma, magnetism, charm. 3 (*There were many sporting personalities at the dinner*) celebrity, dignitary, famous name, VIP.

personnel *n* (*the person in the firm in charge of personnel*) staff, employees, workers, work force.

persuade *vb* (*Could you try to persuade her to go?*) influence, induce, talk into, win over, prevail upon, cajole, wheedle.

pessimistic *adj* (*He has a pessimistic outlook on life*) gloomy, cynical, defeatist, fatalistic, resigned, distrustful.

pest *n* (*He thought the child was a pest*) nuisance, bother, irritant, trouble, worry, problem, inconvenience, trial.

pet *n* (*The boy is teased by the other pupils about being the teacher's pet*) favourite, darling, apple of one's eye.

petty adj (have no time to discuss the petty details of the case) trivial, trifling, minor, unimportant, inconsequential, slight.

phobia n (She has a phobia about spiders) aversion, fear, dread, horror, loathing, revulsion, (inf) thing, (inf) hang-up.

pick vb I (They are picking fruit) gather, collect, harvest, pull. 2 (The little girls was asked to pick a toy) choose, select, single out, opt for, plump for, decide upon, settle on. 3 (The burglar picked the lock) break open, force, prise open.

picture n I (a picture painted by a famous artist) painting, drawing, sketch, likeness, portrait, illustration. 2 (He was paid to take pictures at the wedding) photograph, photo, snapshot, snap. 3 (The novel painted a distressing picture of Victorian England) scene, view, vision, impression, description, portrayal, account, report. 4 (a horror picture) film, movie, motion picture.

pie n (a piece of apple pie) tart, tartlet, pasty, quiche, pastry.

pill n (medicine in the form of pills) tablet, capsule.

piece n I (put the pieces of the jigsaw together) bit, part, section, segment, component, unit. 2 (a quilt made of pieces of cloth) length, bit, remnant, scrap. 3 (a piece of pie) bit, chunk, wedge, hunk, lump, (inf) wodge. 4 (Each of his children will get a piece of his estate) bit, share, slice, portion,

percentage. 5 (The valuable vase smashed to pieces) bit, fragment, smithereens, shard. 6 (an impressive piece of antique furniture) example, sample, specimen, instance, illustration. 7 (a musical piece) work, creation, composition, opus. 8 (The journalist wrote a piece on the war) article, item, story, report.

pierce vb I (Did the knife pierce the skin) penetrate, puncture, prick, perforate, stab, pass through, enter. 2 (pierce the piece of leather to make a leash for the dog) perforate, bore, drill. 3 (The cries of the bird pierced the air) fill, pervade, penetrate.

pile n I (dead leaves in piles around the garden) heap, mound, stack, collection, stockpile, mountain. 2 (We have a pile of homework) great deal, abundance, (inf) lots, (inf) oodles. 3 (He made his pile forging money) fortune, wealth, money.

pillar n (the pillars at the front of the temple) column, post, upright, support, pilaster.

pin n I (Can you pin the brooch to my dress?) fasten, fix, secure, attach. 2 (The man was pinned under the overturned tractor) hold, press, pinion, restrain, immobilize.

pinch vb I (She pinched her friend's arm to wake her up) nip, tweak, squeeze. 3 (Her new shoes are pinching her toes) hurt, crush, squeeze. 4 (She pinched a cake from the baker's shop) steal, take, thieve, rob, filch, pilfer, purloin, (inf) swipe.

pious adj (pious members of the parish)

religious, godly, devout, God-fearing, righteous.

pitch vb 1 (*They pitched their tent in a field*) put up, set up, erect, raise. 2 (*The children began to pitch stones into the lake*) throw, cast, fling, hurl, toss, heave, (*inf*) chuck. 3 (*The ships were pitching in the high winds*) roll, rock, lurch, sway.

pity n 1 (*They felt pity for the poor orphans*) compassion, sympathy, commiseration, distress, sadness. 2 (*The tyrant showed the prisoners no pity*) mercy, leniency, kindness, clemency. 3 (*It was a pity that their bus was late*) shame, crying shame, misfortune.

placard n (*placards advertising the show*) poster, notice, bill, sticker.

place n 1 (*This is the place where she lost the ring/the place where he built the houses*) spot, location, site, setting, position, situation, area, region. 2 (*She won third place in the competition*) position, grade, level, rank. 3 (*It was not his place to sort out the dispute*) responsibility, job, task, function, role. 4 (*The pupil returned to her place*) seat, position.

plain adj 1 (*It was plain to all of us that she was in pain*) clear, crystal-clear, obvious, evident, apparent, manifest, unmistakable, noticeable, conspicuous. 2 (*We need a plain statement of what happened*) clear, straightforward, simple, intelligible, lucid. 3 (*The style of decoration is very plain*) simple, restrained, bare, austere, stark, basic, unadorned, spartan. 4 (*She is very beautiful now and yet she was rather plain as a child*) unattractive, unprepossessing, ugly.

plan n 1 (*They have plans to expand the firm/The prisoners have an escape plan*) scheme, strategy, tactics, system, method, project. 2 (*Their holiday plans have been ruined*) arrangements, schedule, programme, procedure, method, system., 3 (*Their plan was to travel overnight*) aim, intention, objective, scheme, proposal. 4 (*The architect's plans for the new building are on show*) drawing, blueprint, representation, model.

play vb 1 (*Children need time to play*) amuse oneself, enjoy oneself, entertain oneself, have fun. 2 (*The children were playing in the garden with the dog*) play games, frolic, romp, frisk, gambol, cavort. 3 (*He likes to play football*) take part in, engage in, be involved in, participate in. 4 (*Our team is playing against strong opposition*) compete against, take on, oppose, challenge, vie with, contend with. 5 (*She plays the piano*) perform on. 6 (*The children played tricks on their grandfather*) perform, carry out, do, execute, discharge. 6 (*He played Hamlet in the National Theatre production*) play the part of, act the part of, perform, portray.

plead vb (*They pleaded for mercy*) beg, entreat, implore.

pleasant adj 1 (*It was a very pleasant occasion*) agreeable, enjoyable, pleasing, delightful, nice, good, lovely, entertaining, amusing 2 (*Our neighbours are very pleasant*) agreeable, friendly, amiable, affable, likeable, charming.

please vb 1 (We were going to go to the theatre but it is difficult to find a show that will please everyone) give pleasure to, satisfy, suit, delight, amuse, entertain. 2 (Whatever advice you give her she will do as she pleases) wish, want, like, choose, prefer, see fit.

pleasure n 1 (a gift that will bring their mother a great deal of pleasure) happiness, joy, delight, enjoyment, amusement, entertainment, satisfaction. 2 (one of the old man's few pleasures) joy, delight, enjoyment, recreation, diversion.

plentiful adj (plentiful supplies of fuel) abundant, copious, ample, profuse, generous, liberal, large.

plot n 1 (They uncovered a plot to murder the king) conspiracy, intrigue. 2 (The novel has a complicated plot) theme, action, story line, subject. 3 (He grows potatoes on his vegetable plot) allotment, patch.

plump adj (She was plump as a little girl) chubby, tubby, fat.

plunder vb (They crossed the border and plundered the enemy villages) rob, raid, loot, pillage, lay waste.

poetry n (He writes poetry as a hobby) poems, verse, verses.

point n 1 (The spear had a very sharp point) tip, end, top. 2 (She reached a point where she could not go on) stage, position, situation, circumstances, time. 3 (at some point during the meeting) time, juncture, stage. 4 (They discussed the various points in the report) detail, item, particular, issue, subject,

topic. 5 (The speaker spoke at length but few people got the point of his talk) meaning, significance, import, substance, gist, drift. 6 (He took ages to get to the point when he was declaring them redundant) main point, salient point, crux of the matter, crux, heart of the matter, (inf) nitty-gritty. 7 (What is the point of this discussion?) aim, purpose, intention, object, objective, goal. 8 (That is one of the weak points of the argument/He has many good points) aspect, feature, attribute, quality, characteristic, trait. 9 (the team that has most points) mark.

point:— **point out** vb (We pointed out the benefits) draw attention to, call attention to, identify, indicate, show, mention, specify.

pointless adj 1 (It was pointless to continue the search after dark) in vain, useless, futile, to no purpose, senseless, stupid 2 (They made a few pointless comments) worthless, meaningless, insignificant, irrelevant.

poisonous adj 1 (an area with poisonous snakes) venomous. 2 (poisonous chemical substances) toxic, deadly, lethal, fatal.

poke vb 1 (The child tried to poke a pencil in the electric socket) jab, push, thrust, shove, stick. 2 (He poked his friend in the ribs to get him to stop laughing) jab, prod, dig, nudge, elbow.

polish vb 1 (She has to polish the furniture) wax, shine, buff up, burnish. 2 (She wants to polish up her French before she goes on holiday) improve, revise, perfect, brush up.

polite adj 1 (*Children taught to be polite*) well-mannered, mannerly, courteous, civil, well-bred, well-behaved. 2 (*the way things are done in polite society*) well-bred, civilized, cultured, refined, genteel.

pollute vb (*chemicals that pollute the water*) contaminate, taint, infect, adulterate, poison, befoul, dirty.

pompous adj (*They were kept out of the building by a pompous official*) self-important, presumptuous, overbearing, egotistic.

poor n 1 (*poor people with not enough money to live on*) poverty-stricken, penniless, needy, in need, impoverished, deprived, destitute, hard up, badly off. 2 (*It was a poor attempt*) inadequate, unsatisfactory, inferior.

popular adj 1 (*The place is popular with young people*) liked, favoured, approved, in demand, in fashion. 2 (*ideas that were popular at the time*) current, accepted, widespread, common, general.

population n (*The population of the area is mainly elderly*) people, inhabitants, residents, community.

portion n 1 (*Each of his children got an equal portion of his fortune*) part, share, division, piece, bit, quota, percentage. 2 (*The restaurant serves children's portions on request*) serving, helping, quantity. 3 (*They bought four portions of the cake*) piece, bit, slice, section, segment, lump, chunk.

position n 1 (*He had been sitting in an uncomfortable position*) posture, attitude, pose. 2 (*try to find the position of the wrecked ship*) location, whereabouts. 3 (*These trees grow well in a shady position*) situation, location, place, spot, area, setting. 4 (*He is in a very fortunate position*) situation, state, circumstances, condition. 5 (*the position of the team in the league tables*) place, level, grade, status, rank, ranking. 6 (*The position of manager is vacant*) situation, post, job, role. 7 (*people of position in society*) rank, status, influence, standing, prestige.

positive adj 1 (*She is positive that she saw him*) sure, certain, confident, convinced. 2 (*try to give some positive criticism of the essays*) constructive, helpful, useful. 3 (*He should try to have a more positive attitude to life*) optimistic, hopeful, confident, determined. 4 (*The results of the medical tests were positive*) affirmative. 5 (*He is a positive fool*) absolute, utter, complete, total, out-and-out.

possess vb 1 (*They do not possess a car*) own, be the owner of, have. 2 (*He thought that he was possessed by devils*) control, dominate, influence, bewitch.

possessions npl (*Our flat is full of her possessions*) belongings, property, goods, things, personal effects.

possible adj 1 (*It is not possible to get there on time*) feasible, practicable, achievable. 2 (*one possible solution*) likely, potential, conceivable, imaginable.

post n 1 (*He hammered in posts to make a fence*) stake, pole, upright. 2 (*The post has already been filled*) job, position, appointment, situation.

postpone vb (They have had to postpone the wedding) put off, put back, defer, delay, put on ice.

pounce vb (The cat pounced on the mouse) swoop, spring, leap, jump.

pound vb 1 (She pounded the seeds to a powder) crush, smash, beat, pulverize, grind. 2 (She pounded her father's chest with her fists) beat, pummel, strike, hit, hammer. 3 (Her heart was pounding) beat heavily, throb, pulse, pulsate, palpitate. 4 (They pounded the pavements looking for somewhere to live) tramp, tread, trudge.

pour vb 1 (Water began to pour from the burst pipe) rush, gush, stream, spout, spurt, flow. 2 (pour custard over the tart) let flow, splash, spill. 3 (It was pouring) come down in torrents, rain cats and dogs, come down in sheets, (inf) be bucketing.

poverty n need, want, deprivation, hardship.

power n 1 (the power of speech) ability, capability, capacity, faculty. 2 (The tyrant had her in his power) control, command, rule, domination, mastery, authority. 3 (people of power gaining victory over the weak) powerfulness, strength, force, forcefulness, might, vigour, effectiveness. 4 (electricity and other kinds of power) energy.

powerful adj 1 (weight-lifters of powerful build) strong, sturdy, strapping, tough, mighty. 2 (the most powerful members of the community) dominant, controlling, influential, authoritative, strong, forceful, vigorous. 3 (She drew

up a powerful argument against the scheme) strong, forceful, effective, convincing, persuasive, compelling.

practical adj 1 (They want people with practical experience of the job) applied, experienced, skilled, hands-on. 2 (She is very bright academically but not at all practical) sensible, down-to-earth, realistic, businesslike. 3 (wear practical footwear for walking) sensible, functional, useful, utilitarian.

practise vb 1 (She has to practise her piano performances) rehearse, go over, run through, work at, prepare, train for, study for, polish up. 2 (She seems quite unable to practise self-control) carry out, perform, execute, do. 3 (They practise medicine) work in, be engaged in.

praise vb 1 (They praised her performance) applaud, express admiration for, admire, compliment, pay tribute to, sing the praises of. 2 (praise God) worship, glorify, honour, exalt.

precarious adj 1 (It was rather a precarious journey through the jungle) risky, dangerous, hazardous, perilous. 2 (a precarious way to earn one's living) risky, unreliable, uncertain, unsure, chancy, unpredictable.

precious adj 1 (a necklace full of precious stones) valuable, costly, expensive. 2 (family photographs that are very precious to her/her precious memories) valued, treasured, cherished, prized, beloved, dear.

precise adj 1 (We need to know her precise words) exact, actual, literal. 2 (at that precise moment) very, exact, actual, particular. **3** (*He is a very precise person*) exact, careful, accurate, meticulous.

predict vb (*She claimed to be able to predict the future*) foretell, forecast, foresee, prophesy.

predominant adj (*Red is the predominant colour in the pattern*) chief, main, principal, dominant.

prefer vb **1** (*She prefers the blue pattern to the yellow*) like better, favour, choose, select, pick, opt for, plump for. **2** (*They could drive but they prefer to go by train*) like better, would rather, would sooner, favour, choose.

prejudiced adj (*They have a prejudiced attitude towards people of a different race/prejudiced employers*) biased, discriminatory, partial, partisan, bigoted, intolerant, unfair, unjust.

premature adj (*the premature birth of the baby*) too soon, too early.

premonition n (*She had a premonition that something tragic was going to happen*) feeling, foreboding, presentiment, intuition, hunch.

prepare vb **1** (*They must prepare their proposal to present it to the committee*) get ready, arrange, assemble, draw up, put together. **2** (*prepare a meal*) make, cook, put together.

presence n **1** (*the presence of chemical waste in the drinking water*) existence. **2** (*They are asking for our presence at the meeting*) attendance. **3** (*They felt inadequate in the presence of the great man*) company, vicinity, proximity.

present adj **1** (*Pollutants were present in the water supply*) existing, existent.

2 (*There should be a nurse present*) in attendance, here, there, on hand. **3** (*in the present situation*) current, existing, present-day, contemporary.

present n **1** (*thinking about the present rather than the future*) now, today, the present moment. **2** (*a present on her birthday/a present for all their hard work*) gift, reward.

presentable adj (*make yourself presentable before you see the headmaster*) tidy, well-groomed, smart, spruce.

preserve vb **1** (*try to preserve the old village traditions*) keep, keep up, continue, maintain, uphold, conserve. **2** (*a substance to preserve wood*) protect, conserve. **3** (*They had to preserve the city from enemy attack*) protect, save, safeguard, keep, defend. **4** (*preserve some money for one's old age*) keep, put aside, save, retain.

press vb **1** (*You should press the door bell again*) push. **2** (*villagers pressing grapes to make wine*) crush, squeeze, compress. **3** (*need an iron to press her skirt*) iron, smooth. **3** (*The mother pressed the tired child against her*) clasp, hold, pull, squeeze, crush, hug. **4** (*They are pressing the planning committee for a decision*) urge, entreat, implore, pressure, put pressure on, pressurize.

pressure n **1** (*They had to exert a great deal of pressure to get the door open*) force, strength, weight. **2** (*She tried to withstand the pressure of her parents to get her to stay at home*) force, compulsion, constraint, duress. **3** (*the pressures of modern living*) strain, stress, tension.

prestige n (He does not want to lose his prestige in the community) status, kudos, standing, importance, reputation, esteem, influence.

pretence n 1 (She did not really faint—it was just pretence) dissembling, shamming, faking, make-believe. 2 (They left on the pretence that they were going to a meeting) pretext, excuse.

pretend vb (He was not sleeping at all—he was just pretending) put on an act, put it on, play-act, sham, fake, dissemble.

pretty adj (She is a very pretty girl) attractive, good-looking, lovely, nice-looking.

pretty adv (She was feeling pretty annoyed) rather, quite, very.

prevent vb 1 (Her parents tried to prevent her marrying him) stop, halt, restrain, prohibit, bar, hinder, obstruct, impede, hamper. 2 (try to prevent the spread of the infection) stop, halt, arrest, check, block, check, hinder, obstruct, impede.

previous adj 1 (the previous chairman) former, preceding, ex-, foregoing. 2 (We met on a previous occasion) earlier, prior, former.

price n (ask the price of the bookcase) cost, charge.

prick vb 1 (The child pricked the balloon with a pin) pierce, puncture, stab, gash. 2 (She pricked her finger on the needle) jab, jag, stab, wound. 3 (Their eyes began to prick in the smoke from the fire) smart, sting, tingle.

pride n 1 (They take pride in their work) satisfaction, gratification, pleasure. 2 (Her pride was hurt when he left her for another girl) self-esteem, self-respect, ego. 3 (He is guilty of the sin of pride) conceit, vanity, arrogance, egotism, self-importance, (inf) bigheadedness.

prim adj (He is much too prim to join in the fun) proper, demure, strait-laced, stuffy, starchy, prudish, (inf) goody-goody.

prime adj 1 (meat of prime quality) top, best, first-class, superior, choice, select. 2 (His prime ambition was to make money) chief, main, principal. 3 (The prime cause of the infection was the water) basic, fundamental.

prime n (in the prime of life) peak, height, zenith, acme.

principal adj 1 (the principal members of the organization) chief, leading, foremost, dominant. 2 (the principal issues to be discussed) main, major, key, essential.

principle n 1 (the principles of socialism) idea, theory, philosophy, basis, code. 2 (He is a man of principle) morals, ethics, integrity, uprightness, honour.

prison n (He was sent to prison for theft) jail, gaol, lock-up, (inf) clink, (inf) nick.

private adj 1 (a private discussion between cabinet ministers) confidential, secret, privileged, (inf) hush-hush. 2 (She wished to be private to think about things) undisturbed, uninterrupted, alone, solitary. 3 (She would not disclose her private thoughts) personal, intimate, secret. 4 (He found a private place in the large garden) secluded, quiet, out-of-the-way.

privileged adj (She comes from a privileged background) advantaged, favoured, elite.

probable adj (the probable outcome/It is probable that he will lose) likely, expected.

problem n 1 (an arithmetical problem) question, puzzle, poser, brain-teaser. 2 (They have had a few financial problems) difficulty, trouble, complication, predicament. 3 (Their teenage son is a real problem) trouble, bother, nuisance, pest.

proceed vb 1 (We were unsure as to how to proceed) act, take action, move, progress. 2 (We proceeded up the mountain as fast as we could) make one's way, carry on, go on, advance, go forward, progress.

process: n 1 (the manufacturing process) operation, activity, stages. 2 (a new process for cleaning carpets) system, method, technique, procedure.

process: in the process of (something) (They are in the process of moving house) in the midst of, in the course of.

procession n (a procession to celebrate the town's centenary) parade, march, cavalcade.

produce vb 1 (an agricultural area that produces a wide variety of crops) yield, bear, give. 2 (a cat that has just produced kittens) give birth to, bear. 3 (His article produced an angry response) cause, give rise to, evoke, generate, start, spark off. 4 (The country produces a great many goods for export) make, manufacture, turn out. 5 (The police have produced proof that he is guilty) bring forward, present, advance.

product n (a firm specializing in electronic products) commodity, goods, wares, merchandise.

profit n (They made little profit from the sale) gain, return, yield, proceeds, income.

profitable adj (The business is no longer profitable) profit-making, money-making, commercial, lucrative.

programme n 1 (watch the television programme) production, show, performance, broadcast. 2 (the programme of events for the fete) schedule, plan, scheme, list, calendar, syllabus.

progress n 1 (They have been discussing the matter for ages but they have made little progress) headway, advancement. 2 (Her work shows no sign of progress) headway, advancement, improvement.

project n (take part in a project to build a new swimming pool) scheme, plan, undertaking, enterprise, venture, operation.

prominent adj 1 (prominent members of the government) leading, chief, foremost, eminent, top. 2 (The palm trees are a prominent feature of the area) striking, conspicuous, noticeable, obvious, eye-catching. 3 (She has prominent cheekbones) protruding, obvious.

promise n 1 (She made a promise that she would be there) pledge, vow, bond, assurance, commitment. 2 (A young skater of promise) potential, talent, flair. **3** (There was a promise of good times to come) indication, sign, suggestion, hint.

promote vb **1** (They plan to promote him to manager) upgrade, elevate. **2** (The company is promoting a new line in perfume) advertise, publicize, push, (inf) plug. **3** (They need volunteers to promote the cause of animals' rights) support, champion, further, advance, help, assist, boost.

prompt adj (They will expect a prompt reply) rapid, swift, quick, fast, speedy, immediate, instant.

proof n **1** (The police had little proof of his guilt) evidence, confirmation, corroboration. **2** (The workmen had no proof of their identity) evidence, verification, authentication, certification.

proper adj **1** (the proper behaviour on such an occasion) right, correct, suitable, fitting, appropriate, acceptable, conventional. **2** (put the plates in their proper place in the kitchen) right, correct, usual, own.

property n (items that were his property) belongings, possessions, things, goods, goods and chattels.

proportion n **1** (an area with a high proportion of agricultural workers) ratio, distribution. **2** (He gives a large proportion of his earnings to the church) part, share, percentage, measure.

propose vb **1** (We are proposing to go by train) plan, intend, aim, suggest. **2** (They proposed some alterations to the system) put forward, submit, recommend, advocate. **3** (They proposed

him as chairman) put forward, nominate, suggest.

prosper vb (The family began to prosper) thrive, do well, succeed, flourish, make good.

prosperous adj (prosperous people with a great deal of money to spend) well-off, wealthy, affluent, rich, successful.

protect vb (They wished to protect the child from danger) safeguard, guard, keep, preserve, shield, defend.

protest n (They lodged a protest against the closure of the school) objection, opposition, complaint, disagreement, dissent, outcry.

proud adj **1** (He is rich and now too proud to talk to his former neighbours) conceited, vain, arrogant, egotistical, haughty, boastful, supercilious, (inf) snooty. **2** (He was proud of his son's achievement) gratified, appreciative, pleased, happy.

prove vb (evidence that proved his innocence) establish, determine, confirm, corroborate.

provide vb **1** (They provided the money for the trip) give, supply, donate, contribute. **2** (a job that provides opportunity for travel) give, grant, offer, afford, present.

prowl vb (burglars prowling round the house) roam, skulk, slink, sneak.

pry vb (She likes to pry into her neighbours' affairs) interfere, meddle, snoop.

public adj **1** (Public feeling is against the new road) popular, general, common. **2** (make their views public) known, plain. **3** (public figures) well-known, prominent, eminent, influential.

publicity n **I** (*She only did it to get publicity in the press*) public attention, public interest. **2** (*The reception was part of the publicity for her book*) promotion, advertisement, advertising, (*inf*) hype.

pudding n (*have apple tart for pudding*) dessert, sweet, (*inf*) afters.

pull vb **I** (*He pulled the nail out of the wall*) pull out, draw out, take out, extract, remove. **2** (*They began to pull the rope*) haul, tug, (*inf*) yank. **3** (*The child was pulling a toy train behind him*) haul, drag, trail, tow, tug. **3** (*The athlete has pulled a muscle*) strain, sprain, wrench.

punch vb (*The boy punched him on the nose*) strike, hit, box.

punctual adj (*It is important to be punctual at meetings*) on time, prompt, in good time.

punish vb **I** (*She punished the children for being naughty*) discipline, chastise, smack, slap. **2** (*criminals punished for doing wrong*) discipline, penalize.

puny adj (*too puny to fight against such a strong opponent*) weak, weakly, frail, feeble, undersized, stunted, slight, small.

pure adj **I** (*breathing in the pure mountain air*) clean, clear, fresh, unpolluted, uncontaminated, untainted, wholesome. **2** (*dishes of pure gold*) unalloyed, unmixed, unadulterated, true, real. **3** (*people who are expected to be of pure character*) virtuous, honourable, moral, ethical, righteous, blameless, uncorrupted, impeccable, flawless, spotless. **4** (*It was pure folly to do that*) sheer, utter, absolute, downright, total, complete, out-and-out. **5** (*The students are studying pure science*) theoretical, abstract.

purpose n **I** (*What was the purpose of their inquiries?*) reason, point, motivation, cause, grounds, justification. **2** (*The young man should try to get a purpose in life*) aim, goal, objective, object, target, aspiration, ambition. **3** (*The search for the missing goods lacked purpose*) determination, resoluteness, resolve, firmness, perseverance. **4** (*The talks went on all night but to little purpose*) worth, use, usefulness, value, advantage, benefit, avail.

pursue vb **I** (*The policeman pursued the bank robber*) go after, run after, follow, chase, give chase to, trail, stalk, shadow, (*inf*) tail. **2** (*The police are pursuing a line of inquiry in the murder case*) follow, proceed with, go on with, continue with. **3** (*She wishes to pursue a career in medicine*) follow, be engaged in, work in. **4** (*They are pursuing their goal of making a fortune*) strive towards, be intent on.

push vb **I** (*The little boy pushed his friend into the pool*) shove, thrust, propel, ram, drive. **2** (*She pushed her way to the front of the crowd*) force, shove, thrust, press, elbow, shoulder, jostle. **3** (*push the button to start the machine*) press. **4** (*He said that his parents pushed him into going to university*) force, coerce, press, dragoon, browbeat, prod, goad, urge. **5** (*The company held a reception to push their new* *product*) promote, advertise, publicize, boost, (*inf*) plug.

put *vb* **1** (*They were asked to put the books on the desk*) place, lay, set down, deposit. **2** (*They tried to put the blame on their friend*) place, lay, attach, attribute, assign. **3** (*She put the value of the antique vase at £4000*) assess, evaluate, calculate, reckon, guess, (*inf*) guesstimate. **4** (*You should put the idea to your parents*) put forward, propose, present, submit. **5** (*He put a large sum of money on the horse*) place, bet, wager, gamble.

puzzle *vb* (*Her parents were puzzled by the change in her behaviour*) perplex, mystify, baffle, bewilder, nonplus, stump.

Q

qualified adj **1** (a qualified doctor/She is qualified to teach) trained, certificated, equipped. **2** (They gave the plan qualified approval) limited, conditional, modified, restricted.

quarrel n (The sisters have had a quarrel) disagreement, argument, row, fight, difference of opinion, dispute, wrangle, altercation, misunderstanding.

queer adj (Their behaviour seemed very queer) strange, odd, peculiar, funny, weird, bizarre.

question n **1** (She was unable to answer his questions) inquiry, query, interrogation. **2** (We must consider the question of safety) issue, matter, point, subject, topic.

quick adj **1** (You will have to be quick to catch the bus) fast, swift, rapid, speedy. **2** (She wants a quick reply to her letter) prompt, without delay, immediate. **3** (She took a quick look at the instructions) hasty, brief, fleeting, cursory.

quiet adj (It was very quiet in the church) hushed, silent, soundless, noiseless. **2** (He spoke in quiet tones) soft, low, hushed, whispered, inaudible. **3** (lead a quiet life in the country) peaceful, tranquil, calm, serene, placid, untroubled, undisturbed. **4** (They are both rather quiet people) reserved, taciturn, uncommunicative, reticent, placid, unexcitable. **5** (She dresses in quiet colours) restrained, unobtrusive, muted, subdued, subtle, conservative, sober, dull. **6** (They kept the news of their engagement quiet) secret, confidential, private, (inf) hush hush.

quite adj **1** (Has he quite recovered after his accident?) completely, totally, entirely, fully, wholly. **2** (She is quite good at tennis but she will not win the match) fairly, relatively, moderately, somewhat, rather.

R

race *vb* (*runners racing towards the finishing post*) run, sprint, dash, speed, bolt, dart.

race *n* (*Humankind is divided into races*) ethnic group, racial division.

racial *adj* (*racial discrimination*) ethnic, race-related.

racism *n* racial discrimination, racial prejudice.

rack *n* (*a plate rack*) frame, framework, stand, support, holder.

racket *n* 1 (*We couldn't sleep because of the racket from the party next door*) din, noise, commotion, row, hubbub, disturbance. 2 (*They think he was involved in a drugs racket*) fraud, criminal scheme.

radiant *adj* 1 (*They could not see properly in the radiant light*) brilliant, shining, bright, gleaming, irradiant. 2 (*The winners looked radiant*) joyful, elated, ecstatic, delighted.

radiate *vb* 1 (*The fire radiated a fierce heat*) send out, emit, disperse. 2 (*roads radiating out from the town centre*) branch out, spread out, diverge.

radical *adj* 1 (*There have been radical changes in their business methods*) thorough, complete, total, sweeping, exhaustive, drastic, violent. 2 (*She holds radical political views*) extremist, fundamental.

rage *n* 1 (*She went into a rage when they criticized her*) temper, tantrum. 2 (*She was filled with rage at the sight of her rival*) fury, anger, annoyance, exasperation.

rags *npl* (*The homeless woman was dressed in rags*) tatters.

raid *n* 1 (*enemy raids on the town*) attack, assault, onslaught, invasion, foray, sortie. 2 (*a bank raid*) robbery, break-in.

railing *n* (*the railing round the balcony*) rail, paling, barrier, fence.

rain *vb* (*It was raining during the match*) pour, drizzle, (*inf*) rain cats and dogs, (*inf*) come down in stair rods.

rainy *adj* (*We got a rainy day for the picnic*) wet, damp, showery, drizzly.

raise *vb* 1 (*They need a crane to raise the wrecked car*) lift, hoist, heave up, elevate. 2 (*They are going to raise a block of flats there*) put up, build, construct, erect. 3 (*The news raised our hopes*) increase, boost, build up, stimulate. 4 (*They had to raise the temperature in the greenhouse*) put up, increase, augment, intensify. 5 (*The local hotels raise their prices in the summer*) put up, increase, inflate, (*inf*) hike up. 6 (*They raise turkeys*) breed, rear. 7 (*He raises cereal crops*) grow, cultivate, produce, farm. 8 (*They have raised several children*) rear, bring up, nurture.

rake *vb* 1 (*rake up the dead leaves*) scrape up, collect, gather. 2 (*They raked the soil before planting the seeds*) smooth, level, flatten, even out.

3 (*The burglars raked through her things*) search, hunt, ransack, rummage, rifle.

rally n **1** (*They held a rally to demonstrate against the new parliamentary bill*) meeting, mass meeting, gathering, assembly, convention, demonstration, (*inf*) demo. **2** (*Stock market prices fell but then there was a sudden rally*) recovery, revival, improvement, comeback.

rally vb **1** (*The troops rallied to support the king*) assemble, gather, convene, unite. **2** (*The invalid was seriously ill but she has rallied*) recover, recuperate, revive, get better, improve, pull through, take a turn for the better.

ram vb **1** (*ram the clothes into the suitcase in a hurry*) force, cram, stuff, thrust. **2** (*His car rammed ours*) hit, strike, run into, collide with, bump.

ramble vb **1** (*They rambled over the hills for the afternoon*) walk, hike, wander, roam. **2** (*The lecturer rambled on without the students understanding a word*) babble, gibber, rattle on, (*inf*) rabbit on, (*inf*) witter.

rampage vb (*children rampaging around their neighbour's garden*) rush, charge, tear, run riot.

ramshackle adj (*They bought a ramshackle cottage and are going to rebuild it*) tumble-down, broken-down, run-down, dilapidated, derelict, crumbling.

random adj (*ask a random selection of the population how they were going to vote*) haphazard, chance, arbitrary, indiscriminate, unsystematic, unme-

thodical, unplanned, accidental.

range n **1** (*a range of mountains*) row, line, chain. **2** (*It was not within their range of vision*) scope, field, area, limit, reach. **3** (*The corner shop stocks a wide range of goods*) selection, assortment, variety.

range vb **1** (*Prices range from £10 to £200*) extend, stretch, go, vary. **2** (*The books are ranged according to subject*) classify, categorize, group, class. **3** (*sheep ranging over the hills*) roam, rove, ramble, wander, stray.

rank n **1** (*What is the soldier's rank?*) grade, position. **2** (*The salary in the organization is according to rank*) grade, level, position, status. **3** (*The people in the big house were people of rank*) nobility, aristocracy, eminence, power, influence.

ransack vb **1** (*Raiders ransacked the shops after the explosion*) loot, plunder, rob, rifle, pillage. **2** (*We ransacked the house to try to find the lost passport*) search, rummage, scour, turn upside down.

rap vb **1** (*She rapped on the door*) knock, tap, bang. **2** (*The teacher rapped him over the knuckles with a ruler*) hit, strike, tap, bang, whack.

rapid adj (*They set off at a rapid pace*) swift, fast, quick, speedy, hurried, hasty, brisk, lively.

rapture n (*their rapture at the birth of their child*) joy, ecstasy, bliss, euphoria, delight.

rare adj **1** (*The wild flower was a rare specimen*) unusual, uncommon, out of the ordinary, atypical, remarkable.

2 (*He made one of his rare appearances*) infrequent, few and far between, sparse, sporadic.

rascal n **1** (*The child was a real little rascal*) imp, scamp, scallywag. **2** (*Her husband is a rascal who is always in trouble with the police*) scoundrel, villain, rogue, blackguard, ne'er-do-well, good-for-nothing.

rash adj (*Leaving her job to go round the world proved to be a rash decision*) impetuous, reckless, hasty, impulsive, unthinking, incautious, imprudent, foolhardy.

rash n **1** (*She woke up with a rash on her face*) spots, redness, eruption, hives. **2** (*There has been a rash of car thefts in the area*) spate, outbreak, wave, flood, series, run, plague, epidemic.

rasping adj (*She has a rasping voice/the rasping noise of a knife on metal*) grating, discordant, jarring, harsh, rough, gruff, croaky.

rate n **1** (*They walked at a very fast rate*) pace, speed, tempo, velocity. **2** (*the bank's rate of interest*) ratio, proportion, scale, degree. **3** (*The hotel is charging its winter rates*) price, charge, cost, tariff, fee, payment.

rate vb **1** (*How would you rate the team's performance*) judge, assess, evaluate, measure, weigh up, rank, class. **2** (*She rates more respect from them*) deserve, merit, be entitled to.

rather adv **1** (*She would rather go than stay*) for preference, sooner, from choice. **2** (*She is pretty rather than beautiful*) more. **3** (*She tends to be rather blunt but is really rather kind*) quite, fairly, somewhat, slightly.

ratify vb (*The two sides still have to ratify the agreement*) confirm, endorse, sign, approve, sanction.

ratio n (*the ratio of staff to pupils in the school*) proportion, percentage, fraction.

rational adj **1** (*It seemed a rational decision*) sensible, reasonable, logical, sound, intelligent, wise, judicious. **2** (*His mind has been affected but he has a few rational moments*) sane, balanced, lucid, coherent.

rattle vb **1** (*The windows rattled in the wind*) bang, clatter, clank, jangle. **2** (*She rattled the door knocker*) bang, knock, rap. **3** (*He was rattling on about his hobbies and boring everyone*) chatter, babble, prattle, jabber, gibber, blether, (*inf*) rabbit on, (*inf*) witter. **4** (*The speaker was obviously rattled by some of the questions from the audience*) agitate, disturb, fluster, upset, shake.

raucous adj (*the raucous singing of the drunk men*) strident, shrill, grating, jarring, discordant, piercing.

ravenous adj (*They were ravenous after walking all day*) famished, starving, hungry.

raw adj **1** (*She prefers to eat raw vegetables*) uncooked, fresh. **2** (*raw sugar*) unrefined, unprocessed, crude, natural. **3** (*It was a raw winter's day*) cold, chilly, bitter. **4** (*She has a raw place on her elbow from when she fell over*) red, sore, inflamed, tender, abraded, grazed. **5** (*They are raw recruits who have joined the army*) inexperienced, untrained, unskilled, callow, green.

ray n 1 (*The rays of light showed up the dust on the furniture*) beam, shaft, streak, gleam, flash. 2 (*There did not seem to be a ray of hope left*) glimmer, flicker, trace, indication, suggestion.

reach vb 1 (*He reached his hand out for the book*) stretch, extend. 2 (*The child could not reach the door handle*) get hold of, grasp, touch. 3 (*We finally reached our destination*) get to, arrive at. 4 (*He has not reached the required standard*) get to, achieve, attain.

react vb 1 (*How did he react when he discovered that she had gone?*) behave, act, respond. 2 (*The teenagers are reacting against their parents' beliefs*) rebel against.

read vb 1 (*She read a book while she waited*) peruse, study, pore over, browse through. 2 (*Can you read his handwriting?*) decipher, make out. 3 (*They read his silence as consent*) interpret, take to mean.

ready adj 1 (*The meal is ready*) prepared, completed. 2 (*They are ready for battle*) prepared, equipped, organized, all set. 3 (*Her neighbours are always ready to help*) willing, eager, keen, inclined, disposed. 4 (*She was ready to collapse when she got to the bottom of the mountain*) about to, on the point of, in danger of. 5 (*She always has a ready answer*) prompt, quick, rapid, swift, speedy. 6 (*Have you got your ticket ready for collection?*) available, to hand, accessible.

real adj 1 (*things connected with the real world*) actual, factual. 2 (*The coat was made of real leather*) genuine, authentic. 3 (*She showed signs of real emotion*) genuine, authentic, sincere, unfeigned, honest, truthful. 4 (*He has been a real friend*) true, sincere.

realistic adj 1 (*The model of the bear was very realistic*) lifelike, true-to-life, naturalistic, authentic. 2 (*He has to try to be realistic about his job prospects*) practical, down-to-earth, matter-of-fact, sensible, level-headed, unromantic, no-nonsense.

realize vb 1 (*We began to realize that she was ill*) understand, grasp, take in, become aware, appreciate, recognize. 2 (*I hope that she realizes her dreams*) fulfil, achieve, accomplish.

really adv 1 (*It was a really beautiful day*) truly, genuinely, undoubtedly, unquestionably, indeed. 2 (*The performer is dressed as a woman but is really a man*) in fact, in actual fact, in truth.

rear n 1 (*They sat at the rear of the train*) back. 2 (*They were at the rear of the cinema queue*) back, tail, end.

rear vb 1 (*She reared three children on her own*) bring up, raise, care for. 2 (*The farmer rears turkeys*) breed, raise, keep.

reason n 1 (*There seemed no reason for his behaviour*) grounds, cause, basis, motive, justification. 2 (*The old man has lost his reason*) sanity, mind.

reasonable adj 1 (*It seemed a reasonable thing to do*) logical, rational, practical, sensible, intelligent, wise, sound. 2 (*I thought that he was quite a reasonable person*) fair, just, decent, unbiased. 3 (*The prices in the new* restaurant were quite reasonable) inexpensive, moderate, modest, cheap.

rebel vb 1 (The crew are rebelling) mutiny, riot, revolt, rise up. 2 (teenagers rebelling against their parents' authority) defy, disobey.

rebellion n (They joined in a rebellion against the king) revolt, revolution, insurrection, uprising, rising, riot.

rebellious adj (the rebellious troops/the rebellious schoolgirls) defiant, disobedient, unruly, unmanageable, intractable, mutinous, insurgent.

rebuke vb (Her teacher rebuked her for being late) scold, chide, admonish, (inf) tell off.

recall vb 1 (She was unable to recall his name) call to mind, remember, recollect, think of. 2 (The manufacturers have recalled a batch of cars with faulty brakes) call back, withdraw.

recede vb 1 (The flood water began to recede) go back, retreat, subside, ebb. 2 (The danger seems to have receded) grow less, lessen, fade, diminish.

receive vb 1 (She said that she posted the goods but we never received them) get, be in receipt of. 2 (She received many benefits from the scheme) get, obtain, gain, acquire. 3 (She received the best of treatment in the hospital) get, experience, undergo, meet with. 4 (She got ready to receive her dinner guests) welcome, greet, entertain.

recent adj (The doctor tries to keep up with recent medical developments) new, fresh, latest, modern.

recite vb (The little girl was asked to recite a poem) say, repeat, speak, deliver.

reckless adj (He later regretted his reckless action) rash, careless, thoughtless, inattentive, incautious, irresponsible, negligent.

reclaim vb 1 (They went to the police station to reclaim their property) get back, recover, retrieve. 2 (They reclaimed some land from the sea to build a bird sanctuary) get back, recover, retrieve, regain, store, save, salvage, rescue.

recline vb (The invalid reclined on a sofa) lie down, lie, stretch out, lean back, be recumbent, rest, repose, lounge.

recognize vb 1 (I failed to recognize my cousin after all these years) know, know again, identify, recall, call to mind, recollect, remember. 2 (The authorities are refusing to recognize his claim to the title) acknowledge, accept, allow, grant, validate. 3 (He recognized that he had been at fault) realize, be aware, appreciate, admit, acknowledge. 4 (His genius as a composer was not recognized in his lifetime) appreciate, honour, pay homage to, reward.

recoil vb (He recoiled when he realized that his fellow thief had a gun) flinch, shrink, draw back, wince.

recollect vb (I cannot recollect his name) remember, recall, call to mind, think of.

recommend vb 1 (He recommended a cure for a cold) commend, advocate, speak favourably of, approve, vouch for. 2 (They recommend caution in that case) advise, urge.

reconcile vb 1 (The couple separated for a time but have now been reconciled) bring together, reunite. **2** (*They quarrelled but have now reconciled their differences*) settle, resolve, put to rights. **3** (*We have now reconciled ourselves to our misfortune*) resign oneself, accept, make the best of it.

record n **1** (*He is using parish records to write a history of the area*) register, documents, information, data, chronicles, annals. **2** (*She kept a diary of her holiday experiences*) account, note, description, report, diary, register. **3** (*She played a dance record*) gramophone record, disc, album, vinyl.

record vb **1** (*All births, marriages and deaths must be recorded*) register, enter, note, document, minute, catalogue. **2** (*The group have recorded some folk songs*) make, cut, tape, videotape, video.

recount vb (*They recounted the tale of their holiday adventure*) tell, relate, narrate, unfold, repeat.

recover vb **1** (*She has been seriously ill but she is now recovering*) get well, get better, recuperate, improve, rally, pull through. **2** (*They recovered some of their stolen property*) get back, regain, recoup, retrieve, reclaim, repossess, redeem. **3** (*They recovered land from the sea*) reclaim, restore, salvage, save.

recreation n **1** (*His recreations include wind-surfing as well as theatre-going*) hobby, pastime, diversion, amusement, distraction. **2** (*What does he do for recreation?*) leisure, relaxation, amusement, entertainment, fun,

pleasure, diversion, distraction.

recruit vb (*The club is hoping to recruit new members*) enrol, enlist, sign up, take on.

recur vb (*His illness has recurred*) come back, return, reappear.

recurrent adj (*a recurrent fault*) recurring, repeated, repetitive, periodic, frequent.

recycle vb (*recycle paper products*) re-use, use again, reprocess, salvage.

red adj **1** (*She was red with embarrassment*) flushed, blushing. **2** (*Her face goes red in the cold*) ruddy, florid.

reduce vb **1** (*reduce the amount of food they eat*) cut, curtail, decrease, lessen, diminish. **2** (*Drivers should reduce speed*) decrease, moderate, lessen, lower. **3** (*Prices have been reduced*) cut, lower, mark down, take down, slash, cheapen.

redundant adj **1** (*The introduction of the new technology in the firm made many of the workers redundant*) unemployed, jobless. **2** (*a piece of writing full of redundant words*) unnecessary, superfluous, surplus.

refer vb **1** (*He referred to the difficulty of the task in his speech*) mention, allude to, touch on, speak of. **2** (*She referred the complaint to the manager*) pass, hand on, direct, transfer. **3** (*If you do not know the meaning of the word you should refer to a dictionary*) consult, look up, turn to.

referee n (*select a referee for the match*) umpire, judge, adjudicator, arbiter, arbitrator, (*inf*) ref.

reference n **1** (*She made no reference*

to the previous day's quarrel) mention, allusion. **2** (His comments have no reference to the case being discussed) relation, relevance, connection, bearing, application. **3** (She asked her former teacher for a reference when she applied for a job) character reference, testimonial, commendation.

refined adj **1** (refined sugar) processed, purified, treated. **2** (She felt she was too refined to mix with them) polished, cultivated, cultured, civilized, well-bred.

reflect vb **1** (Glass reflects light) send back, throw back, diffuse. **2** (His expression reflected his mood) show, indicate, reveal, communicate. **3** (She needed time to reflect on her problems) think about, consider, contemplate, mull over, ponder.

reflection n (his reflection in the mirror) image, likeness.

reform vb (make efforts to reform the educational system) improve, make better, better, amend, rectify, reorganize, revolutionize.

refreshing adj **1** (a refreshing cool drink/ a refreshing cool breeze) invigorating, reviving, bracing, exhilarating. **2** (Some of his ideas seemed very refreshing) fresh, new, novel, original, different.

refuge n **1** (They sought refuge from their enemies/seek refuge from the storm) asylum, sanctuary, protection, safety, shelter, cover. **2** (The building was a refuge for the homeless) safe house, sanctuary, shelter, retreat, haven.

refugee n (refugees from the famine area) fugitive, exile, displaced person, stateless person.

refuse vb (She refused their invitation) turn down, reject, decline.

refuse n (dispose of household refuse) rubbish, waste, debris, litter, (esp Amer) garbage.

regard vb **1** (The policeman was regarding them closely as they tried to get into the car) look at, watch, observe, study, eye. **2** (He regards his job prospects with optimism) look on, view, consider. **3** (They regard him as rather a fool) consider, judge, rate, assess.

regard n **1** (They paid no regard to his advice) heed, notice, attention. **2** (He is looked upon with regard in the firm) respect, esteem, admiration.

region n (the cold regions of the world) area, territory, section, tract, zone, part, place.

register vb **1** (The hotel guests were asked to sign the register) list, record, directory. **2** (He used the parish registers for his research) record, chronicle, annal. **3** (the register of her voice) range, scale, reach, gamut.

register vb **1** (They registered the birth of their son/They had to register their arrival on the list) record, put on record, enter, write down. **2** (The thermostat registered twenty degrees) read, indicate, show, display. **3** (Her face registered her surprise) show, express, display, reveal.

regret vb (She regrets that she did it) feel sorry, feel repentant, feel remorse, repent, to be ashamed of.

regretful adj (She gave a regretful smile) apologetic, repentant, contrite, remorseful, penitent.

regular adj 1 (The postman did not follow his regular route) usual, customary, accustomed, habitual, normal. 2 (The breathing of the patient is regular) even, steady, rhythmic. 3 (They planted the trees at regular intervals) even, fixed, uniform. 4 (You will have to apply through the regular channels) usual, standard, official, conventional, orthodox.

regulation n (traffic regulations) rule, order, law, decree.

rehearse vb (The actors were rehearsing the play) practise, try out, go over, run through.

reject vb 1 (She has rejected their invitation) refuse, turn down, decline. 2 (She rejected the baby at birth) abandon, forsake, renounce, cast aside.

rejoice vb (They rejoiced on hearing that they had won) be joyful, be happy, be glad, be delighted, be overjoyed, celebrate.

relapse n (The patient was improving but then suffered a relapse) set-back, turn for the worse.

relate vb 1 (He related the story of his misfortune) tell, recount, describe, narrate, report. 2 (information not relating to the matter) apply, be relevant, concern, have a bearing on.

relations npl 1 (She has no relations in the area) family, kin. 2 (They have business relations) dealings, associations.

relationship n. 1 (I don't think there is any relationship between the two events) connection, association, link. 2 (Their relationship is over) friendship, partnership, love affair.

relax vb 1 (He relaxes by swimming) rest, unwind, take it easy, be at leisure, amuse oneself. 2 (He relaxed his grip on the dog's leash) loosen, lose, slacken, weaken 3 (The police will not relax their efforts to find the criminal) reduce, lessen, decrease, diminish.

release vb 1 (The police have released the accused) free, set free, let out, set loose, liberate. 2 (They were tied up by the burglars and could not release themselves) set free, free, untie, undo. 3 (They have released the news of the royal engagement) make public, make known, issue, announce, disclose, put out, circulate, publish.

relentless adj 1 (The judge was completely relentless) ruthless, unmerciful, merciless, pitiless, unforgiving, harsh, cruel. 2 (their relentless efforts to persuade him) persistent, persevering, unremitting, non-stop, unceasing.

relevant adj (the information was not relevant to the discussion) applicable, pertinent, apposite, appropriate.

reliable adj 1 (her most reliable friends) dependable, trustworthy, true, loyal, devoted. 2 (The evidence was not considered reliable) dependable, trustworthy, well-founded, sound.

relieve vb 1 (a drug to relieve the pain) alleviate, soothe, assuage, ease, reduce. 2 (collect money to relieve the distress of the famine victims) help, assist, aid, bring aid to. 3 (She was to relieve the nurse on duty) take over from, take the place of, stand in for, substitute for. **4** (*look for something to relieve the monotony of her life*) break up, interrupt, vary, lighten.

religious adj **1** (*take part in a religious ceremony/a religious discussion*) church, holy, divine, theological. **2** (*She comes from a religious family*) church-going, pious, devout, God-fearing.

relinquish vb (*He relinquished his right to the title*) give up, renounce, surrender.

reluctant adj **1** (*a reluctant witness*) unwilling, unenthusiastic, grudging **2** (*She was reluctant to go*) unwilling, disinclined, loath, averse.

rely vb (*She was relying on her parents for help*) depend on, count on, bank on, trust, put one's faith in.

remain vb **1** (*She remained calm in the emergency*) stay, keep, continue. **2** (*Only a few of the original inhabitants remained*) be left, survive, last, endure. **3** (*He has to remain in hospital*) stay, wait.

remark n (*She made some critical remarks*) comment, statement, observation.

remarkable adj (*It was a remarkable achievement for one so young*) extraordinary, unusual, exceptional, outstanding, impressive.

remedy n (*a remedy for the common cold*) cure, treatment.

remember vb **1** (*I cannot remember his name*) recall, call to mind, recollect, think of. **2** (*Try to remember to post the letter*) keep in mind, bear in mind.

reminisce vb (*old people reminiscing about their youth*) call to mind, recall, remember, recollect, think back on.

remorse n (*She showed remorse for her wrongdoing*) regret, penitence, compunction, contriteness.

remote adj **1** (*They live in a remote mountain village*) distant, far-off, out-of-the-way, isolated. **2** (*She is rather a remote person*) distant, aloof, reserved, unfriendly. **3** (*There is a remote possibility that he will win*) outside, unlikely, slender, slight.

remove vb **1** (*They removed their shoes*) take off. **2** (*She was asked to remove her books from the table*) move, shift, take away, carry away. **3** (*They tried to remove him from his post*) get rid of, throw out, dismiss, sack, expel, evict, oust. **4** (*She has had a tooth removed*) take out, pull out, extract.

renounce vb **1** (*He renounced his claim to the title*) give up, relinquish, surrender, waive. **2** (*He renounced the smoking habit*) give up, swear off, abstain from, desist from. **3** (*They renounced their religion*) give up, abandon, turn one's back on, forsake.

renovate vb (*They are renovating an old country cottage*) modernize, restore, recondition, overhaul.

renown n ((*Her renown as a singer spread*) fame, acclaim, reputation, eminence, prestige.

rent vb (*They rented a boat*) hire, lease, charter.

repair vb **1** (*The mechanic repaired the ancient car*) mend, fix, put right, overhaul. **2** (*They repaired the torn clothes*) mend, sew, darn, patch.

repeal vb (They have repealed that law) revoke, annul, declare null and void, cancel, retract.

repeat vb 1 (He was asked to repeat his statement to the committee) say again, iterate, restate, recapitulate. 2 (The boy repeated his father's words) say again, echo, quote, parrot. 3 (They have to repeat the task) re-do, do again, duplicate.

repel vb 1 (They succeed in repelling their attackers) drive back, push back, repulse, fend off, ward off. 2 (The sight of the rotting meat repelled them) revolt, disgust, nauseate, sicken.

repent vb (She committed a sin but she has repented) feel regret, feel remorse, be sorry, be repentant, be penitent, be contrite.

repercussion n (He could not have foretold the repercussions of his actions) consequence, effect, result, reverberation.

repetitive adj (His work consists of repetitive tasks) repeated, unchanging, monotonous.

replica n (The original of the necklace is in the bank—this is a replica) copy, duplicate, reproduction, imitation, model.

reply n 1 (She gave no reply to his question) answer, response, retort, rejoinder. 2 (He received a reply to his letter) answer, response, acknowledgement.

report n 1 (the firm's annual financial report) statement, record, register. 2 (a newspaper report of the accident) account, article, piece, story, write-up. 3 (They heard the report of a gun) bang, explosion, blast, boom, crack.

report vb 1 (They reported that they had been successful) announce, communicate, tell, relate. 2 (The soldiers were to report to the sergeant at noon) present oneself, announce oneself, appear, arrive. 3 (They reported him to the police) inform on, accuse, tell on, complain about, (inf) rat on, (inf) grass on.

repose n (enjoy some repose after his hard work) rest, relaxation, respite, time off, sleep.

represent vb 1 (A closed fist represents violence) symbolize, stand for, epitomize, personify. 2 (The queen was represented in the picture as a warrior) depict, portray, picture, show. 3 (His lawyer represented him) appear for, act for, speak for, be the representative of.

repressive adj (a repressive regime) repressing, tyrannical, despotic, dictatorial, oppressive, harsh, stern.

reprieve vb (The woman was reprieved because she had killed in self-defence) pardon, let off, spare.

reprimand vb (The pupils were reprimanded for being late) scold, chide, reprove, admonish, reproach, (inf) tell off, (inf) tick off.

reprisal n (When their village was attacked they took reprisals on the attackers) retaliation, vengeance, revenge, retribution, redress, requital.

reproach n (She was upset by his words of reproach) criticism, censure, condemnation, reprimand, reproof.

reproduce vb 1 (*Can the photocopier reproduce coloured documents?*) copy, photocopy, duplicate. 2 (*We were unable to reproduce the lighting effect we produced last week*) repeat, recreate, emulate. 3 (*Rabbits reproduce quickly*) breed, bear young, procreate, multiply.

repulsive adj (*It was a repulsive sight*) revolting, repellent, disgusting, nauseating, offensive, objectionable, loathsome, nasty, horrible, foul.

reputable adj (*get a reputable firm to do the work*) respected, respectable, well-thought-of, esteemed, reliable, dependable.

reputation n 1 (*The firm has a bad reputation for shoddy work*) name, character. 2 (*The incident damaged their reputation*) good name, respectability, esteem.

request vb (*They requested more help*) ask for, seek, apply for, demand, beg for, plead for, petition.

require vb 1 (*They require more money*) need, have need of, be short of, lack, want. 2 (*The job requires concentration*) need, involve, take, call for. 3 (*The police required him to go to the police station*) order, instruct, command.

rescue vb (*They rescued the drowning man from the river/They rescued the men from prison*) save, get out, extricate, free, liberate.

research n (*They were carrying out medical research into new drugs*) investigation, exploration, inquiry, study, analysis.

resemble vb (*She resembles her mother*) look like, be like, bear a semblance to, be similar to, take after, put one in mind of, remind one of.

resent vb (*She resents the fact that her sister earns more money than she does*) begrudge, grudge, be bitter, feel aggrieved, envy, be jealous.

reserve vb 1 (*We reserved seats for the play*) book, order. 2 (*You should reserve some fuel for the winter*) keep, put aside, conserve, save, store. 3 (*They should reserve judgement until they have heard all the facts*) postpone, delay, defer.

reserved adj (*She is very reserved and does not speak to many people*) shy, retiring, diffident, reticent, aloof, distant, unsociable, uncommunicative.

reside vb (*He resides in a large house in London now*) live in, stay in, occupy, inhabit, dwell in.

residence n 1 (*They have an impressive Georgian residence*) house, dwelling place, domicile. 2 (*They take up residence next week*) occupation, occupancy, tenancy.

resident n 1 (*the residents of the new block of flats*) occupant, occupier, inhabitant. 2 (*the hotel residents*) guest, visitor.

resign vb 1 (*He resigned yesterday*) give notice, hand in one's notice, leave. 2 (*He resigned from his job yesterday*) leave, quit, give up.

resist vb (*The troops resisted the invading army*) fight against, stand up to, withstand, hold out against, defy, oppose, repel.

resolve vb 1 (*She resolved to try harder*)

decide, make up one's mind, determine, settle. **2** (*They seemed unable to resolve the problem*) solve, sort out, work out, clear up, answer.

resourceful adj (*resourceful people who made do with what they had*) ingenious, inventive, creative, imaginative, clever, capable.

respect n **1** (*They had great respect for him as a painter*) esteem, high regard, admiration, reverence, deference. **2** (*With respect to the matter under discussion*) reference, relevance, regard, relation. **3** (*The plan was not perfect in all respects*) aspect, facet, feature, way, sense, particular, point, detail.

respectable adj (*Her neighbours do not think that she is very respectable*) of good reputation, upright, honourable, honest, decent, worthy.

response n (*They asked several questions but received no response*) answer, reply, acknowledgement, reaction.

responsible adj **1** (*They said that he was responsible for the damage*) blameworthy, to blame, guilty, at fault, accountable, answerable. **2** (*They need a responsible person to look after the children*) mature, sensible, level-headed, stable, reliable, dependable, trustworthy.

rest n **1** (*a period of rest after work*) repose, relaxation, leisure, ease, inactivity, sleep. **2** (*She is going away for a rest*) break, holiday, vacation.

restless adj **1** (*The children got restless in the afternoon*) fidgety, restive, agitated. **2** (*They passed a restless night*) wakeful, fitful.

restrain vb **1** (*They tried to restrain him from jumping off the bus*) prevent, hold back, impede. **2** (*She tried to restrain her laughter*) suppress, curb, check, stifle, contain. **3** (*It was her job to restrain the dogs*) control, keep under control, subdue, curb.

restrict vb **1** (*The long tight skirt restricted her freedom of movement*) hinder, hamper, impede, obstruct. **2** (*He was told by the doctor to restrict his consumption of salt*) limit, regulate, control, moderate.

restricted adj **1** (*a restricted space*) cramped, confined. **2** (*There is a restricted area around the military camp*) out of bounds, off limits, private.

result n (*His illness was a result of overwork*) effect, consequence, upshot, outcome, repercussion.

retain vb **1** (*They were asked to retain their train tickets*) keep, hold on to, hang on to. **2** (*The village still retains some of the old traditions*) keep, maintain, continue, preserve.

retaliate vb (*They hit the new boy and he retaliated*) take revenge, seek retribution, take reprisals, get even, give tit for tat.

reticent adj (*He was very outgoing but his wife was very reticent*) reserved, diffident, uncommunicative, taciturn, unforthcoming, silent.

retiring adj (*Very few people know her as she is very retiring*) shy, diffident, bashful, self-effacing, unassertive.

retreat vb **1** (*The army retreated before the enemy*) withdraw, go back, fall back, take flight, flee, beat a retreat.

2 (*The tide retreated*) go back, recede, ebb.

retrieve vb (*He tried to retrieve his stolen property*) get back, recover, regain, recoup, reclaim.

return vb **1** (*Their parents will return tomorrow*) come back, go back, reappear. **2** (*She asked him to return the book which she had lent him*) give back, send back.

reveal vb **1** (*She took off her coat and revealed a white dress*) show, display, exhibit, expose, uncover. **2** (*The press revealed the truth about the affair*) disclose, divulge, tell, let out, make known.

revenge n (*He wanted revenge for his brother's murder*) vengeance, retribution, retaliation, reprisal.

reverse vb **1** (*They reversed their roles for the day*) change, exchange, swap, trade. **2** (*They have reversed their previous decision*) alter, change, overturn, repeal, revoke. **3** (*He reversed the car*) back. **4** (*reverse the coat*) turn round, put back to front.

revise vb **1** (*The pupils are revising the term's work*) go over, reread, (*inf*) swot up. **2** (*She had to revise the text of the manuscript*) amend, emend, correct, alter, edit. **3** (*We have had to revise our holiday plans*) reconsider, review, alter, change.

revolt vb **1** (*The sight of the dried blood revolted her*) disgust, repel, nauseate, sicken, (*inf*) turn one off. **2** (*The citizens are revolting against the tyrant*) rebel, rise up, take up arms, mutiny.

revolution n **1** (*There was a revolution against the king*) rebellion, revolt, uprising, insurrection, mutiny, riot. **2** (*There has been a revolution in the computer industry*) complete change, transformation, reformation, innovation. **3** (*one revolution of the wheel*) rotation, round, whirl, spin. **4** (*The satellite made a revolution of the sun*) orbit, circuit, turn.

revolve vb **1** (*The wheel revolved slowly*) go round, turn, rotate, spin, whirl. **2** (*The planet revolves round the sun*) orbit, circle. **3** (*His world revolves round his family*) centre on, focus on, concentrate on.

reward n (*He received a reward for bravery*) award, prize, recompense, gift, decoration, medal.

rhythm n (*The tune had a fast rhythm*) beat, pulse, throb, tempo, cadence.

rich adj **1** (*rich people who owned several houses*) wealthy, affluent, well off, prosperous, well-to-do, moneyed. **2** (*a house with rich furnishings*) costly, expensive, opulent, luxurious, sumptuous, splendid, magnificent. **3** (*The area has a very rich soil*) fertile, fruitful, productive, fecund. **4** (*curtains of a very rich colour*) strong, deep, vivid, intense, brilliant. **5** (*The country has rich supplies of oil*) abundant, copious, ample, plentiful.

rid:— get rid of vb (*She should get rid of those old clothes*) dispose of, throw away, throw out, jettison, dump.

riddle n (*unable to solve the riddle*) puzzle, conundrum, poser, brain-teaser.

ridiculous adj **1** (*It was a ridiculous thing to do*) absurd, pointless, senseless, foolish, inane. **2** (*He told us a ridiculous story about his holiday/She always wears ridiculous hats*) absurd, comical, funny, laughable, humorous, ludicrous. **3** (*It is ridiculous that he got away with the crime*) shocking, outrageous, monstrous, preposterous, incredible.

right adj **1** (*They all gave the right answer*) correct, accurate. **2** (*He was not the right person for the job*) suitable, appropriate, fitting, desirable. **3** (*He is not in his right mind*) sane, sound, rational, sensible. **4** (*They thought the judge did not make the right decision*) just, fair, impartial, good, honest, virtuous.

rigid adj **1** (*It was made of a rigid substance*) stiff, hard, taut, inflexible, unbending. **2** (*The headmaster was a rigid disciplinarian*) strict, severe, stern, stringent, harsh, inflexible.

ring n **1** (*She wore a gold ring*) band, hoop. **2** (*They saw a ring around the moon*) circle, loop. **3** (*He jumped into the boxing ring*) arena, area, enclosure. **4** (*The police have discovered a spy ring*) gang, organization, league, combine, syndicate.

ring vb **1** (*church bells ringing*) toll, sound, peal, chime. **2** (*The hall rang with music*) resound, reverberate, echo, resonate. **3** (*He said that he would ring back*) call, phone, telephone.

riot n (*There was a riot in the crowd when their leader was arrested*) rebellion, revolt, uprising, insurrection, mutiny, uproar.

ripe adj (*ripe fruit in the fruit bowl*) ma-

ture, ready to eat, ready, mellow.

rise vb **1** (*The balloon will rise into the air*) go up, climb, ascend. **2** (*the mountains rising behind the village*) rear up, tower, soar, loom. **3** (*She always rises early*) get up. **4** (*Prices are set to rise*) go up, increase, mount, escalate, rocket. **5** (*The dough for the bread failed to rise*) puff up, swell, expand. **6** (*The stream rises in the mountains*) originate, begin, start, flow from.

risk n **1** (*There is a risk of flooding*) danger, chance, possibility, likelihood. **2** (*Their actions put lives at risk*) danger, peril, jeopardy.

rival n (*her rival in the competition*) opponent, opposition, adversary.

roar vb **1** (*The lion roared*) bellow. **2** (*He roared in rage*) bellow, yell, bawl, shout.

robbery n (*The criminals committed robbery*) burglary, theft, stealing, larceny.

robust adj (*in robust health*) strong, vigorous, tough, rugged, sturdy, stalwart.

rock vb **1** (*The boat began to rock in the storm*) roll, lurch, pitch, swing, sway, wobble. **2** (*rock the cradle*) sway, swing.

rogue n (*He was a rogue who ended up in prison*) villain, scoundrel, rascal.

role n **1** (*her role in the play*) part, character. **2** (*He attended in his role as chairman*) capacity, position, function, post.

roll vb **1** (*The wheels began to roll*) turn, go round, rotate, revolve, spin. **2** (*roll up a newspaper to swat a fly*) furl, coil, fold. **3** (*roll the lawn*) flatten level, smooth, even out. **4** (*as time rolls on*) pass, go by. **5** (*as the ship rolled*) rock, lurch, pitch, toss, swing, sway.

romantic *adj* **1** (*She has a very romantic idea of what it is like to live in a remote village*) unrealistic, impractical, idealistic, starry-eyed. **2** (*romantic words on a greetings card*) loving, amorous, sentimental. **3** (*She seemed to them a romantic figure*) fascinating, glamorous, mysterious, exotic, exciting.

rope *n* (*tie the logs up with a rope*) string, cord, cable, line.

rotate *vb* **1** (*The wheels rotate*) turn, go round, revolve, spin. **2** (*The two doctors rotate between the two wards*) alternate, take turns.

rotten *adj* **1** (*rotten food*) bad, mouldy, decaying, decomposed, putrid, rancid, stinking. **2** (*rotten wood*) decaying, crumbling, disintegrating, corroding. **3** (*What a rotten thing to do!*) nasty, mean, foul, despicable, contemptible.

rough *adj* **1** (*sand down the rough surface of the table*) uneven, bumpy, jaggy, rugged, irregular. **2** (*They have a dog with a rough coat*) shaggy, bushy, hairy, coarse, bristly. **3** (*people with rough voices*) gruff, hoarse, harsh, husky. **4** (*rough weather at sea*) stormy, squally, wild, inclement. **5** (*He goes around with a rough crowd*) rowdy, disorderly, wild, uncouth, coarse, loutish, boorish. **6** (*at a rough estimate*) approximate, inexact, imprecise. **7** (*He made a rough sketch of the house*) rough-and ready, hasty, quick, sketchy, rudimentary.

round *adj* (*a round shape*) circular, ring-shaped, spherical.

route *n* (*They went home by a different route*) way, road, course.

routine *n* (*He hates to have his routine upset*) custom, habit, practice, procedure.

row *n* **1** (*children standing in rows*) line, column, queue, series. **2** (*empty rows of seats in the theatre*) line, tier, rank.

row *n* **1** (*The two brothers had a row over money*) argument, disagreement, dispute, squabble, fight. **2** (*the row coming from the party*) noise, din, rumpus, uproar, commotion.

rowdy *adj* (*the rowdy drunks in the pub*) unruly, disorderly, noisy, boisterous, loud, wild.

rub *vb* **1** (*She rubbed his sore neck*) massage, knead. **2** (*The child began to rub the cat's back*) pat, caress, fondle. **3** (*rub off the dirty mark*) wipe off, remove, erase. **4** (*rub the ointment into the skin*) apply, work in, spread.

rude *adj* **1** (*The children were very rude*) ill-mannered, bad-mannered, impolite, discourteous, impertinent, impudent, cheeky. **2** (*They told rude jokes*) vulgar, coarse, smutty, dirty, bawdy, blue. **3** (*The peasants had only a few rude tools*) crude, primitive, rough, rudimentary, simple.

ruffian *n* (*The old man was attacked by a gang of ruffians*) rogue, thug, villain, hooligan, scoundrel.

rugged *adj* **1** (*a rugged landscape*) rough, uneven, irregular, bumpy, rocky, jagged. **2** (*rugged men who do hard physical work*) tough, strong, stalwart, robust, sturdy, muscular, brawny.

rubbish n 1 (*They put the rubbish in sacks*) refuse, waste, litter, debris, junk. 2 (*She talks a lot of rubbish*) nonsense, drivel, balderdash, gibberish, twaddle.

ruin vb 1 (*The storm ruined the crops*) spoil, damage, wreck, wreack havoc on, destroy, lay waste. 2 (*The recession ruined many small businesses*) bring to ruin, bankrupt, make insolvent, impoverish.

rule vb 1 (*The emperor ruled over several countries*) govern, preside over, have control over, have authority over, be in command of. 2 (*The judge ruled that the accused be released*) order, command, direct, decide.

rumour n (*Rumour has it that he has gone*) gossip, hearsay, the grapevine.

run vb 1 (*They had to run to catch the bus*) race, sprint, dash, rush, bolt, charge. 2 (*Do the trains run on Sundays?*) operate, go, travel. 3 (*water running down the walls*) flow, stream, pour, gush. 4 (*The dye from the black trousers ran on to the white shirt*) spread, mix with. 5 (*He runs a successful business*) operate, conduct, carry on, manage, administer, control, be in charge of, rule. 6 (*They left the engine running*) go, operate, function.

rural adj (*a house in a rural setting*) country, rustic, pastoral.

ruse n (*He gained entrance to the house by a ruse*) trick, stratagem, subterfuge, dodge, ploy, deception, hoax.

rush vb (*They rushed to switch off the water*) hurry, hasten, make haste, run, race, dash.

ruthless adj (*He was a ruthless tyrant*) merciless, pitiless, relentless, unforgiving, harsh, severe, heartless, cruel.

S

sacred adj **1** (*playing sacred music*) religious, church, spiritual, devotional. **2** (*The temple was a sacred place*) holy, blessed, hallowed, consecrated, godly, divine. **3** (*In Hinduism the cow is a sacred animal*) sacrosanct, protected.

sad adj **1** (*She felt sad when her friend went away*) unhappy, miserable, wretched, dejected, downcast, in low spirits, depressed, gloomy, melancholy. **2** (*She tried to forget the sad events of her childhood*) unhappy, unfortunate, distressing, tragic. **3** (*He thought that the country was in a sad state*) sorry, wretched, unfortunate, regrettable, deplorable, disgraceful.

safe adj **1** (*The children are safe indoors*) safe and sound, secure, protected, uninjured, unscathed, free from harm, free from danger, out of harm's way. **2** (*Is the building a safe place for the children to play?*) secure, sound, risk-free. **3** (*She is a safe person to look after the children*) reliable, dependable, trustworthy. **4** (*a safe driver*) careful, cautious, prudent.

sail vb (*We sail at dawn*) set sail, embark, put to sea, put off.

salary n (*He earns a good salary*) wage, pay, earnings, remuneration.

same adj **1** (*That is the same dress which she wore yesterday*) identical, selfsame, the very. **2** (*We ate the same old food, week after week*) identical, similar, unchanging, unvarying.

sample n **1** (*The artist showed the advertising agency a sample of her work*) specimen, example, illustration, instance. **2** (*They gave the questionnaire to a sample of the population*) cross-section, sampling, random sample.

sane adj (*He said that he had not been sane when he committed the murder*) of sound mind, in one's right mind, rational, compos mentis, rational, lucid, (*inf*) all there.

sarcastic adj (*They were hurt by her sarcastic remarks*) caustic, acerbic, sardonic, sneering, mocking, scoffing, derisive.

satisfactory adj (*They did not find her work satisfactory*) adequate, good enough, all right, acceptable, passable, up to scratch, up to standard.

satisfied adj **1** (*They were satisfied with the results/The shop satisfied customers*) pleased, happy, content. **2** (*The police were satisfied that he was innocent*) convinced, sure, certain, positive. **3** (*They felt satisfied after one course of the meal*) full.

satisfy vb **1** (*students who satisfy the university entrance requirements*) fulfil, meet, be sufficient for. **2** (*products that satisfy the demands of the customers*) fulfil, gratify. **3** (*find some cool water to satisfy their thirst*) quench, slake, satiate. **4** (*He was able to satisfy her parents that she was telling the truth*) convince, persuade, assure.

savage adj 1 (attacked by a savage animal) ferocious, fierce, wild. 2 (During the attack she received a savage blow to the head) vicious, brutal. 3 (He was really savage to his family) brutal, cruel, vicious, harsh, grim, barbarous, merciless. 4 (The explorers were attacked by a savage tribe) primitive, uncivilized, wild.

save vb 1 (try to save some money for a holiday) put aside, set aside, put by, keep, reserve, conserve, stockpile, hoard. 2 (It will save a lot of inconvenience) prevent, obviate, rule out. 3 (He saved his friend from death) rescue, deliver, snatch, free.

say vb 1 (say a few words) speak, utter, voice, pronounce. 2 (You should say what you are thinking) express, tell, put into words, state, communicate, make known, articulate. 3 ('It's snowing heavily,' she said) state, remark, announce.

scandalous adj 1 (a politician who had to resign because of his scandalous behaviour) disgraceful, dishonourable, shocking, outrageous, disreputable, improper. 2 (scandalous rumours circulating about the family) slanderous, defamatory, libellous, scurrilous.

scant adj (take scant notice of what her mother said) little, slight, minimal, inadequate, insufficient.

scar n (The accident left him with a scar on his face) blemish, mark, blotch, disfigurement.

scarce adj (Copies of the book are scarce now—it was published so long ago) rare, few, few and far between, in short supply, scant, uncommon, unusual.

scare vb (The sight of the man scared the children) frighten, make afraid, alarm, startle, terrify, terrorize.

scatter vb 1 (scatter the breadcrumbs for the birds) spread, disseminate, sow, sprinkle. 2 (The crowd scattered when the police arrived) disperse, break up, separate, disband.

scene n 1 (They visited the scene of the battle) site, location, position, spot. 2 (The photographs were taken against a winter scene) background, setting, landscape, view, vista, outlook. 3 (It was a moving scene when child and mother were reunited) event, incident, happening, situation. 4 (The child made a scene when she did not get her own way) fuss, outburst, commotion, exhibition, to-do, upset, row.

scenery n (tourists admiring the scenery) view, outlook, prospect, vista, landscape.

scent n 1 (He bought her an expensive scent for her birthday) perfume, fragrance. 2 (the scent of roses in the room) perfume, fragrance, smell. 3 (the scent of newly baked bread) aroma, smell, bouquet, odour. 4 (dogs following the scent of the fox) trail, track, spoor.

sceptical adj (She was sceptical about her chances of success) doubtful, dubious, distrustful, mistrustful, unconvinced.

scheme n 1 (They have developed a new training scheme for young people) plan, programme, project, system, procedure, strategy, design, tactics.

2 (*a modern colour scheme*) arrangement, system.

scoff vb (*They began to scoff at his efforts to bake a cake*) jeer at, mock at, laugh at, ridicule.

scold vb (*Her parents scolded her for being late*) rebuke, reprimand, chide, upbraid.

score n **1** (*What was the score at half-time?*) result, outcome. **2** (*She noticed a deep score on the table*) scrape, scratch, groove, cut, mark.

scorn n (*He treated everyone else's ideas with scorn*) contempt, disdain, mockery, derision.

scowl vb (*He scowled when they disagreed with him*) frown, glower, glare, look daggers.

scrap n **1** (*use scraps of material to make a patchwork quilt*) remnant, fragment, bit, piece, snippet. **2** (*feed the dog scraps of food*) piece, bit, morsel, particle. **3** (*He is a scrap merchant*) waste, junk. **4** (*There was not a scrap of sincerity in what she said*) bit, grain, iota, trace, whit.

scrape vb **1** (*scrape the surface of the table*) scratch. **2** (*The child fell and scraped her knee*) graze, scratch, abrade, cut.

scratch vb **1** (*try to scratch an itchy spot on her back*) rub, tear at. **2** (*She scratched her hand on a rusty nail*) graze, cut, abrade, skin, lacerate, wound.

scream vb (*He screamed when the heavy weight fell on him*) shriek, shout, yell, howl, squeal, yelp, wail.

screen n **1** (*a screen at the window to stop people looking in*) curtain, blind. **2** (*trees to act as a screen from the wind*) shelter, shield, protection, guard. **3** (*The business was a screen for his drug-dealing*) front, façade, blind, disguise, camouflage, cover, cloak.

scruffy adj (*He was told to tidy up, that he was too scruffy to go to school*) untidy, unkempt, dishevelled, messy, slovenly.

scurry vb (*The children were late and scurried home*) hurry, hasten, rush, run, race, dash, scamper.

seal vb **1** (*They sealed the parcel before posting it*) fasten, secure, close up, shut. **2** (*They filled the jars with fruit and sealed them*) make airtight, close, shut, cork. **3** (*The police sealed off the area*) cordon off, shut off, close off. **4** (*They have sealed a bargain*) settle, secure, clinch.

search vb **1** (*The police are searching for clues to the crime*) look for, seek, hunt for, ferret out. **2** (*They searched the building for the missing jewels*) look through, hunt through, rifle through, scour.

secluded adj (*a secluded part of the large garden*) sheltered, private, remote, out-of-the-way.

secret adj **1** (*They were told to keep the matter secret*) confidential, private, under wraps, (*inf*) hush-hush. **2** (*a desk with a secret drawer*) hidden, concealed.

secretive adj (*She is very secretive about where she is going*) reticent, uncommunicative, unforthcoming, taciturn, silent.

section n **1** (*He bought the wood in sections*) part, segment, piece, portion, bit. **2** (*a book divided into sections*) part, division, chapter. **3** (*the children's section of the bookshop*) part, department.

secure adj **1** (*The children feel secure at their grandparents' house*) safe, protected, free from danger, out of harm's way. **2** (*They can no longer look forward to a secure future*) safe, settled, solid, dependable, reliable. **3** (*The stepladder is not very secure*) steady, stable, sturdy, sold.

see vb **1** (*They could not see the cottage through the mists*) make out, catch sight of, spot, glimpse, look at, discern, perceive, notice, observe, view. **2** (*I see what he means*) understand, grasp, get, comprehend, follow, take in. **3** (*I will go and see where he is*) find out, discover, learn, ascertain. **4** (*We asked her to see that the children went to bed early*) make sure, be sure, ensure, mind, see to it, take care. **5** (*When she asked if she could go on holiday her parents said that they would have to see*) think, have a think, give it some thought, consider, reflect. **6** (*The two friends see each other once a week*) meet, arrange to meet. **7** (*He saw his mother to her door*) escort, accompany, usher, guide, lead. **8** (*Did you see the documentary on TV last night?*) watch, look at, view.

seek vb **1** (*The police are seeking more information*) search for, look for, hunt for. **2** (*After the accident she was advised that she should seek help from a counsellor*) request, ask for, solicit.

seem vb (*They seem rather pleasant people*) appear to be, look to be, give the impression of being.

seemly adj (*They thought that her behaviour was far from seemly*) decent, proper, decorous, fitting, suitable, appropriate, becoming.

seize vb **1** (*He seized a hanging branch to pull himself out of the water*) grab, grab hold of, take hold of, grasp, grip, clutch at. **2** (*Kidnappers seized the children*) snatch, kidnap, abduct.

seldom adv (*We seldom see them*) rarely, hardly ever, infrequently.

select vb (*The little boy was asked to select a toy as a present*) choose, pick, opt for, decide on, settle on, plump for.

selfish adj (*The child is selfish and will not share anything with his friends*) self-centred, self-seeking, egotistic, egocentric.

sell vb **1** (*They plan to sell their house soon*) put on sale, put up for sale. **2** (*shops selling foodstuffs*) offer for sale, stock, carry, deal in, market.

send vb **1** (*send a parcel by airmail*) dispatch, convey, transport, remit, post, mail. **2** (*She sent her parents a message that she was well*) communicate, convey, transmit.

sensational adj (*tabloid newspapers with a sensational story about a politician*) spectacular, exciting, dramatic, startling, shocking, scandalous.

sense n **1** (*a sense of smell*) sensation, faculty, feeling. **2** (*They have no sense of honour*) awareness, understanding, appreciation. **3** (*He now has a sense of shame*) feeling. **4** (*The child had the sense to wait for her mother*) common sense, intelligence, cleverness, wisdom, practicality. **5** (*a word with more than one sense*) meaning, definition.

sensitive adj **1** (*She has very sensitive skin*) delicate, fine, soft. **2** (*She is very sensitive to noise*) easily affected by, susceptible to. **3** (*She is a very sensitive person*) responsive, perceptive, sympathetic, understanding. **4** (*She is too sensitive to work in such a competitive firm*) over-sensitive, thin-skinned, touchy. **5** (*The two sides were discussing a very sensitive issue*) delicate, difficult, problematic, thorny.

sentence n **1** (*The judge delivered his sentence*) judgement, verdict, ruling, decision. **2** (*Her attacker is serving a ten-year sentence*) prison sentence, prison term, (*inf*) porridge.

sentimental adj **1** (*The vase is not valuable but she has a sentimental attachment to it*) emotional, nostalgic. **2** (*The group were singing sentimental love songs*) emotional, overemotional, romantic, mawkish, maudlin, (*inf*) soppy, (*inf*) schmaltzy.

separate adj **1** (*The two issues are quite separate*) unconnected, unrelated, divorced, distinct, different. **2** (*They have separate flats*) individual, independent, rite, ritual.

series n (*a series of sporting events/a series of misfortunes*) succession, progression, sequence, chain, train, run, cycle, order.

serious adj **1** (*The headmaster was looking very serious*) solemn, grave, earnest, unsmiling, sombre, sober. **2** (*The accident victim has serious injuries*) bad, grave, critical, acute, dangerous. **3** (*They have several serious matters to discuss*) grave, important, weighty, of consequence, urgent, pressing, crucial, vital. **4** (*make a serious attempt at the championship*) earnest, determined, resolute, honest, sincere.

serve vb **1** (*He has served his master loyally for many years*) be in the service of, work for, be employed by. **2** (*people who have served the community*) be of service to, be of use to, help, assist, benefit, support. **3** (*He served three years as a plumber's apprentice*) spend, carry out, fulfil, complete. **4** (*a sofa that will also serve as a bed*) function, act as, do duty as. **5** (*The hostess is just about to serve the first course*) dish up, give out, deal out. **6** (*She is trying to find a salesperson to serve her*) attend to, assist.

service n **1** (*She retired after forty years' service with the firm*) work, employment. **2** (*We did him a service by telling him the truth about his friends*) good turn, benefit, advantage, help, assistance. **3** (*His car is due for a service*) overhaul, check-up, repair, maintenance. **4** (*guests at the wedding service*) ceremony, rite, ritual.

session n (*old friends having a good gossip session*) time, period, spell.

set vb **1** (*set their suitcases down on the pavement*) put, put down, lay down, place, deposit. **2** (*set the jewel in a gold ring*) fix, embed, arrange, mount.

3 (*set the thermostat*) regulate, adjust. **4** (*set the house on fire*) put, cause to be, start. **5** (*The jelly will not set*) solidify, thicken, harden, gel. **6** (*At what time does the sun set?*) go down, sink, subside. **7** (*The runner set a new record for the course*) set up, establish, create, institute. **8** (*We must set a date for the annual dinner*) fix, establish, settle, agree on, decide on, select. **9** (*His behaviour set them talking*) start, cause. **10** (*The teacher set the children an exam*) assign, allot.

settle vb **1** (*We must settle on a date for the annual dance*) set, decide on, agree on, fix, arrange, choose, select. **2** (*I hope they settle the dispute soon*) clear up, resolve, bring to an end, conclude. **3** (*He wants to settle his financial affairs before he dies*) set to rights, put in order, arrange, clear out, straighten up. **4** (*enough money to settle their bills*) pay, meet. **5** (*The coffee dregs had settled at the foot of the cup*) sink, subside, fall. **6** (*She was so upset that the doctor had to give her something to settle her*) calm, calm down, quieten, sedate, compose, tranquillize. **7** (*The family emigrated from Ireland to settle in America*) make one's home, take up residence, go to live, move to. **8** (*a part of America settled by Scots*) establish, colonize, occupy, inhabit, populate.

sever vb **1** (*In the accident he severed his leg at the knee*) cut off, chop off, lop off. **2** (*He had to sever the logs in two*) divide, split. **3** (*The two families quarrelled and severed relations with each other*) break off, suspend, end, terminate.

several adj **1** (*She has invited several people to dinner*) some, a number of, a few. **2** (*Eventually we all went our several ways*) separate, different, respective, individual, particular.

severe adj **1** (*He wore a very severe expression*) stern, grim, forbidding, disapproving, sombre, serious. **2** (*The tyrant ruled over a severe regime*) harsh, hard, strict, cruel, brutal, savage, merciless. **3** (*She always wore severe clothes*) plain, simple, unadorned, austere. **4** (*We have had a severe winter*) harsh, hard, extreme. **5** (*She suffers from severe pain in her legs*) extreme, intense, fierce, strong, violent, very bad.

shabby adj **1** (*She wore shabby clothes*) worn, threadbare, scruffy. **2** (*The house is looking rather shabby*) dilapidated, run-down, broken-down, tumbledown, ramshackle, dingy, seedy, squalid, slum-like. **3** (*The way he treated her was shabby*) despicable, dishonourable, mean, shoddy.

shade n **1** (*They sat in the shade of a tree*) shadow, cover. **2** (*a shade of blue*) colour, tint, tone, hue. **3** (*a shade against the light*) screen, shield, cover, blind.

shadow n **1** (*We sat in the shadow of the tree*) shade, cover. **2** (*the shadow of the children on the wall*) silhouette, outline, shape.

shady adj **1** (*sit in a shady part of the garden on a hot day*) shaded, shadowy, sheltered, screened, dark, dim. **2** (*The* *shop is run by rather a shady character*) suspicious, suspect, questionable, devious, underhand, dishonest, dishonourable.

shake vb 1 (*The child shook her piggy bank to hear the coins jingling*) rattle, jolt, jerk. 2 (*The car shook as we drove over the stony roads*) bump, jolt, bounce, rock, roll. 3 (*The child was feverish and was shaking*) shiver, quiver, tremble, quake, shudder. 4 (*Her failure had shaken her confidence for future tournaments*) undermine, lessen, weaken. 5 (*She was obviously shaken by the news of the accident*) disturb, upset, shock, agitate, perturb, disquiet, disconcert.

shame n 1 (*He seemed to feel no shame at his crime*) guilt, remorse, compunction, discomfiture, humiliation. 2 (*It was a shame that it rained on the picnic*) pity, misfortune, bad luck, ill-luck. 3 (*She felt that he had brought shame to the school by his action*) disgrace, dishonour, scandal, discredit, disrepute, ignominy.

shape n 1 (*children playing with pieces of cardboard of different shapes*) form, formation, outline. 2 (*Help came in the shape of a passing motorist*) form, guise, appearance. 3 (*Put the jelly in shapes*) mould. 4 (*The players must be in good shape for tomorrow's game*) condition, state, fettle, trim.

share n (*Each of them will receive a share of the profits*) portion, part, quota, percentage, division, allocation.

sharp adj 1 (*need a sharp knife to carve the meat*) keen, razor-edged. 2 (*The child was injured by a sharp length of metal*) pointed, spiky. 3 (*She felt a sharp pain in her side*) acute, intense, keen, piercing, stabbing, severe. 4 (*The sauce had rather a sharp taste*) pungent, sour, tart, bitter, biting. 5 (*There is a sharp drop to the sea just there*) steep, sheer, abrupt, precipitous. 6 (*He was sharp enough to realize that they were trying to swindle him*) clever, shrewd, bright, smart, intelligent. 7 (*She sounded rather sharp on the phone*) abrupt, brusque, curt, short.

sheer adj 1 (*It was sheer stupidity to behave like that*) utter, downright, total, complete, out-and-out. 2 (*It was a sheer drop to the sea*) steep, abrupt, sharp, precipitous.

sheet n 1 (*sheet of glass*) piece, length, panel. 2 (*a sheet of ice on the roadway*) layer, coat, coating, cover, covering, film, blanket, carpet. 3 (*sheets of water left after the flood*) expanse, stretch.

shelf n (*build a shelf for the books*) ledge.

shield vb (*try to shield her eyes from the sun/shield the children from danger*) protect, screen, guard, safeguard.

shine vb (*The street lights were shining*) gleam, glow, glint, sparkle, flash, glitter, shimmer.

shiver vb (*They began to shiver with cold*) shake, quiver, tremble, shudder, quake.

shock vb 1 (*She was shocked by the state of the slum housing*) appal, horrify, outrage, disturb, amaze, astound, traumatize.

short adj **1** (He is too short to reach the branch) small, tiny, diminutive. **2** (short holiday/a short relationship) brief, short-lived, short-term, fleeting, transitory, transient, ephemeral. **3** (She was asked to write a short account of the incident) brief, concise, succinct, terse. **4** (She was rather short on the phone) sharp, brusque, abrupt, curt. **5** (Their supply of money is getting a bit short) deficient, insufficient, scarce, scanty, sparse, meagre, tight.

shot n **1** (hear a shot) gun-fire, report of a gun, bang, blast, explosion. **2** (have a shot at winning) try, attempt, effort, (inf) go, (inf) stab. **3** (take shots at trying to hit the target) turn, opportunity. **4** (tourists taking shots of the beauty spot) photograph, photo, snapshot, snap, film. **5** (have to have several shots before going on a trip to the tropics) vaccination, inoculation, injection, (inf) jab.

shout vb (They shouted to attract his attention/He shouted out in pain) cry, call, yell, howl, roar, scream, bellow.

show vb **1** (show the new products to the customers) display, exhibit, present, demonstrate, set forth. **2** (show them how to use the machine) demonstrate, point out, explain, teach, instruct. **3** (He showed his displeasure by leaving the meeting early) indicate, demonstrate, express, manifest, make known, reveal. **4** (The effects of his illness are beginning to show) be visible, be seen, be obvious, appear. **5** (The ushers showed the guests to their seats at the wedding service) escort, accompany, guide, usher, conduct.

shrewd adj (a shrewd businessman) astute, clever, smart, sharp.

shrill adj (a shrill voice) high-pitched, high, sharp, piercing, penetrating, screeching, shrieking.

shrink vb **1** (That blouse might shrink in the wash) get smaller. **2** (The market for goods like that will shrink) grow less, become smaller, contract, diminish, fall off, drop off. **3** (They shrank from him in fear) draw back, coil, flinch, cringe.

shut vb (Please shut the door when everyone is here) close, fasten, secure, lock.

shy adj (She is too shy to say much in public) bashful, diffident, reserved, reticent, retiring, withdrawn, self-effacing, self-conscious, timid.

sick adj **1** (She has been sick and is off work) ill, unwell, indisposed, poorly, ailing, below par, (inf) under the weather. **2** (She felt sick on the sea voyage) nauseated, queasy, bilious. **3** (He is sick of his present job) tired, weary, bored, jaded, (inf) fed up. **4** (That was rather a sick joke) morbid, macabre, ghoulish, gruesome.

side n **1** (flowers growing by the side of the river) edge, border, verge. **2** (the upper side of the desk) surface, part. **3** (They live on the north side of the town) part, area, region, district, quarter, section, neighbourhood. **4** (discuss all sides of the problem) aspect, angle, facet, point of view, viewpoint, standpoint. **5** (on his side in the dispute) camp, faction, party, group, wing. **6** (the side that is playing against them tomorrow) team, squad.

sight n 1 (It was her first sight of the old family house) view, glimpse. 2 (The child was told to stay within sight of her parents) view, range of vision, field of vision. 3 (Her sight is now poor) eyesight, vision, eyes, power of sight. 4 (visitors going on a tour of the town's sights) spectacle. 5 (What a sight she was in that hat) spectacle, eyesore, mess, (inf) fright.

sign n 1 (Her thinness was a sign of her illness) indication, symptom, evidence, clue. 2 (a sign indicating the way to the museum) signpost, notice, placard. 3 (He gave them a sign to stay still) signal, gesture, motion, movement, gesticulation. 4 (mathematical signs) symbol. 5 (They believed that they would be given a sign of forthcoming tragedy) omen, portent, warning, presage.

silent adj 1 (It was very silent on the hills at night) quiet, hushed, peaceful, tranquil. 2 (They were completely silent as he told them the news) speechless, wordless, unspeaking, without speaking, mute, taciturn, mum, uncommunicative. 3 (She was upset by their silent reproach) unspoken, wordless, unsaid, unexpressed, tacit, implicit.

silly adj 1 (She is a very silly person) foolish, stupid, irresponsible, giddy, frivolous, immature. 2 (It was a very silly thing to do) foolish, stupid, senseless, idiotic, unwise, foolhardy, irresponsible, ridiculous, absurd.

simple adj 1 (It was a very simple task) easy, uncomplicated, elementary, straightforward, effortless. 2 (You will have to explain it to them in simple language) plain, uncomplicated, clear, straightforward, direct, intelligible. 3 (They are wealthy but lead a very simple life) ordinary, modest, unpretentious, humble. 4 (She was a simple peasant girl) unsophisticated, innocent, naive, ingenuous, inexperienced. 5 (The boy is a bit simple) simple-minded, feeble-minded, backward, retarded.

sin n (They will be punished for their sin) wrong, wrongdoing, evil, evildoing, badness, crime, offence, immorality.

sincere adj 1 (Her apology was obviously sincere) genuine, real, true, honest, wholehearted, heartfelt.

single adj 1 (Only a single flower was left blooming) sole, solitary, one, lone, isolated, by itself. 2 (He is still single) unmarried, unwed, unattached, free.

sink vb 1 (The ship began to sink) go under, submerge, founder, capsize. 2 (He sank to his knees to ask forgiveness) fall, drop, slump. 3 (The invalid is thought to be sinking rapidly) decline, deteriorate, fail, fade.

sit vb 1 (The audience were asked to sit) sit down, take a seat, be seated. 2 (Their suitcases were sitting on the pavement) be placed, be situated. 3 (Parliament was sitting all night) be in session, meet, assemble. 4 (We require a table that sits twelve people) seat, accommodate, hold, have room for.

situation n 1 (a cottage in a picturesque situation) place, position, location, setting, site. 2 (The firm is in an unstable financial situation) circumstances, state, state of affairs, condition, predicament. **3** (*There is a vacant situation in the accounts department*) post, position, job, place.

size n (*measure the size of the room*) dimensions, measurements, proportions, area, extent.

skilful adj (*He is a very skilful carpenter*) skilled, able, good, competent, adept, accomplished, expert, deft, masterly.

slack adj **1** (*She has lost a lot of weight and her clothes are now slack*) loose, baggy. **2** (*Since he stopped exercising his muscles have got slack*) limp, flabby, flaccid. **3** (*Business is slack just now*) slow, quiet, inactive, sluggish. **4** (*The pupils have got rather slack about their work*) negligent, neglectful, remiss, careless, slapdash, slipshod.

slap vb (*She slapped his face*) strike, hit, whack, cuff (*inf*) wallop.

sleep n (*have a short sleep after lunch*) nap, doze, rest, (*inf*) snooze, (*inf*) forty winks.

sleepy adj **1** (*She had not had much rest and was feeling sleepy*) tired, drowsy, lethargic, sluggish. **2** (*a sleepy little village*) quiet, peaceful, inactive.

slight adj **1** (*There had been a slight improvement*) small, little, minute, subtle, modest. **2** (*slight matters*) unimportant, minor, insignificant, trifling, trivial. **3** (*She was very slight*) slightly built, slender, slim, small, delicate.

slip vb **1** (*The old lady slipped on the ice and broke her leg*) slide, skid, slither, lose one's footing. **2** (*The cup slipped from her grasp*) fall, slide, drop. **3** (*She*

became upset and slipped from the room*) steal, creep, sneak. **4** (*She just had time to slip on some clothes*) put on, pull on. **5** (*Some people think that educational standards have slipped*) drop, fall, decline, deteriorate, degenerate.

slope n **1** (*The floors of the building are on a slight slope*) slant, angle, inclination, tilt, dip. **2** (*They had picnic on a grassy slope*) hill, hillock, bank, rise.

slow adj **1** (*They moved along at a very slow pace*) slow-moving, leisurely, unhurried, dawdling, snail-like. **2** (*Getting planning permission can be a slow process*) slow-moving, drawn-out, long-drawn-out, prolonged, protracted, time-consuming. **3** (*pupils who are rather slow*) slow-witted, backward, retarded, stupid, unintelligent. **4** (*Business is rather slow*) slack, quiet, sluggish.

sly adj (*It is difficult to know what he is doing—he is very sly*) cunning, crafty, wily, artful, sneaky, devious, underhand, scheming, shifty, furtive.

small adj **1** (*The child is very small for her age*) little, tiny, slight, short, diminutive, under-sized, (*inf*) pint-sized. **2** (*It was just a small mistake*) slight, minor, unimportant, insignificant, trifling, trivial. **3** (*He is rich and powerful but came from small beginnings*) humble, low, lowly, modest, poor, inferior.

smart adj **1** (*You must try to look smart for your job interview*) well-dressed, elegant, neat, spruce, (*inf*) natty. **2** (*The child is smart for her age*) clever, bright, intelligent, sharp.

smash vb **1** (*She smashed several plates when washing up*) break, shatter. **2** (*He smashed his father's car*) crash, wreck, collide. **3** (*Our hopes of success were smashed*) shatter, ruin, wreck.

smell n **1** (*the smell of roses*) scent, perfume, fragrance. **2** (*The smell of freshly baked bread*) aroma, odour. **3** (*The smell of rotting meat*) stink, stench.

smooth adj **1** (*smooth surfaces*) even, level, flat, plane. **2** (*The sea was very smooth*) calm, still, flat, tranquil. **3** (*He is responsible for the smooth running of the firm*) trouble-free, steady, regular, effortless. **4** (*young men with smooth faces*) clean-shaven, hairless. **5** (*She was approached in the shop by a smooth salesman*) smooth-tongued, suave, glib, urbane, courteous, gracious.

smother vb **1** (*She was accused of trying to smother the old lady with a pillow*) suffocate, stifle, asphyxiate. **2** (*She tried to smother a giggle*) suppress, stifle, muffle.

snag n (*He did not see the possible snags in his plans*) drawback, hitch, catch, obstacle, stumbling-block.

snap vb **1** (*The branch suddenly snapped*) break, splinter, fracture, crack. **2** (*She snapped her fingers*) click, crack. **3** (*The dog snapped at our ankles*) bite, snarl, growl. **4** (*She was tired and began to snap at the children*) speak irritably, shout, growl, snarl. **5** (*She was behaving very calmly and then she suddenly snapped*) collapse, break down.

snatch vb **1** (*She was late and had to snatch a piece of toast from the table and run for the bus*) grab, seize, take hold of. **2** (*The thief snatched my hand-bag at the airport*) rob, steal, make off with. **3** (*They snatched the millionaire's child and demanded a ransom*) kidnap, abduct, seize, grab.

sneer vb (*sneering at her attempts*) smirk, snicker, snigger, scoff, scorn, mock, jeer.

snobbish adj (*She has a very snobbish attitude towards people who are badly off*) arrogant, haughty, proud, disdainful, condescending, supercilious, (*inf*) snooty, (*inf*) uppity.

soak vb **1** (*They got soaked in the storm*) drench, wet through, saturate. **2** (*soak the dress in cold water to remove the stain*) steep, immerse. **3** (*blood soaking through the bandage*) penetrate, permeate.

sob vb (*She began to sob as her mother left*) weep, cry, wail.

sociable adj **1** (*Our neighbours are very sociable people*) friendly, affable, social, gregarious, communicative, outgoing.

soft adj **1** (*The car got stuck in soft mud*) spongy, mushy. **2** (*The ground by the river was very soft*) swampy, spongy, boggy. **3** (*soft substances such as plasticine*) pliable, pliant, flexible, malleable. **4** (*a dress of a soft material*) smooth, silky, velvety. **5** (*dresses in soft colours*) pale, light, pastel, muted, subdued, restrained. **6** (*The lighting in the room was very soft*) low, dim, faint, muted, subdued. **7** (*She spoke in a soft voice so that the others would not hear*) quiet, hushed, low, faint, whispered. **8** (*parents accused of being too soft with* their children) lenient, indulgent, easygoing, permissive, liberal.

soil n 1 (*The soil is very poor in that area*) earth, ground, dirt. 2 (*troops killed on foreign soil*) land, country.

solemn adj 1 (*She wore a solemn expression*) grave, serious, unsmiling, sombre. 2 (*It was a solemn occasion*) serious, grave, important, formal, grand, stately, dignified, ceremonious. 3 (*a solemn promise*) earnest, sincere, genuine, honest.

solid adj 1 (*a solid rather than a liquid substance*) firm, hard, dense, thick. 2 (*jewellery made of solid gold*) pure, unalloyed, complete. 3 (*solid houses made of stone and built to last*) substantial, strong, sturdy.

solitary adj (*He leads a solitary life with no family or friends*) lonely, lonesome, friendless, unsociable. 2 (*A solitary tree in the barren landscape*) single, lone, sole, by oneself/itself.

solution n 1 (*unable to find the solution to the mathematical problem*) answer, result, resolution. 2 (*a solution of salt and water*) suspension, mixture.

soothe vb 1 (*an ointment to soothe the painful sunburn*) ease, alleviate, assuage, lessen, reduce. 2 (*He tried to soothe the crying baby*) quieten, calm, pacify.

sophisticated adj 1 (*She regards herself as being a sophisticated city-dweller*) worldly, experienced, cultivated, cultured, urbane, suave, cosmopolitan. 2 (*an office equipped with sophisticated electronic equipment*) advanced, complex, complicated, elaborate.

sore adj 1 (*She has a sore patch on her arm*) painful, in pain, aching, tender, raw, smarting, inflamed, bruised. 2 (*people in sore need of somewhere to live*) urgent, pressing, desperate, critical, dire.

sorry adj 1 (*He is not at all sorry for his misdeeds*) apologetic, regretful, ashamed, repentant, penitent, remorseful, contrite. 2 (*We were sorry to hear that she was ill*) sad, unhappy, distressed, regretful. 3 (*They felt sorry for the homeless people*) sympathetic, compassionate, full of pity, moved.

sort n (*several different sorts of vegetable/a new sort of computer*) kind, variety, type, class, category, make, brand.

sound n 1 (*There was not a sound from the children's room*) noise. 2 (*The sound of someone playing the recorder*) noise, music. 3 (*We did not like the sound of their plans for improvement*) impression, idea.

sour adj 1 (*a sauce that was rather sour*) tart, acid, bitter, sharp. 2 (*milk that had turned sour*) curdled, bad, rancid, off. 3 (*He is a sour old man*) ill-tempered, disagreeable, irritable, cross.

space n 1 (*travel in space*) outer space, infinity. 2 (*large pieces of furniture that take up a great deal of space*) room, expanse, area, scope. 3 (*There was only a narrow space between each house*) gap, interval, opening, break. 4 (*There is a space on the form to explain why you want the job*) blank space, blank, empty space, gap. 5 (*They both died within the space of* *two years*) time, period, span, interval, duration. **6** (*There are no spaces left on the course*) place, room.

spare *adj* **1** (*take a spare pair of socks*) extra, additional, reserve, supplementary, surplus. **2** (*She works long hours and has little spare time*) free, unoccupied, leisure.

sparse *adj* (*a sparse covering of grass*) scanty, meagre, slight.

spasm *n* **1** (*He is in agony with stomach spasms*) contraction, cramp. **2** (*limb spasms*) twitching, convulsion. **3** (*a sudden spasm of coughing*) fit, paroxysm, convulsion, bout, attack.

speak *vb* **1** (*Did he speak the truth?*) say, tell, state, utter, voice, express, pronounce. **2** (*The two sisters quarrelled and have not spoken to each other for years*) talk to, converse with, communicate with, chat. **3** (*The lecturer is to speak for an hour*) talk, lecture, deliver a speech.

special *adj* **1** (*We were asked to take special care of the book*) especial, particular, exceptional, extra special. **2** (*It was a special occasion for the old people*) unusual, exceptional, remarkable. out-of-the ordinary, notable, outstanding, memorable, significant, important, momentous.

spectacular *adj* (*a spectacular firework display*) striking, remarkable, impressive, magnificent, splendid, sensational, breathtaking, dramatic.

speech *n* **1** (*the power of speech*) talk, communication. **2** (*He was drunk and his speech was slurred*) diction, enunciation, pronunciation. **3** (*He gave a speech thanking everyone*) talk, lecture, address.

speed *n* **1** (*the speed at which they were going*) rate. **2** (*They moved with amazing speed*) rapidity, swiftness, fastness, quickness, haste, hurry.

spend *vb* **1** (*They will have to spend a great deal of money on that house*) pay out, lay out, expend, (*inf*) fork out, (*inf*) shell out. **2** (*They spend hours on the beach*) pass, while away, fill, occupy. **3** (*A great deal of effort was spent on the task*) use, employ, apply, devote.

spill *vb* (*Water was spilling from the bucket as she walked*) flow, pour, overflow, brim over, run over, slop over.

spirit *n* **1** (*His spirit was troubled*) soul, psyche, inner self. **2** (*They were people of determined spirit*) character, temperament, disposition, quality. **2** (*He required spirit to undertake the journey*) courage, bravery, mettle, pluck, determination. **4** (*The children performed the play with spirit*) liveliness, animation, enthusiasm, energy, vivacity, verve.

spite *n* (*She damaged her friend's bike out of spite*) malice, maliciousness, ill-will, hostility, resentment, vindictiveness.

splendid *adj* **1** (*We had a splendid holiday*) excellent, fine, first-class, superb, marvellous, wonderful, great. **2** (*a splendid royal palace*) magnificent, sumptuous, imposing, impressive, glorious, luxurious.

split *vb* **1** (*split the logs for the fire*) break, chop, cut. **2** (*The plate seemed

just to *split in two*) break, snap, splinter.
3 (*The robbers split the profits from the burglary amongst themselves*) divide, share, apportion, distribute. **4** (*The argument over the local school split the village into two groups*) divide, separate. **5** (*The couple have split up*) separate, part, divorce, break up.

spoil vb **1** (*a substance that spoiled the surface of the table*) damage, mar, impair, blemish, deface, ruin, destroy. **2** (*She spoils her daughter*) over-indulge, indulge, pamper, cosset, coddle, mollycoddle.

spot n **1** (*spots of soot on the washing on the line*) mark, speck, fleck, dot, smudge, stain, blotch. **2** (*get ointment for the spots on her chin*) pimple, pustule, boil, blemish. **3** (*a pleasant spot for a country cottage*) place, area, location, site, situation, setting.

spread vb **1** (*They spread rumours*) circulate, disseminate, transmit, propagate, publicize. **2** (*Feeling against the new road is spreading*) extend, increase, proliferate, escalate, mushroom. **3** (*The farmer spread fertilizer on the fields*) lay, put, apply, cover. **4** (*The bird spread its wings and flew off*) stretch, extend, open out, unfurl.

squeeze vb **1** (*squeeze limes to make a cool drink*) squash, crush, compress. **2** (*She squeezed his arm to attract his attention*) pinch, press, grip. **3** (*She squeezed the water from the dress and hung it up*) wring, twist, press. **4** (*They squeezed the water from the wet sweaters*) extract, press, force, express. **5** (*The speaker was so popular that the audience was squeezed into the hall*) crush, squash, pack, crowd, cram, jam, wedge.

stage n **1** (*the stages in the production process*) point, step, period, level, phase. **2** (*the first stage of the journey*) lap, leg, phase. **3** (*She was too nervous to go on the stage*) platform, dais, rostrum, podium.

stand vb **1** (*The audience was asked to stand*) rise, get to one's feet, get up, be upright, be erect, be vertical. **2** (*The block of flats that used to stand here*) be, be situated, be located. **3** (*stand the bookcase against the wall near the fireplace*) place, put, position, erect, set up. **4** (*They appealed against the judge's ruling but the sentence stood*) remain, stay, hold, hold good, prevail. **5** (*She cannot stand loud noise*) put up with, tolerate, bear, endure, abide.

start vb **1** (*before the war started*) begin, commence, get underway, come into being. **2** (*start the machine*) turn on, put on, set in motion, activate. **3** (*She started a new society*) begin, commence, set up, establish, found, launch.

state n **1** (*a system in a state of chaos*) condition, situation, circumstances, position, state of affairs, predicament. **2** (*She was in a tearful state*) condition, mood, humour, frame of mind. **3** (*His mother got into a state when he did not come home*) panic, fluster, (*inf*) flap. **4** (*occasions of state attended by the queen*) pomp, ceremony, majesty, grandeur. **5** (*the various states in the world*) country, nation, land.

state vb (state their reasons for going) express, voice, utter, say, declare, tell, announce.

stay vb 1 (They left but we decided to stay) remain, wait, linger. 2 (She stayed angry a long time) remain, continue. 3 (They stayed at a small hotel) put up, reside.

steady adj 1 (drive at a steady pace) uniform, even, regular, consistent. 2 (try to keep the table steady on the moving ship) stable, immovable, unmoving, motionless. 3 (her steady love for him) constant, unchanging, unfaltering, continuous, endless. 4 (require a steady young person for the job) sensible, level-headed, calm, reliable.

step n 1 (take one step nearer the sea) stride. 2 (She listened for her father's steps on the stairs) footstep, footfall, tread. 3 (She took a rash step) act, course of action, move, deed. 4 (looking for the next step in his promotion) stage, level, grade, rank, degree. 5 (a rotten step on the ladder) rung, tread.

stick vb 1 (The child began to stick the pictures in a book) glue, paste, gum, attach, fix, pin, tack. 2 (She stuck a knife in the meat to see if it was cooked) thrust, push, jab, poke, insert. 3 (The machine has stuck) jam, stop, halt, come to a halt.

stiff adj 1 (a piece of stiff card) rigid, hard, unyielding, inflexible. 2 (Her muscles are stiff after the long climb) tight, tense, taut. 3 (The robbers received a stiff sentence) severe, harsh, hard, heavy, drastic, stringent. 4 (She was rather stiff when the young couple arrived) formal, cold, aloof.

still adj 1 (It was a still day) calm, windless. 2 (They were asked to stay completely still) motionless, immobile, stationary. 3 (The house was still) quiet, peaceful, silent, hushed.

stop vb 1 (They tried to stop the fight) bring to a halt, halt, end, finish, terminate, bring to a standstill, wind up. 2 (She could not stop shivering) refrain from, desist, cease, leave, hinder, impede, obstruct.

story n 1 (a story about dragons) tale, fairy story, myth, legend, fable. 2 (the story of how he got home) account, report.

straight adj 1 (The picture is not straight) level, in line. 2 (a straight line) uncurving, unbent. 3 (They would not give a straight answer) direct, forthright, frank, candid, honest, sincere.

strange adj 1 (It was a strange sight) peculiar, odd, queer, bizarre, weird. 2 (a market stocking strange fruits) exotic, foreign, alien, unfamiliar.

strong adj 1 (require someone strong to lift the heavy furniture) powerful, muscular, well-built, burly, sturdy, strapping, robust. 2 (strong doors at the castle entrance) solid, heavy, sturdy. 3 (They have a very strong argument against closing the station) sound, powerful, cogent, compelling. 4 (There is a strong similarity between the two styles) marked, noticeable, pronounced, distinct, definite, striking. 5 (They have strong feelings on the subject of education) intense, fervent, passionate. 6 (wearing strong colours) bright, vivid, deep, intense. **7** (*strong coffee*) concentrated. **8** (*take strong measures*) active, firm, severe, drastic, extreme.

stupid *adj* **1** (*He is too stupid to follow the instructions*) unintelligent, thick, dense, dim, dull-witted, foolish. **2** (*It was a stupid thing to do*) foolish, absurd, silly, idiotic, unwise, unintelligent.

suggest *vb* **1** (*suggest a plan of action*) propose, put forward, recommend, advocate. **2** (*What are you suggesting?*) hint at, insinuate, imply.

suit *vb* **1** (*find a time for the meeting that suits both of them*) be suitable for, be convenient for. **2** (*a style of dress that does not suit her*) become. **3** (*You must try to suit your speech to the occasion*) fit, tailor, adapt, adjust.

suitable *adj* **1** (*The books are not suitable for the course*) suited, right, appropriate, apt, in keeping with. **2** (*come at a suitable time*) convenient, acceptable.

supply *n* (*have a supply of fuel for the winter*) store, stock, reserve, pile, mass, heap, hoard, stockpile.

supply *vb* (*They supply us with fuel*) give, provide, furnish, equip.

support *vb* **1** (*the uprights that support the bridge*) bear, prop up, hold up, shore up, underpin. **2** (*He supported the local candidate in the election*) back, champion, assist, aid, help, be on the side of, vote for. **3** (*support the cause of animal rights*) back, champion, promote, further, favour, defend. **4** (*evidence to support his point of view*) back, bear out, substantiate, corroborate,

confirm. **5** (*She works long hours to support the family*) maintain, provide for, look after, sustain.

suppose *vb* (*I suppose he will get there as soon as he can*) assume, presume, think, believe, expect, imagine.

sure *adj* **1** (*The police have to be sure that he is guilty*) certain, definite, positive, convinced, confident. **2** (*He felt that the project was a sure winner*) certain, definite, guaranteed, inevitable, (*inf*) in the bag. **3** (*a sure remedy for warts*) certain, unfailing, infallible, reliable, dependable.

suspicious *adj* **1** (*We are a bit suspicious of his story*) doubtful, distrustful, mistrustful, sceptical, disbelieving. **2** (*The circumstances of the case are rather suspicious*) odd, strange, queer, questionable, (*inf*) fishy. **3** (*a house now occupied by a suspicious character*) shady, shifty.

sweet *adj* **1** (*children who love sweet foods*) sugary, syrupy. **2** (*the sweet smell of roses*) fragrant, perfumed, scented. **3** (*the sweet sound of the flute*) musical, tuneful, dulcet, melodious. **4** (*What a sweet little girl*) delightful, charming, appealing, attractive. **5** (*She was always very sweet to us*) charming, pleasant, friendly, generous, kind, kindly, amiable.

sympathy *n* **1** (*They expressed their sympathy to the widow*) compassion, commiseration, pity, condolence, support, concern, consideration. **2** (*They have some sympathy for the cause of the protesters*) good will, approval, favour, support.

synthetic adj (objects made of synthetic material) man-made, manufactured, artificial, fake, mock.

system n 1 (the public transport system) structure, organization, arrangement, set-up. 2 (a new system for filing information) method, process, means, technique.

T

table n 1 (*pupils doing their homework at a table*) counter, bench, desk. 2 (*a book containing many tables*) diagram, chart, figure. 3 (*a table of contents at the front of the book*) list, catalogue, index.

tablet n 1 (*take tablets for a headache*) pill, capsule. 2 (*The hotel provided tablets of soap*) bar, cake.

tackle vb (*He is going to tackle the job alone*) deal with, undertake, attempt, take on, apply oneself to.

tactful adj (*You will have to be tactful as she is very sensitive*) diplomatic, discreet, delicate, subtle, sensitive.

tactics npl (*They used dishonest tactics to win*) strategy, manoeuvres, scheme, plan, policy.

tail n 1 (*a fox's tail*) brush, scut. 2 (*We were at the tail of the queue*) end, rear, back. 3 (*The police were on his tail*) trail, scent.

tail vb 1 (*police tailing the crook*) follow, shadow, stalk. 2 (*Business tails off at the end of autumn*) dwindle, decrease, drop off, fall away, peter out, die away.

take vb 1 (*The child took his mother's hand*) take hold of, grasp, seize, grip, grab, clutch, 2 (*The soldiers took several prisoners*) seize, catch, capture, arrest. 3 (*Someone has taken the teacher's pen*) remove, go off with, pick up, move, steal, (*inf*) pinch. 4 (*She took her sister to the pictures*) escort, accompany, conduct, guide.

5 (*The journey takes two hours*) take up, use, need, require, call for. 6 (*The bus will take you right there*) transport, carry, convey. 7 (*He took the books to school with him*) carry, bear, fetch, convey. 8 (*She decided to take the red dress*) choose, pick, select, buy, purchase. 9 (*She took the bad news well*) receive, accept, deal with, cope with. 10 (*She takes Latin at school*) study, learn, be taught. 11 (*I take it that you do not agree*) understand, gather, assume, believe.

tale n 1 (*a fairy tale*) story, anecdote, legend, fable, narrative. 2 (*We hear tales of his bad behaviour*) talk, rumour, gossip.

talented adj (*They are very talented musicians*) gifted, accomplished, able, capable, expert.

talk vb 1 (*The children were scolded for talking in class*) speak, express oneself, communicate, chatter, chat, gossip. 2 (*He was talking nonsense*) speak, say, utter, voice. 3 (*People are talking about her wild behaviour*) gossip, comment, spread rumours.

talk n 1 (*The lecturer gave an interesting talk*) lecture, speech, address. 2 (*She wanted to have a talk with him about her career*) chat, discussion, conversation, tête à tête, (*inf*) confab.

talkative adj (*so talkative that no one else gets a chance to say anything*) garrulous, loquacious, voluble.

tall adj **1** (*Many good basketball players are tall*) big. **2** (*a town with many tall buildings*) high, lofty, towering.

tame adj (*The animal is quite tame*) domesticated, gentle.

tamper vb (*Someone had tampered with the papers on her desk*) interfere with, meddle with, fiddle with.

tangled adj **1** (*tangled hair/tangled wool*) entangled, twisted, knotted, matted. **2** (*tangled financial affairs*) confused, muddled, jumbled, complicated, involved.

tap vb **1** (*tap on the door*) knock, rap, bang. **2** (*Someone tapped me on the shoulder*) touch, pat.

target n **1** (*The archer failed to hit the target*) mark, bull's eye. **2** (*The target for the appeal is £50,000*) goal, aim, objective. **3** (*The new girl is the target of all their teasing*) butt, victim, scapegoat.

task n (*tasks to be done around the house*) job, chore, duty, assignment.

take (someone) to task to reprimand or criticize (someone) (*The teacher took the student to task for his untidy homework*).

taste n **1** (*The pudding had an odd taste*) flavour, tang. **2** (*her taste in literature*) like, liking, preference, inclination, predilection. **3** (*a house furnished with great taste*) stylishness, elegance, refinement, discrimination.

tasteless adj **1** (*The soup was tasteless*) flavourless, bland, insipid, watery. **2** (*tasteless Christmas decorations in the shops*) vulgar, tawdry, flashy, garish. **3** (*She made a few tasteless remarks*) unseemly, indelicate, vulgar.

teach vb **1** (*She teaches the younger children*) educate, give lessons to, instruct, coach, train. **2** (*He teaches history*) give lessons in, give instruction in. **3** (*His father taught him how to ride a bike*) instruct, train, show.

tease vb **1** (*The cat will scratch you if you tease it*) torment, annoy, bother, provoke. **2** (*She was upset by his remark but he was only teasing*) joke, fool.

technique n **1** (*The tennis player is trying out a new technique*) method, system, approach. **2** (*We admired the technique of the sculptor*) skill, expertise, artistry, proficiency, knack.

tedious adj (*The work is tedious*) boring, monotonous, dull, wearisome.

tell vb **1** (*We told them the news*) inform, make known, impart, communicate, announce, disclose, declare. **2** (*He told the children a story*) recount, relate, narrate. **3** (*The children were told to go home*) instruct, order, command, direct. **4** (*They know her secret but promised not to tell*) tell tales, blab, give the game away, let the cat out of the bag, (*inf*) spill the beans, (*inf*) grass. **5** (*We could not tell which twin was which*) distinguish, differentiate.

temper n **1** (*She is in a temper*) bad mood, ill humour, rage, fury, tantrum. **2** (*He is of uncertain temper*) temperament, disposition, nature, character, mood. **3** (*She lost her temper*) composure, self-control, coolness, calm, good humour.

temperamental adj (*She is a good*

worker but she is very *temperamental*) excitable, emotional, volatile, moody.

temporary adj **1** (*They have got temporary jobs*) short-term, provisional, impermanent. **2** (*His interest in golf was only temporary*) short-lived, brief, fleeting, ephemeral, transient.

tempt vb (*She was on a diet but was tempted by the sight of the chocolates*) entice, lure, attract, seduce.

tendency n **1** (*They have a tendency to tell lies*) inclination, leaning, propensity. **2** (*The upward tendency of the temperature graph*) movement, direction, trend, bias.

tender adj **1** (*The meat was tender*) not tough, juicy, succulent, soft. **2** (*She has a tender area on her head*) sore, painful, aching, irritated, inflamed. **3** (*The old man seems fierce but has a tender heart*) compassionate, softhearted, kind, sympathetic, caring, gentle.

tense adj **1** (*They are feeling tense as they wait for the results of the exam*) strained, under a strain, under pressure, overwrought, distraught, worked up, anxious, uneasy. **2** (*You have to keep the rope tense*) tight, taut, rigid, stretched, strained.

tentative adj **1** (*The toddler took a few tentative steps*) hesitant, hesitating, faltering, uncertain, cautious. **2** (*She asked if she could make a tentative suggestion*) speculative, exploratory, experimental, trial, untried.

term n **1** (*a document full of technical terms*) word, expression, phrase, name, title. **2** (*the mayor's term of office*) period, time, spell, interval, duration.

terrible adj **1** (*refugees who endured terrible hardship*) dreadful, appalling, shocking, horrible, horrific, grim. **2** (*the terrible heat from the fire*) extreme, severe, intolerable. **3** (*There was a terrible smell from the drains*) nasty, foul, vile, offensive, obnoxious. **4** (*He is a terrible dancer*) very bad, poor, incompetent, useless, dreadful, (*inf*) rotten.

terrify vb (*Walking through the churchyard at night would terrify her*) frighten, scare, alarm, petrify, terrorize.

terror n **1** (*She was gripped with terror when she heard noise*) fear, dread, alarm, panic. **2** (*That boy's a little terror*) rascal, rogue, imp, hooligan.

test n **1** (*The children are having an English test*) exam, examination. **2** (*a hearing test*) examination, check, assessment, appraisal, investigation, exploration. **3** (*the test of a successful film*) criterion, touchstone, yardstick, standard, measure.

test vb **1** (*test the child's hearing*) examine, check, assess, appraise, investigate, explore, analyse. **2** (*The children's behaviour really tested his patience*) try, tax, strain. **3** (*test the car*) try out, try.

text n **1** (*The text of his speech was world poverty*) topic, subject, subject matter, theme. **2** (*in the introduction, not in the text of the book*) body, main part. **3** (*He is responsible for the text but not the illustrations of the book*) words.

thankful adj (Her parents were thankful that she was safe) grateful, full of gratitude, appreciative, relieved.

thaw vb (The ice began to thaw) melt, defrost, liquefy.

theft n (There have been a series of thefts from shops) stealing, robbery, thieving, burglary, larceny, pilfering, (inf) pinching.

theoretical adj (He was describing a theoretical situation rather than an actual one) hypothetical, speculative, assumed.

thick adj 1 (Thick snow lay on the roads) deep. 2 (She was reading a very thick book) fat, substantial. 3 (She thinks that she has thick legs) broad, wide, fat, large, solid. 4 (a thick rope to tie up the logs) strong, stout, sturdy. 5 (A thick mist descended) dense, heavy, sold. 6 (a voice thick with emotion) husky, gruff, hoarse, rough, guttural, throaty. 7 (He is too thick to understand the instructions) stupid, dense, unintelligent, dim, dull-witted.

thief n (The thief got away with his watch) robber, pickpocket, burglar, housebreaker, larcenist.

thin adj 1 (She is thin and ill-looking) underweight, skinny, scrawny, emaciated, gaunt, skeletal. 2 (She is on a diet to try to get thin) slim, slender, svelte, light. 3 (a design formed of thin lines) fine, narrow, delicate. 4 (a dress made of a very thin material) light, lightweight, delicate, flimsy, sheer, filmy. 5 (She is worried about having thin hair) sparse, scanty, wispy. 6 (The custard was too thin) dilute, watery, runny.

7 (They had hoped for a large crowd but the audience was rather thin) sparse, scarce, scanty, meagre. 8 (rather a thin voice) weak, low, feeble, faint. 9 (It was rather a thin excuse) flimsy, weak, feeble, poor, unconvincing, inadequate.

thing n 1 (There was a huge pile of things on the table) article, item, object. 2 (It was a sensible thing to do) action, act, deed, undertaking. 3 (It was a dreadful thing to happen) incident, event, occurrence, happening. 4 (Calmness is a useful thing to have in a crisis) quality, characteristic, attribute, trait. 5 (There are a few things which we should discuss) fact, point, detail, particular. 6 (The poor thing had nowhere to go) wretch, creature. 7 (She has a thing about spiders) phobia, fear, aversion, dislike, horror.

think vb 1 (You must think before you act) reflect, deliberate, concentrate, contemplate, ponder, ruminate. 2 (The old lady was thinking about the past) remember, recall, call to mind, reminisce. 3 (We think that they will arrive tomorrow) believe, expect, suppose, imagine, assume. 4 (He is thought to be brilliant) consider, regard, hold, deem.

thirst adj 1 (They nearly died of thirst in the desert) thirstiness, dehydration. 2 (They had a great thirst for knowledge) desire, craving, longing, yearning, avidity, eagerness, keenness.

thorough adj 1 (The police conducted a thorough investigation) exhaustive, in depth, comprehensive, intensive, extensive. 2 (He is a slow worker but he is *thorough*) meticulous, painstaking, punctilious, assiduous, careful. **3** (*He is a thorough villain*) thoroughgoing, utter, out and out, absolute, sheer, complete.

thought n **1** (*He is now incapable of rational thought*) thinking, powers of reasoning. **2** (*She was deep in thought*) thinking, reflection, contemplation, deliberation, musing. **3** (*I had a sudden thought as to what we should do*) idea, line of thought, notion. **4** (*We shall give the matter some thought*) consideration, attention, heed, regard. **5** (*We asked her for her thoughts on the subject*) idea, opinion, view, feeling. **6** (*In giving gifts it is the thought that counts*) thoughtfulness, consideration, care, kindness, compassion.

thoughtful adj **1** (*He seemed in a thoughtful mood*) reflective, contemplative, meditative, introspective, absorbed, in a brown study. **2** (*She is a thoughtful daughter*) considerate, attentive, caring, solicitous, helpful, kind, kindly.

threaten vb **1** (*The bully threatened the younger children*) make threats, menace, intimidate, browbeat, bully, pressurize. **2** (*Pollution threatens the environment*) be a threat to, menace, be a danger to, endanger, put at risk, jeopardize, put in jeopardy, imperil. **3** (*Rain was threatening*) be imminent, loom, be impending.

thrifty adj (*They have to be thrifty as they do not have much money*) economical, careful, frugal, sparing.

thrill vb (*The children were thrilled by the display of acrobatics*) excite, stimulate, arouse, stir, electrify, give joy to, (*inf*) get a kick out of.

thrive vb **1** (*The house plants thrive in that room*) flourish, do well, burgeon. **2** (*The firm is now thriving*) flourish, proper, do well, boom.

throb vb (*His pulse throbbed normally/ Her heart throbbed*) beat, pulse, palpitate, pound, vibrate, thump.

throw vb **1** (*He threw a brick through the window*) hurl, fling, toss, cast, lob, sling, (*inf*) chuck. **2** (*She threw him a warning glance*) cast, send, give, bestow on. **3** (*She threw away all her old clothes*) throw out, discard, dispose of, get rid of, dispense with, (*inf*) dump. **4** (*The question completely threw him*) baffle, bamboozle, dumbfound, disconcert, astonish.

thrust vb **1** (*He thrust the present into her hands*) push, shove, ram. **2** (*They thrust the door open*) push, shove, drive, press, propel. **3** (*They thrust their way to the front of the queue*) push, shove, press, force, shoulder, elbow, jostle.

thud n (*The box fell with a loud thud*) thump, bang, crash, wham.

thug n (*The thug attacked the old man*) ruffian, villain, hoodlum, rogue, rough, tough.

thump vb **1** (*He turned round and thumped his attacker*) strike, hit, punch, wallop, smack, slap, batter. **2** (*Her heart was thumping in terror*) thud, pulse, pulsate, throb, palpitate. **3** (*He thumped on the table*) bang, batter, beat, crash, knock.

thwart vb (*Their plans for expansion were thwarted*) frustrate, foil, baulk, check, block, obstruct, impede, hamper, stop.

tidy adj 1 (*The room was very tidy*) neat, orderly, in order, in good order, clean, shipshape, spick and span, spruce. 2 (*Everyone had to be tidy for the school photograph*) neat, well-groomed, spruce. 3 (*He is not a tidy person*) neat, orderly, organized, methodical, systematic.

tie vb 1 (*He tied the string*) knot, make a bow in. 2 (*They tied the parcel with string*) bind. 3 (*They had to tie the dog to the gate*) tie up, tether, fasten, secure, attach, fix. 4 (*The two teams tied for first place*) draw, be equal, be even, be neck and neck.

tight adj 1 (*She wore a tight skirt instead of a full one*) tight-fitting, close-fitting, figure-hugging, narrow. 2 (*You must keep the rope tight*) taut, rigid, stiff, tense, stretched, strained. 3 (*She kept a tight grip on her mother's hand*) fast, secure. 4 (*We need a jar with a tight lid*) airtight, watertight, sealed, hermetically sealed. 5 (*make sure that the screws are tight*) secure, fast, fixed. 6 (*a tight mass of fibres*) compact, compressed. 7 (*Space was tight in the small house*) cramped, restricted, limited. 8 (*Security was tight at the meeting of the presidents*) strict, rigorous, stringent. 9 (*Money was tight*) scarce, scant, in short supply, limited, inadequate, insufficient.

time n 1 (*in the time of the cavemen*) period, age, era, epoch. 2 (*He seemed fine the last time I saw him*) occasion, point, juncture. 3 (*He felt that it was time to leave*) moment, point, stage. 4 (*I worked in Spain for a time*) while, period, spell. 5 (*It was a tune in waltz time*) rhythm, measure, tempo, beat.

timetable n (*give out copies of the conference timetable*) schedule, programme, list, agenda.

timid adj 1 (*The pupils were too timid to stand up to the bullies*) timorous, fearful, afraid, apprehensive, frightened, scared, cowardly. 2 (*She was too timid to ask the pop star for his autograph*) timorous, shy, bashful, diffident, reticent, retiring.

tingle vb (*Her fingers were tingling*) prickle, tickle, itch, sting, quiver, tremble.

tint n 1 (*The artist had several tints to chose from*) colour, shade, tone. 2 (*an auburn hair tint*) dye, colorant, colouring.

tiny adj 1 (*a tiny insect*) minute, diminutive, miniature, microscopic, infinitesimal, minuscule. 2 (*a tiny amount of water*) small, trifling, negligible, minor, insignificant.

tip vb 1 (*The dog tipped over the rubbish bin*) upset, overturn, topple, capsize. 2 (*She tipped the water into the bucket*) pour, empty. 3 (*The wardrobe tends to tip*) tilt, lean, list, cant. 4 (*He tipped the horse to win*) back, put one's money on, recommend. 5 (*tip the waiter*) give a tip to, reward.

tip n 1 (*the tip of the iceberg*) point, peak, top, apex. 2 (*the tips of his fingers*) end, extremity. 3 (*give the waiter* *a tip*) gratuity, reward, remuneration. **4** (*She gave him a few tips on cooking*) hint, suggestion, advice. **5** (*a racing tip*) recommendation.

tired adj **1** (*They were tired after their long walk*) weary, fatigued, worn out, exhausted. **2** (*The comic told a series of tired jokes*) stale, hackneyed, outworn, trite, banal. **3** (*They were tired of her endless complaints*) bored, weary.

tiresome adj (*She finds the work tiresome*) wearisome, tedious, boring, dull, monotonous, unexciting, uninteresting.

title n **1** (*the title of the book*) name. **2** (*What title does the king's nephew have?*) form of address, name, designation.

toilet n (*public toilets*) lavatory, WC, (*inf*) loo.

tolerate vb **1** (*We could not tolerate the noise from next door*) put up with, stand, bear, endure. **2** (*People should be able to tolerate views that are different from theirs*) permit, allow, recognize, sanction, brook.

tone n **1** (*He enjoys the sweet tone of the flute*) sound, pitch, timbre. **2** (*He spoke in a whispered tone*) voice, intonation, inflection. **3** (*The tone of his letter was threatening*) mood, spirit, manner, tenor, vein, gist. **4** (*She was dressed in tones of blue*) tint, shade, tinge.

tool n (*The workman forgot one of his tools*) implement, instrument, utensil, gadget, appliance.

top n **1** (*They reached the top of the mountain*) peak, summit, crest, apex.

2 (*They are at the top of their careers*) height, peak, pinnacle, zenith, acme, culmination, climax. **3** (*replace the top on the bottle*) lid, cap, stopper, cork. **4** (*They were at the top of the queue*) head, front. **5** (*The child wore a white summer top*) sweater, jumper, jersey, blouse, shirt, T-shirt.

topical adj (*The pupils were asked to write about something topical*) newsworthy, in the news, current, contemporary, up to date.

toss vb **1** (*She tossed the book on the sofa*) throw, fling, hurl. **2** (*ships tossing on the waves*) rock, roll, sway, lurch, pitch, heave. **3** (*The horse tossed its head*) throw back, jerk. **4** (*They tossed and turned unable to sleep*) thrash, writhe, tumble.

total adj **1** (*the total amount of money*) complete, entire, whole, full. **2** (*He's a total fool*) complete, thorough, utter, absolute, downright.

touch vb **1** (*The two wires should touch*) be in contact, come together, meet. **2** (*She touched his arm*) put her hand on, tap, pat. **3** (*You shouldn't touch his private things*) handle, pick up, hold, fiddle with, interfere with. **4** (*They were touched by the orphan's sad story*) affect, move, upset, disturb. **5** (*Some firms were not touched by the recession*) affect, have an effect on, concern, have a bearing on.

tough adj **1** (*objects made of a tough substance*) strong, durable, solid, sturdy, rigid, stiff. **2** (*The meat was tough*) chewy, leathery, gristly, sinewy. **3** (*They had to be tough to survive the* *weather conditions*) hardy, rugged, robust, sturdy, strong. **4** (*The job was very tough*) difficult, hard, arduous, strenuous, laborious. **5** (*They had a tough life*) hard, harsh, austere, rugged, rough, grim, difficult. **6** (*the tough kids of the district*) rough, rowdy, unruly, disorderly, wild, violent, law-breaking.

tourist n (*foreign tourists visiting the city*) visitor, traveller, sightseer, holiday-maker.

tower n (*a church tower*) spire, steeple, belfry, turret.

trace n **1** (*We could find no trace of where they had camped*) mark, sign, remains, vestige, indication, evidence. **2** (*There was not a trace of shame in his expression*) bit, hint, suggestion, suspicion, shadow, jot, iota. **3** (*follow the animal's traces*) track, trail, spoor, scent.

trace vb (*They were unable to trace their lost son/We tried to trace the missing letter*) find, discover, detect, track down, unearth, ferret out.

track n **1** (*The hunters were following the tracks of the bear*) marks, traces, prints, trail, spoor, scent. **2** (*They followed the track up the mountain*) path, road, trail, **3** (*The train suddenly left the track*) rail, line. **4** (*The runners had to run ten times round the track*) course, running track, racetrack.

trade n (*He is in the export trade*) commerce, business.

tradition n (*keep up the old village traditions*) custom, habit, belief, practice, convention, institution.

traffic n (*The noise of traffic kept him awake*) vehicles, cars.

tragedy n (*She was sad because of some tragedy in her life*) disaster, calamity, misfortune, adversity.

tragic adj **1** (*appalled at her tragic story about her childhood*) sad, unhappy, pathetic, moving, distressing, pitiful. **2** (*She was killed in a tragic accident*) disastrous, calamitous, catastrophic, terrible, dreadful, appalling, dire.

trail vb **1** (*They trailed the fallen trees behind them*) tow, pull, drag, haul, draw. **2** (*They trailed the fox to its earth*) follow, pursue, track, trace, tail, shadow.

train vb **1** (*She is training the pupils in cooking techniques*) teach, coach, instruct, educate, give lessons to. **2** (*She is training to be a vet*) study, learn. **3** (*The football players have to train every evening*) work out, do exercises, practise.

tramp n **1** (*tramps sleeping rough*) vagrant, derelict, down-and-out. **2** (*go for a tramp over the moors*) hike, trek, march, ramble, wander, roam, walk.

tranquil adj **1** (*a tranquil country scene*) peaceful, restful. quiet, still, serene. **2** (*a very tranquil person*) calm, serene, placid, composed.

transfer vb (*He transferred the furniture from one house to another*) move, shift, take, carry, convey, transport.

transform vb (*The new furnishings transformed the room*) change, alter, transfigure, revolutionize.

transmit vb (*transmit the information electronically*) pass on, transfer, communicate, spread, send, carry.

transparent adj 1 (things made of a transparent material) clear, see-through. 2 (They were impressed by his transparent honesty) obvious, clear, unmistakable, evident, noticeable, apparent.

travel vb 1 (They travel a lot in the course of their work) journey, move around, take a trip. 2 (the speed at which sound travels) be transmitted, proceed, progress. 3 (They travel the country begging) journey, cross, traverse, roam, wander.

treacherous adj (He was betrayed by a treacherous friend) traitorous, disloyal, faithless, double-dealing, untrustworthy.

treasure n (They looked for buried treasure) riches, valuables, wealth, fortune.

treat vb 1 (He treated his children badly) act towards, behave towards, deal with, cope with, use. 2 (They treated his remarks as a joke) regard, consider, view. 3 (The doctor treated the patient) attend to, cure, heal, give treatment to, give medication to. 4 (treat the wood with something to preserve it) apply to, put on. 5 (They treated us to dinner) pay for, stand, entertain, take out. 6 (She treats the subject in an original way) deal with, discuss, consider, write about, speak about.

tremble vb (They were trembling with fear) shake, quiver, quake, shudder.

tremendous adj 1 (It made a tremendous difference to their lives) huge, enormous, great, immense, vast, colossal. 2 (She is a tremendous cook) excellent, exceptional, remarkable, wonderful, fabulous.

trend n 1 (witness an upward trend in prices) tendency, drift, swing, course. 2 (She always follows fashion trends) fashion, style, fad.

trial n 1 (She was a witness at a murder trial) court case, case, hearing. 2 (He is giving the young man a trial as a trainee mechanic) trial period, probation. 3 (cars having passed safety trials) test, try-out, check. 4 (facing the trials of life) trouble, worry, burden, hardship, suffering.

trick n 1 (He gained entry to her house by a trick) deception, hoax, ruse, stratagem, subterfuge. 2 (The children played tricks on each other) practical joke, joke, hoax, prank.

trick vb (He was tricked into giving her his life's savings) cheat, deceive, delude, mislead, hoodwink, dupe, swindle, defraud.

trip vb (She tripped over her shoe laces) stumble, lose one's footing, lose one's balance, slip, fall, tumble.

trip n (They went on a trip to the seaside) excursion, outing, jaunt, expedition.

triumphant adj 1 (He gave a triumphant shout when he won) exultant, joyful, jubilant. 2 (the triumphant team) winning, victorious, successful.

trivial adj (They quarrelled over something trivial) unimportant, insignificant, inconsequential, petty, minor, negligible.

trouble n 1 (Their teenage children are causing them some trouble) worry, bother, anxiety, disquiet, unease, inconvenience, difficulty, problems. **2** (*There has been a great deal of trouble in her life*) misfortune, difficulty, hardship, distress, suffering, unhappiness, sadness. **3** (*Our hosts went to a great deal of trouble*) bother, inconvenience, disturbance, fuss, effort. **4** (*There was a bit of trouble in the restaurant last night*) disturbance, disorder, strife, fighting, commotion. **5** (*He has chest trouble*) disorder, disease, illness.

trust vb **1** (*We do not trust his judgement*) place one's trust in, have confidence in, have faith in, believe in, be convinced by. **2** (*You can trust them to help if they offer*) rely on, bank on, depend on, count on, be sure of. **3** (*We trust that you will be there*) hope, assume, presume, expect, suppose.

true adj **1** (*What she said is true*) truthful, accurate, right, correct, genuine, reliable. **2** (*They have been true friends since childhood*) real, genuine, loyal, faithful, trustworthy, reliable, dependable. **3** (*The book gives a true account of the war*) accurate, correct, exact, precise, faithful, close.

trustworthy adj (*He thinks that all his employees are trustworthy*) reliable, dependable, loyal, staunch, faithful, trusty, honest, honourable.

truth n **1** (*There seemed little truth in what he said*) truthfulness, accuracy, correctness, rightness, validity, veracity. **2** (*Truth is often stranger than fiction*) reality, actuality.

try vb **1** (*You must try to do well*) attempt, aim, endeavour, make an effort, exert oneself, strive, struggle. **2** (*We tried a new kind of cereal*) try out, test, evaluate. **3** (*The children are trying her patience*) tax, strain, exhaust. **4** (*He was the judge who tried the case*) hear, judge, adjudicate.

trying adj **1** (*They had had a trying day*) taxing, demanding, difficult, stressful, hard, tough, arduous. **2** (*The children were particularly trying that day*) troublesome, tiresome, annoying, irritating, exasperating.

tuck vb **1** (*She tucked her blouse into her skirt*) push, ease, insert, stuff. **2** (*tuck the child up in bed*) cover up, wrap up. **3** (*They tucked into a hearty meal*) eat, devour, wolf down, gobble up.

tug vb **1** (*She tugged at the rope*) pull, jerk, yank. **2** (*The child tugged a toy cart behind him*) drag, draw, tow, lug.

tumble vb **1** (*Watch that the child does not tumble*) fall over, fall headlong, topple, stumble, trip. **2** (*Prices have tumbled*) fall, drop, plummet, plunge, slump. **3** (*acrobats tumbling*) turn somersaults, go head over heels.

tune n (*a group playing a folk tune*) melody, air, song.

turn vb **1** (*The wheel began to turn*) go round, rotate, revolve, spin, whirl, twirl. **2** (*He turned the car in the driveway*) turn round, reverse, make a U-turn. **3** (*He turned the steaks over on the grill*) turn over, flip over, invert, reverse. **4** (*The weather turned stormy*) become, grow, get. **5** (*Tadpoles turn into frogs*) become, change into. **6** (*The car turned the corner*) go round, round. **7** (*He turned the attic into a* *bedroom*) convert, change, transform, alter, modify.

tussle n (*The two boys had a tussle to gain possession of the bag*) struggle, fight, scuffle, skirmish.

tweak vb (*The boy tweaked his friend's ear*) twist, pinch, nip, pull, jerk.

twilight n (*They walked home at twilight*) dusk, half-light.

twinkle vb (*The stars twinkled*) sparkle, glitter, glint, flicker, shimmer.

twist vb 1 (*The extreme heat had twisted the metal*) bend, warp, distort, buckle. 2 (*He twisted the string round his finger*) wind, coil, curl, twine, twirl, loop.

3 (*The road twists up the mountain*) curve, wind, zigzag, snake, meander. 4 (*The ropes became twisted*) entangle, tangle, entwine. 5 (*They twisted his words*) distort, garble, misrepresent, falsify. 6 (*She twisted her head round to look at him*) turn, swivel, screw.

type n 1 (*a type of plant/a type of person*) kind, variety, sort, form, class. 2 (*in italic type*) print, face, fount.

twitch n 1 (*Her arm gave a twitch*) spasm, jerk, jump, quiver, tremor. 2 (*He has a twitch in his eye*) blink, flutter, tic.

U

ugly adj 1 (an ugly monster/ugly buildings) hideous, unattractive, unprepossessing, horrible, frightful. 2 (The war situation grew more ugly) dangerous, threatening, menacing, ominous, hostile, nasty.

umpire n (The umpire in the tournament) referee, judge, adjudicator, arbitrator, (inf) ref.

unanimous adj (The committee was unanimous in its decision to close down the club) agreed, united, like-minded, at one, in harmony, with one voice.

unaware adj (They were unaware of what people were saying about them) unconscious, ignorant, oblivious, heedless, (inf) in the dark.

uncanny adj 1 (There were uncanny happenings in the graveyard at night) strange, odd, queer, mysterious, eerie, weird, unnatural, supernatural. 2 (She bore an uncanny resemblance to her grandmother) remarkable, striking, extraordinary, astonishing, incredible.

uncertain adj 1 (The result of the talks is still uncertain) unknown, undetermined, unsettled, up in the air. 2 (We are uncertain about whether to go or stay) unsure, doubtful, undecided, dubious, unresolved, indecisive, wavering, in two minds. 3 (The future is uncertain) unpredictable, risky, chancy.

uncouth adj (uncouth table manners) rough, coarse, uncivilized, unrefined, unpolished, boorish, ill-bred.

under prep 1 (She sat under the tree) below, underneath, beneath. 2 (prices under £10) below, less than, lower than. 3 (army ranks under major) low, lower than, inferior to, subordinate to, junior to.

underclothes npl (wear warm underclothes in the winter) underwear, underclothing, undergarments, lingerie, (inf) smalls.

undergo vb (undergo a terrible experience) go through, experience, be subjected to, endure.

underground adj 1 (an underground shelter) subterranean, sunken. 2 (an underground organization) secret, clandestine, undercover, surreptitious.

undergrowth n (The animals emerged from the undergrowth) thicket, brushwood.

underhand adj (She got the job by underhand methods) deceitful, devious, crafty, cunning, sneaky, furtive, dishonest.

underline vb (The burglary underlined the need for security staff) emphasize, stress, highlight.

undermine vb (They tried to undermine the authority of the manager) weaken, impair, damage, destroy.

understand vb 1 (We did not understand his instructions) comprehend, grasp, take in, follow, fathom, interpret. 2 (She failed to understand how the homeless people felt) appreciate, sympathize with. **3** (*We understand that he has left*) gather, hear, be informed, learn, believe.

understanding n **1** (*have a poor understanding of the facts*) comprehension, grasp, knowledge, awareness. **2** (*His powers of understanding are poor*) reasoning, brain power, (*inf*) grey matter. **3** (*The two businessmen did not sign a contract but they had an unofficial understanding*) agreement, gentleman's agreement, arrangement, deal, pact. **4** (*She treated the difficult situation with great understanding*) sensitivity, consideration, insight, compassion, sympathy. **5** (*It was our understanding that he was leaving*) belief, opinion, feeling.

undertake vb (*They agreed to undertake the difficult task*) take on, assume, tackle, set about, enter upon.

underwear n (*wear warm underwear in winter*) underclothes, underclothing, undergarments, lingerie, (*inf*) smalls.

undo vb **1** (*She undid the hook on her dress*) unfasten, unhook, unbutton, untie, loosen, open. **2** (*They undid all his good work*) destroy, ruin, wreck, upset. **3** (*She rang to undo the arrangements for the meeting*) cancel, annul, revoke, set aside.

unearth vb **1** (*The police have unearthed new information about the murder*) uncover, discover, find, come across, bring to light, expose, turn up. **2** (*The dog unearthed an old bone*) dig up, excavate, exhume.

unearthly adj (*They heard an unearthly shriek*) eerie, uncanny, supernatural, ghostly, weird.

uneasy adj (*They felt uneasy when their son did not arrive home*) anxious, worried, concerned, troubled, nervous.

unemployed adj (*He has been unemployed for a year*) jobless, out of work, (*inf*) on the dole.

unfasten vb (*unfasten the gate/unfasten the knot*) undo, open, loose, untie, unlock.

unfortunate adj **1** (*in unfortunate circumstances*) adverse, disadvantageous, unfavourable. **2** (*The unfortunate girl lost all her money*) unlucky, out of luck, luckless, wretched, unhappy. **3** (*It was a most unfortunate remark*) regrettable, inappropriate, tactless.

unhappy adj (*She was unhappy when her dog died*) sad, miserable, sorrowful, dejected, gloomy.

uniform adj **1** (*pieces of cloth of uniform length*) same, alike, like, equal, identical. **2** (*keep the room at a uniform temperature*) constant, unvarying, unchanging, regular, even.

union n (*a union of youth clubs*) association, alliance, league, federation.

unique adj **1** (*a unique specimen*) one and only, single, sole, solitary, exclusive. **2** (*The salesmen pointed out the unique features of the dishwasher*) distinctive, unequalled, unparalleled.

unit n **1** (*The English course is divided into units*) component, part, section, portion, element. **2** (*The metre is a unit of length*) measurement, measure, quantity.

unite vb **1** (*The two sides united to fight their common enemy*) join, join together, get together, join forces, amalgamate, combine, merge. **2** (*They decided to unite the two teams*) join, combine, amalgamate, merge, link, fuse.

universal adj (*Poverty is a universal problem*) general, widespread, common, global, international, worldwide.

universe n (*the wonders of the universe*) world, cosmos.

unlikely adv (*It is unlikely that they will arrive on time*) improbable, doubtful.

unlucky adj **1** (*He was unlucky not to win/a most unlucky young man*) out of luck, luckless, down on one's luck, unfortunate, hapless. **2** (*By an unlucky set of circumstances they failed to arrive on time*) unfortunate, adverse, disadvantageous, unfavourable.

unmarried adj (*She is unmarried and lives with her parents*) single, unwed, unattached.

unpleasant adj (*an unpleasant experience/an unpleasant person*) disagreeable, nasty, horrible.

unreal adj (*a story about an unreal world*) imaginary, fictitious, make-believe, mythical.

unruly adj (*The teacher could not control the unruly children*) rowdy, wild, disorderly, noisy, uncontrollable, unmanageable.

unsightly adj (*unsightly modern blocks of flats in a historical area*) ugly, unattractive, hideous, horrible.

unsuccessful adj (*Their attempt to save the firm was unsuccessful*) without success, in vain, failed, futile, useless, ineffective.

untangle vb (*untangle the knots*) disen-

tangle, unravel, straighten out.

untidy adj **1** (*The room where the children were playing was very untidy*) in disorder, disordered, disarranged, chaotic, disorganized. **2** (*The children were scolded for being untidy*) dishevelled, unkempt, rumpled, messy.

untie vb (*untie the gate/untie the string*) undo, unfasten, loosen.

untrue adj (*We felt that his account of the accident was untrue*) false, fallacious, erroneous, wrong, inaccurate.

unusual adj (*His behaviour was unusual*) uncommon, out of the ordinary, abnormal, odd, different, irregular.

unwell adj (*She is unwell and is off work*) ill, sick, ailing, unhealthy, (*inf*) under the weather.

unwilling adj (*They were unwilling to set off so late*) reluctant, disinclined, loath, averse.

upbringing n (*They had a very strict upbringing*) rearing, training.

upheaval n (*Moving house caused a terrible upheaval*) disturbance, disruption, disorder, turmoil, chaos, confusion.

upkeep n (*pay for the upkeep of the house*) maintenance, running, support.

upper adj **1** (*the upper shelf*) higher. **2** (*the upper ranks in the army*) higher, superior, senior.

upright adj **1** (*the upright posts in the fence*) erect, vertical, perpendicular. **2** (*He is an upright member of the community*) honest, honourable, decent, respectable, law-abiding, upstanding.

uproar n (*There was uproar when the*

football player kicked the ball into his own goal) disturbance, turmoil, tumult, commotion, pandemonium, bedlam, riot, rumpus

upset *vb* **1** (*His remarks upset her*) hurt, distress, worry, bother. **2** (*The animals were upset by the thunderstorm*) agitate, alarm, frighten. **3** (*He got a new job and upset our holiday plans*) disorganize, disarrange, (*inf*) mess up. **4** (*The child upset the pail of water*) overturn, knock over, upend, capsize, tip over.

upshot *n* (*The upshot of the quarrel was that he left*) result, outcome, end, conclusion.

up-to-date *adj* (*His ideas are very up-to-date*) modern, current, contemporary, fashionable.

urban *n* (*urban areas*) city, town, metropolitan, inner-city.

urbane *adj* (*an urbane man whom women found charming*) suave, smooth, sophisticated, elegant, cultivated, polished, refined, gracious, courteous.

urge *vb* **1** (*urge the cattle to the milking shed*) drive, propel, force, push, hurry. **2** (*We urged her to accept the invitation*) advise, encourage, prompt, entreat, exhort. **3** (*The applause of the crowd urged the players on to greater effort*) spur, incite, stimulate, prod, goad, encourage, egg on.

urge *n* (*She had a sudden urge to laugh*) desire, compulsion, need, wish, impulse, longing.

urgent *adj* **1** (*It is urgent that we get him to hospital*) imperative, a matter of life or death, vital, crucial, critical, essential. **2** (*We have urgent matters to discuss*) important, crucial, vital, serious, grave, pressing.

use *n* **1** (*The lotion we bought at the chemist is for external use only*) application, utilization, employment. **2** (*What use is this old chair?*) usefulness, good, benefit, service. **3** (*We have no use for this old bike*) need, purpose.

use *vb* **1** (*Do you know how to use this machine?*) make use of, utilize, work, operate, employ, wield. **2** (*You will have to use tact*) exercise, employ, apply. **3** (*Have you used all the flour?*) consume, get through.

used *adj* (*a shop selling used clothing*) second-hand, nearly new, cast-off.

useful *adj* (*This is a useful kitchen gadget*) of use, practical, of service, handy, convenient.

usual *adj* **1** (*the postman's usual route*) regular, accustomed, customary, habitual, normal, routine, set, established. **2** (*The weather was usual for the time of year*) common, typical, standard, normal, average, run-of-the-mill.

usually *adv* (*We usually go out to lunch on Saturday*) generally, as a rule, normally, mostly, for the most part.

utter *vb* (*We heard him utter threats*) say, speak, voice, pronounce, express.

utter *adj* (*They are utter fools*) complete, absolute, total, thorough, out-and-out, perfect.

utterly *adv* (*We were utterly delighted at the news*) absolutely, completely, totally, thoroughly, perfectly.

V

vacant adj 1 (*The house is vacant*) empty, unoccupied, uninhabited, to let, deserted. 2 (*several vacant posts in the firm*) free, available, unfilled, unoccupied, empty. 3 (*look for a vacant seat*) empty, free, unoccupied, unused. 4 (*He wore a vacant look*) expressionless, blank, inexpressive, deadpan.

vagrant n (*vagrants begging for money for food*) tramp, homeless person, person of no fixed abode, itinerant.

vague adj 1 (*She has only a vague idea about her duties in her new job*) hazy, imprecise, ill-defined, uncertain, nebulous. 2 (*Our holiday plans are still rather vague*) hazy, uncertain, undecided, indefinite, (*inf*) up in the air, doubtful. 3 (*He gave rather a vague description of the person who attacked him*) imprecise, inexact, loose, hazy, woolly. 4 (*A vague shape loomed out of the mist*) indistinct, indeterminate, shadowy, unclear, hazy, dim, fuzzy. 5 (*She is rather a vague person*) absent-minded, dreamy, with one's head in the clouds.

vain adj 1 (*They made a vain attempt to save the drowning man*) unsuccessful, futile, useless, ineffective, abortive, unprofitable. 2 (*He is a very vain young man*) conceited, proud, arrogant, egotistical, narcissistic, cocky, (*inf*) big-headed.

valiant adj (*He made a valiant attempt to save his friend's life in the war*) brave, courageous, gallant, heroic, bold.

valid adj 1 (*The school regulation is still valid*) in force, effective, in effect, legal, lawful. 2 (*He has valid reasons for lodging an objection*) sound, well-founded, reasonable, justifiable, authentic.

valuable adj 1 (*The burglars took some valuable jewellery*) expensive, costly, high-priced, precious, priceless. 2 (*The old man gave them some valuable advice*) useful, helpful, beneficial, worthwhile.

value n 1 (*It is difficult to place a value on the antique table*) price, market price, cost. 2 (*She tried to convince the children of the value of a balanced diet*) worth, benefit, merit, advantage, gain, importance.

value vb 1 (*They asked him to value their house*) set a price on, price, place a value on. 2 (*She values the contribution that parents make to sports events*) appreciate, think highly of, rate highly, set store by.

vanish vb 1 (*The figure seemed to vanish into the mist*) disappear, fade, melt. 2 (*They were talking about a way of life that has now vanished*) go, die out, disappear, end, come to an end.

vanquish vb (*They vanquished the enemy army*) conquer, defeat, triumph over, overcome, crush, trounce.

varied adj (*a varied selection of magazines*) assorted, mixed, miscellaneous, diversified.

variety n 1 (*They tried to introduce some variety into the diet*) variation, diversity, diversification, change. 2 (*A huge variety of flowers were on display*) assortment, miscellany, mixture, range, collection.

various adj 1 (*The dress comes in various colours*) varying, diverse, different, many, assorted. 2 (*For various reasons we are unable to attend the meeting*) numerous, several, many, varied.

vary vb 1 (*They tend to vary slightly in size*) differ, be different, be unlike, be dissimilar. 2 (*The temperature varies throughout the day*) change, alter. 3 (*try to vary your speed on a long journey*) change, alter, modify.

vast adj 1 (*the vast plains covered in ripe corn*) extensive, immense, expansive, wide, sweeping. 2 (*A vast shape suddenly loomed out of the fog*) huge, enormous, massive, colossal, gigantic.

vegetation n (*an area of the world with little vegetation*) plant life, plants, greenery, flora.

vehement adj (*a vehement denial*) emphatic, vigorous, forceful, strong, fervent, passionate.

vehicle n 1 (*no parking for unauthorized vehicles*) conveyance, car, bus, lorry, means of transport. 2 (*They use the magazine simply as a vehicle for spreading their political views*) medium, means of expression, agency, instrument.

veil n (*The mountain peaks were hidden under a veil of mist/They moved the body under a veil of secrecy*) cover, covering, screen, curtain, blanket, cloak, mantle, mask, shroud, cloud.

vein n 1 (*Blood gushed from the vein*) blood vessel. 2 (*a vein of ore in the rocks*) seam, lode, stratum. 3 (*The marble fireplace had a pink vein in it*) streak, stripe, strip, line, thread. 4 (*There was a vein of humour in her criticism*) streak, strain, dash, hint. 5 (*The poem was in a serious vein*) mood, tone, tenor.

vengeance n (*They sought vengeance for the murder of their brother*) revenge, retaliation, reprisal, retribution, tit for tat.

venom n 1 (*find an antidote for the snake's venom*) poison, toxin. 2 (*She spoke with venom about her fellow competitor*) spite, malice, ill will, animosity.

venture n (*a business venture*) enterprise, undertaking, project.

verbal adj (*asked to give a verbal account of the accident*) oral, spoken, in speech.

verdict n (*The jury delivered its verdict*) decision, findings, conclusion, judgement, ruling, opinion.

verge n (*the grass verge by the road*) edge, border, boundary.

verify vb (*He was asked to verify that he had been present*) confirm, corroborate, endorse, ratify.

versatile adj 1 (*a versatile kitchen gadget*) adaptable, multipurpose. 2 (*She is a very versatile musician*) adaptable, adjustable, flexible, resourceful.

version n 1 (*She gave us her version of what happened in court*) account, story, report, side, interpretation. 2 (*There are several versions of that* *song around)* variant, variation, form.

vertical n *(hammer vertical posts into the ground to make a fence)* upright, erect, perpendicular.

very adj **1** *(Those were her very words)* actual, exact, precise. **2** *(The beauty of the dress lay in its very simplicity)* sheer, utter, pure. **3** *(He has been a member from the very beginning)* absolute.

vessel n **1** *(There was a foreign flag flying from the vessel)* ship, boat, craft. **2** *(We need some kind of vessel to give the dog a drink)* container, receptacle.

veto vb *(Some members vetoed his membership of the club)* ban, bar, place an embargo on, forbid, disallow, reject, turn down, give the thumbs down to.

vex vb *(Her mother was vexed by her refusal to come home for Christmas)* annoy, irritate, upset, put out, distress, *(inf)* peeve, *(inf)* miff.

vibrate vb **1** *(The music vibrated throughout the hall)* throb, pulsate, resonate, reverberate, ring, echo. **2** *(The whole bus vibrated as the driver tried to start the engine)* shudder, tremble, shake, quiver, shiver.

vice n **1** *(Vice seems to be on the increase in the modern world)* sin, sinfulness, evil, wickedness, badness, wrongdoing, iniquity. **2** *(one of his many vices)* sin, offence, misdeed, failing, flaw, defect.

vicious adj **1** *(The postman was attacked by a vicious dog)* fierce, ferocious, savage, dangerous. **2** *(The attack on the old man was a particularly vicious one)* violent, savage, brutal, fierce, ferocious, inhuman.

victim n **1** *(They were victims of a vicious attack)* casualty, sufferer. **2** *(tracking down their victims)* prey, quarry.

victorious adj *(the victorious army/the victorious team)* conquering, winning, triumphant, champion.

victory n *(We celebrated our victory)* win, success, conquest, triumph, achievement.

view n **1** *(The view from our balcony was beautiful)* outlook, prospect, panorama, vista. **2** *(A strange figure came into view)* sight, range of vision, eyeshot. **3** *(Our view is that he is dishonest)* opinion, point of view, viewpoint, belief, feeling, idea.

vigorous adj *(a vigorous attempt at winning the game)* strong, powerful, forceful, determined, enthusiastic, lively, energetic, strenuous.

vile adj *(What a vile thing to do)* nasty, foul, unpleasant, disagreeable, horrible, dreadful, disgusting, hateful, shocking.

villain n *(The police have caught the villains)* rogue, scoundrel, wrongdoer, ruffian, *(inf)* crook.

violent adj **1** *(a violent attack)* brutal, ferocious, cruel, savage, vicious. **2** *(He has a violent temper)* uncontrollable, unrestrained, wild, passionate, forceful. **3** *(He took a violent dislike to her at first sight)* strong, great, intense, extreme, vehement.

virtually adv *(Traffic was virtually at a standstill)* more or less, nearly, practically, as good as, effectively, in effect, in essence, for all practical purposes.

virtue n **1** *(The church admires virtue*

and discourages vice) goodness, righteousness, morality, integrity, uprightness, honesty, decency.

visible *adj* 1 (*The hilltops were scarcely visible in the mist*) in view, discernible, perceptible. 2 (*His unhappiness was visible to us all*) obvious, evident, apparent, noticeable, plain, clear, unmistakable.

vision *n* 1 (*Certain jobs call for good vision*) eyesight, sight. 2 (*He claims to have seen a vision in the graveyard*) apparition, ghost, spectre. 3 (*He saw his dead brother in a vision*) dream, hallucination. 4 (*men of vision*) insight, perception, discernment, intuition.

visit *vb* (*He visits his aunt once a year*) pay a visit to, go to see, pay a call on, call on, (*inf*) drop in on.

vital *adj* 1 (*It is vital that you attend the meeting*) imperative, essential, necessary, crucial. 2 (*hold vital discussions*) indispensable, urgent, essential, necessary, key. 3 (*She was a very vital person*) lively, energetic, vivacious.

vitality *n* (*well-nourished children full of vitality*) energy, liveliness, vigour, zest, vivacity.

vivacious *adj* (*She is so vivacious that everyone else seems dull beside her*) lively, animated, sparkling, scintillating, dynamic, vibrant.

vivid *adj* 1 (*vivid colours*) bright, brilliant, strong, intense. 2 (*a vivid description*) clear, graphic, powerful, dramatic.

vocabulary *n* (*the difficult vocabulary in the piece*) language, words.

voice *n* 1 (*She lost her voice when she had a cold*) speech. 2 (*They finally gave voice to their feelings*) expression, utterance. 3 (*governments refusing to listen to the voice of the people*) opinion, view, comment.

volume *n* 1 (*an encyclopedia in several volumes*) book. 2 (*measure the volume*) capacity, bulk. 3 (*the sheer volume of water pouring out*) amount, quantity, mass. 4 (*We asked them to turn down the volume of their radio*) loudness, sound.

voluntary *n* 1 (*Attendance at the meeting is entirely voluntary*) of one's own free will, optional, non-compulsory. 2 (*She is unemployed but does voluntary work*) unpaid, without payment, volunteer.

vote *vb* 1 (*They are voting to elect a new president*) cast one's vote, go to the polls. 2 (*She voted for the woman candidate*) elect, opt for, select.

vote *n* (*have a vote on who should lead the team*) ballot, poll, election.

voucher *n* (*lunch vouchers*) token, ticket, slip.

vow *n* (*marriage vows*) oath, promise, pledge.

vow *vb* (*He vowed to be true*) swear, promise, pledge, give one's word.

vulgar *adj* 1 (*They objected to his vulgar language*) rude, indecent, obscene, bawdy, smutty. 2 (*vulgar table manners*) rude, impolite, unmannerly, ill-mannered. 3 (*They thought her clothes were vulgar*) tasteless, flashy, gaudy, tawdry.

vulnerable *adj* (*They felt vulnerable camping out in that area*) exposed, unprotected, defenceless.

W

wad *n* **1** (*The nurse used a wad of cotton wool to clean the wound*) lump, chunk, plug. **2** (*wads of banknotes*) bundle, roll.

wadding *n* (*use cotton-wool wadding to pack the jewellery*) filling, packing, padding, lining, stuffing.

waddle *vb* (*The very fat lady waddled down the street*) wiggle, sway, totter.

wade *vb* **1** (*The children were wading in the pool in the park*) paddle, splash. **2** (*There was no bridge and they had to wade across the stream*) ford, cross.

waffle *vb* (*She did not have much to say about the subject but she waffled on*) ramble, babble, prattle, (*inf*) witter, (*inf*) rabbit.

wag *vb* **1** (*The dog's tail was wagging*) swing, sway, shake, twitch, quiver. **2** (*The teacher wagged her finger angrily at the children*) waggle, wiggle.

wage *vb* (*wage war*) carry on, conduct, engage in, undertake.

wager *n* (*He laid a wager that she would not win*) bet, gamble, stake, (*inf*) flutter.

wager *vb* (*She wagered that the horse would come first in the race*) bet, place a bet, lay a bet, lay odds, put money on, gamble.

wages *npl* (*She has asked for a rise in her wages*) pay, salary, earnings, income, remuneration.

wail *vb* (*The children were wailing because their mother would not give them*) sweets) cry, weep, sob, lament, howl, whine.

wait *vb* **1** (*The children were told to wait at the side of the road*) stay, remain, stop, halt. **2** (*She does not know if she has got the job—she will just have to wait and see*) be patient, stand by, hang fire, mark time, (*inf*) sit tight. **3** (*They asked us to wait for them*) await, watch out for, expect. **4** (*They are employed to wait at table*) serve, be a waiter/waitress.

wake *vb* **1** (*He asked us to wake him early*) wake up, waken, rouse. **2** (*We woke at dawn*) awake, waken, wake up, get up, arise.

walk *vb* **1** (*We were able to walk to the shops*) go by foot, go on foot, take shanks's pony, (*inf*) hoof it. **2** (*The children were told to walk and not to run*) stroll, saunter, amble, march.

walk *n* **1** (*They went for a walk after lunch*) stroll, saunter, amble, ramble, hike. **2** (*I recognized him by his walk*) gait, step, stride.

walker *n* (*We passed a few walkers as we drove to the village*) pedestrian, hiker, rambler.

wall *n* **1** (*The garden had a wall around it*) enclosure, barrier. **2** (*We tore down a wall of the house to knock two rooms into one*) partition. **3** (*tourists who went to visit the old city walls*) fortifications, ramparts, barricade, bulwark.

wallet *n* (*His wallet was stolen and he*

now has no money) pocketbook, note case, purse.

wallow vb **I** (*The animals were wallowing in mud*) roll, splash, tumble. **2** (*She was wallowing in self-pity*) bask, luxuriate, revel, delight.

wan adj (*She looked wan after having had flu*) pale, white, pallid, (*inf*) peaky.

wand n (*The fairy godmother waved her wand*) stick, baton, rod.

wander vb **I** (*The child wandered off while his mother was shopping*) go off, get lost, stray, lose one's way. **2** (*They loved to wander over the hills when they were on holiday*) roam, ramble, rove, range. **3** (*The old man does not recognize his family and has started to wander*) ramble, rave, babble.

wane vb **I** (*The moon is waning*) decrease, diminish, dwindle. **2** (*The power of ancient Greece waned*) decrease, decline, diminish, dwindle, fade, subside, dim, vanish, die out.

want vb **I** (*The children wanted some sweets*) wish for, desire, demand, long for, crave, yearn for, hanker after. **2** (*poor people wanting food*) lack, be lacking in, be without, be devoid of, be short of.

war n **I** (*The war between the countries lasted many years*) warfare, fighting, conflict, struggle, hostilities, battles. **2** (*There was a state of war between the two nations*) conflict, strife, hostility, enmity, ill-will. **3** (*She took part in the war against poverty in the area*) battle, fight, crusade, campaign.

ward n **I** (*The hospital ward holds four beds*) room, cubicle, compartment.

2 (*Which ward does the councillor represent?*) district, division. **3** (*Her parents are dead and she is a ward of her uncle*) charge, dependant.

ward vb **I** (*She succeeded in warding off his attack*) fend off, stave off, deflect, avert, rebuff. **2** (*They warded off the intruders*) drive back, repel, beat back.

warden n **I** (*She is employed as traffic warden*) supervisor, superintendent, overseer. **2** (*He is a game warden in Africa*) keeper, custodian, guardian, guard. **3** (*The prisoners attacked a warden*) warder, prison officer, guard, jailer, gaoler, (*inf*) screw.

wardrobe n **I** (*She hung her clothes up in the wardrobe*) cupboard. **2** (*She is buying a new wardrobe for her holiday*) clothes, trousseau.

warehouse n (*They collected the books from the warehouse*) store, depot, stockroom.

wares npl (*There were many people selling their wares in the market*) goods, products, merchandise, stock, commodities.

warlike adj (*They encountered warlike tribes in the jungle*) belligerent, aggressive, pugnacious, hostile.

warlock n (*a story about a warlock*) wizard, sorcerer, magician, witch.

warm adj **I** (*She bathed the wound in warm water*) heated, tepid, lukewarm. **2** (*go for a swim on a warm day*) sunny, hot, close, sultry. **3** (*She has a warm heart*) kind, kindly, sympathetic, tender, loving, affectionate. **4** (*We received a warm welcome*) hearty, cordial, friendly, enthusiastic.

warm vb 1 (*The mother warmed the food for the baby*) heat, heat up. 2 (*The competitors warmed up for the race*) loosen up, limber up, exercise.

warn vb (*They were warned that they were entering a dangerous area*) advise, caution, make aware, notify, inform, (*inf*) tip off.

warning n 1 (*They had no warning of the terrible storm*) forewarning, notification, notice, information, indication, hint. 2 (*He was superstitious and regarded his experience as a warning of things to come*) omen, signal, threat.

warrior n (*a book about the deeds of ancient warriors*) fighter, combatant, champion, soldier, knight.

wary adj (*The children were taught to be wary of strangers*) cautious, careful, on one's guard, watchful, chary, suspicious, distrustful.

wash vb 1 (*They washed their hands before dinner*) clean, cleanse, scrub. 2 (*The children washed before going to bed*) have a wash, wash oneself, clean oneself, sponge oneself down. 3 (*They washed their clothes and hung them out to dry*) launder, clean. 4 (*waves washing against the boats*) splash, dash, beat.

waste vb 1 (*They waste a lot of money/Try not to waste time*) squander, fritter, misuse, misspend. 2 (*Because of his illness his limbs are wasting away*) grow weak, grow thin, wither, atrophy.

waste n 1 (*find a way of getting rid of the waste*) rubbish, refuse, debris, (*esp Amer*) garbage. 2 (*doing research in the wastes of the Antarctic*) wasteland, wilderness, desert, vastness.

wasteful adj (*a wasteful use of money*) thriftless, extravagant, spendthrift, profligate, prodigal.

watch vb 1 (*We watched the sun going down*) look at, observe, view, contemplate, survey, stare at, gaze at. 2 (*If you watch what the teacher does you will be able to do the experiment yourself*) pay attention to, take notice of, to heed, concentrate on. 3 (*The police are watching him*) keep watch on, keep an eye on, keep under surveillance, follow, spy on. 4 (*Watch and don't get attacked in that area of the town*) take care, look out, take heed, beware, be alert. 5 (*She asked her mother to watch the children*) mind, take care of, look after, keep an eye on, tend.

watchman n security guard, guard, caretaker, custodian, sentry.

water n 1 (*have a glass of water with the meal*) tap water, bottled water, mineral water. 2 (*children playing by the water*) pond, pool, lake, river, sea.

watery adj 1 (*The gravy was watery/The soup was watery*) thin, weak, dilute, runny, tasteless, flavourless. 2 (*watery eyes*) wet, moist, damp, tearful, weepy.

wave vb 1 (*flags waving in the breeze*) flutter, flap, ripple, shake, undulate. 2 (*He waved his sword angrily*) shake, swing, brandish. 3 (*He waved his hand to his friends*) flutter, waggle. 4 (*He waved to the driver*) gesture. 5 (*Her hair waves*) curl, kink, undulate.

wave n 1 (*The children were splashing in the waves*) breaker, swell, surf, billow.

2 (*the waves in her hair*) curl, kink, undulation, **3** (*a town hit by a crime wave*) upsurge, surge, rash, outbreak.

waver *vb* **1** (*His courage did not waver*) falter, vary, change. **2** (*We had been determined to go but then we began to waver*) hesitate, think twice, vacillate, shilly-shally. **3** (*lights wavering*) flicker, tremble, quiver.

wax *vb* (*The moon was waxing*) increase, enlarge.

way *n* **1** (*They asked which was the way to London*) road, route, direction. **2** (*She said that it was a long way to London from there*) distance, journey. **3** (*They were taught the correct way to change the wheel of a car*) method, procedure, technique, system, manner, means. **4** (*The children laughed at the way the old lady dressed*) manner, fashion, style, mode. **5** (*They have old-fashioned ways*) habit, custom, practice, conduct, behaviour. **6** (*His business affairs are in a bad way*) state, condition, situation. **7** (*In some ways I will miss them although mostly I am glad that they've gone*) respect, aspect, feature, detail, point.

weak *adj* **1** (*She felt very weak after her long illness*) weakly, frail, delicate, feeble, shaky, debilitated, tired. **2** (*Their leader was too weak to stand up to the enemy*) cowardly, timid, soft, spineless, powerless. **3** (*She made a weak excuse for being late*) feeble, lame, pathetic, unconvincing, unsatisfactory. **4** (*The tea was too weak*) dilute, watery, tasteless, wishy-washy.

weaken *vb* **1** (*The illness had obviously weakened her*) make weak, debilitate, tire, wear out. **2** (*Our chances of winning were weakened*) lessen, decrease, reduce, diminish, undermine. **3** (*Our parents refused to let us go but then they weakened*) relent, come round, give in.

weakness *n* **1** (*A tendency to lie is her major weakness*) fault, failing, flaw, defect, shortcoming, imperfection, foible. **2** (*She has a weakness for chocolate*) fondness, liking, love, soft spot, preference, penchant.

wealth *n* (*He shared his great wealth among his family*) riches, fortune, money, capital, assets.

wealthy *adj* (*an area of the town where wealthy people live*) affluent, rich, well-off, well-to-do, moneyed, (*inf*) well-heeled.

wear *vb* **1** (*The children were wearing warm coats*) be dressed in, be clothed in, have on. **2** (*She wore a gloomy expression*) have, show, display. **3** (*rocks worn away by water*) erode, eat away, rub away. **4** (*She was worn out by the long walk*) tire, fatigue, exhaust.

weary *adj* **1** (*The children were weary at the end of the long school day*) tired, fatigued, exhausted, worn out, (*inf*) deadbeat. **2** (*She is weary of her present job*) bored, discontented, jaded, (*inf*) fed up.

weather *n* (*What is the weather like there in August?*) climate.

web *n* (*a spider's web*) mesh, net, network, lattice.

wedding *n* wedding ceremony, marriage, marriage ceremony.

wedge vb 1 (*Since it was very hot they wedged the door open*) jam, secure. 2 (*Four of them were wedged in the back seat*) squeeze, jam, cram, pack.

wedge n (*a wedge of cheese*) chunk, hunk, lump, (*inf*) wodge.

weep vb (*The child wept when her mother went away*) cry, sob, shed tears.

weight n 1 (*estimate the weight of the cake*) heaviness. 2 (*A weight fell on his toe*) heavy object. 3 (*When their daughter returned it was a weight off their minds*) burden, load, onus, worry, trouble. 4 (*They attach a great deal of weight to his opinion*) importance, significance, value, substance.

weird adj 1 (*We heard weird noises in the cellar*) eerie, strange, queer, uncanny, creepy, ghostly, unearthly, (*inf*) spooky. 2 (*She always wears weird clothes*) strange, queer, odd, bizarre, eccentric, outlandish, off-beat.

welcome vb 1 (*They welcomed their guests at the door*) greet, receive, meet. 2 (*We welcomed the news*) be pleased with, be glad at.

welfare n (*She was worried about her children's welfare*) well-being, health, happiness.

well adj 1 (*She has been ill but is now quite well*) in good health, healthy, fit, strong. 2 (*They found that all was well*) all right, satisfactory, fine, (*inf*) OK.

well adv 1 (*He plays the piano well*) competently, skilfully, expertly. 2 (*The children behaved well*) properly, correctly, suitably, satisfactorily. 3 (*They speak well of him*) highly, admiringly,

approvingly, favourably. 4 (*They may well be right*) probably, likely, possibly.

wet adj 1 (*The ground was wet after the rain/Her clothes were wet*) damp, moist, soaked, drenched, saturated, sopping. 2 (*We had wet weather on holiday*) rainy, damp, showery.

wet vb 1 (*She wet the shirts before ironing them*) dampen, moisten, sprinkle, spray. 2 (*The rain really wet them*) soak, drench, saturate.

wharf vb (*ships being unloaded at the wharf*) dock, quay, pier, jetty, landing stage.

wheeze vb (*She had a bad cold and was wheezing*) pant, puff, gasp.

whimper vb (*The dog was sitting whimpering on the doorstep*) whine, cry.

whine vb (*The children were bored and began to whine*) wail, cry, whimper, complain, (*inf*) grizzle.

whip n (*The jockey used his whip on the horse*) switch, crop, scourge, lash, horsewhip, cat o' nine tails.

whip vb 1 (*They used to whip people who had done wrong*) lash, flog, scourge, birch, beat, thrash. 2 (*She whipped the cream*) beat, whisk, mix, blend. 3 (*He whipped his handkerchief from his pocket*) pull, yank, jerk, snatch, whisk.

whirl vb (*They watched the dancers whirling round the floor*) turn, spin, rotate, revolve, wheel, circle, twirl.

whisper vb (*She whispered to her friend at the back of the classroom*) murmur, mutter, breathe.

white adj 1 (*She was white with fear*) pale, wan, pallid, ashen, peaky. 2 (*Her* *hair is white with age*) grey, silver, snowy white.

whole adj **1** (*We asked her to tell us the whole story*) full, entire, complete, unabridged. **2** (*Not a single wine glass was left whole*) intact, in one piece, undamaged, unbroken.

wholesome adj (*wholesome food*) health-giving, healthy, nutritious, nourishing.

wholly adv **1** (*We are not wholly against the scheme*) entirely, completely, fully, thoroughly, utterly. **2** (*The responsibility lies wholly with him*) only, solely, purely, exclusively.

wicked adj (*the wicked people who attacked and robbed the old man*) evil, bad, sinful, vicious, immoral, unethical, villainous, criminal.

wide adj **1** (*a city with wide streets*) broad, spacious. **2** (*A wide range of subjects is available at the school*) broad, large, extensive, comprehensive, wide-ranging. **3** (*He always wears very wide trousers*) loose, baggy, roomy.

widespread adj (*There were widespread rumours of war*) general, common, universal, extensive, prevalent, rife.

width n **1** (*measure the width of the material*) wideness, breadth, broadness, span. **2** (*We admired the width of his knowledge*) wideness, breadth, scope, range, comprehensiveness.

wield vb **1** (*a knight wielding a sword*) brandish, flourish, wave, swing. **2** (*It is the deputy president who wields the power*) have, hold, exercise, exert.

wife n spouse, partner, (*inf*) better half.

wild adj **1** (*an area where wild animals roamed*) untamed, undomesticated, fierce, savage, ferocious. **2** (*the wild flowers of the area*) uncultivated, native, indigenous. **3** (*The ship sank in wild weather*) stormy, rough, blustery, turbulent, windy. **4** (*They had to travel across wild country*) rough, rugged, desolate, waste. **5** (*the wild behaviour of the football crowd*) rowdy, disorderly, unruly, violent, turbulent, uncontrolled.

wilful adj **1** (*a nanny finding it difficult to cope with such wilful children*) headstrong, strong-willed, obstinate, stubborn, determined, disobedient, contrary. **2** (*The jury decided that it was a case of wilful murder*) deliberate, intentional, planned, premeditated, calculated.

will n **1** (*He seems to have lost the will to live*) desire, wish, inclination, determination. **2** (*He died without making a will*) last will and testament, testament.

willing adj **1** (*They had a lot of willing helpers at the church fête*) eager, keen, enthusiastic, avid. **2** (*There was no one willing to take responsibility for the organization of the event*) ready, prepared, disposed, agreeable, amenable.

wilt vb (*The flowers in the vase were wilting*) droop, wither, shrivel, dry up.

wily adj (*He was wily enough to convince the old lady that he was a representative of the church*) cunning, crafty, artful, scheming, sly, sharp.

win vb **1** (*We were not surprised when*

wince vb (She winced when they reminded her of her tactless remark) grimace, flinch, cringe, recoil.

wind n (The wind blew the papers all around the room) breeze, gale, gust, blast, draught.

wind vb 1 (Her grandmother asked her to wind her wool) twist, twine, coil, roll. 2 (The road winds up the mountain) twist, twist and turn, curve, loop, zigzag, spiral, snake, meander.

wing n 1 (The family occupy just the west wing of the castle) side, annex. 2 (They are on the right wing of the party) section, side, group, segment.

wink vb 1 (He winked an eye) blink, flutter, bat. 2 (lights winking on the water) twinkle, flash, sparkle, glitter, gleam.

winner n (They were the winners in the battle/the winner in the tennis tournament) victor, champion, conqueror, vanquisher.

wipe vb (wipe the kitchen surfaces) clean, sponge, mop, rub, brush.

wisdom n 1 (admire their wisdom in getting out of the industry at the right time) sense, common sense, prudence, good judgement, shrewdness, astuteness, smartness. 2 (The young people benefited from the wisdom of their grandparents) knowledge.

wise adj 1 (We thought it wise to leave early when it began to snow) sensible, well-advised, prudent, shrewd, astute, smart. 2 (They asked the wise old men of the village for advice) knowledgeable, learned, well-informed, enlightened, sage.

wish vb (They could not have wished for friendlier neighbours) want, desire, long for, yearn for, covet, (inf) have a yen for.

wish n 1 (They were supposed to obey the king's every wish) want, desire, demand, request. 2 (At last she was able to satisfy her wish to travel) desire, longing, yearning, fancy, inclination, craving, (inf) yen.

wistful adj (She had a wistful expression as she watched them leave on holiday) yearning, longing, forlorn, sad, pathetic.

wit n 1 (He did not have the wit to realize that she was teasing him) intelligence, brains, sense, common sense, shrewdness. 2 (We had to admire his wit as he kept us all amused) wittiness, humour.

witch n (a story about a witch and her broomstick) enchantress, sorceress.

withdraw vb 1 (She withdrew from the tennis match because of ill health) pull out, come out, retire. 2 (They withdrew their son from the school) remove, take away, pull out. 3 (The troops withdrew when they were defeated) pull back, fall back, move back, retreat, retire, depart.

wither vb (The flowers in the vase had withered) fade, dry up, dry out, shrivel, die.

witness vb (They witnessed a terrible accident) see, observe, look on at, watch, view, be present at.

witness n (*The police asked for witnesses at the scene of the accident*) eye-witness, onlooker, observer, spectator, bystander.

witty adj (*witty stories/witty people*) amusing, funny, humorous, comic, clever.

wizard n (*a fairy story about wizards*) warlock, sorcerer, magician, enchanter.

wobble vb 1 (*This table wobbles*) rock, teeter, shake. 2 (*wobble down the street on stiletto heels*) totter, teeter, sway, stagger, waddle. 3 (*Her voice wobbled and she began to cry*) shake, tremble, quiver.

woe n (*We listened to her tale of woe*) misfortune, distress, suffering, trouble, misery, unhappiness.

wonder n 1 (*watched with wonder as the acrobats performed*) amazement, astonishment, awe, bewilderment, curiosity. 2 (*The acrobats are a wonder*) marvel, miracle, prodigy, surprise.

wonder vb 1 (*wondering at the immensity of the sky*) admire, gape, marvel. 2 (*I wonder if they will marry*) conjecture, ponder, query, question, speculate.

wonderful adj 1 (*The church ceiling was a wonderful sight*) marvellous, remarkable, extraordinary, amazing, astonishing, fantastic. 2 (*She was a wonderful pianist*) superb, marvellous, brilliant, excellent, first-rate, outstanding.

wood n 1 (*houses made of wood*) timber. 2 (*go for a walk in the wood*) woods, forest, copse, thicket.

woolly adj 1 (*buy the child a woolly toy*) fluffy, fleecy, furry. 2 (*woolly thoughts*) hazy, vague, muddled, confused, indefinite, uncertain.

word n 1 (*She was trying to think of another word for 'work'*) term, expression. 2 (*She gave him her word that she would be there*) promise, pledge, assurance, guarantee, undertaking. 3 (*They have had no word about their missing son*) news, information, communication.

work n 1 (*Making a doll's house for his daughter involved a lot of work*) effort, exertion, labour, toil, trouble, elbow grease. 2 (*Her work involves meeting a great many people*) job, employment, occupation, profession, trade.

work vb 1 (*He works in banking*) be employed, have a job. 2 (*The pupils will have to work at their studies to pass the exams*) exert oneself, apply oneself, make an effort, labour, toil. 3 (*Can you work this machine?*) operate, use, control, handle. 4 (*This machine does not work*) go, operate, function, run. 5 (*That idea will not work*) succeed, be successful, go well, be effective.

world n 1 (*the peoples of the world*) earth, globe, planet. 2 (*The world was shocked by the terrorist attack*) people, everyone, the public. 3 (*the medical world*) society, sector, section, group.

worry n 1 (*His behaviour caused her a lot of worry*) anxiety, trouble, bother, distress, disturbance, upset, uneasiness. 2 (*She was a real worry to her parents*) trouble, nuisance, pest, problem, trial, thorn in the flesh.

worsen vb 1 (*The situation between workers and management has worsened*) get worse, take a turn for the worsen, deteriorate, degenerate. 2 (*His efforts to help simply worsened the situation*) make worse, aggravate, exacerbate, increase.

worship vb 1 (*go to church to worship God*) pray to, praise, glorify, pay homage to. 2 (*He simply worships his wife*) idolize, adore, be devoted to, cherish, dote on.

worth n 1 (*The jewellery is of little financial worth but is of sentimental value*) value. 2 (*We regarded his advice as being of little worth*) value, use, advantage, benefit, gain.

worthy adj 1 (*They were not worthy of respect*) deserving, meriting. 2 (*the worthy people in the community*) good, decent, honourable, upright, virtuous, admirable, commendable, deserving.

wound n 1 (*He got his wound dressed in hospital*) injury, sore, cut, laceration, lesion. 2 (*Her remark was a wound to his pride*) blow, injury, hurt, damage, slight.

wrap vb 1 (*Wrap the child in a blanket and take him to a hospital*) cover, bundle up, swathe, enfold. 2 (*She wrapped the Christmas presents*) wrap up, parcel up, package, tie up, gift-wrap.

wrath n (*They had to face the wrath of the teacher when they played truant*) anger, rage, fury, indignation, annoyance.

wreck vb 1 (*He wrecked his father's car*), smash, demolish, ruin, damage, (*inf*) write off. 2 (*His illness wrecked their holiday plans*) ruin, destroy, spoil, shatter.

wrench vb (*He wrenched the lid from the container*) twist, pull, tug, jerk, force.

wretched adj 1 (*She was feeling wretched about being away from home*) miserable, depressed, unhappy, sad. 2 (*He felt wretched when he had flu*) ill, unwell, sick, (*inf*) under the weather. 3 (*He has a wretched cold*) nasty, unpleasant, disagreeable.

wriggle vb 1 (*children wriggling with impatience in their seats*) twist, squirm, writhe. 2 (*She tried to wriggle out of helping with the housework*) dodge, evade, avoid, duck out of.

wring vb 1 (*wring the clothes out*) squeeze, twist. 2 (*His enemies wrung the information from him*) extract, force, wrench.

wrinkle n (*She ironed her blouse to remove the wrinkles*) crease, pucker, fold, furrow.

write vb 1 (*write an essay*) compose, pen. 2 (*She wrote down the names of the people present*) put down, take down, note, list, record.

writer n (*He is a professional writer*) author, novelist, journalist.

writing n 1 (*She teaches children writing*) handwriting, penmanship, script. 2 (*a list of his writings*) work, book, publication.

wrong adj 1 (*It is wrong to steal*) bad, wicked, sinful, illegal, unlawful, criminal, crooked. 2 (*There is something* *wrong with the computer*) broken, faulty, defective, out of order. **3** (*It was the wrong way to deal with the problem*) incorrect, improper, inappropriate, unsuitable. **4** (*She gave the wrong answer to the mathematical question*) incorrect, inaccurate, erroneous, mistaken.

wrong *n* **1** (*be taught right from wrong*) badness, evil, sin, sinfulness, unlawfulness. **2** (*He committed several wrongs*) misdeed, offence, crime.

Y

yearn vb (They yearned for some sunshine) long, pine, crave, desire, covet, fancy, hanker after, (inf) have a yen for.

yield vb **1** (They refuse to yield to the invading army) submit, give in, surrender, concede defeat. **2** (They finally yielded to his demands) give in, comply with, consent to, grant. **3** (investments which yield a good return) bring in, earn, return, produce. **4** (an area which yields heavy crops) produce, give, bear, grow, supply.

young adj (young people) youthful, juvenile, adolescent.

Z

zealous adj (zealous followers of the sport/zealous in their efforts to gain support) eager, keen, enthusiastic, passionate, fervent, earnest, fanatical.

zenith n (when the Roman empire was at the zenith of its power) peak, height, top, pinnacle, acme, apex.

zero n 1 (How many zeroes are there when you write a million in figures?) nought, nothing. 2 (We won absolutely zero) nothing, naught, nil, (inf) zilch.

zest n (the old lady's zest for life) enthusiasm, eagerness, relish, energy.

zone n (a traffic-free zone) area, sector, region.